CONFLICT AND SOCIAL PSYCHOLOGY

PRIO is an independent international institute of peace and conflict research, founded in 1959 as one of the first of its kind. It is governed by an international Governing Board of seven individuals, and it is financed mainly by the Norwegian Ministry of Education, Research and Church Affairs. The results of all PRIO research are available to the public.

International Peace Research Institute, Oslo
Fuglehauggata 11, N-0260 Oslo, Norway
Telephone: 472-55 71 50
Cable address: PEACERESEARCH OSLO
Telefax: 472-55 84 22

Soual Y .

CONFLICT AND SOCIAL PSYCHOLOGY

Edited by
Knud S. Larsen

PRIO

International Peace Research Institute, Oslo

S SAGE Publications
London · Newbury Park · New Delhi

SAGE Publications Ltd
6 Bonhill Street
London EC2A 4PU

SAGE Publications Inc
2455 Teller Drive
Newbury Park, California 91320

SAGE Publications India Pvt Ltd
32, M-Block Market
Greater Kailash – I
New Delhi 110 048

ISBN 0-8039-8745-5

Typeset by Sage Publications, London

Printed by The Cromwell Press,
Broughton Gifford, Melksham, Wiltshire SN12 8PH

Contents

To my mother

Gerda Larsen

for lifelong inspiration

Preface

Throughout history, conflict has been the human experience. Social psychology has particularly important contributions to make to the understanding of conflict, and of equal importance to the resolution of conflict. We live in changing times, but one fact is certain: the potential to destroy is ever-increasing, in step with the technological revolution. Recent changes in the relationships between East and West may give some cause for hope. Yet the very rapidity of these events also demonstrates the fragility of peace and how major social change outcomes may depend on perceptual, i.e. psychologically based, miscalculations.

Images are mediators of intergroup conflict. But images are constantly changing: yesterday's ugly American or duped Russian becomes tomorrow's appealing friend. Useful psychological constructs underlie all social change and, most would agree, lawful and predictive behavior as well. Psychologists have been preoccupied with understanding hostile intergroup or enemy images – a focus reflected in the current volume. Since much conflict derives from miscalculations regarding the intentions of the 'enemy', having realistic images is crucial.

Research on images suggests that we rarely have completely accurate perceptions of other groups or nations. This distortion is due primarily to the syndrome of interrelated traits we call 'ethnocentrism'. From such an ethnocentric perspective, we rank other peoples and cultures according to their relationship to us, the in-group. Having negative inter-group images is the consequence of seeing a large array of ideas and beliefs as different and foreign, and only a rather narrow range as familiar and acceptable. Contributing to inter-group hostility are psychological processes that include information simplicity, a paranoid perspective on the world, feelings of personal insecurity, and conformity pressures. These processes combine to create a perception of psychological distance and ethnocentrism.

A social-psychological model of hostile inter-group images would view ethnocentric group identification as a function of cognitive perceptual habits: paranoid and ego-defensive thinking which induces a contrast between the familiar and the foreign. By 'cognitive simplicity' we mean the absence of a sufficient number of constructs with which to differentiate the world. Such inadequate cognition predisposes individuals and groups toward simplistic and ego-defensive judgements.

Child-rearing practices are also important in the development of ethnocentric group identification. Simplistic experiences, where the individual is confined to a narrow range of social opportunities, can be one factor. Children also mediate to others what they have experienced, and punitive child-rearing leads to hostile orientations. When these factors are combined with emotional conditioning to ethnocentric symbols, inter-group hostility is a likely outcome. Child-rearing practices influence personality development; and practices which result in personal insecurity and low self-esteem are more likely to produce an ethnocentric personality.

Much is known about conflict from the psychological perspective. This volume has been developed to produce an up-to-date review of major psychological contributions to conflict theory. Its chapters have come in response to an international call, and are meant as a contribution to international theoretical development. The authors represent a variety of countries and viewpoints. From that perspective, I hope that this book may prove a model for international cooperation in social science.

Ultimately, this discussion should lead to a better understanding of global conflict and inter-group conflict. Researchers who engage in this work are also motivated by the need for conflict resolution. Conflict is complex, and theories which seek to understand the source must reflect that reality. Will the ideas presented in this volume assist in conflict resolution? One thing is certain: no lasting peace can be achieved without an understanding of the underlying dynamics and nuances of intergroup conflict.

To appreciate the chapters in this volume, some familiarity with social psychological theory is necessary. Social cognition, emphasized in the *first section*, is concerned with understanding how we notice, utilize memory, interpret information, and implement social information – in short, how we form inferences about our social environment, and subsequently make social judgements.

Early work on social cognition emphasized rational models of inference, on the assumption that there are logical ways of utilizing information in making social judgements. Unfortunately, subsequent research has shown that the rational model is a poor predictor, as people's integration of information is often illogical and may include serious biases. Alternative information processors are called schemas. These cognitive structures help organize information processing, recall important facts, and provide expectations.

In general, social psychology has shown that people will seek to minimize the effort involved in complex social judgement. Mental short-cuts include rule-heuristics which allow for rapid decisions. There is also a long-established relationship between affect and cognition. All in all, then, rational models describe abstract and ideal conditions rarely found in the real world. Schemas, on the other hand, help people make decisions and may in some cases become a self-fulfilling prophecy.

The chapter by *Boehnke et al.* examines how the threat of war affects mental well-being within a cognitive-phenomenological theory of stress. In the nuclear age uncontrollable or unpredictable events are not only possible, but also perceived as more stressful. The reason is clear: if conflict is unpredictable, it becomes particularly difficult to develop plans or find ways of coping. The cognitive-phenomenological theory suggests that stress is in the eye of the beholder. Events are stressful only when the individual regards them as such. Boehnke and his co-workers combine these ideas with basic social psychological determinants of appraisal and coping.

The second chapter, by *Maoz*, focuses on decision-theoretic studies of the initiation, management, and termination of international conflict. The rational model suggests that there are logical and even correct ways to understand conflict. However, decisions are in fact often illogical. Maoz's review seeks a synthesis of rational and cognitive models of conflict.

Wallbaum discusses the role of integrative complexity during international crises. In general, crises which end in war show reduced complexity among policy-makers, whereas increases in integration complexity tend to precede international agreement. Ideally, of course, policy-makers should function at a level of complexity appropriate to the situation. The concept of integrative complexity suggests that belief systems should produce more rational decisions if based on sound information and if well integrated. Integration complexity therefore refers to a differentiation process (the number of elements in a problem), and integration (the ability of the social perceiver to see various parts of the problem as interrelated).

Kruglanski et al. suggest that the way in which individuals react to conflict depends on at least two types of knowledge. Not only must we understand what a conflict connotes, but we must also be able to identify a situation as conflictual. This chapter advocates a social cognitive model of how knowledge is acquired, and shows its relevance in terms of changing people and resolving conflict. The main idea behind the cognitive approach is that behavior is based on a person's social perception. Research has shown that social perceivers frequently let prior expectations override the perception of social situations; further, social information is often unreliable.

Hazani offers a focus on a specific conflict in discussing the demonization and rigidity of Israeli concepts of Palestinians. It is suggested that Zionism has arisen as a response to the Jewish sense of symbolic immortality. In Israeli social cognition, Palestinians, by their very presence, prevent Jewish unification, thus perpetuating death and replacing the Nazis as 'villains'.

In the final chapter of section 1, *Moore* discusses the basic processes of social categorization. This concept suggests that we group people together on the basis of some shared attributes or common characteristics. Social categorization as a basis for social identity has considerable psychological salience. However, according to Moore, these processes are essentially defective coping mechanisms which produce stereotyping, intergroup bias, and biased information gathering. Mutual misperception (mirroring) is a major impediment to equitable conflict revolution. Conflict is more difficult to reduce when one is influenced by the powerful mechanism of misperception.

The *second section* of the book applies classical social psychological approaches to the topic of conflict. The scope of social psychology is quite broad. Among the many topics social psychologists study are how people act in groups and in what ways groups affect the behavior of their members. Social psychologists are not the only ones to study social processes, of course. Sociologists are concerned about the societal level of analysis, and may focus on such broad factors as class conflict or intergroup violence. At the other extreme, the focus of clinical psychology is on personality and individual processes. Social psychology plays an intermediate role in studying interpersonal relations and the overall social situation – the latter including the contextual structure of society, other people, and the social environment. In defining this territory, social psychology is saying that social behavior and thought rest ultimately with individuals. Our focus, then, as social psychologists, is on the variety of social conditions which shape the ways in which individuals behave to other individuals and to social groups. In short, we seek to understand the causes of social behavior and thought within the framework of social situations.

Many of the chapters in this section draw on theories of group behavior. A 'group' is generally defined as two or more individuals who share common goals, possess a perception of interdependent fates, and have ongoing stable relationships. A major function of groups is to create conformity with respect to established norms and goals. At times group cohesiveness may take on a dysfunctional form known as 'group think'. That situation may occur when groups have very high levels of cohesiveness combined with dynamic and powerful leaders. 'Group think' puts priority on consensus as the overriding motivation; groups in this cognitive frame fail to evaluate decisions accurately or realistically.

An important topic in group research is social categorization. This is the experience of 'us' versus 'them', the in-group as distinguished from the out-group. Many social dimensions may be utilized in the social categorization process, including race, age, sex, and political persuasion. Experimental research has shown that people evaluate their own in-group more favorably and are negative toward out-groups, even when distinctions are made on the basis of unimportant or nonsensical categories. Why do people categorize? One reason is that individuals seek to enhance their self-esteem by identifying with specific social groups.

Groups therefore contribute social identity, a psychological construct of considerable importance. The psychological relevance of group identification is manifested in peoples' attitudes. For many people it is a comforting thing to see themselves reflected vicariously in the status and glory of the in-group.

An outcome of the identity process is interdependence and competition between groups. Competition occurs when two groups are in a relationship where the outcome depends on what the other group gets – a zero-sum game. Competition for resources may lead to conflict, whereas defining superordinate goals may lead to cooperation. Many group reward-structures are a mixture of both cooperation and competition.

Rabbie, in the initial chapter of section two, provides a conceptual distinction between social groups and social categories. Group categorization is examined and favoritism toward the ingroup is evaluated within the framework of a behavioral interaction model.

The chapter by *Fisher* offers a comprehensive social psychological model for the study of conflict. Some research has played an important role in the development of theory. Typically, games simulate key features of everyday interaction. A common finding of this research is that middle class participants will tend to compete even when cooperation would produce greater rewards. The model presented by Fisher also evaluates social identity and social categorization. He argues that conflict theory in social psychology is fragmentary and often restricted, hence the need for an integrative and eclectic model of inter-group conflict. Fisher offers a dynamic description of causation, escalation, and resolution of conflict.

Inter-group relations is the focus of the chapter by *Roux et al.* Inter-group relations often display prejudice, in the form of negative attitudes toward out-groups. Other products include stereotypes (generalized beliefs about the out-group) and discriminatory behavior. *Roux et al.* argue that the study of groups shows that in-group members tend to be xenophobic. However, when people are allowed to make independent approaches to inter-group relations, an attitude of solidarity develops.

The contributions of community psychology to understanding and promoting of world peace are examined in the chapter by *Criss and Johnson*. The authors argue for a social systems approach, since behavior in larger national systems is more complex and contains features that resist change. We need meta-perspectives and a program of 'people empowerment' to prevent war.

Attitudes play a central role in social psychology. As defined, attitudes contain affective beliefs as well as behavioral components. Attitudes refer to general evaluations people make about a variety of specific objects in the external world. Acquired through experience, they guide or direct people's behavior to some extent. The contribution by *Auerbach and Agid* provides a conceptual framework for an attitude in an existence conflict. Focusing on Israeli leaders, the authors outline an analysis of nuances that distinguish each over time.

Louche is interested in problems of inter-group negotiations, in particular labor negotiations in France. Group decisions represent another significant field in social psychology. It is often possible to predict the final decisions of groups if we have knowledge of initial opinions, since group discussion frequently serves only to strengthen the majority viewpoint. From a common-sense point of view, groups are thought to produce 'better' decisions, as they may contain a variety of viewpoints reflecting complex social reality. Research has shown, however, that groups in fact make riskier decisions. Groups often display a shift toward polarization, leading to more extreme viewpoints. Group members convince themselves of the correctness of these viewpoints, and are therefore willing to adopt stronger views which can lead to 'group think'. In intergroup negotiations Louche notes that the 'representation' role obligation can hinder agreement. Since negotiations often result in compromises, this means that further intra-organizational conflicts ensue between negotiators and constituents.

To complete this section, *Eskola* provides a critique of the deterministic-mechanistic paradigm in peace research. In general, the scientific paradigms of social science are derived from models developed in 19th century physics. Social science provides a mechanistic model of human beings as passive organisms, whereas real people display functions of language and purpose. Behavior is often seen as a reaction to external factors, but people initiate change. Neopositivists fail to take into account contextual history, or researcher influence on experimental results, and they are naive in representing social reality. Eskola provides a critique of the deterministic-mechanistic paradigm. His chapter argues for a reconciliation between traditional methods employed in the search for scientific laws and approaches concerned with meanings and logic.

In the *final section* of the book we see examples of current research on major conflict-related topics.

The contribution by *Olsen* applies theories from cognitive psychology and attribution theory to analyze the ethnic conflict in Sri Lanka. We have already mentioned social cognition. 'Attributions' refer to ways in which people use information to determine causes of social behavior. Uncertainty or unexpected events create a greater need for predictability. Attributions help people make predictions, determine attitude and behavior, and control the social environment. In the Sri Lanka conflict, we see that expectations of the future are largely influenced by attributions for past events.

National identity is the cutting edge for changes in Eastern Europe and other parts of the world today. That people are influenced by the groups to which they belong is 'old news'. An emotional attachment to the nation-state encourages people to identify with national values for behavioral guidance. We know from social identity theory that people have a basic tendency to form in-groups and out-groups, and that this categorization process provides the basis for social attitudes. National identity is also fundamental to self-esteem: we feel proud when 'our' nation is successful and powerful. Unfortunately, such national identity may also bring on de-individuation, when personal identity is replaced by the objectives of the nation-state. We can see such a loss of personal responsibility in the Nazi and Stalinist outlooks, and certainly also in other xenophobic societies. De-individuation is facilitated by anonymity and reduced self-awareness. The study by *Larsen et al.* suggests the presence of a common national identity which transcends socio-political differences in the United States. Other national samples suggest both unique national identity, as well as international concordance indicating the presence of universal values.

Johnson et al. examine a range of patriarchal, moral, and nationalistic beliefs. Their survey analysis yields four factors, where the war system is predicted by positive attitudes toward patriotism-nationalism and by negative perspectives on social connectedness. The acceptance of war is seen as partly dependent on a range of moral and nationalistic beliefs.

The final chapter by *Berger Gould* examines differences in the attitudes of men and of women to the stress of living under the threat of war. Gender difference is a valuable contribution to the understanding of conflict and its consequences. Gender not only forms a basis for identity and the self-concept, it also perpetuates the division of labor and social roles. Moreover, all research points to the greater destructiveness of the males of the species.

The reader is now invited to study these chapters. Conflict may be our history – but it is born into our social identities and social psychology. Thus it is neither inevitable nor inherent in human nature. We humans have purposive qualities and are capable of initiating and completing social change. This book has been compiled in the hope that it may offer useful thoughts for the ultimate quest of mankind: peace on earth.

Notes on the Contributors

Ludmilla Andrejeva, PhD (University of Sofia, 1992). Assistant Professor, University of Sofia.

Yehudit Auerbach, Bar Ilan University, Ramat Gan, Israel.

Daniel Bar-Tal, Tel-Aviv University

Hemda BenYehuda Agid, Bar Ilan University, Ramat Gan, Israel.

Klaus Boehnke, PhD, Associate Professor, Department of Education, Free University of Berlin, Germany.

Julie E. Criss, PhD, Centinela Family and Child Guidance Clinic, Inglewood, CA

Gyorgy Csepeli, PhD (University of Budapest, ELTE, 1972). Chair, Department of Social Psychology.

Antti Eskola, PhD, Professor of Social Psychology, University of Tampere, Finland.

Ronald J. Fisher, PhD, Professor of Psychology, University of Saskatchewan, Saskatoon, Canada.

Wolfgang Frindte, PhD, Professor of Social Psychology, Department of Psychology, Friedrich Schiller University, Jena, Germany.

Benina Berger Gould, PhD, Adjunct Professor of Psychology, Saybrook Institute, San Francisco, CA and Research Associate, University of California, Berkeley, Center for Slavic and East European Studies.

Scott B. Hamilton, PhD, Professor of Psychology, Department of Psychology, Colorado State University, Fort Collins, USA.

Andy Handler, graduate student at the California School of Professional Pyschology, Los Angeles

Moshe Hazani, Department of Criminology, Bar Ilan University, Ramat-Gan, Israel

Paula B. Johnson, PhD, Professor of Psychology, California School of Professional Psychology, Los Angeles, CA

Nadia Kashlakeva, M.A. (University of Sofia, 1991). Assistant Professor, University of Sofia.

Carolyn Killifer, M.A. (Oregon State University, 1990). Professional Counselor.

Yechiel Klar, Tel-Aviv University

Arie W. Kruglanski, University of Maryland

Krum Krumov, PhD (University of Sofia, 1981). Chair, Department of Social Psychology, University of Sofia.

Knud S. Larsen, PhD (Brigham Young University, 1973). Professor, Oregon State University.

Claude Louche, Centre de Recherche en Psychologie, Equipe de Psychologie Sociale et du Travail, Université Paul Valéry, Montpellier, France.

Zeev Maoz, University of Haifa

Alexander V. Melnikov, PhD, Senior Researcher, Institute for the Problems of Higher Education, Academy of Pedagogical Sciences, Moscow, Russia.

Michael Moore, Department of Education in Science and Technology, Technion – Israel Institute of Technology

Gabriel Mugny, PhD, Professor of Social Psychology, Faculté de Psychologie et des Science de l'Education, University of Geneva, Switzerland.

Bendigt Olsen, Affiliated, Department of Social Science and Development, Chr. Michelsen Institute, Bergen, Norway

Juan Antonio Pérez, PhD, Professor of Social Psychology, Departamento de Psicologia, University of Valencia, Spain.

Laszlo Pordany, M.A. (Attila Jozsef University, 1973). Hungarian Ambassador to Australia.

Jacob M. Rabbie, Department of Social and Organizational Psychology, University of Utrecht, The Netherlands.

Patricia Roux, PhD in Sociology, Faculté des Sciences Sociales et Politiques, University of Geneva, Switzerland.

Zlatka Russinova, PhD (University of Sofia, 1987). Associate Professor, University of Sofia.

Margarita Sanchez-Mazas, Faculté de Psychologie et des Science de l'Education, University of Geneva, Switzerland.

Tytti Solantaus, MD, PhD, Senior Lecturer, Department of Child Psychology, University of Helsinki, Finland.

Ulrike Unterbruner, PhD, Associate Professor, Department of Didactics of the Natural Sciences, University of Salzburg, Austria.

Alistair B.C. Wallbaum, Doctoral student of Health Psychology, School of Social Ecology, University of California, Irvine.

PART 1:

Cognitive and Perceptual Approaches

Introduction to Part 1

This section opens with a chapter that centers around a question vividly debated over the past decade or so: how threat of war or other global threats can affect the psychic well-being of people. *Boehnke et al.* postulate a way of conceptualizing threat within a cognitive-phenomenological theory of stress as outlined by Lazarus. They also point out, however, that cognitive stress theory can be applied only if certain qualifications are made. First, threat of war has to be classified as macro-social stress, as opposed to other types of stressors like everyday hassles. Furthermore, remote threats of war have to be distinguished psychologically from immediate threats of war. The authors then argue that the original cognitive-phenomenological theory of stress has one central deficit, in that it ignores the social determinants of appraisal and coping. On the basis of thoughts by Tajfel, suggestions are made on how to integrate social-psychological ideas into the theory of stress. The chapter closes with brief propositions in regard to design and methodology in future research on the psycho-emotional effects of global crises.

The review essay by *Maoz* examines decision-theoretic studies of the initiation, management, and termination of international conflict, focusing on the traditional distinction between rational choice models and cognitive ones. The main arguments of this chapter are threefold. First, contrary to conventional wisdom, rational and cognitive models of international conflict provide not mutually exclusive but rather complementary explanations. Second, it is therefore constructive to view these models as context-dependent explanations of actual conflict behavior of national decision-makers. Third, we can get a better understanding of the decision-making processes by which conflicts are being made and unmade if these two approaches are synthesized.

The chapter by *Wallbaum* reviews the literature on integrative complexity during international crises. In several archival studies, crises that ended in war showed reduced complexity among the policy-makers. Conversely, increases in integrative complexity have been shown to precede international agreements. Political longevity is associated with the ability to maintain or increase complexity during crisis situations – although this ability seems to be quite rare. The optimal approach to international politics thus is not always to function at maximal complexity, but rather to be a 'cognitive manager', functioning at the complexity appropriate to the situation. For example, successful revolutionary leaders will operate at a low complexity level during the revolution, and then at a higher level once in power. And finally, Wallbaum proposes possible ways to create an environment compatible with optimal cognitive management, in which the full range of information-processing complexity is available to the policy- maker.

Reactions of individuals to conflict situations depend on two types of knowledge, as discussed in the chapter by *Kruglanski, Bar-Tal and Klar*. These are general knowledge of what the term 'conflict' connotes emotionally and behaviorally, and the specific knowledge that a particular situation indeed is conflictual. A social cognitive understanding of processes whereby knowledge is acquired and modified is, therefore, highly relevant to possible attempts to alter persons' reactions to conflicts.

In the chapter by *Hazani*, two intertwined features of Israeli attitudes in the Israeli-Arab conflict are discussed: rigidity, and demonization of the Palestinians, who are often compared to the Nazis. Employing Lifton's paradigm of symbolic immortality, Hazani asserts that Zionism is, in part, a response to the Jewish sense of immortality that emerged in Eastern Europe in the late 19th century. Zionism, which exhibited a totalistic nature, clung to a new version of the traditional Jewish immortalizing system, shifting the emphasis from the theological to the spatial and institutional modes of immortality. By creating a Jewish nation-state in the Promised Land, it sought to bring about Jewish rebirth – badly needed before but particularly so after the Holocaust. However, the indigenous Palestinian population has impeded Jewish reunification with the Holy Land, thereby perpetuating Jewish symbolic death. Israeli consciousness thus sees Palestinians as replacing the Nazi arch-villain.

In the final chapter in this section, *Moore* suggests the basic process of social categorization as a defective coping mechanism likely to produce stereotyping. The latter, itself rooted in biased perception, is related to further distortions, such as intergroup bias and biased information gathering. Along with numerous derived misperceptions, these distortions are extremely wide-spread in intergroup perception. This review considers mutual misperception or the mirror image phenomenon in more detail. Moore shows that such complementary stereotypes range from general intergroup bias ('We are good; they are evil') to specific mirroring, and include varieties such as parallelisms, mutual misconceptions, and ignorance. Though intergroup conflict is based on additional factors, reducing such conflict is made more difficult through the powerful psychological mechanisms that underlie misperception and mirroring.

1

Can the Threat of War be Conceptualized as Macro-Social Stress?

Theoretical Considerations

Klaus Boehnke
Wolfgang Frindte
Scott B. Hamilton
Alexander V. Melnikov
Tytti Solantaus
Ulrike Unterbruner

1. The Peace Issue as a Part of the Global Crises Issue

It is now widely accepted that the survival of humanity is severely challenged by various global crises (World Commission on Environment and Development, 1987). The prospect of a world-wide war (recently inflamed by the Gulf crisis) and the grave ecological problems all over the planet are only the most prominent symptoms. Hunger crises in various parts of the world, for example, should by no means be forgotten, neither should unemployment. All these pose serious political and economic problems. They are the result of political and economic decisions in the past; they form the basis for political and economic decisions at the present and in the future. Aside from their political and economic importance, they also influence the well-being of humans on a daily basis, even for those not living in a war zone or in an area immediately challenged by ecological problems. Although debated by some authors (e.g., Coles, 1986), it seems generally accepted that the prospects of nuclear war (see Fiske, 1987) and of ecological catastrophes pose a serious threat to psychic well-being all over the world.

Psychology, thus, has the obligation to furnish a better understanding of

* This chapter is the by-product of the formulation of an invited research proposal to the committee for Psychological Study of Peace (CPSP – Chairman M. Wessells) of the International Union of Psychological Sciences (IUPsyS).

the principles at work in the perception and handling of these threats. Additionally, it is our firm belief that psychology also should offer assistance in developing better tools to enable humankind to minimize or abolish these threats. Psychology should aim at laying the groundwork for a better theoretical understanding of the perception and handling of the war threat and of ecological crises in various social groups and cultures. It should also make suggestions for improvement of – broadly conceived – health and peace education programs. Both these objectives – of gaining a better understanding of theoretical psychic aspects of macro-social stress and of improving education programs in the field – are basically cross-cultural, in that the macro-social stressors which are of primary interest are clearly global phenomena.

2. Global Crises as Macro-Social Stress

The two main theoretical approaches for dealing psychologically with the above-mentioned threats have been the cognitive-phenomenological approach to stress, originally formulated by Lazarus (1966), and a psychoanalytically-oriented approach, originally proposed by Janis & Leventhal (1968). Haan's (1977) work can be seen as an attempt to reconcile both approaches by introducing the psychoanalytic concepts of defense mechanisms (repression, displacement etc.) into a cognitively oriented theory of stress.

If global crises are conceptualized in terms of environmental stressors, it seems necessary to define them more clearly as macro-social stressors in order to distinguish them from (individual) critical life events (Holmes & Rahe, 1967) and from everyday hassles (Lazarus, 1986). Macro-social stress is viewed as a long-term threatening condition originating in the political and/or economic domain – as opposed to 'social stress' (Levine & Scotch, 1973) which may also be a long-term threatening condition, but with its primary origin in person-to-person social interaction.

If macro-social stress is conceptualized as a long-term threatening condition, several problems arise when it comes to studying the effects within the framework of a psychoanalytically enriched cognitive-phenomenological theory of stress. The latter decision seems appropriate, since several studies have shown that, from a mental health perspective, the prospect of war and ecological catastrophes cannot be seen as noxious stimuli quasi-automatically leading to health disturbances, as might be postulated in a mechanistic biological theory of stress. Studies by Boehnke et al. (1989) and by Meyer-Probst et al. (1989) have shown that the reverse appears true: Those adolescents who express most fears with regard to war and ecological catastrophes seem to be the most healthy in terms of psychiatric or psychosomatic symptoms.

2.1. Immediate vs. Remote Stressors

This finding sheds light on a central theoretical problem in dealing with macro-social stressors from a cognitive-phenomenological perspective. Any new research must indicate exactly to which extent macro-social stress is immediate vs. remote. By 'immediate', we mean to what extent a macro-social stressor has immediate personal relevance. In psychological terms, this may be addressed as the salience issue (see Fiske, 1987; Hamilton et al., 1988). Two examples: Because of the Vietnam and Afghanistan wars, the threat of war seemed more immediate to US citizens in the late 1960s and early 1970s and to Soviet citizens in the early 1980s, than, for example, to Austrians or to Finns. Secondly, the threat of radiation after the 1986 Chernobyl disaster was, of course, much more immediate for Eastern and Central Europeans than, for example, for Australians. In this sense, an immediate macro-social stressor is a threatening condition which is *likely to acquire immediate physical relevance* to a person. This type of stress condition must be distinguished from remote stressors. The latter could be defined as stressors with *no immediate physical relevance* to persons. An example would be the accident at Bhopal in India, for North Americans. Immediate and remote stressors must furthermore be distinguished from noxious stimuli. It does not seem appropriate to conceive of, say, Bhopal or Chernobyl as macro-social stressors for the people directly physically affected by them. For them, the catastrophes had death-bringing consequences which it would be cynical to view as macro-social stress within the framework of cognitive-phenomenological stress research.

Classifying a given macro-social stressor as remote, immediate, or noxious depends on the persons involved and their unique environmental circumstances. The classification into remote and immediate macro-social stressors can be seen as a reference to spatial as well as temporal immediacy. For example, the Bhopal accident was a remote stressor for Europeans in general, but it may have been an immediate stressor for people living adjacent to other chemical factories. Ecological problems will always have the character of noxious stimuli when they reach a certain level of local intensity. Smog conditions over big cities may be remote stressors for people living in non-industrialized areas with low population density; they may be immediate stressors for inhabitants of big cities on a normal fall or early winter day, but they may also become noxious stimuli on smog-alert days especially for people with chronic lung ailments. Psychological thinking would not seem to offer the optimal frame of reference for situations in which macro-social stressors have become acutely hazardous noxious stimuli requiring urgent medical attention.

2.2. Cognitive Appraisal and Coping

Let us now return to the theoretical assumptions underlying cognitive-phenomenological stress theory. Lazarus & Launier (1978) proposed that in dealing with potentially stressful events or conditions, two principal components are involved: cognitive appraisal and coping. Cognitive appraisal can be subdivided into three components: primary appraisal, secondary appraisal, and reappraisal. Primary appraisal can take three directions: irrelevance, benign-positive appraisal, and stressful appraisal. In the first case, a potential stressor is judged to be of no interest. In terms of macro-social stressors, they may be irrelevant for certain groups of a society. For example, in West Germany civil servants are granted a life-time contract after having been a member of the civil service for a certain time-period; thus, unemployment may become irrelevant as a macro-social stressor for these individuals. Even positive appraisals of macro-social stressors are possible if one focuses on certain groups within a society. Military personnel, for example, may evaluate the war threat as positive, because it gives them a feeling of being needed. A stressful primary appraisal seems most apt for macro-social stressors – at least, in cases where they have the quality of an immediate stressor.

If an event or a condition is appraised as stressful, Lazarus & Launier (1978) assume that three types of stressful stimuli have to be distinguished: harm/loss, threat, and challenge. For psychological stress research of the type outlined here, threats are the center of interest. Of course, macro-social stressors can cause harm and/or loss in various ways. The arms race, for example, is one primary reason for economic disturbances in many societies; it creates harms and losses for many people. Moreover, macro-social stressors may be appraised as stressful challenges by certain groups. If ecological problems were not, to a certain extent, challenges for so many, how could organizations like Greenpeace remain so active over the years? But, in general, macro-social stressors must psychologically be classified as threats. The danger of a nuclear war, of a nuclear power plant leak, or of a climate catastrophe – such things are usually not evaluated as harms, losses, or challenges, but as remote or immediate threats.

The second phase of dealing with stressful events or conditions, according to cognitive-phenomenological stress theory, is that of secondary appraisal. In this phase the stressed person evaluates his or her resources and options for coping with the stressor. At first glance, secondary appraisal would seem a very person-centered phase of dealing with stress. Trait-like personal tendencies in interpreting and evaluating resources and options could be seen as the prime focus of research on secondary appraisal processes. But this narrow perspective is not a very fruitful approach to the question of how people deal with macro-social stressors. A focus on personal appraisal tendencies may be adequate when dealing with everyday hassles – for example, if we are interested in what happens if it starts raining and someone realizes that he or she forgot an umbrella. In case of macro-social stressors, the social circumstances of resource evaluation must be included (see Section 3).

The third phase of the appraisal process is that of reappraisal. Feedback processes as well as defense mechanisms in the deep-psychological sense are subsumed by this category. In the course of cognitive appraisal, an originally threatening stressful condition may be reappraised as non-threatening or as less threatening, because of secondary appraisal processes (e.g., if the cognitive evaluation of resources and options for coping showed the individual that there are numerous options available). In this sense, air pollution as a macro-social stressor may be reappraised as less threatening than military or non-military nuclear power, because there seem to be more personal and societal options available to deal successfully with pollution than with radiation.

The reappraisal process may, however, function in reverse. A person may sense that he or she has no options for dealing successfully with a macro-social stressor which was primarily appraised as threatening. This person may then react cognitively by redefining the original stimulus (e.g., reconceptualizing the danger of an all-out nuclear war as non-existent or non-threatening). Theoretically and empirically, a defensive reappraisal and a primary appraisal of irrelevance are very difficult to distinguish. One attempt to tackle the problem involves the use of psycho-physiological assessment and contrasting its results with self-report data. A pattern of high psycho-physiological arousal and low self-reported emotionality would be viewed as an indication of defensive reappraisal, whereas a synchronous pattern of low arousal and low self-reported emotionality would be interpreted as a 'true' primary appraisal of irrelevance (Keilin & Hamilton, 1989).

If the process of all three phases of cognitive appraisal shows that an event or condition is threatening and that there are viable options for dealing with the stressor, then action – that is, the actual coping – begins. Lazarus & Launier (1978) point out that coping processes tend to focus on the self, the environment, or both; and that they are directly related to the troubled transaction (instrumental coping) or to the emotions accompanying the transaction (palliative coping).

A few examples should clarify what is meant. First, let us point out again that macro-social stressors are threats anticipated to bring about harm or loss in the future. One instrumental self-oriented way of coping with the macro-social stressor air pollution would be to stay indoors during a smog-alert. A palliative self-oriented way of coping with the threat of war would be to concentrate actively on other things, by joining a sports club or a religious sect or by retreating into a very close personal relationship (Solantaus, 1989). An instrumental environment-oriented way of coping with air pollution could be to sell one's car and use public transportation instead. A palliative environment-oriented way of coping with the threat of war would be to organize discussions and workshops on the topic of war and peace, thereby attempting to change public opinion on the topic. We will not delve deeper into separate coping modes here, but refer the reader to the monograph by Lazarus & Folkman (1984).

3. Social Determinants of Appraisal and Coping

To us, a major shortcoming of the theoretical approach of Lazarus and his research group seems to be that appraisal and coping are conceptualized more or less exclusively as individual processes. We agree with Lazarus (1986) that individual meanings of stressors and their place in coping and adaptation have to be explored. But although Lazarus includes the 'sociodynamics of hassles and uplifts' (1986, p. 45) in his theoretical considerations, the sociological and/or social-psychological aspects of a cognitive-phenomenological theory of stress seem clearly underdeveloped. As indicated above, we view the social circumstances of an individual as an extremely important factor in determining how a particular stressor will be appraised and subsequently coped with.

Tajfel (1981) and Moscovici (1984) have forwarded plausible assumptions and empirical material on how social stereotypes come about. We hypothesize that the cognitive appraisal of macro-social stressors has much in common with the generation of social stereotypes. This should be the case especially for primary appraisals of irrelevance and defensive reappraisals, but also for the secondary appraisal of resources for coping. More concretely this means that we consider primary appraisals like 'no panic on the Titanic' (= no serious threat present), but also like 'our endangered species' (= threats in abundance) as symbolic appraisals which function as group-specific social stereotypes.

Our considerations take what may be called a *systemic* starting point. In detail, the following processes must be examined in order to incorporate the thoughts of Tajfel (1981) and Moscovici (1984) as well as the elaborations of von Cranach et al. (1987), who offer empirical material on the theory of social representations, into a cognitive-phenomenological theory of stress:

The potentially stressed individual, and the social units in which he or she lives and acts (groups, organizations, and societies) are seen as interconnected complex systems. The global problems briefly outlined above, their local manifestations, and attitudes, norms, and values at work when dealing with global threats in various societies, organizations, and social groups cannot be conceptualized as a linear causal chain. Neither is there such a chain when one looks at individual coping strategies. These more or less axiomatic propositions can be organized into four separate hypotheses (see also Frindte et al., 1989).

1. *Individuals and their social forms of living (which are both seen as complex systems) have analogous basic functions.*
For our purposes, the functions of information processing and appraisal (IP) and of organization of action and activity itself (OA) are of primary interest. Information processing and action are interconnected in 'functional circles'. This means:

A. In order to act successfully against (potentially) stressful environmental conditions or events, a human being resorts to currently available or formerly accumulated information, evaluates this information emotionally, and tests its applicability by initiating action. Experience acquired through acting leads to new learning processes and to a restructuring of the individual's memory. We consider social processes in groups, organizations, and societies to be regulated analogously. Group-related, collective, or societal processes of IP and OA are interconnected as well in forms of societally-organized communication and interaction. A clear example of this can currently be seen in the restructuring process of the society of former East Germany into a marked-oriented economy.

B. When analyzing individual ways of dealing with stress, we should, therefore, look at IP (cognitive appraisal) and OA (coping – as is indeed done by Lazarus, 1966, and Haan, 1977); *and* we should take into consideration the various levels of social organizations – a step more or less omitted by Lazarus and adherents of his theoretical approach. Relevant social organizations could be the family, the work group, the ethnic group, the social class, the region, the state etc., and their influence on individual appraisals of macro-social stress. In analyzing these higher levels of social organizations, we will have to keep in mind that they are not aggregates, but develop specific properties of their own. A work group is not merely the sum of its members: it has its very own 'individual' characteristics which have to be measured in empirical research.

2. *Complex systems develop actively, on the basis of their internal dynamics.* This means:

A. As a result of their pre-existing inner complexity, and aided by the basic functions described above, complex systems generate their structural properties by themselves, constrained only by certain contextual limits. Therefore, complex systems may remain surprisingly inactive in the face of various external stimuli or general parameters. On the other hand, every system has its special straining points which will be responsible for a very sensitive reaction to external influences. A somewhat far-fetched example could be that of a coalition government in which the partners reach decisions that are at odds with the principles of one of the partners, if not both – and yet nothing happens. At other times, however, minor departures from the platform of one party can lead to a split-up of the government, because external influences have changed.

B. Global crises are not experienced, evaluated, and coped with congruently as macro-social stressors by individuals, groups, and organizations. Whether and how a person or a group deals with a global stressor depends primarily on the frame of reference of IP and OA indigenous to the complex system. Psychologists will therefore need to study an enormous diversity of interindividual and intergroup modes of dealing with potential macro-social stressors. The analysis of the phenomenology and the causation of the various modes lies at the core of empirical research in the field of coping with macro-social stressors, like, for example, the threat of (nuclear) war.

3. *Complex systems form hierarchical networks.*
The functioning of every higher system depends on interconnected lower or partial systems. Every lower or partial system, on the other hand, deduces its ways of functioning from properties of higher order systems and/or partial systems. Thus the information processing (IP) and the organization of action (OA) of a system are always interconnected in a network with other partial systems and higher order systems. This means:

A. The IP and OA of individuals or groups are primarily a part of the autonomous activity of the very system. The various systems (individuals, groups, etc.) do, however, exist in mutual interrelation based on communication and interaction. Their specific IPs and OAs, thus, form a hierarchically-organized network as well. The IP and the OA of a single person will be co-determined by the retrospective, current, and prospective 'anchors' cast by the various social units to which that person belongs. Of special relevance for the individual IP and OA are the so-called social representations (SRs) which exist in social groups, organizations, and societies and which an individual can and usually will acquire.

> The term social representations stands for the organized, abstracted, and typified body of knowledge of a society or of a sub-unit (social group) of it. Social representations, thus, always need a social 'carrier-system'. They are related to certain social circumstances and contain the central conceptions about these circumstances in the form of values, norms, attitudes, and knowledge. They constitute superindividual systems of symbols shared by all members of the social unit (Thommen et al., 1988, p. 48) (our translation).

Individuals acquire the various social representations through interaction and communication with other individuals within social groups and organizations and convert them into person-specific social representations (into individual social categories, schemata, stereotypes, etc.). According to von Cranach et al. (1987), and explicated more extensively by Tajfel (1981) in his social identity theory, individual social representations (ISRs) serve the following purposes:

1 They serve as a frame of reference for the individual's perception and evaluation of environmental influences. *We assume* that a person will act more efficiently and carefree the more his or her ISRs are in congruence with the SRs of his or her reference group. Social conventions advance the efficiency of action and tend to reduce stress.
2 They stabilize the individual's self-concept and social identity. *We assume* that a person acquires the SRs of certain groups in order to gain the social support of these groups and to stabilize his or her own sense of self.
3 They serve as a means of delimiting from other social groups and organizations, those SRs the person does not want to identify with. *We assume* that a person will try to reject, denounce, reinterpret, or change those SRs of a social group with which he or she does not identify, in order to acquire congruence of ISRs and the SRs of a group to which he or she belongs. A person or a group can, therefore, influence the SRs of hierarchically higher complex social systems by changing the SRs of another individual, and this may eventually lead to a change in the SRs of a group with regard to this topic (e.g., opinions regarding global crises). The changed SRs of a group may in turn change the SRs of an organization, and, in the long run, those of a society and even of humanity as a whole.
4 They assist the individual's organization of action. *We assume* that a person who identifies with certain social groups, organizations, etc. will plan actions and eventually act in a way valued highly by his or her reference group, relatively independent of the options of action available in principle. Socially-shared intended actions have an increased probability of happening. For example, Boehnke & Macpherson (1989) demonstrated that how a child acts with regard to the threat of nuclear war is determined largely by how his or her parents have acted with regard to this threat.

B. Individual cognitive evaluations (appraisals and reappraisals) of global threats, as well as the search for and utilization of various coping strategies, will be decisively co-determined by the SRs available. Thus, it depends largely on the social values, norms, and attitudes of the reference group

1 whether a person will evaluate global problems positively, as stressful, or as irrelevant (primary appraisal);
2 how he or she will assess the available options for action (secondary appraisal);
3 which defense mechanisms he or she will prefer (reappraisal); and
4 which coping strategies he or she will employ.

Global threats may be upgraded, down-graded, or reinterpreted in accordance with the SRs of the reference group in order to enhance the positive social identity of the individual. The fewer opportunities a person has to identify with a relevant social reference group in the process of dealing with macro-social stress, the greater will be the emotional, cognitive, and behavioral efforts necessary to cope with the threatening circumstances. This is one reason why individuals spontaneously form groups in stressful situations (as was the case in many European countries immediately after the Chernobyl accident – see Schmidt et al., 1990). As Haste (1989) has indicated, this tendency should not be seen as a sign of successfully coping with the macro-social stressor, but as one step in the secondary appraisal process. It lowers the individual's emotional/cognitive efforts by offering accepted and shared SRs as a frame of reference.

C. Additionally, by means of person- or group-specific evaluations, re-evaluations, and the handling of stressors, individuals and/or their reference group take a conscious stand with regard to the SRs offered by hierarchically higher social systems (organizations, societies) concerning the approach to global threats. This means that individuals and groups do not just deal with the global stressor itself, but simultaneously examine the social forms of dealing with macro-social stress. Via this process, individuals and groups can also influence the SRs of hierarchically higher social systems and can change them under certain circumstances: an assumption which gathered overwhelming empirical support during recent changes in East Germany. (See also Moscovici's 1976 monograph on the influences of minorities on social change.)

4. *The development of complex systems is based on internal inconsistencies and disequilibria.*
This means that (as was stressed in Hypothesis 3) the SRs of a reference group are acquired in an individual manner and are incorporated in the individual's memory as ISRs. As a person can simultaneously be a member of different social groups (family, work group, interest group, etc.), he or she is confronted with different SRs. As a result of the autonomous internal development of systems, ISRs, SRs of the reference group, and SRs of other groups, are

seldom fully compatible. The greater the discrepancy between the ISRs and the SRs of the reference group and of other groups, the greater the emotional, cognitive, and social contradictions to be overcome in order to uphold a stable and positive self-concept. With increasing discrepancies between SRs and ISRs, whether a person will (re)act with an enhanced capacity for action or with learned helplessness, frustration, anxiety, and/or depression in the face of global threats and macro-social stress in general will depend on the following factors:

- the social influence of the reference group (which determines the capability to enforce its SRs as dominant values, norms, etc.).
- the transparency of the general societal system and the individual's opportunities to gather information on global threats and ways of coping with them.
- the individual's degree of freedom in choosing among various stress reducing alternatives.
- the societal relevance of individual stress-reducing actions (i.e., on the individual's general capacities to influence hierarchically higher social systems).

4. Brief Practical Conclusions and Summary

The theoretical explications forwarded thus far imply that psychological peace research as well as research on macro-social stress, in general, should be interested in gathering data as to how macro-social stressors are cognitively appraised and coped with. The social determinants of appraisal processes and modes of coping must be examined orthogonically, so to speak. This means that methodologies will have to be implemented which focus both on the primary appraisal of macro-social stressors *and* on the social determinants of primary appraisal; on the secondary appraisal of coping resources *and* on the social availability of resources; and on modes of reappraisal *and* their social origin.

Furthermore, on the basis of the hypothesis that complex social systems form hierarchical networks, it is necessary not only to gather data on one systemic level, but to include at least two such levels 'above the individual' – to employ *vertical stratification*). Together with the above-mentioned necessity of dealing with global crises on a worldwide scale, this means that studies must employ a cross-cultural and multi-group design and methodology. On the cultural level of social systems, a further differentiation seems appropriate: horizontal stratification – drawing samples from more than one socio-political system e.g., First, Second, Third World; East, West, Neutral or Non-aligned; North, South. It is not sufficient, however, to include culture as a stratified quasi-experimental variable by simply drawing one sample each from various countries of different socio-political systems. The propositions of social identity theory – of group determination of social representations – should lead to the conclusion that at least two different types of groups ought to be studied in every culture. One type of group could consist of people actively engaged in the fields of peace or ecology. Another type of group could consist of people active in a field that has nothing to do with macro-social stress, for example, a sports club. Such a design could serve as a substitute for a control group design, which is not possible in the case of macro-social stress, since every human being is potentially affected by global crises. To study a non-topical group, however, can provide the opportunity to study a group for whom decisions regarding membership and group alignment have not been based on the perception of global threats. Again, we emphasize that entire groups should be included in future research, so that group processes with regard to the appraisal of and the coping with macro-social stress can be *studied*, instead of having to be inferred statistically.

As to the question posed in the title of this chapter, we can answer in a more or less straightforward way: Yes, the threat of war and, even more, the threat of nuclear war *can* be seen as macro-social stress. But several qualifications have to be made. Firstly, to deal psychologically with the consequences of the war threat, we have to be very precise in identifying the quality of the stressor and the modes of appraisal and coping. Secondly, in dealing with the war threat as macro-social stress, it is crucial to take into consideration the social determinants of these modes of appraisal and coping. This calls for a change in cognitive-phenomenological studies in the field of psychological peace research: Studies can no longer be one-shot studies – they need to employ a multi-group design and preferably be set up as cross-cultural endeavors from the very beginning.

References

Boehnke, Klaus & Michael J. Macpherson, 1989. 'Zum Einfluß der atomaren Bedrohung auf das politische Engagement – Literaturüberblick und interkulturelle Vergleichsstudie', pp. 227–245 in Boehnke et al., 1989.

Boehnke, Klaus; Michael J. Macpherson, & Folker Schmidt, eds., 1989. *Leben unter atomarer Bedrohung – Ergebnisse internationaler psychologischer Forschung*. Heidelberg: Asanger.

Boehnke, Klaus; Michael J.Macpherson, Margarete Meador & Horst Petri, 1989. 'How West German Adolescents Experience the Nuclear Threat', *Political Psychology*, vol. 10, no. 4, pp. 419–443.

Coles, Robert, 1986. *The Political Life of Children*. Boston, MA: Atlantic Monthly Press.

Cranach, Mario v.; Guy Ochsenbein, Franziska Tschan & Heinz Kohler, 1987. 'Untersuchungen zum Handeln sozialer Systeme. Bericht über ein Forschungsprogramm', *Schweizerische Zeitschrift für Psychologie*, vol. 46, no. 3/4, pp. 213–226.

Fiske, Susan, 1987. 'People's Reactions to Nuclear War: Implication for Psychologists', *American Psychologist*, vol. 42, no. 3, pp. 207–217.

Frindte, Wolfgang; Horst Schwarz & Frank Roth, 1989. 'Selbst- und Fremdorganisation in sozialen Systemen – ein neuer sozialpsychologischer Ansatz', *Forschungsbericht der Friedrich-Schiller-Universität Jena*. Jena: Friedrich Schiller University.

Haan, Norma, 1977. *Coping and Defending*. New York: Academic Press.

Hamilton, Scott B.; Susan Van Mouwerik, Eugene R. Oetting, Frederic Beauvais & William G. Keilin, 1988. 'Nuclear War as a Source of Adolescent Worry: Relationships with Age, Gender, Trait Emotionality, and Drug Use', *Journal of Social Psychology*, vol. 128, no. 6, pp. 745–763.

Haste, Helen, 1989. 'Politisches Engagement gegen atomare Bedrohung: Erfolgreiche Angstbewältigung oder Zwischenschritt der Streßverarbeitung?', pp. 91–109 in Boehnke et al., 1989.

Holmes, Thomas H. & Richard H. Rahe, 1967. 'The Social Readjustment Scale', *Journal of Psychosomatic Research*, vol. 11, no. 2, pp. 213–218.

Janis, Irving L. & Howard Leventhal, 1968. 'Human Reactions to Stress', pp. 1041–1085 in E.F. Borgatta & W.W. Lambert, eds, *Handbook of Personality Theory and Research*. Chicago: Rand McNally.

Keilin, William G. & Scott B. Hamilton, 1989. 'Zum Umgang mit der Gefahr eines Atomkriegs: Eine Laboruntersuchung zu Abwehrprozessen und anderen emotionalen Reaktionen', pp. 127–148 in Boehnke et. al., 1989.

Lazarus, Richard S., 1966. *Psychological Stress and the Coping Process*. New York: McGraw-Hill.

Lazarus, Richard S. 1986. 'Puzzles in the Study of Daily Hassles', pp. 39–53 in R.K. Silbereisen, K. Eyferth, & G. Rudinger, eds, *Development as Action in Context*. Berlin: Springer.

Lazarus, Richard S. & Susan Folkman, 1984. *Stress, Appraisal, and Coping*. New York: Springer.

Lazarus, Richard S. & Raymond Launier, 1978. 'Stress-related Transactions between Person and Environment', pp. 287–327 in L.A. Pervin & M. Lewis, eds, *Perspectives in Interactional Psychology*. New York: Plenum.

Levine, Seymour & Norman A. Scotch, 1973. *Social Stress*. Chicago: Aldine.

Meyer-Probst, Bernhard; Helfried Teichmann & Helga Engel, 1989. 'Wünsche und Befürchtungen 14jähriger Jugendlicher: Phänomenologie und Abhängigkeitsbeziehungen', *Pro Pacem Mundi*, vol. 5 – *Psychologie und Frieden*, pp. 36–46.

Moscovici, Serge, 1976. *Social Influence and Social Change*. London: Academic Press.

Moscovici, Serge, 1984. *Das Zeitalter der Masse*. München: Hanser.

Schmidt, Folker; Michael J. Macpherson & Klaus Boehnke, 1990. 'Bedrohungsängste – Ergebnisse internationaler psychologischer Forschung', pp. 149–156 in J. Schlootz, ed., *Wir sind noch einmal davongekommen?* Berlin: Freie Universität.

Solantaus, Tytti, 1989. 'The Global World – a Domain for Development in Adolescence?', *Journal of Adolescence*, vol. 12, no. 1, pp. 27–40.

Tajfel, Henri, 1981. *Human Groups and Social Categories – Studies in Social Psychology*. Cambridge: Cambridge University Press.

Thommen, Beat; Xaver Ammann, & Mario v. Cranach, 1988. *Handlungsorganisation durch soziale Repräsentationen. Welchen Einfluß haben therapeutische Schulen auf das Handeln ihrer Mitglieder*. Bern: Huber.

World Commission on Environment and Development, 1987. *Our Common Future*. Oxford: Oxford University Press.

2

Choosing War, Choosing Peace

Decision-Theoretic Contributions
to Peace Research

Zeev Maoz

1. Introduction

The study that may well have launched decision-theoretic-based research in international politics dealt with the relations between national choices and war initiation. Theodore Abel (1941, p. 855) argued that most wars are the result of calculated decisions of states to engage in sustained combat with other states in order to achieve political objectives; and that most decisions to initiate war are made far prior to the outbreak of overt hostilities. Irrespective of the empirical validity of this statement, decision-theoretic research in international politics has been intimately linked to a variety of questions concerning the initiation, management, termination, and resolution of international conflict.

This chapter aims at a critical review of decision-theoretic contributions to peace research. It identifies two major streams of scholarship that characterize this literature: the rational choice approach, and the cognitive approach. My main argument is that, though both bodies of theory are often seen as mutually exclusive explanations of the conflict process, they also share many compatibilities. A thorough understanding of the causes, courses, and consequences of international conflict should emerge from a synthesis of these two approaches.

In section 2, I discuss the main features of the rational and the cognitive approaches. The three sub-sections that follow review, respectively, decision-theoretic research on the causes, management, and outcomes of international conflict. I distinguish between rational choice theories and cognitive ones, and review both theoretical and empirical research. The fourth and final section offers some basic ideas for a synthesis of choice-related theories of international conflict.

2. Rational and Cognitive Approaches in the Study
of International Conflict

At the outset, I should like to make very clear what I consider to be a 'psychological' contribution to the study of peace and war. Contrary to the popular use of the term in international politics (cf. Achen & Snidal, 1989; Lebow & Stein, 1989) that takes 'psychological' to be any kind of analysis that emphasizes the extra- or non-rational aspects of individual or group behavior, I view as psychological those studies that focus on the reasoning processes of individuals and on the interaction among individuals in groups, organizations, and international (e.g., bargaining and negotiation) settings. Anyone focusing on biases and deviations from an ideal-type pattern of logic and behavior in a descriptive study of behavior, must also treat the ideal-type pattern – either as a standard to which we should aspire (Kahneman & Tversky, 1982; Fischoff, 1982), or as a rival hypothesis (Simon, 1985). From this definition it follows that decision-theoretic studies of international conflict are treated as psychological in one way or another, irrespective of their epistemological or methodological orientation: wherever there is room for decision, the factors that go into action – personality, motivation, 'hot' and 'cold' cognitive mechanisms, rational calculations, interpersonal interaction – are inherently psychological.

Before distinguishing between these two approaches, let us note some of the similarities between them in the context of conflict studies. First, both cognitive and rational choice models are 'bottom-up' approaches. They focus on the reasoning processes of individuals and on the interaction within policy groups as explanations of the causes, courses, and consequences of international conflict. This is in contrast to systemic approaches, the focus of which is a set of forces outside the decision-makers and beyond their control (such as the structure of the international system, the distribution of power within it, the pattern of international alignments, and so forth). The immediate implication of this is that conflict is man-made and could be unmade by man. There is an underlying normative assumption here: Understanding international conflict is a prerequisite for managing or resolving it (Nardin, 1980). Hence, psychological approaches should be contrasted to systemic approaches rather than to rational choice ones.

Second, both approaches assume an inherent association between decision process and outcomes. Specifically, both approaches state that the better (and both agree that 'better' means 'more rational') the process by which a decision is made – other things being equal – the more likely is the outcome to meet the goals of the unit making the decision (Janis & Mann, 1977; Janis, 1989; Brecher, 1979a; Stein & Tanter, 1980; Bueno de Mesquita, 1981). In fact, both approaches, by and large, view the rational choice model as the normative ideal type of decision-making.

Psychological factors operate in conflict-related decisions at two levels: One is the cognitive and affective level, consisting of the processes of perception, cognition, reasoning, and emotional arousal that operate on the individual mind. The second is the social level, wherein the perceptions, cognition, and emotions of different individuals interact with one another to produce a decisional outcome. Both levels represent distinct areas of research in psychology, as well as aspects in the study of conflict-related decision making (Maoz, 1990a, pp. 41–43).

The main difference between rational and cognitive approaches lies at the descriptive level: in terms of what they view as the 'best' approximations to the kind of processes that characterize conflict decision-making. There are two main versions of the rational decision-making model. The first and most common version is the formal one that focuses on the utility-maximization principle or its close relatives in game theory (dominant strategies, maximin, etc.). This version accepts as exogenous the nature of the alternatives considered by the decision-maker, the elements making up his or her values and preferences, and the nature of the process by which decision-makers assign probability estimates to various outcomes. The issue of rationality is simply whether – given an array of alternatives, outcomes, a probability distribution over these outcomes, and a set of utility scores assigned to each – a decision-maker (or a decision-making unit) chooses that alternative which maximizes his or her subjectively expected utility (SEU). (See, for example, Brams & Kilgour, 1988; Zagare, 1987; Bueno de Mesquita, 1981, 1985.)

The second version has been termed 'procedural rationality' (Maoz, 1990b). It views rational decision-making as an analytic process that includes the definition of the situation, the selection of alternatives and assignment of outcomes to the alternatives under consideration, the assignment of probabilistic estimates to outcomes, the trading-off of different value dimensions in the process of evaluating outcomes, and, only as the final stage, the selection of the SEU-maximizing alternative. Analytic decision-making consists of a set of procedures which include unbiased definitions of the situation, parallel and comprehensive exploration of multiple alternatives, systematic and unbiased (i.e. Bayesian) revision of probability estimates in the light of new information, trade-off calculations of multiple criteria in the process of assigning utilities to outcomes, and SEU maximization, as a natural result. This perspective of rational choice is characteristic of more empirical studies of conflict decision-making (e.g., Stein & Tanter, 1980; Brecher, 1980; Anderson, 1981; Maoz, 1981).

The cognitive approach, on the other hand, focuses on the same aspects of the decision-making process as does the procedural rationality approach. Its emphasis, however, is on the factors that cause deviation from the procedural rationality mode of behavior in each of the stages of the decision-making process. First, this approach emphasizes the biased uses of analogies and historical examples as tools of definition of the situation (May, 1973; Vertzberger, 1986; Neudstadt & May, 1987). Second, it examines types of improper strategies of reducing the number of available alternatives, such as premature closure (Jervis, 1976) or sequencing (Simon, 1957). Third, it explores cognitive heuristics and affective processes that bias information processing, predictions and judgements (Kahneman & Tversky, 1982; Jervis, 1976; Vertzberger, 1990). Lastly, it examines cognitive and affective processes that bias the process of outcome evaluation, such as the tendency to avoid or suppress value trade-offs (Holsti & George, 1975; Janis

& Mann, 1977). This often results in suboptimal decision-rules that lead to non-SEU maximizing choices.

Both models also describe group decision-making in radically different terms. The rational choice approach examines group decision-making in terms of open and unconstrained exchanges among individuals that lead to broad examination of all available alternatives by the group. Decisions at the group level reflect some sort of weighted aggregation of individual preferences into an optimal group decision. By contrast, cognitive models focus on group-induced constraints on dissenting views that often results in incomplete analysis of alternatives by the group and in suboptimal decisions (Janis, 1982).

The analytic-rational approach attributes to decision-makers and decision-making bodies, high calculation skills and sophisticated problem solving. The cognitive approach emphasizes the psychological, bureaucratic, and political constraints on rationality in foreign policy settings. The models appear to be fairly distinct, and hence seem to require some sort of assessment of their relative empirical validity in conflict-related decisions.

3. Decision-Theoretic Research: Three Aspects

3.1 Conflict Initiation

Causes of conflict can be divided into two types: underlying causes and immediate ones (Lebow, 1981; Levy, 1986; Maoz, 1989). Underlying causes refer to long-term processes that serve to generate, perpetuate, or increase hostility and mistrust among the parties to the conflict, but which – in and of themselves – do not determine when a conflict of interest will be transformed from a low level to one involving intense violence. Arms races, deterrence policies, and cognitive dynamics responsible for generating of hostile perceptions are among the key examples of underlying causes of war (Maoz, 1989). Immediate causes of war consist of situational conditions or short-term processes which determine the course of the conflict. The initiation of international crises, and how these are managed, is the single most important immediate cause of war. Decision-theoretic studies of international conflict focus, for the most part, on international crises and their relationship to the outbreak of war.

Some of the typologies of international crises rest on the nature of the initiation process. Lebow (1981) and Maoz (1982b) offer fairly similar typologies. The first category is that of a calculated crisis (or what Lebow, [1981, p. 25] calls 'justification of hostility' crises). The second category is that of unintended crises (or 'brinkmanship crises' in Lebow's terminology) wherein the crisis erupts (or escalates) despite the wishes of all participants.[1]

From a decision-theoretic perspective, an international crisis is defined as a change in the internal or external environment which entails: (a) perception of high threat to basic national values, (b) a short time for decision responding to this threat, and (c) a sharp increase in the subjective or collective probability of violence (Brecher, 1980).[2] This definition emphasizes the need for crucial decisions and the strict time-limits and psychological stress that characterize the conditions under which these decisions must be made.

The essential argument of rational choice models of conflict initiation is that decision-makers carefully weigh the risks and benefits associated with the initiation of a crisis, including the risk that the crisis will escalate into an all-out war. These pros and cons are compared to the benefits and costs associated with the present status quo. Decision-makers will resort to options which entail a high potential for violence only if they think that they might be generally better off starting a crisis than maintaining the status quo.

Perhaps the most explicit articulation of the argument that war is a rational act is the work of Bueno de Mesquita (1981) that lays out and empirically tests a formal rational choice model of conflict initiation. The model envisions the decision process as not only rational, but unitary as well. Bueno de Mesquita assumes that war (and peace) decisions can be conceived of as if they were made by a single all-powerful individual.[3] Decision-makers will not embark on a conflict initiation path if they think that this alternative has a negative expected utility. Furthermore, conflict initiated as a result of a careful consideration of costs and benefits usually ends in victory for the initiator.

Bueno de Mesquita's theory was found to have a marked degree of empirical support when tested on a dataset including all international conflicts involving at least one major power, and all interstate wars in the 1815–1975 period. However, this theory has also invoked substantial criticism. Some critics have attacked the assumptions and measurement procedures of the theory (Majeski & Sylvan, 1984) while others have pointed out problems in the internal logic of the theory and its empirical tests (Simowitz & Price, 1990; Wagner, 1984; Maoz, 1984). One criticism of the theory has been that the model of conflict initiation was misspecified in that it relied on decision theory instead of game theory. Decision theory is not useful for modeling situations characterized by intrinsic interdependence, where the outcome of one's decision depends on the choices of other actors (Wagner, 1984).

To rectify this problem, a model of conflict initiation has been developed which starts out with a decision-theoretic approach and moves on to a game theoretic setting (Maoz, 1985). The logic of dispute initiation entailed in the model yields propositions regarding the types of preference structures of actors likely to be associated with the outbreak of international conflict. It has also been shown that this logic can be extended to examine the dynamics of conflict management and conflict termination.

Anderson & McKewon (1987) offer a bounded rationality satisficing alternative to the rational choice model of Bueno de Mesquita. In their model, states are said to act upon perceptions of attainment gaps. According to this model, attainment gaps are defined in terms of gaps between states' expectations from their environment and their actual achievements in the international arena. When this gap goes beyond a certain critical threshold, states are prone to initiate conflict (cf. Maoz, 1982a). Tested against the predictions of the rational choice model of Bueno de Mesquita, this model has been found to provide a considerably better fit to the data. This model, though relying on a non-rational choice logic, has features similar to the rational choice models in that it attempts to identify static conditions for conflict initiation rather than the underlying dynamics of initiation processes.

Rational models focus on the factors that make the conflict initiation alternative viable from the perspective of the decision-makers. They do not, however, enable dynamic determination of the timing and form of initiative, nor do these models attempt to account for the process by which national preference structures are formed associated with conflict initiation.[4]

According to this line of approach, Saddam Hussein's calculus of the Kuwaiti invasion was based on a careful analysis of the possible consequences of this action, including the possible outbreak of war with the United States. According to the information he had at the time, Hussein may have assessed the chances of such an eventuality as low, and the (national and personal) benefits of a successful takeover of the oil-rich state as extremely high. Alternatively, his bet might have included a second stage wherein parts of Kuwait, the two islands at the outlet of the Shatt el-Arab, or annulment of Iraq's debt to Kuwait and Saudi Arabia, would be traded for Iraqi withdrawal from Kuwait. Accordingly, the analysis of options may well have suggested to him that the SEU of the crisis initiation option outweighed that of the status quo option. Reports suggesting that the operational plans of the Kuwaiti invasion had been laid out as early as 1988, would indicate that the decision was not taken hastily and under crisis-induced stress.

The theme of cognitive studies is that crisis initiation is, in many cases, the result of some human error in the decision-making process that caused things to get out of control and escalate well beyond the point any of the actors involved desired. If it is the case that both sides of a conflict often go to war under the impression that they would emerge as victors (Blainey, 1988, p. 127), then someone must have the wrong impression. When we consider the costs of war and the fact that sometimes victory in war may itself be a major disaster (Maoz, 1989, pp. 251–252), then even the eventual winner may have grossly miscalculated the value of conflict and the wisdom of engaging in such a process (Levy, 1983).

Cognitive models of conflict initiation are intimately related to the study of deterrence failure. These studies focus on decisions to violate a given status quo in the face of an existing commitment of an adversary to defend such a status quo through the use of force. Cognitive models of conflict agree that conflict initiation is often a result of some sort of miscalculation. The responsibility for such miscalculation is often shared by the initiator and by the target. The initiator may be driven to crisis by domestic pressures which evoke patterns of wishful thinking. Lebow (1981, p. 274) points out that '[p]erceiving the need to pursue a policy of brinkmanship, these leaders rationalized the conditions for its success and sought to insulate themselves from information that challenged their expectations of success.' This thesis is demonstrated in several of the cases studied by Lebow (1981) and by a subsequent study of Argentina's decision to occupy the Malvinas/Falkland Islands (Lebow, 1985).

Motivated by perceptions of opportunity, initiators may also miscalculate the extent to which the target is committed to preserving the status quo. They may be guided by an unfounded belief that the risks associated with crisis initiation are controllable (George & Smoke, 1974, pp. 524–532). Finally, initiators' partial successes may blind them into a notion that they can push their luck further, by ignoring the fact that their past successes may deepen the commitment of the target to preserve the status quo. Such, for example, was the interpretation of Nasser's decision process in the May–June 1967 crisis (Lebow, 1981) or the cumulative diplomatic coups that Hitler staged in Europe during the second half of the 1930s (Maoz, 1983, pp. 226; 1990, pp. 518–528).[5]

The target's side of the blame for initiation is due to three principal factors. First, the target may fail to define clearly the nature of its commitments. The initiator's action may provoke a crisis not due to its awareness that this action challenges the target's commitment but because it has been led to believe that such an action might seem acceptable to the target (George & Smoke, 1974). Second, the target may define its commitment in a manner that provokes the initiator. Specifically, an initiator may believe that deterrence is likely to be converted into compellence; hence crisis initiation becomes a pre-emptive measure (Maoz, 1989, pp. 75–77). Third, the target's unwillingness to supplement deterrence measures (designed to increase the initiator's costs of initiation) with measures of positive inducement (which are designed to increase the initiator's valuation of the status quo), may cause the initiator increased frustration. Over time, this frustration is translated into a willingness to take risks (Stein, 1985, pp. 58–59; 1987, pp. 7–8; Maoz, 1989, pp. 77–78).

The cognitive explanation of the outbreak of the Gulf crisis focuses therefore on false notions of quick and easy victory, based on the 'last war analogy' (Jervis, 1976, pp. 266–270). The 'lesson' of the Iran–Iraq war in which Iraq had secured the financial and political support of most Arab nations, was that – despite enormous difficulties and numerous sacrifices – bold initiatives meet eventual success. This analogy gave Saddam Hussein unfounded optimism, and – more importantly – prevented him from seeing the fact that the United States, as well as the Arab League,[6] were committed to preserving the sovereignty and territorial integrity of this Kuwait. Saddam Hussein, therefore, ignored or downgraded the threats issued by President Bush as well as the movement of two US vessels into the Gulf prior to the invasion. He may also have been made blind to warnings by Arab regimes that he would find himself isolated if he invaded Kuwait.

There might also have been a deterrence failure on the part of the United States. Though the USA may well have had good intelligence suggesting that the Iraqis had been massing troops along the Kuwaiti border, the President issued only a mild warning that did not clearly specify how far the USA would be willing to go to secure Kuwaiti independence. An important quantitative study on the determinants of success and failure of deterrence has demonstrated that a key factor that determines whether a threat will deter is not the overall balance of capabilities between the defender and the would-be aggressor, but rather the available capabilities at the location of the crisis (Huth & Russett, 1984). Hence, the failure of the USA to bring to bear sufficient capabilities to Kuwait itself (for example, the deployment of the 82nd airborne division in Kuwait as a trip-wire), may well have caused Hussein to believe that the risks of invasion were calculable and controllable. The implication of this is of course that errors by both parties contributed to the outbreak of the crisis.[7]

The principal criticism of cognitive studies of conflict initiation has focused not so much on the approach or on the findings, but rather on the methodology. Most cognitive studies of conflict have relied on a case study approach; most of the cases studied consisted of deterrence failures. Hence the criticism has been that the findings of this approach are due to a bias in case selection (Achen & Snidal, 1989). Another problem entailed in these studies is the implicit notion of a link between defective decision-making and conflict initiation. Virtually all of the studies that have used a cognitive approach have revealed some deficiencies in the decision to initiate conflict. Hence a logical implication might be that had decision-makers been more rational, conflict would have been averted. This proposition is very difficult to substantiate because one would have to analyze peaceful relations and to show that they have been characterized by rational behavior.

Taken together, cognitive studies of conflict initiation imply that attempts to design a rational policy to prevent the eruption of crises may encounter considerable difficulties. Even if designed and implemented with great care, deterrence policy may contain built-in seeds of failure (Maoz, 1989, pp. 96–99; Jervis, 1985, p. 33; Lebow & Stein, 1989). Likewise, Bueno de Mesquita (1985) showed that war might break out when misperceptions regarding the risk-propensity of the opponent enters an otherwise rational decision calculus.[8]

3.2 Conflict Management

The focus of studies of conflict management is on 'how strategy is used in the service of politics' (Maoz, 1989, p. 3). A broader definition of management views this aspect of conflict as consisting of decision-making from the initial act to the actual termination of hostilities. The chief problem of conflict management is how cope with the tradeoff between the risk of escalation and the benefits of coercive diplomacy (George, 1984; George, Hall, & Simmons, 1972). Much of the 'crisis decision-making' literature concerns this stage of conflict (Tanter, 1978; Holsti, 1979). Here, too, the two approaches present seemingly polarized images of the characteristics of this stage.

Rational choice models of crisis management are impaired by a fundamental problem. If decision-makers are rational, and if they are capable of reasonable forecasts about the outcome of the crisis, then one of the parties knows that it will lose, the other knows that it will win: hence both should exchange the values or assets at stake without prolonging the crisis or escalating it (Maoz, 1985). This is the key result of a study of bargaining among rational agents with differential costs for time. If one of the parties pays for each unit time an iota more than the other, the former should rationally yield to the latter at the very outset of the bargaining process (Rubinstein, 1982). The implication is, of course, that conflict can arise only in settings characterized either by misperception or by incomplete information, wherein both parties think they stand a reasonable chance of emerging winners (Morrow, 1989).

However, even if misperception does affect crisis decision-making, this may not be as serious as to suggest to a vastly inferior party that it could win the conflict. Japanese decision-makers had no illusion that they could win a war with the United States. Neither did Egypt's Sadat expect an easy victory when he initiated the October 1973 war. Rather, the key function of conflict management is to use strategy in a manner that can compensate for inferiority in capabilities, in the opening stages of the conflict (Maoz, 1983, 1985, 1989, pp. 137–167), or as a device for making more reliable assessments of how far to push an adversary in the absence of complete information (Moore, 1991; Morrow, 1989).

Rational choice models focus on the substantive dynamics of conflict management rather than on the characteristics of crisis decision-making. The issues addressed by these models represent a mix of normative and descriptive facets of the basic management dilemma. For example, states wish to use threats and limited force to demonstrate resolve; at the same time, they also wish to signal to the opponent that they may be willing to reach some sort of compromise before war breaks out.

Just what is the optimal mixture of threats, physical demonstrations of resolve, and prudence is the key issue discussed by game theoretic models of crisis management (Brams & Kilgour, 1988; Leng, 1988; Snyder & Diesing, 1977). Rational-choice students of conflict management agree that, to the extent that actual management parallels the rationally prescribed mixture of threats and accommodative measures, actors might reach a Pareto-optimal resolution, typically short of war. It is quite possible that the mixing of probabilistic (contingent) threats, demonstrations of resolve, and accommo-dative measures might lead to rational 'winding down' processes even if initial attempts to prevent the crisis from escalating have failed (Brams & Kilgour, 1988).[9]

However, in order to enable such accommodation, decision-makers must be non-myopically rational; their decisions must be based on careful assessment of both the short-term and long-term consequences of their decisions. Only by adopting a long-range perspective can they manage some crises in a manner that prevents unwanted escalation. An illuminating models of this problem is the Dollar Auction game (O'Neill, 1986; Brockner & Rubin, 1985; Maoz, 1989, pp. 106–118; 276–282). In this game, players bid for a dollar, with the 'prize' going to the highest bidder for the price of the bid. However, contrary to a typical auction, the second-highest bidder also pays his or her bid but gets nothing in return. O'Neill (1986) has shown that the game has an equilibrium solution whereby one player bids an amount smaller than a dollar (just what is that amount is a function of the stake – a dollar – and the bankroll of the two players) and the other stays out.

However, if players are incapable of such long-range foresight, then short-term rationality drives this process into an infinite escalation which neither side desired. What is suggested by this case is that the problem of crisis management from a short-term rational perspective is inherently paradoxical: in their effort to recover the sunk costs represented in their initial entry into the crisis, the parties deepen their involvement. Because neither party has a short-term incentive to remain second, both end up losing far more than the dollar. The explanation of this paradox is that the parties are driven by prior commitments that prevent them from slowing down or terminating the escalation sequence. Experimental studies based on the Dollar Auction game (Teger, 1980) and other games of entrapment (Brockner & Rubin, 1985), as well as case studies of various international wars (Maoz, 1989) support this conclusion quite robustly.[10]

The recent Gulf crisis suggests a similar logic. Because both parties had invested tremendously in the management of their crisis, each step taken immediately caused a deepening of commitments, which, in turn, raised the risks of escalation. The more committed each of the parties, the more it had to rationalize in terms of the advisability of previous steps. Iraq had to rationalize its Kuwaiti invasion in light of the international uproar this caused. The United States had to justify its overreaction in light of the inability of UN economic sanctions to lead to an unconditional Iraqi withdrawal. Both parties were thus thrust into a spiral of unwanted escalation.

Cognitive models of conflict management focus on two main topics: how crisis decisions are made, and how these decisions affect the course of the crisis. There exist several good reviews of crisis decision-making (Tanter, 1978; Holsti, 1979; Maoz, 1990a), all of which generally agree on a major point regarding the structure of crisis decision-making. The quality of decision-making processes is a function of several variables, but most typically, it is a function of the level of stress which decision-makers experience. The relationship between stress and crisis behavior has been found to be curvilinear, resembling an inverse U-shaped function: both low and high levels of stress are associated with poor-quality decision-making, whereas a medium level of stress is associated with high-quality decision making (Maoz, 1990a). However, the definition of decisional stress does not necessarily involve situations with high threat, short time and high probability of violence (Brecher, 1977; 1979a; Janis & Mann, 1977, pp. 46–47). Stress may be evoked by perceptions of opportunities as much as it may be evoked by threats (Maoz, 1990a, pp. 64–66).

This point is significant because it resolves an ongoing debate on the quality of crisis decision-making. Much of the initial literature on this topic (e.g., Holsti, 1972a, 1972b; Hermann, 1969, 1972) suggested that crisis decision-making tends to be of particularly low quality due to the distorting effects of high levels of decisional stress. High stress invokes both 'hot' (motivated) and 'cold' (unmotivated) cognitive biases (Holsti & George, 1975; Janis & Mann, 1977). However, more recent investigations (Brecher, 1980; Stein & Tanter, 1980; Maoz, 1981) have found that crisis decisions may be highly analytic in nature, in some cases best represented by a rational choice model. Still others (Saris & Gallhofer, 1984) found little or no relationship between stress and decision quality. The explanation for the persistence of this debate is that initial crisis decision-making studies focused on high-stress situations which exhibited low-level decisional performance. More recent investigations have focused on a more refined differentiation of crisis stages which exhibited more variability in terms of decisional stages (Brecher, 1980; Maoz, 1990a, pp. 335–337).

Another aspect highlighted by recent research is the susceptibility of decision-making groups to manipulation of decisions. Some of these manipulations may be rational in that they lead to the expansion of the array of alternatives considered by the group. For example, splitting a majority that supports an undesirable alternative by introducing a new alternative, is a tactic of this sort. Other strategies of political manipulation build on the tendency of individuals and groups to deviate from the canons of rationality. One case in point is splitting a major decision with little or no support in the group, into a series of small and incremental decisions, each of which commits the group to support of the next decision in the series.

Another manipulation tactic which makes use of the known tendencies of individuals and groups to violate the axioms of rational choice is the 'framing' effect (Tversky & Kahneman, 1981; Quattrone & Tversky, 1988). Framing group decisions refers to manipulating the way the decision problem is presented to the group. If a decision problem is presented as a choice among gains, individuals tend toward riskless alternatives. However, if the same problem is framed as a choice among potential losses, decisions tend to be risk-acceptant. The ability to control the definition of the situation provides a decision-maker with substantial power to induce favorable choices without misrepresenting the data (Maoz, 1990b, pp. 88–90). It has been argued that crisis conditions, especially the short time-frame characteristic of crisis, tend to facilitate the task of the manipulator and make it difficult to detect or counter manipulation attempts (Maoz, 1990b, pp. 92–94).

Recent studies suggest a relationship between the quality of crisis decision-making and the quality of crisis outcomes. Herek, Janis, & Huth (1987), and Janis (1989) have studied 19 crises in US foreign policy since World War II in terms of the presence or absence of symptoms of defective decision-making, and then used expert polling technique to examine the quality of the outcomes of these crises in terms of: (a) the effectiveness of crisis management by US policy-makers in terms of US interests, and (b) the subsequent level of conflict invoked by this decision. They found substantial support for the hypothesis linking the decision process to crisis management and crisis outcomes. A study of the Arab-Israeli conflict during the 1970–73 period, based on analysis of 42 decisions made by Israel, Jordan, Egypt, Syria, the PLO and the United States, has corroborated some of these conclusions (Maoz & Astorino, 1991).

3.3 Conflict Termination

Blainey (1988, p. 3) points out a key problem when he argues that: 'For every thousand pages published on the causes of wars there is less than one page directly on the causes of peace.' This also applies to decision-theoretic studies of conflict termination. Nonetheless, some interesting works exist on this topic.

Before we review these studies, it is important to note that most of the literature on conflict resolution does not focus specifically on decision-making processes; much of it is concerned with bargaining theory, or with conflict theory in more general terms.

On the rational-choice side of the fence, probably the most directly relevant work is that of Wittman (1979), who examines the factors that may affect decisions to end wars. He develops a decision-theoretic model that examines the choice problem facing the actors as one between continued warfare and war termination. Actors are said to decide to choose to end the war if the expected utility of war termination exceeds that of continued fighting. The calculus is based on states' estimates of the likelihood of winning the war eventually, the cost of continued warfare, and the stakes of the war. Changes in any one of these factors may at some point tip the balance in favor of the war termination choice. The key problem of this analysis is that it really lacks a bargaining component. That is, the expected utility of war is a well-defined function of capability and stakes of war. Yet the expected utility of war termination is a function of the post-war agreement, which is a matter of bargaining. Indeed one of the most interesting works on war termination treats the problem entirely in terms of bargaining theory, showing the continuous and interdependent features of such processes (Pillar, 1983).

Building on Wittman's and Pillar's work, Maoz (1985) has formulated a tentative dynamic model of war termination as a bargaining problem. The decision of the parties to end the war is a function of an expected utility calculus. However, each side can affect the opponent's calculus in two ways: First, through the conduct of war operations, a party can raise the costs of resistance and lower the opponent's probability of winning. Second, through the use of diplomacy, a state can raise the value of the post-war settlement for the opponent.

These rational-choice models tend to convey the message that the problem of war termination is one of optimization: when both parties realize that a settlement is preferable to continuation of the war, they sign a peace treaty. However, subsequent work has shown that on several occasions states tend to fight well beyond the point of diminishing marginal returns from war. Moreover, sometimes it takes a state less time and fewer casualties to realize that it is going to lose the war, than the time and casualties it takes the would-be loser to extricate itself out of the war once this realization has set in (Maoz, 1989, pp. 276–297). This is the sunk-cost paradox of war termination.

The rational explanation of this paradox focuses on the short-sighted nature of the war management process, and on the fact that the would-be loser increases its losses because it is bound by its commitments both to allies and to a part of its constituency to accomplishment of at least some of its war aims.

The cognitive explanation, however, focuses on the need for 'justification and rationalization' of previous costs and losses which serves to increase present costs and losses (cf. Brockner & Rubin, 1985). In order to justify the deaths of the people already lost, decision-makers will attempt to recover some of the sunk cost by trying to prove to their constituency that the war has not been fought in vain. In order to present proof to that effect, additional troops must be sent in, and more be killed in the process. The original aim of the war had been to win; once realization of defeat sets in, the new aim is to reach a 'honorable solution'; when this is not possible, getting out without humiliation becomes the next step in the process, and so on. At each stage, more casualties are incurred. And at each stage, the state's political and military situation only worsens.

War termination decisions are neither easy nor clear-cut. Psychological factors often combine with political factors to produce delays in termination of hostilities, and in more fundamental processes of conflict resolution. It is often this combination of the psychological reluctance of decision-makers who started a war and the political fact that they are still in power that causes difficulties for a nation to extricate itself from a war. Hence, more often than not, it takes leadership change to bring about war termination. This has been the case in many of the long and difficult wars of the nuclear era (Korea, Algeria, Vietnam, Egypt–Israel, the Israeli invasion of Lebanon, Afghanistan, Iran–Iraq). This itself suggests that to make a rational decision about war termination requires a leadership that does not have the same psychological dispositions of rationalization and justification as the leadership that originally got the nation into war.

Another difficulty is entailed in the psychological implications which protracted conflict can have for the images (at both elite and mass levels) of the parties. Prolonged conflict tends to produce stereotypes of the enemy, with tendencies to dehumanize it, lack of understanding of its motives, and lack of acceptance of the notion that some of the opponent's claims may have some validity. This often causes the parties to misperceive one another and to entrench themselves in their positions (White, 1971; Jervis, 1976; Heradstveit, 1978; Saunders, 1985). Conflict resolution, therefore, will often require very heroic efforts to eradicate psychological barriers of mistrust and suspicion (Sadat, 1977).

4. Decision-Theoretic Contributions to Peace Research: Is the Glass Half Full or Half Empty?

A key issue in much of the decision-theoretic research on international conflict has been the question of which of these models provides a better account of the conflict process, which model leads to more accurate prediction, and which is more generalizable. If that is the right question, then the jury is still out: we do not have a definite verdict.

However, this may well be the wrong way of addressing the issue of the extent to which decision-making approaches have contributed to the study of international conflict. Perhaps rational-choice models provide a better account of one aspect of the conflict process, while cognitive models can provide a more persuasive account of other aspects of the conflict process.

More importantly, asking which model provides the *best* account of the conflict process leads one to ignore the compatibilities between these two models. There are issues which are ignored, assumed away, or otherwise treated as given by rational-choice models, but which serve as key elements of a cognitive explanation of conflict behavior. For example, rational-choice models do not deal with the determinants of national preferences (or even the preferences of national elites when the unitary actor assumption is relaxed). On the other hand, cognitive models of decision focus on the belief-related sources of preferences. In some cases, decisions that can be seen as rational in the expected utility maximization sense can have an irrational foundation because the processes by which the preferences were formed were biased in some fundamental ways (Maoz, 1989, pp. 43–51).

In terms of the issues discussed in this chapter, it seems evident that the two models are not mutually exclusive. Rather, they seem to complement one another quite well in many cases. Hence a combination of both might provide a better account of the conflict process than the use of each or either of them as a single explanation.

Viewed in this light, the emerging picture of the foregoing review is not all that bleak. Rather, several points summarize this study. First, both models address various stages of conflict. If both models have some claim to validity, then in order to manage or resolve conflict successfully, we must understand both its strategic aspects, properly modeled by rational choice models, and its psychological aspects, as explained by the cognitive model. Second, a cumulative body of knowledge based on the decision-theoretic approach is beginning to emerge regarding various aspects of conflict. The point of decision-theoretic approaches is that people and their choices make a difference in world politics in general, and in processes of international conflict in particular. Finally, there are areas – such as the study of decisions to end conflict, or decisions to fundamentally transform conflictual relations into peaceful ones – where there is still substantial work to be done, because the decision-theoretic foundations of these aspects are not sufficiently understood.

What are the components of a synthesis of the two approaches? Space constraints preclude a detailed discussion, but a brief outline of its main elements might be constructive. First and foremost, we must dispense with the false notion that one approach can universally provide a 'better' description of conflict decision-making processes than the other. Rather, we know from the available literature that both approaches have substantial empirical validity, and that the applicability of a rational explanation or of a cognitive one is context-dependent. Some decision-makers, under some types of political, situational, and psychological conditions, are more prone to one type of decision-making than to another (see, e.g., the findings on the relationship between crisis-induced stress and decision behavior). The task of future research is to understand better the relationship between contextual variables and decision-making strategies at various stages of the conflict process.

Integrating the implications of the two approaches of decision-making is also important. We know that not all the consequences of cognitive styles of decision-making are negative; nor does rational decision-making invariably yield cooperative or otherwise desirable outcomes. A synthesis of these two approaches would enable us to assess better the relationship between the processes by which conflict decisions are made and the individual or collective (that is, national or international) adaptability of their outcomes.

Notes

1 The third category is that of crises that arise out of domestic precipitation. These are crisis situations that emerge for decision-makers in one nation as a result of some domestic change in another nation. This resembles Lebow's third category which concerns spinoff crises that typically arise in the context of an ongoing war (Maoz, 1982b).

2 Some (e.g., Maoz, 1982b) view this definition as defender-oriented and as predicated on a reactive bias. An alternative definition focuses on an intentional or forced need to accept a value trade-off between the risks of escalation and the benefits of coercive diplomacy.

3 This could also be interpreted as an outcome of a collective decision process wherein the preferences of the individual participants were highly homogeneous.

4 An exception is Moore (1990) who discusses in detail the kind of perceptual dimensions that determine preferences in the context of adversarial relations and how these dimensions shape crisis-initiation decisions. This study combines cognitive and rational choice analysis of crisis decision-making.

5 For an interesting analysis of the effects that prior crisis outcomes have on bargaining behavior in subsequent crises, see Leng (1983, 1988).

6 In 1961, with the granting of independence to Kuwait, Iraq mobilized troops and threatened to invade Kuwait, which it regarded as an illegitimate entity. The Arab League organized a multilateral force and, in cooperation with Great Britain, successfully deterred the Iraqi invasion.

7 An alternative interpretation of the crisis focuses on the personal characteristics of Saddam Hussein, his megalomania, his sense of Iraqi grandeur, and his authoritative and dogmatic leadership style. While definitely valid in many ways, the personality-based approach cannot account for the timing and form of the initiation of the crisis. What it does is suggest that Saddam Hussein has certain personality traits that make him likely to launch high-risk ventures like the Iran-Iraq war and the Kuwaiti invasion. On this literature see Maoz (1990a, pp. 51–59).

8 See also Intrilligator & Brito (1984) and Brito & Intrilligator (1985) for a rational-choice model of arms races suggesting that war may be a rational outcome of arms racing when, under conditions of incomplete information, actors may misperceive each other's best strategy.

9 This discussion shows why rational-choice models of international conflict are

clearly consistent with the more traditional notion of 'psychological' or cognitive models. These studies serve to show that the management problem is essentially what Schelling (1963) called 'competition in risk-taking': parties use strategy to induce fear, thereby forcing the opponent to give in before the war breaks out.

10 It is noteworthy that some studies of strategically rational management of international crisis have found that the choice of 'just' the optimal mixture of escalatory and de-escalatory strategies might cause unwanted war, due to misperception of the latitude of choice available to the opponent and due to lack of accurate signaling of intentions by the opponent (Bueno de Mesquita, 1985; Moore, 1991).

References

Abel, Theodore, 1941. 'The Element of Decision in the Pattern of War', *American Sociological Review*, vol. 6, no. 4. December, pp. 853–859.

Achen, Christopher. H. & Duncan Snidal, 1989. 'Rational Deterrence Theory and Comparative Case Studies', *World Politics*, vol. 41, no. 2., January, pp. 143–169.

Anderson, Paul A., 1981. 'Justification and Precedents as Constraints in Foreign Policy Decision Making', *American Journal of Political Science*, vol. 25, no. 4., December, pp. 738–781.

Anderson, Paul A. & Timothy J. McKewon, 1987. 'Changing Aspirations, Limited Attention, and War', *World Politics*, vol. 40, no. 1, October, pp. 1–29.

Blainey, Geoffrey, 1988. *The Causes of War* (Third ed.). New York: Free Press.

Brams, Steven J. & D. Marc Kilgour, 1988. *Game Theory and National Security*. New York: Basil Blackwell.

Brecher, Michael, 1980. *Decisions in Crisis: Israel, 1967 and 1973*. Berkeley and Los Angeles, CA: University of California Press.

Brecher, Michael, 1979a. 'State Behavior in International Crises', *Journal of Conflict Resolution*, vol. 23 no. 3, September, pp. 446–480.

Brecher, Michael, (ed.) 1979b. *Studies in Crisis Behavior*. New Brunswick, NJ: Transaction Press.

Brecher, Michael, 1977. 'Toward a Theory of International Crisis Behavior'. *International Studies Quarterly,* vol. 21, no. 1, March, pp. 39–74.

Brito, Dagobert L. & Michael D. Intrilligator, 1985. 'Conflict, War, and Redistribution', *American Political Science Review*, vol. 79, no. 4, December, pp. 943–957.

Brockner, J. & Jeffery Rubin, 1985. *Entrapment in Escalating Conflicts: A Social Psychological Analysis*. New York: Springer Verlag.

Bueno de Mesquita, Bruce, 1985. 'The "War Trap" Revisited: A Revised Expected Utility Model', *American Political Science Review*, vol. 79, no. 1, March, pp. 156–173.

Bueno de Mesquita, Bruce, 1981. *The War Trap*. New Haven, CT: Yale University Press.

Fischoff, Baruch, 1982. 'Debiasing', pp. 422–444 in D. Kahnenman, P. Slovic, and A. Tversky, eds, *Judgment Under Uncertainty: Heuristics and Biases*. Cambridge: Cambridge University Press.

George, Alexander L., 1984. 'Crisis Management: The Interplay of Military and Political Considerations', *Survival*, vol. 26, no. 5, pp. 223–234.

George, Alexander L., David K. Hall & William Simmons, 1972. *The Limits of Coercive Diplomacy*. Boston, MA: Little, Brown.

George, Alexander L. & Richard Smoke, 1974. *Deterrence in American Foreign Policy: Theory and Practice*. New York: Columbia University Press.

Heradstveit, Daniel, 1978. *The Arab-Israeli Conflict: Psychological Barriers to Peace*. Oslo: Universitetsforlaget.

Herek, Gregory M.; Irving L. Janis, & Paul Huth, 1987. 'Decision Making During International Crises: Is Quality of Process Related to Outcome?' *Journal of Conflict Resolution*, vol. 31, no. 2, pp. 203–226.

Hermann, Charles F., 1972. 'Threat, Time, and Surprise: A Simulation of International Crises', pp. 187–211 in C. F. Hermann, ed., *International Crises: Insights from Behavioral Research*. New York: Free Press.

Hermann, Charles F., 1969. *Crises in Foreign Policy: A Simulation Analysis*. New York: Bobbs Merrill.

Holsti, Ole R., 1979. 'Theories of Crisis Decision Making', pp. 99–136 in P.G. Lauren, ed., *Diplomacy: New Approaches in History, Theory and Policy*. New York: Free Press.

Holsti, Ole R., 1972a. *Crisis, Escalation, War*. Montreal: McGill University Press.

Holsti, Ole R., 1972b. 'Time, Alternatives, and Communications: The 1914 and Cuban Missile Crises', pp. 58–80 in C.F. Hermann, ed., 1972.

Holsti, Ole R. & Alexander L. George, 1975. 'The Effects of Stress on Foreign Policy Makers', pp. 255–319 in C. P. Cotter, ed. *Political Science Annual*. Indianapolis, IN: Bobbs Merrill.

Huth, Paul & Bruce M. Russett, 1984. 'What Makes Deterrence Work? Cases from 1900 to 1960', *World Politics*, vol. 36, no. 4, July, pp. 496–526.

Intrilligator, M. D. & Brito, D. L., 1984. 'Can Arms Races Lead to the Outbreak of War?', *Journal of Conflict Resolution*, vol. 26, no. 1, pp. 123–128.

Janis, Irving L., 1989. *Crucial Decisions: Leadership in Policymaking and Crisis Management*. New York: Free Press.

Janis, Irving L., 1982. *Groupthink* (Second edition). Boston, MA: Houghton Mifflin.

Janis, Irving L. & Leon Mann, 1977. *Decision Making: A Psychological Analysis of Conflict, Choice, and Commitment*. New York: Free Press.

Jervis, Robert, 1985. 'Perceiving and Coping with Threat', pp. 13–33 in R. Jervis, R.N. Lebow, & J.G. Stein, eds, *Psychology and Deterrence*. Baltimore, MD: Johns Hopkins University Press.

Jervis, Robert, 1976. *Perception and Misperception in International Politics*. Princeton, NJ: Princeton University Press.

Kahneman, Daniel & Amos Tversky, 1982. 'Intuitive Prediction: Biases and Corrective Procedures', pp. 414–421 in D. Kahnenman, P. Slovic, & A. Tversky, eds, *Judgment Under Uncertainty: Heuristics and Biases*. Cambridge: Cambridge University Press.

Lebow, Richard N., 1985. 'Miscalculation in the South Atlantic: The Origins of the Falklands War', pp. 89–124 in R. Jervis, R.N. Lebow, & J.G. Stein, eds, 1985.

Lebow, Richard N., 1981. *Between Peace and War: The Nature of International Crisis*. Baltimore, MD: Johns Hopkins University Press.

Lebow, Richard N. & Janice Gross-Stein, 1989. 'Rational Deterrence Theory: I Think, Therefore I Deter', *World Politics*, vol. 41, no., 2 January, pp. 208–224.

Leng, Russell J., 1988. 'Crisis Learning Games', *American Political Science Review*, vol. 82, no. 1, March, pp. 179–194.

Leng, Russell J., 1983. 'When Will They Ever Learn? Coercive Bargaining in Recurrent Crises', *Journal of Conflict Resolution*, vol. 27, no. 3, September, pp. 379–419.

Levy, J.S., 1986. 'Organizational Routines and the Causes of War', *International Studies Quarterly*, vol. 30, no. 2, June, pp. 193–222.

Levy, J.S., 1983. 'Misperceptions and the Causes of War', *World Politics*, vol. 35, no. 1, October, pp. 76–99.

Majeski, Steven J. & Donald J. Sylvan, 1984. 'Simple Choices and Complex Calculations: A Critique of "The War Trap"', *Journal of Conflict Resolution*, vol. 28, no. 2, June, pp. 316–340.

Maoz, Zeev, 1990a. *National Choices and International Processes*. Cambridge: Cambridge University Press.

Maoz, Zeev, 1990b. 'Framing the National Interest: The Manipulation of National Decisions in Group Settings', *World Politics*, vol. 43, no. 1, October, pp. 77–110.

Maoz, Zeev, 1989. *Paradoxes of War: On the Art of National Self-Entrapment*. Boston, MA: Unwin Hyman.

Maoz, Zeev, 1985. 'Decision Theoretic and Game Theoretic Models of International Conflict', pp. 77–111 in U. Luterbacher & M.D. Ward, eds, *Dynamic Models of International Conflict*. Boulder, CO: Lynne Riener Publishers.

Maoz, Zeev, 1983. 'Resolve, Capabilities, and the Outcomes of Interstate Disputes, 1816–1976', *Journal of Conflict Resolution*, vol. 27, no. 2, June, pp. 195–225.

Maoz, Zeev, 1982a. *Paths to Conflict: International Dispute Initiation, 1816–1976*. Boulder, CO: Westview Press.

Maoz, Zeev, 1982b. 'Crisis Initiation: a Theoretical Exploration of A Neglected Topic in International Crisis Theory', *Review of International Studies*, vol. 8, no. 4, October, pp. 215–232.

Maoz, Zeev, 1981. 'The Decision to Raid Entebbe: Decision Analysis Applied to Crisis Behavior', *Journal of Conflict Resolution*, vol. 23, no. 4, December, pp. 677–707.

Maoz, Zeev & Allison Astorino, 1991. 'Waging War, Waging Peace: Decision Making and Bargaining in the Arab-Israeli Conflict, 1970–73', *Political Psychology* (forthcoming).

May, Ernest, 1973. *'Lessons' of the Past: The Uses and Misuses of History in American Foreign Policy*. New York: Oxford University Press.

Mor, Benjamin D., 1990. 'Crisis Games: A Game Theoretic Analysis of Strategic Choices in International Crises', Ph.D. Dissertation, New York University.

Mor, Benjamin D., 1991. 'Nasser's Decision Making in the 1967 Middle East Crisis: A Rational-Choice Explanation', *Journal of Peace Research*, vol. 28, no. 4, December.

Morrow, James D., 1989. 'Capabilities, Uncertainty, and Resolve: A Limited Information Model of Crisis Bargaining', *American Journal of Political Science*, vol. 33, no. 4, December, pp. 941–972.

Nardin, Terry, 1980. 'Theory and Practice in Conflict Research', pp. 461–489 in T.R. Gurr, ed., *Handbook of Political Conflict*. New York: Free Press.

Neudstadt, Richard & Ernest May, 1987. *Thinking in Time*. New York: Free Press.

O'Neill, Barry, 1986. 'International Escalation and the Dollar Auction', *Journal of Conflict Resolution*, vol. 30, no. 1, March, pp. 33–50.

Pillar, Paul, 1983. *Negotiating Peace: War Termination as a Bargaining Process*. Princeton, NJ: Princeton University Press.

Quattrone, George A. & Amos Tversky, 1988. 'Contrasting Rational and Psychological Analyses of Political Choice', *American Political Science Review*, vol. 82, no. 3, September, pp. 719–736.

Rubinstein, Ariel, 1982. 'Perfect Equilibrium in a Bargaining Model', *Econometrica*, vol. 50, no. 1, March, pp. 90–109.

Sadat, Anwar el, 1977. 'Speech to the Israeli Knesset', November 20. Cited in Sadat, A., 1979, *In Search of Identity*. New York: Harper and Row.

Saris, Willem E. & Irmtraud N. Gallhofer, 1984. 'Formulations of Real-Life Decisions: A Study of Foreign Policy Decisions', *Acta Psychologica*, vol. 56, no. 2, June, pp. 247–265.

Saunders, Harold H., 1985. *The Other Walls: The Politics of the Arab-Israeli Peace Process*. Washington, DC: American Enterprise Institute.

Schelling, Thomas C., 1963. *The Strategy of Conflict*. Cambridge, MA: Harvard University Press.

Simon, Herbert A., 1985. 'Human Nature in Politics: The Dialogue of Psychology with Political Science', *American Political Science Review*, vol. 79. no. 2., June, pp. 293–304.

Simon, Herbert A., 1957. *Models of Man: Social and Rational*. New York: Wiley.

Simowitz, Roslyn & Barry L. Price, 1990. 'The Expected Utility Theory of Conflict: Measuring Theoretical Progress', *American Political Science Review*, vol. 84, no. 2, May, pp. 439–460.

Snyder, Glenn H. & Paul Diesing, 1977. *Conflict Among Nations*. Princeton, NJ: Princeton University Press.

Stein, Janice G., 1987. 'Deterrence and Reassurance'. Paper presented to the Committee on the Contribution of the Behavioral Sciences to the Prevention of Nuclear War, National Research Council.

Stein, Janice G., 1985. 'Calculation, Miscalculation, and Conventional Deterrence', pp. 34–88 in R. Jervis, R.N. Lebow, & J.G. Stein, eds, 1985.

Stein, Janice Gross & Raymond Tanter, 1980. *Rational Decision Making: Israel's Security Choices, 1967*. Columbus, OH: Ohio State University Press.

Tanter, Raymond, 1978. 'International Crisis Behavior: An Appraisal of the Literature', *Jerusalem Journal of International Relations*, vol. 3, nos. 2–3, Spring–Summer, pp. 340–374.

Teger, Alfred, 1980. *Too Much Invested to Quit*. New York: Basic Books.

Tversky, Amos & Daniel Kahneman, 1981. 'The Framing of Decisions and the Psychology of Choice', *Science*, no. 211, pp. 453–458.

Vertzberger, Yaacov, 1990. *The World in Their Minds: Information Processing, Cognition, and Perception in Foreign Policy Decisionmaking*. Stanford, CA: Stanford University Press.

Vertzberger, Yaacov, 1986. 'Foreign Policy Decisionmakers as Practical-Intuitive Historians: Applied History and Its Shortcomings', *International Studies Quarterly*, vol. 30, no. 2, June, pp. 223–247.

Wagner, R. Harrison, 1984. 'War and Expected Utility Theory', *World Politics*, vol. 36, no. 3, July, pp. 407–423.

White, Ralph K., 1971. *Nobody Wanted War: Misperception in Vietnam and Other Wars*. Garden City, NY: Anchor Press.

Wittman, Donald, 1979. 'How a War Ends', *Journal of Conflict Resolution*, vol. 23, no. 4, December, pp. 743–763.

Zagare, Frank C., 1987. *The Dynamics of Deterrence*. Chicago, IL: University of Chicago Press.

3

Integrative Complexity, International Crises, and Cognitive Management

Alistair B.C. Wallbaum*

1. Introduction

Psychological analyses of political decisions have traditionally focused on the personality of the decision-maker(s), to the relative exclusion of the particular situation. Jervis's (1976) criticism of early psychological studies of international relations is still valid – there is a tendency to 'overpsychologize', and ignore environmental demands. As Hermann (1986) has pointed out, it is vital to study political leadership in context. Another of Jervis's (1976) criticisms is that most psychological theories of high-level decision-making are based on simple laboratory research that is far removed from the complex world of foreign policy. Many of the laboratory experiments, he argues, have been based on questions of little importance to the subjects, who have been given little information, and to whom the consequences of the decision are minor anyhow. In contrast, high-level policy-makers are often over-loaded with information (see e.g. Suedfeld & Tetlock, 1977) and deal with issues of critical importance in which a poor decision could be disastrous.

Integrative complexity is one construct that allows researchers to measure the information-processing structure of actual high-level decision-makers across a variety of situations, without having to infer the emotional or motivational state, or personality traits, of the individuals involved. Through the systematic analysis of archived letters, speeches, and proclamations, researchers have been able to compare policy-makers' integrative complexity across and within specific situations. The proliferation of archives may allow researchers to analyze the complexity levels of the same policy-maker during various situations, as well as those of different policy-makers dealing with one particular problem.

This chapter reviews some of the literature on integrative complexity of

* I am grateful to Peter Suedfeld for his extensive assistance with this manuscript, and to Susan Bluck for her insightful editorial suggestions.

communications during political crises, and uses the findings as a basis for suggesting ways in which high-level policy-makers can create an environment conducive to improving cognitive management. Before continuing, however, let us describe integrative complexity, its origins, and measurement.

Integrative complexity theory evolved from Kelly's (1955) theory of personal constructs. His seminal work led to conceptual systems theory (Harvey et al., 1961) which in turn led to conceptual complexity theory (Schroder et al., 1967), interactive complexity (Streufert & Streufert, 1978), and eventually integrative complexity (Suedfeld et al., 1992).

The *Manual for Coding Integrative Complexity* (Baker-Brown et al., 1992) outlines a method for coding the structure of written or spoken material on a 7-point scale, derived from the original scoring system for the Sentence (later Paragraph) Completion Test (Schroder et al., 1967). The scale is built around the measurement of cognitive differentiation and integration. Differentiation is the recognition of different perspectives and/or dimensions of a stimulus, problem, or decision; it is a prerequisite for integration, the recognition of interrelations among these perspectives or dimensions. A score of 1 reflects no differentiation, 3 reflects high differentiation and no integration, 5 reflects high differentiation and moderate integration, and 7 reflects both high differentiation and high integration.[1] Scores of 7 are quite rare, and most group results are positively skewed (that is, most scored materials are low in integrative complexity). Scores of 2, 4 and 6 represent levels of complexity intermediate between the adjacent nodes.

2. Complexity and Political Crises

The measurement of integrative complexity has been applied to the communications of such diverse political figures as US Civil War generals (Suedfeld et al., 1986), Canadian Prime Ministers (Ballard, 1983), revolutionary leaders (Suedfeld & Rank, 1976), UN ambassadors (Suedfeld et al., 1977), and Soviet statesmen (Tetlock & McGuire, 1984).[2] One of the most consistent findings in complexity research is that stress tends to lower the level of integrative complexity:

> This impairment includes a lessened likelihood of accurately distinguishing between relevant and irrelevant information, reduced search for novel information, the suppression or ignoring of unpleasant inputs, and greater concentration of both incoming and outgoing communications to the ingroup. Long-term plans tend to be ignored in favor of stimulus-bound reactions, fine distinctions among items of information or among other participants in the crisis are abandoned, and responses and attitudes become increasingly stereotyped. (Suedfeld & Tetlock, 1977, p. 171)

However, as Tetlock and McGuire (1986) argue, stress does not automatically induce simplicity. Both individual differences and situational variables must be considered. For example, Wallace and Suedfeld (1988) measured the integrative complexity of sixteen leaders before, during, and after seven international crises that occurred between 1958 and 1983. Fifteen of the leaders exhibited lowered levels of complexity during crises. The exception was Andrei Andreyevich Gromyko, whose complexity level actually increased during the crises.

Wallace and Suedfeld then hypothesized that Gromyko's lengthy tenure (since 1938) in key diplomatic positions was associated with this finding. To test their hypothesis, they studied the complexity of six other leaders (Prince Talleyrand, Lord Castlereagh, Prince Metternich-Winneburg, the Duke of Welllington, Prince Otto von Bismarck, and Lester B. Pearson) who had served for at least 20 years in positions of responsibility for foreign affairs. Like Gromyko, this second sample of leaders generally exhibited crisis complexity levels that were equal to or greater than pre-crisis levels. Thus, it seems that an ability to maintain (or increase) complexity during crisis situations is associated with political longevity.

Integrative complexity may also be a useful predictor of conflict. It has been found that complexity tends to drop during crises that end in war (Suedfeld & Tetlock, 1977; Suedfeld et al., 1977) and rise during crises that are resoved peacefully (Raphael, 1982; Suedfeld & Tetlock, 1977). Tetlock (1985) also found that Soviet interventions abroad have been associated with a drop in integrative complexity for the quarter-year period preceding the action, and that Soviet foreign policy rhetoric tends to be higher in complexity one quarter-year before major US-USSR agreements.

Perhaps the best example of the potential utility of integrative complexity as a predictor of future conflict is the Suedfeld and Bluck (1988) study of nine surprise military attacks from 1941 ('Case Barbarossa' and Pearl Harbor) to 1982 (Falklands/Malvinas War). Suedfeld and Bluck scored public statements made by governments of both the attacker and the attacked nation from five time-periods, ranging from five years before, to the day of (or few days immediately after) the attack. They found that the attackers' level of integrative complexity decreased significantly between three months and two to four weeks before attacking. Interestingly, the complexity of the receiving countries increased between two to four weeks and one week before the attack, presumably as they increased their efforts to be understanding and flexible, and then dropped rapidly at the time of the attack.

The consistent finding in crisis research is that lowered levels of integrative complexity tend to precede armed conflict, while international agreement and peaceful crisis resolution are usually associated with increases in complexity.

3. Cognitive Managers

Integrative complexity is both a personality trait (the range of information processing available to the person) and a temporary state in response to the environmental context. Fiske and Taylor (1984) posit that humans are 'cognitive misers' who expend the least possible cognitive effort they can get away with. While not rejecting the model outright, I prefer to think that people tend to be 'cognitive managers', who respond to specific situations with the level of complexity they find most appropriate (see Suedfeld, 1992). The best exemplar of the political figure as a 'cognitive manager' comes from Suedfeld and Rank's 1976 study of revolutionary leaders. Revolutions are (to quote Hoffer) 'pioneered by men of words, materialized by fanatics and consolidated by men of action' (Hoffer, 1958, p. 134).

Suedfeld and Rank studied the archival materials of nineteen revolutionary leaders in five successful revolutions (English Civil War, US Revolution, Bolshevik Revolution, Chinese Revolution, Cuban Revolution). Of the nineteen, the eleven leaders who retained power until voluntary retirement or natural death exhibited low complexity during the revolution and high complexity after its success. The eight leaders who lost their positions after the revolution showed no such change in complexity. Successful leaders not only had to exhibit absolute, single-minded dedication to the cause (pre-takeover phase), but also had to process information in a complex manner after forming the new government. Whether this single-mindedness is an example of impression management (Tetlock et al., 1984), or a genuine cognitive response to the situation (Suedfeld, 1988), it provides strong support for the notion that complex information processing is not necessarily the best approach to all situations.

Similarly,

> ... (an) example is that of the decision maker confronting an implacable and determined antagonist. In such cases, it may be necessary to present an equally impervious front to the enemy. Would a simplistic show of unyielding resistance by Great Britain and France have stopped Germany's sequence of aggressions leading to World War II? Chamberlain's maneuvering certainly failed to do so; and his level of integrative complexity in one sample of reports from the 1938 Munich conference was almost 50 percent higher than that of Hitler. (Suedfeld, 1988, p. 27)

Nor are complex solutions (e.g., negotiated peace) always optimal. The Munich agreement, which resulted in peace (albeit a very brief peace), serves as an appropriate example to expose a bias in the literature. Almost all psychological (and political) research on decision-making in times of crisis assumes that the ultimate failure of decision-makers is the beginning of war. While it may often be true that 'to avoid war should be the highest ambition of statesmanship' (Gentz, 1805), it must also be noted that war can have certain positive aspects for the countries involved, and especially for certain leaders (Heraclides, 1989). In some cases war may even be the optimal solution to a country's problems (Suedfeld, 1988), or a necessity to prevent future conflict. As Friedrich Gentz (1805) also wrote:

> The more vigorously and courageously injustice and force are attacked at their first appearance, the less often will it be necessary to take the field against them in battle. (p.8)

In summary, cognitive managers adopt different information-processing strategies depending on the specific environment. Researchers should resist the temptation to evaluate the quality of political decisions without considering the contexts in which they were made. We cannot arbitrarily posit what complexity level is 'right' for a particular situation. Instead, we need further study of the complexity levels associated with decisions that, historically, are judged to have been successful or unsuccessful.

The real test of the applicability of the cognitive manager model to international politics will come with more longitudinal studies cf career politicians, officials, and diplomats. If the model is good, successful leaders should exhibit a greater range of integrative complexity, and be more likely to use all levels within that range, than unsuccessful leaders.

4. Cognitive Management During Political Crises

Several scholars have suggested that decision-makers might use cognitive mapping (Axelrod, 1976) and/or formal decision analysis (Fischoff et al., 1981) as tools in solving problems. While both techniques have made important contributions to the understanding and improvement of decision-making in general, their applicability in actual crisis situations seems limited. Political decision-makers are almost always under time pressure; not only do decisions have to be made quickly (especially in a crisis situation), extensive examination of one issue necessarily results in the neglect of other challenges of office.

Furthermore, there is the not trivial point that having to draw flow charts to make a decision hardly inspires confidence. An example of popular attitudes towards this kind of decision-making comes from Royko's (1971) portrait of former Chicago mayor Richard Daley:

> To the gullible Daley offers this version: after the election, he set up a blackboard in the basement of his home, and he and Sis spent the evening chalking in the pluses and minuses of retaining both posts; they found that the pluses exceeded the minuses, and together they agreed that for the good of the city he should hold all the power. Picture that: a man who has spent most of his adult life in politics and government, a man so professional that he was able to rise to the top of the most competitive municipal organization in the country, having to jot on a blackboard what it all means. (p. 96)

Janis (1972) has outlined ten points to improve high-level decision-making that are not only theoretically useful, but may also be practical in political situations. He intensively studied the decision-making processes which preceded six US foreign-policy decisions, four of which were categorized as 'fiascoes' (Bay of Pigs, escalation of the Korean War, Pearl Harbor, escalation of the Vietnam War) and two of which were successful (Marshall Plan, Cuban Missile Crisis). In the policy-making groups that made poor decisions, Janis observed a phenomenon he calls 'groupthink', characterized by a collective effort to maintain group harmony and unanimity, to the detriment of the decision-making process. Among his guidelines, Janis suggests that the group leader should avoid stating his preferences at the outset of the discussion, encourage others to express criticisms, and periodically assign the role of 'devil's advocate' to one member of the group.

More recently, Janis and colleagues (Janis, 1989; Herek, Janis & Huth, 1987; Janis & Mann, 1977) have outlined a schema for judging the quality of decision-making. Criteria for poor decision-making include gross omissions in surveying alternatives; gross omissions in surveying objectives; failure to examine major costs and risks of the preferred choice; poor information search; selective bias in processing information at hand; failure to reconsider originally rejected alternatives; and failure to work out detailed implementation, monitoring, and contingency plans. Herek et al. (1987) analyzed US presidential decision-making during 19 international crises from 1947–1973 and found that the presence of the above criteria was related to poor crisis outcomes. Recently, both the criteria and conclusions of this study have been questioned (Welch, 1989), although it appears that most of this criticism is based on an erroneous interpretation of the criteria (Herek et al., 1989).

Janis's standards for high-quality group decision-making tend to correspond with the decision-making approaches found in cognitively complex individuals. Streufert and Swezey (1986) have compiled a series of studies that differentiate between the more and the less cognitively complex. The cognitively complex person engages in more effective information search, is more likely to accept and integrate non-supporting information, and does not under- (or over-) plan. Further, Streufert and Swezey postulate that the capacity an individual has for complex information processing can be modified through training. Again, the optimal strategy is not higher complexity, but maximal flexibility:

> In our view, any increase in managerial capaciaty to differentiate and integrate can be of value, if it is associated with the flexibility to use those processes when they are appropriate, retaining, however, the capacity to shift toward more unidimensional functioning as required (Streufert & Swezey, 1986, p. 224)

The usefulness of being moderate in integrative complexity in international relations has already been indirectly argued for by White in his call for 'empathy ... understanding the thoughts and feelings of others' (1984, p. 160), which is similar to recognizing alternate perspectives (high differentiation). According to White, there are five 'motivated misperceptions' that interfere with peaceful international relations. One of these is the 'pro-us' illusion, characterized by:

> the tendency to assume that others see things as we do, with no special effort to empathize realistically or to explore differences between their perception and ours ... (p. 147)

White's argument for greater empathy in US-Soviet relations is almost a direct call for moderate integrative complexity in international communications, and is supported by the research findings, noted earlier, that low-complexity (little or no differentiation) communications often precede armed conflict, while moderately complex (more differentiation and perhaps some integration) communications precede peaceful resolutions of conflict. Communications that are consistently high in integrative complexity are relatively rare, and their impact cannot yet be generalized. But how to ensure that policy-makers process information in a moderately complex way? Probably the best way to avoid the oversimplification of international affairs is to follow Janis's guidelines for policy-making groups. By encouraging group members to explore possible drawbacks of any decision, and to recognize options and possibilities, we may be able to avoid the dynamics of 'concurrence-seeking' (Janis, 1972) which have led to fiascoes in the past. Another guideline also encourages policy-makers to see the situation as the other side does:

> Whenever the policy issue involves relations with a rival organization or out-group, a sizable bloc [sic] of time (perhaps an entire session) should be spent surveying all warning signals from the rivals and constructing alternative scenarios of the rival's intention (Janis, 1972, p. 216)

Encouraging the examination of possible alternatives, in conjunction with a dedication to understanding the perspective of one's rivals, may help to prevent the 'groupthink' sometimes characteristic of crucial foreign-policy decisions. These conditions do not induce complex cognition, but may preserve an environment in which moderately complex decisions can be made.

5. Conclusion

The usefulness of the cognitive complexity construct in studying political decision-making seems quite clear. It allows researchers to examine information-processing at the highest levels, and has shown promise as a predictor of behavior. In addition, the complexity data suggest that some successful leaders are also adept cognitive managers.

The good cognitive manager is capable not only of generating and integrating a variety of ideas, but also of unwavering commitment to an ideal. Yet, while low complexity may be optimal in some situations – for example when negotiating with an unyielding opponent (Suedfeld, 1988) or when leading a revolution (Suedfeld & Rank, 1976) – complexity research indicates that, in most cases, the clearest road to preventing international conflict is through the flexible approach inherent in a moderately complex level of information-processing (see e.g. Suedfeld & Tetlock, 1977). Unfortunately, during crisis situations, the majority of policy-makers studied exhibited lowered levels of complexity. It seems likely that the range of integrative complexity available to the would-be cognitive manager tends to be severely restricted during crises. Probably the best way to maintain the range of possible complexity in difficult times is to create an environment that can avoid rapid closure and encourage 'the recognition of alternative perspectives or different dimensions, and the acceptance of these as being relevant, legitimate, justifiable, valid, etc. (Baker-Brown et al., 1992). As White tentatively posits:

> One is tempted to say that in the business of preventing war the most vital kind of learning is to see the world in a more and more differentiated way, with more and clearer distinctions between its various parts and aspects. (1984, pp. 174–175)

Although this report has focused on crisis situations, the development of a decision-making environment that tolerates different perspectives on fundamental issues would probably be advantageous in more harmonious moments, as well. In light of Tetlock's (1985) findings that complex diplomatic communications lead to similarly complex responses, and that complex communications tend to precede international agreements, creating an environment conducive to differentiated and integrative thinking may be even more important in peacetime than it is during hostilities. The best way to deal with international crises, after all, is to try to ensure that they do not happen very often.

Notes

1 Examples of paragraphs that scored 1, 3, 5 and 7 on the integrative complexity coding scale (from Tetlock, 1984): Scores of 1 reflect low differentiation and low integration. For instance:

> The key problem is that we (the British) have been living way beyond our means for far too long. We have to tighten our belts. Nobody likes to face this unpleasant truth, but that's the way it is. Our standard of living will inevitably fall. It is as straightforward as that. I don't think anyone in touch with current economic reality can deny that.

Scores 3 reflect moderate or high differentiation and low integration. For instance:

> In politics, of course, it is not only a question of doing what is right or best for the country. It's also a question of what you can carry. An incomes policy (limits on wage increases) is needed to get our economic house in order. But it would be political suicide to go whole hog and impose a straight-jacket policy.

Scores of 5 reflect moderate or high differentiation and moderate integration. For instance:

> The Opposition responded in two seemingly contradictory ways to the steel bill (to nationalize the industry). They had to go through some ritual posturing to show the colonels in their constituencies they were doing a good job. But they also had some serious suggestions for improving the bill which they knew full well was going to pass. So they behaved constructively in committee working on technical details, but were strident opponents when more in the public eye.

Scores of 7 reflect high differentiation and high integration. For instance:

> We always have to deal with competing priorities in making up the budget. Most basically, we face the tension between the need to fund social welfare programmes to which we are committed and the need to stimulate private sector expansion. But there is no simple rule to resolve that tension. A lot depends on factors that are to some extent beyond our control: the state of the pound, our trade balance, unemployment, and those sorts of thing. Usually no one is very satisfied: we end up

with different priorities in different years and wind up looking rather inconsistent. (Tetlock, 1984, p. 369)

2 The archival study of integrative complexity often relies on the public presentations of leaders. Thus, the question arises as to whether speeches or letters accurately reflect the internal mind states of the policymakers. Tetlock, Hannum & Micheletti (1984) suggest that, as a safeguard, researchers look at statements delivered to as many different groups as possible. It must again be emphasized, however, that integrative complexity is a measure of the structure of information processing; while the content of speeches may well be affected by impression management, it is less likely that any world leaders have consciously attempted to manage the structure of their arguments.

References

Axelrod, Robert, 1976. *Structure of Decision*. Princeton, NJ: Princeton University Press.

Baker-Brown, Gloria; Elizabeth J. Ballard, Susan Bluck, Brian de Vries, Peter Suedfeld & Philip E. Tetlock, 1992. 'The Conceptual/Integrative Complexity Scoring Manual', pp. 401–418 in C.P. Smith (ed.) *Motivation and Personality: Handbook of Thematic Content Analysis*. Cambridge: Cambridge University Press.

Ballard, Elizabeth J., 1983. 'Canadian Prime Ministers: Complexity and Political Issues', *Canadian Psychology*, vol. 24, no. 2, April, pp. 125–130.

Fischoff, Baruch; Sarah Lichtenstein, Paul Slovic, Stephen L. Derby & Ralph L. Keeney, 1981. *Acceptable Risk*. Cambridge: Cambridge University Press.

Fiske, Susan T. & Shelley E. Taylor, 1984. *Social Cognition*. New York: Random House.

Gentz, Friedrich, 1805. *A History of the Balance of Power in Europe*. Quoted in Wheeler-Bennett, John W., 1948. *Munich: Prologue to Tragedy*. London: Macmillan & Co.

Harvey, O.J.; David E. Hunt & Harold M. Scroder, 1961. *Conceptual Systems and Personality Organization*. New York: Wiley.

Heraclides, Alexis, 1989. 'Conflict Resolution, Ethnonationalism and the Middle East Impasse', *Journal of Peace Research*, vol. 26, no. 2, May, pp. 197–212.

Herek, Gregory M.; Irving L. Janis & Paul Huth, 1987. 'Decision Making During International Crises: Is Quality of Process Related to Outcome?', *Journal of Conflict Resolution*, vol. 31, no. 2, June, pp. 203–226.

Herek, Gregory M.; Irving L. Janis & Paul Huth, 1989. 'Quality of U.S. Decision Making During the Cuban Missile Crisis: Major Errors in Welch's Reassessment', *Journal of Conflict Resolution*, vol. 33, no. 3, September, pp. 446–459.

Hermann, Margaret G., 1986. 'Ingredients of Leadership', pp. 167–192 in Margaret G. Hermann, ed., *Political Psychology*, San Francisco, CA: Jossey-Bass.

Hoffer, Eric, 1958. *The True Believer*. New York: Mentor.

Janis, Irving L., 1972. *Victims of Groupthink: A Psychological Study of Foreign-Policy Decisions and Fiascoes*. Boston, MA: Houghton Mifflin.

Janis, Irving L., 1989. *Crucial Decisions: Leadership in Policymaking and Crisis Management*. New York: Free Press.

Janis, Irving L. & Leon Mann, 1977. *Decision Making: A Psychological Analysis of Conflict, Choice, and Commitment*. New York: Free Press.

Jervis, Robert, 1976. *Perception and Misperception in International Politics*. Princeton, NJ: Princeton University Press.

Kelly, George A., 1955. *The Psychology of Personal Constructs*. New York: W.W. Norton & Co.

Raphael, Theodore D., 1982. 'Integrative Complexity Theory and Forecasting International Crises: Berlin, 1946–1962', *Journal of Conflict Resolution*, vol. 26, no. 3, September, pp. 423–450.

Royko, Mike, 1971. *Boss: Richard J. Daley of Chicago*. New York: New American Library.

Schroder, Harold M.; Michael J. Driver & Siegfried Streufert, 1967. *Human Information Processing*. New York: Holt, Rinehart and Winston.

Streufert, Siegfried & Susan C. Streufert, 1978. *Behavior in the Complex Environment*. Washington DC: Winston.

Streufert, Siegfried & Robert W. Swezey, 1986. *Complexity, Managers, and Organizations*. Orlando, FL: Academic Press.

Suedfeld, Peter, 1988. 'Are Simple Decisions Always Worse?', *Society*, vol. 25, no. 5, July/August, pp. 25–27.

Suedfeld, Peter, 1992. 'Cognitive Managers and Their Critics', *Political Psychology*, vol. 13, no. 3, pp. 435–453.

Suedfeld, Peter & Susan Bluck, 1988. 'Changes in Integrative Complexity Prior to Surprise Attacks', *Journal of Conflict Resolution*, vol. 32, no. 4, December, pp. 626–635.

Suedfeld, Peter & Alistair B.C. Wallbaum, 1992. 'Modifying Integrative Complexity in Political Thought: Value Conflict and Audience Disagreement', *Interamerican Journal of Psychology*, vol. 26, no. 1, pp. 19–36.

Suedfeld, Peter; Raymond S. Corteen, & Carol McCormic, 1986. 'The Role of Integrative Complexity in Military Leadership: Robert E. Lee and His Opponents', *Journal of Applied Social Psychology*, vol. 16, no. 6, pp. 498–507.

Suedfeld, Peter & A. Dennis Rank, 1976. 'Revolutionary Leaders: Long-Term Success as a Function of Changes in Conceptual Complexity', *Journal of Personality and Social Psychology*, vol. 34, no. 2, August, pp. 169–178.

Suedfeld, Peter & Philip Tetlock, 1977. 'Integrative Complexity of Communications in International Crises', *Journal of Conflict Resolution*, vol. 21, no. 1, March, pp. 169–184.

Suedfeld, Peter; Philip E. Tetlock & Siegfried Streufert, 1992. 'Conceptual/Integrative Complexity', pp. 393–409 in Charles P. Smith, ed., *Motivation and Personality: Handbook of Thematic Content Analysis*. Cambridge: Cambridge University Press.

Suedfeld, Peter, Philip E. Tetlock & Carmenza Ramirez, 1977. 'War, Peace, and Integrative Complexity: UN Speeches on the Middle East Problem, 1947–1976', *Journal of Conflict Resolution*, vol. 21, no. 3, September, pp. 427–442.

Tetlock, Philip E., 1985. 'Integrative Complexity of American and Soviet Foreign Policy Rhetoric: A Time-series Analysis', *Journal of Personality and Social Psychology*, vol. 49, no. 6, pp. 1565–1585.

Tetlock, Philip E.; Kristen A. Hannum, & Patrick M. Micheletti, 1984. 'Stability and Change in the Complexity of Senatorial Debate: Testing the Cognitive Versus Rhetorical Style Hypotheses', *Journal of Personality and Social Psychology*, vol. 46, no. 5, May, pp. 979–990.

Tetlock, Philip E. & Charles B. McGuire, Jr., 1984. 'Integrative Complexity of Societ Rhetoric as a Predictor of Soviet Behavior', *International Journal of Group Tensions*, vol. 14, no. 1–4, pp. 113–128.

Tetlock, Philip E. & Charles B. McGuire, Jr. 1986. 'Cognitive Perspectives of Foreign

Policy', pp. 255–273 in Ralph K. White, ed., *Psychology and the Prevention of Nuclear War*. New York: New York University Press.

Wallace, Michael D. & Peter Suedfeld, 1988. 'Leadership Performance in Crisis: The Longevity-Complexity Link', *International Studies Quarterly*, vol. 32, no. 4, December, pp. 439–451.

Welch, David A., 1989. 'Crisis Decision Making Reconsidered', *Journal of Conflict Resolution*, vol. 33, no. 3, September, pp. 430–445.

White, Ralph K., 1984. *Fearful Warriors: A Psychological Profile of U.S.-Soviet Relations*. New York: Free Press.

4

A Social Cognitive Theory of Conflict

Arie W. Kruglanski
Daniel Bar-Tal
Yechiel Klar

1. Introduction

The term conflict usually calls to mind clashing passions, intense emotial upheaval, the turmoil of battle and the tension of struggle. Thus, one might think that the cognitive metaphor, cold and rationalistic as it appears, would be singularly unifit to express what the essence of conflict is all about. Nonetheless, conflict theorists of different persuasions have found it useful to employ cognitive terms in their analyses, and have stressed the role of cognitions in determining the course of various conflicts and their outcomes.

Previous work in this domain has emphasized the perceptions that the parties in conflict have of each other (Jervis, 1976), and the cognitions that they hold on matters relevant to the conflict (Holsti, 1962). Further work has considered ways in which psychological insights into the *process* of cognitive change may suggest new avenues of conflict resolution (Bar-Tal, Kruglanski, & Klar, 1989). The present essay, though a continuation of those prior efforts, takes the social cognitive analysis of conflict one step further. Specifically, rather than addressing cognitions surrounding a particular conflict (e.g. the parties' perceptions of each others intentions) this chapter elaborates the importance of persons' general understanding of the *concept of conflict* and its implications for their emotional and behavioral reactions to a situation labeled as conflictual.

We argue here that the behaviour of individuals in conflict situations depends on two types of knowledge: general or categorical knowledge of what the very term 'conflict' means, and specific knowledge of whether a particular situation indeed represents a conflict.

Though general (categorical) knowledge of conflict takes logical precedence over situational knowledge (one must first know what conflict means before deciding whether a given situation is a conflict), we shall assume that both types of knowledge are attained via the same epistemic process. This is the process whereby all types of knowledge are attained or modified (Kruglanski, 1989). The epistemic process involving the intertwined operation of several cognitive and motivational factors will be described in some detail later. The role of such a process in forming categorical and situational knowledge of conflicts may have important implications for preventing, resolving, and dissolving undesirable conflicts. Such implications too will be discussed in some detail.

2. Conflict as a Category

When asked explicitly, most people would probably state that the term 'conflict' denotes an incompatibility of goals between the parties.[1] However, while the *denotative* meaning of the conflict category may be widely shared, persons or groups of people may vary in the *connotations* they attach to this category. Such differences may relate to the affective significance of conflict and to the action implications that conflict may have for various individuals.

Differences in the affective meanings of conflict are illustrated by the divergent reactions to the Israeli-Palestinian feud of former Israeli Prime Minister Golda Meir on the one hand, and former Israeli Defense Minister Moshe Dayan on the other hand. Ms. Meir regarded the conflict situation as highly undesirable, and the perennial cost in human lives a terrible tragedy. Her frequent pronouncements to that effect inspried considerable gloom among Israeli audiences, and the feeling that the situation was basically abnormal and untolerable. Dayan, by contrast, felt that conflict could be normal or at least represent a protracted state. His persistent attempt was to educate the Israeli public to 'live' with conflict, to inure the people to its possible costs, and to accept it unflinchingly as an inevitable part of everyday existence.

Beyond its affective connotations, the conflict category may have different behavioral implications for different persons. For some people, being in conflict may imply a need to escape it as soon as possible through attempts at appeasement and conciliation; for others, it may suggest a need to display courage, strength, and aggressiveness. An individual may also have different conflict categories for different classes of situations. For example, for some persons, conflict with members of the same sex may have different affective and behavioral connotations than conflict with members of the opposite sex. Similarly, the boss who is extremely aggreesive at work and rather docile at home may exemplify a person with possibly different conflict categories for the 'work' and 'home' situations, respectively.

Possible individual differences in the subjective connotations of conflict may be clustered, according to personality, cultural, and situational factors. Thus, the pattern of reactions to conflict situations may not be uniform. Instead, variability can be predicted in accordance with the possible multifarious contents of conflict categories to different persons. Further research along these lines might aim at a devising measurement techniques to map interpersonal, situational, and intergroup differences in the meaning of conflict and empirically study the ways in which those determine people's reactions to instances of conflict.

3. Applying the Conflict Category to Specific Situations

So far the discussion has centered on the categorical knowledge of conflict – on the meaning that the conflict notion has for the individual denotatively and connotatively. Let us now briefly consider the situational knowledge of conflict – the individual's judgement that a given social relationship is conflictual. Such judgement is largely contingent on what the conflict category means to the person: a situation will be judged as an instance of the category if its features fit the definitve properties of that category. That is, individuals will perceive the specific case as a conflict when they believe that the goals of two persons or two groups are indeed incompatible.

However, the conflictual interpretation of the situation may prove ambiguous if other, competing, interpretations also seem to provide a good fit to the situational features. The decision between competing hypotheses consitutes an integral part of the general epistemic process whereby human knowledge is crystallized. This process pertains both to the formation of our knowledge of conflict as a category, and the formation of knowledge regarding a given instance of conflict. As the general epistemic process is applicable to other (non-conflictual) types of knowledge as well, we shall temporarily abandon the topic of conflict and turn to a more general discussion describing the process whereby all human knowledge is formed and changed.

4. The Process of Knowledge Acquisition

Let us assume (with Kruglanski, 1989) that all knowledge – including knowledge of what conflict means and whether a given situation represents a conflict – is formed in the course of a two-phase process in which hypotheses are first generated and then validated. Hypotheses are genereated on the basis of external information and/or an internal stream of ideas. Later, they are validated by reference to subjectively relevant evidence. By 'subjective' we mean that what represents legitimate evidence for a given assertion is largely in the 'eye of the beholder'. For some persons in some situations, a pronouncement by a revered authority would be considered as evidence. Thus, if a political leader, a priest, or a parent declared conflict as unfortuante and something to be avoided, some people would consider this sufficient testimony and hasten to accept the declarations as valid. Similarly, such persons might accept an authority's pronouncement that a given situation is conflictual. For instance, Hitler's pronouncement that Germany was in conflict with the rest of Europe may have established this as a firm fact for many devout Nazis.

Other persons in some situations might accept only the evidence of hard empirical observations. For instance, they might consider conflict as deleterious only if all past conflicts could be demonstrated to have had destructive effects. Similarly, they might consider a given situation as conflictual only if the parties' goals appeared glaringly incompatible.

However, as implied earlier, any type or amount of evidence can fit *many alternative hypotheses*. Thus, even if the evidence were suggestive or consistent with a given interpretation, a clear conclusion would be drawn only if no competing interpretation appeard to provide an equally compelling account of the 'data'. For instance, an authority's pronouncement that conflict is deleterious would lose much of its persuasive power, if the alternative hypothesis was advanced that this pronouncement had been made under duress, and the souce had not actually meant what was said. Similarly, the same set of goals may be alternatively viewed as compatible or incompatible. Thus, if two women whished to marry the same man this might be regarded as conflictual in a monogamous society, but not in a polygamous one. In short, much of our knowledge is based on some kind of evidence. And as the *relevance* of evidence is subjective, the same evidence may be more or less compelling to different individuals. Furthermore, whether a given body of evidence is considered to warrant a given conclusion may depend on the existence of alternative hypotheses that are also consistent with the evidence. Let us, therefore, consider more closely the factors that determine the number and type of alternative hypotheses considered by the individual in course of a given knowledge-acquisition sequence.

5. Factors Affecting Hypothesis Consideration

According to the present model, the factors that affect the type and number of hypotheses considered by the individual fall into two categories; the category of cognitive capability and that of epistemic motivation.

Cognitive capability. The readiness with which a person may come up with ideas in a given domain may depend on their momentary accessibility (Higgins, Bargh & Lombardi, 1985). In turn, this may depend on whether the ideas were generally available in the individual's conceptual repertory or long-term memory, and were retrieved at the right moment. Alternatively, it may depend on the person's mental flexibility and creativity or the ability to search for and absorb information from external sources. Otherwise, one might be unable to conceive that things could be other than they presently are, or to imagine possible worlds distinct from current 'realities'. Holsti's (1962) analysis of the events that led to the outbreak of World War I is a good example of such epistemic 'freezing' (Kruglanski, 1988) due to cognitive capability factors. During the crucial and tense days following the Sarajevo assassination, the incapacity of various European heads of state to generate alternative ideas to those already so well thought out and rehearsed may have contributed to the outbreak of the war.

Motivational factors. Beyond cognitive capability factors having to do with the accessibility of various constructs, the tendency to consider alternative hypotheses may depend on a person's epistemic motivations. Three motivational forces are particurlarly relevant in this regard: the need for non-specific cognitive closure, the need for a specific cognitive closure, and the need to avoid non-specific cognitive closure. Let us consider them in turn. By the need for non-specific cognitive closure we mean the desire to have clear and firm knowledge on a given topic – any knowledge, as opposed to ambiguity, doubt or confusion. This need may stem from various sources. Thus, a person might desire closure when under time pressure, when the costs of further information processing appear prohibitive, or when the situation calls for immediate action. Arousal of a need for closure in a given domain may dispose the individual to generate a pertinent hypothesis quickly and then refrain from probing it too deeply or confronting it with further, potentially embarrassing evidence or alternative explanations.

A heightened need for closure may promote the 'freezing' of any subjective knowledge, including knowledge about conflict. For instance, labeling the situation as 'conflict' provides a simple and clear-cut definitioin, dispelling whatever ambiguity may have existed. This allows for well-defined responses and removes the need for time-consuming information search and deliberation. There exists today much evidence from real and simulated international and intergroup conflicts to show that in confrontational situations, where indecision might prove dangerous, intolerance towards abiguity increases (e.g. Driver, 1962; Singer, 1958; Streufert & Fromkin, 1969; Suedfeld & Tetlock, 1977). According to the present analysis, this might intensify the tendency to freeze on a clear-cut hypothesis, for instance a conflict hypothesis, which may provide the individual with the desired cognitive closure.

So far we have considered the motivation for closure per se. Often, however, individuals may prefer some types of closure over others – they may have the need for specific closure. For instance, a party may have a stake in believing that conflict is generally deleterious, if this party also sees its changes of gaining the upper hand are slim. Similarly, a person may prefer to believe that a given situation is conflictual, if such a belief may justify various desired moves – for instance, leaving the relationship, or taking punitive action. If the need for cognitive closure per se promotes the tendency to freeze on a given bit of knowledge, the need for a specific closure may promote either freezing or unfreezing, depending on whether the individual's initial notions were or were not congruent with such a closure. If the initial notion was desirable or pleasing, the person might be reluctant to search any furhter or consider further alternative hypotheses on a topic. And the reverse: if the initital notions were incongruent with the specific closure favored, the individual might be strongly motivated to seek alternative interpretations and/or be vigilant to such interpretations if these were suggested – by an external source, that is.

A handful of specific wishes and fears may serve to feed and maintain (i.e. freeze) conflictual interpretations in the context of numerous intergroup and international relations. One such wish might be to preserve the preferred ideology, image of self and other and of reality. In this vein, Finlay, Holsti & Fagen (1967) traced a large part of the policies of former US Secretary of State, John Foster Dulles, to his Puritan ideology and commitment to Christian ethics. These factors induced a strong aversion to Soviet Communism (and a concommittant readiness to accept a conflictual interpretation of the Soviet-US relations) as Communism, according to Dulles, rejected

Christian principles, promoted atheism, and preached a new and dangerous social order.

Inspired by the dictum of 'better safe than sorry', a party to a conflict may be motivated to adopt the worst-case scenario of the unfolding events. This may lead to the perception of the other party as harboring malevolent intentions, and to a rejection of possible benign interpretations of its actions. Such patterns are readily recognizable in several long-standing international conflicts. Thus, Bronfenbrenner (1964) has suggested that many Soviet beliefs about the West can be understood from the vantagepoint of fears of a Western attack. Similarly, Gamson (1968) has analyzed three US positions with regard to Soviet intentions in the Cold War and concluded that assumed level of threat is a major determinant of remaining beliefs related to the US-Soviet conflict.

Several studies (e.g., Bar-Tal, 1984; Heradstveit, 1981; Mroz, 1980) have revealed parallel perceptions of threat among Palestinian and Israeli reposndents. Specifically, deep-seated Palestinian fears of Israeli supremist attitudes and discriminatory behaviors, and Israeli Jews' fears of anti-semitism, holocaust, and annihilation by the Arabs, have been served by adopting beliefs about the inevitability of the Israeli-Palestinian conflict. Such beliefs have allowed both parties to assume that their own fears represent an appropriate response to an objective threat (that is controllable in principle) rather than constituting a (less controllable) outbreak of irrational or 'psychologically-based' anxieties.

Occasionally, the preferential feature of given closures might relate to aspects other than their contents, for instance to their novelty. Thus, people may become bored with ideas that they have held for a long time, in the same way that they may grow weary of old garments. Accordingly, a new idea might be adopted simply because it is different from the old ones. Likewise, people might tire of a conflictual interpretation of a given situation and welcome an opportunity to exhange it for an alternative conception that is exciting because of its novelty. Sadat's dramatic visit to Jerusalem in 1977, following decades of bitter strife between Egypt and Israel, represents one instance in which the attractiveness of an 'off-beat' idea might have facilitated reduction of a firmly entrenched conflict. We should remember here that Sadat's conception was utterly different from conventional notions about reducing the Egyptian-Israeli conflict in a piecemeal, gradual fashion through mutual concessions.

Finally, the third motivational force relevant to the process of consideration and/or generation of alternative hypotheses is the need to avoid cognitive closure. Such tendency toward cognitive openness may often stem from a concern with the validity of one's interpretation (Kruglanski & Freund, 1983). Thus, the individual may wish to make sure of carefully considering every conceivable angle before forming an opinion about a situation. One condition that might contribute to a more critical test of conflict-related beliefs is the parties' desire to be (or appear) moral and righteous – whether to satisfy a demanding self-image, or to vindicate oneself in the eyes of a judgemental world, especially when support and sympathy are badly needed.

Another condition under which a fear of invalidity might be aroused is when confidence in previous beliefs has been upset by overwhelming evidence to the contrary. Consider for instance, Janis' 1972 analysis of transformation in the decision-making process of the Kennedy Administration between the Bay of Pigs fiasco and the October Missile Crisis. According to Janis, the trauma of the former event shocked the US Administraion into adopting a more careful approach to crisis management. Just as the fear of invalidity notion would imply, this led to the consideration of alternative scenarios, with a closer examination of evidence inconsistent with accepted views and systematic playing of the role of a devil's advocate.

A need to avoid cognitive closure may be also aroused by a reluctance to make a firm commitment to a position. For example, a professional diplomat may find it limiting to hold overly firm opinions on various topics; hence he or she might be quite willing to consider all possible views and interpretations offered.

In summary, then, the need for non-specific closure per se is assumed to induce freezing on a given interpretation. Further, the need to avoid non-specific closure is assumed to induce the tendency to unfreeze one's views; and that for specific closure is assumed to induce selective freezing and unfreezing in accordance with congruence between existing and desired notions.

Passive epistemic process. So far, we have described an *active* process of knowledge acquisition – one in which the individual initiates the generation of hypotheses, attentively considers the proposals of others, and searches for relevant evidence, all in the interest of forming informed knowledge on a topic.

However, changes in knowledge may occur also via a passive route – one which pertains to the dissolution of existing knowledge structures rather than the formation of new knowledge. The main idea here is that when a given knowledge structure remains inactive for long, not only does it become less mentally accessible to the individual (Higgins, Bargh, & Lombardi, 1985) but also its internal and external linkages to other cognitive structures are much weakened. Thus, following long periods of inactivity, the connotative meaning of the conflict category becomes less clear to the individual, the category less likely to figure in the explanation which the individual offers for various events, and it becomes less clear to the individual whether a given situation or relationship previously labeled as 'conflict' was indeed conflictual. All this, because the linkage of the conflict hypothesis with the relevant evidence may not be as clear after considerable time has elapsed. Indeed, a person's confidence that the conflict even existed may wane considerabely with the passage of time.

6. Implications for Conflict Reduction and Management

The present epistemic analysis has several implications for ways in which conflict phenomena can be managed or controlled. We can discuss implications at the level of the general conflict category as well as at the level of the specific conflictual instance. Let us consider these two in turn.

Preventive approach. At the level of the general conflict category, it is possible to discuss a *preventive* approach to dealing with conflicts. By altering a person's subjective connotations of conflict as a category it should be possible to effect an in-advance alteration of the individual's reactions to situations subsequently labeled as conflictual. To the extent that the person's current conflict behaviours are considered inappropriate or dysfunctional, one might attempt systematically to modify the corresponding connotations of the conflict construct. Such attempts at introducing conceptual change may be assisted by our notions of the epistemic process whereby all knowledge is formed and changed. For instance, attempts at changing persons' conceptions of conflict may take as their point of departure our notions of the types of evidence they may consider relevant and compelling. Furthermore, such attempts may be based in part on our knowledge of the cognitive and motivational factors that affect the processes of 'freezing' and 'unfreezing' to induce more socially constructive conceptions of conflict.

Empirical research may be carried out to ascertain whether such preventative procedures indeed modify, in desirable ways, people's subsequent reactions to conflictual situations. For example, one might take a sample of what Kelley and Stahelski (1970) called 'competitors' (persons whose predominant reaction to conflict is the attempt to defeat the other party) and change them into 'cooperators' (persons whose predominant reaction to conflict is to look for ways for preserving both parties' interests) via the appropriate cognitive and motivational procedures. The conflict behavior of such individuals could then be comparatively studied.

7. Conflict Resolution and Dissolution

Beyond the *preventive* mode of dealing with conflict, the present epistemic analysis seems pertinent to dealing with extant conflictual situations. The active and passive processes of knowledge modification may be utilized here as well. Attempts to actively modify the conflictual interpretation will be referred to as *conflict resolution*; those based on the passive cognitive process will be referred to as *conflict dissolution*.

Conflict resolution. In this attempt to resove a conflict, the conflict interpretation is attacked head on. This might be accomplished by rendering accessible evidence inconsistent with the interpretation, and/or by arousing epistemic motivations that may work to 'unfreeze' the interpretation. On the basis on the core contents of the conflict notion, its undermining might often require one of three types of evidence: (a) that one's goal is not really to attain the object believed incompatible with the other party's goal; (b) that the other party is not actually striving to achieve its assumed goal; (c) that the two goals are not actually incompatible.

Elimination of one's own goal (incompatible with another's) might be accomplished in any number of ways. A goal may be abandoned because it no longer appears attractive, because it is believed to have been attained, or, conversely, because it appears unattainable and therefore is likely to engender only frustration and pain. An example of the elimination of a goal is recognizable in the change in US policy between the Carter Administration and the first Reagan Administration. A great number of conflicts involving US foreign policy during the Carter years originated from the goal of preserving human rights, especially in South America. When this goal was abandoned with onset of the Reagan era, many international conflicts in which the US was embroiled simply vanished.

An interesting form of goal change is goal partition, where a major goal is separated into a more attainable group of subgoals. Fisher (1969), who advocated this mode of conflict resolution, cites several instances in which it appears to have led to an abatment of conflict. For example, an air rights agreement was struck between the United States and the Soviet Union during the Cold War because of a decision to exclude this issue from the broad concerns on which the major powers were divided. The technique of goal-partition characterized Kissinger's mediation of the Middle-East disengagement negotiations in 1973–75 (Brown, 1980). Specifically, Kissinger initiated a series of limited agreements breaking the large objectives into smaller issues, whose resolution was more readily attainable, until the final goals of each side were realized to an acceptable degree.

Conflict may also be resolved through change in the perception of the other party's goals. Thus, one might come to believe that the other party has abandoned its goals, or come to realize that it never had those goals to begin with. This type of shift is exemplified in the gradual transformation of Japanese perceptions of the West in the latter part of the 19th century. Formal proclamations depicting the Westerners as 'beasts' and 'barbarians' gave way to a different approach that valued the technological advancements of the foreigners and de-emphasized conflictual relations with Westerners in general.

Another major route to conflict resolution is to bring about change in the assessment that the goals are, in fact, incompatible. One example is the Israeli-Egyptian Peace Treaty, signed when both sides were willing to believe that their goals could be concurrently achieved. Israel achieved security whitout occupying the Sinai Penisula, and Egypt regained its territory without striking against Israel.

Conflict dissolution. While conflict resolution involves an active focusing on the conflict interpretation in ways that may lead to a reassessment of its validity, conflict dissolution may occur when the conflict schema is put out of the focus of attention and moved into relative obscurity. Research by Higgins, Bargh and Lombardi (1985) suggests that *recency* as well as *frequency* of activating a construct determines its subsequent accessibility. Conversely, it follows that a conflict interpretation left inactive for long periods of time might become relatively inaccessible and thus cease to exert any appreciable influence on judgements and behavior. For instance, a married coupe could at one time experience intense conflict and react to it by negative affect, derogatory cognitions, and possible negative actions as well. At a different time, however, after the conflict schema has been left alone for a while, awareness of conflict might be abated and the negative thoughts supplanted by more positive notions of 'love' or 'partnership'. If that occurred, the same couple that only recently was on the verge of breaking up could now exhibit authentic affection and mutual commitment.

The same principle applies in reverse as well: that is, to parties who maintained amicable relations until the conflict schema was activated. Thus, people from two opposing groups – say, Israelis and Palestinians – may maintain relatively positive everyday contacts (e.g. in the domains of commerce or labor) until such time when the Palestinian-Israeli conflict notion surfaced in a group member's mind. Should this occur, the individual's attitude might shift drastically, to the point of undertaking hostile and violent actions toward persons to whom under different circumstances he or she might exhibit genuine humanity and friendship. Similarly, two groups may at one time be in intense conflict, whereas at some subsequent time they may experience warm and friendly relations, even though no systematic resolution of the conflict has taken place. Relations between China and the United States, or France and West Germany, represent salient cases in point.

Reduced accessibility of the conflict construct may take place if an alternative construct has asserted its place at the forefront of the person's attention. For example, the appearance of a superordinate goal common to hitherto conflicting groups may reduce the awareness of conflict. Thus, in the classical research by Sherif, Harvey, White, Hood and Sherif (1961), conflict between two competing groups of boys was reduced by introducing a series of different superordinate goals that they shared in common. Of course, a decline in the accessibility of a given conflict schema may be temporary rather than permanent. For example, the United States and the Soviet Union put their disagreements aside during World War II in order to work together against a common enemy; however, immediately following the victory over Nazi Germany, the two nations reverted to their conflictual relations that have persisted until recently.

'Setting aside' a conflictual interpretation of a given relationship may weaken its linkages with the evidence on which it rested in the first place. Ample social psychological research on the 'sleeper effect' (starting with Hovland, Lumsdain & Sheffield, 1949) attests that such dissociations are widespread. Presumably, this may weaken the individual's confidence in the conflictual interpretation and render it easier to reinterpret the relationship in alternative terms. Those notions, too, are amenable to empirical research.

8. Summary and Conclusions

In sum, then, we have tried to delineate a framework in which conflict is treated as a form of knowledge. This framework has implications for understanding and predicting behavior in conflictual situations as well as for ways of preventing possible undesirable consequences of conflicts, and of resolving or dissolving particular conflicts. The present apporach is not intended to replace alternative analyses of conflict and conflict resolution. It purports to add a perspective that may allow new avenues of pertinent research and application. It also implies that the cognitive pradigm in social psychology need not divest research in the area of its social significance. If anything, interpersonal conflict is a distinctly social phenomenom, rather than a purely individualistic one. Yet a cognitive-epistemological analysis can illuminate it in novel and, let us hope, fruitful ways.

Notes

1 In its present usage the term 'conflict' is meant to denote an *interpersonal* incompatibility between goals rather than intrapersonal incompatibility between one's goals, or a mere inconsistency (inter or intra-personal) between cognitions.

References

Bar-Tal, D., 1984. *Israeli-Palestinian Conflict: A Cognitive Analysis.* Unpublished manuscript. Tel Aviv University.

Bar-Tal, D.; A.W. Kruglanski & Y. Klar, 1989. 'Conflict Termination: An Epistomological Analysis of International cases', *Political Psychology*, vol. 10, no. 2, pp. 233–255.

Bar-Tal, D. & A.W. Kruglanski, eds, 1988. *The Social Psychology of Knowledge.* New York: Cambridge Univerisity Press.

Bronfenbrenner, U., 1964. 'Allowing for Soviet Perceptions', in R. Fisher, ed., *International Conflict and Behavioral Science.* New York: Basic Books.

Brown, W.R., 1980. *The Last Crusade: A Negotiator's Middle East Handbook.* Chicago: Nelson-Hall.

Driver, M.J., 1962. 'Conceptual Structure and Group Processes in an International Stimulation: Part 1. The Perception of Simulated Nations.' (ONP Technical Report No. 9). Princeton, NJ: Princeton University & Educational Testing Service.

Finlay, D.J.; O.R. Holsti & R.R. Fagen, 1967. *Enemies in Politics.* Chicago: Rand McNally.

Fisher, R., 1969. *International Conflict for Beginners.* New York: Harper and Row.

Gamson, W.A., 1968. *Power and Discontent.* Homewood, IL: Dorsey.

Heradstveit, 1981. *The Arab-Israeli Conflict*, 2nd ed. Oslo: Universitetsforlaget.

Higgins, E.T.; J.A. Bargh & W. Lombardi, 1985. 'The Nature of Priming Effects on Categorization', *Journal of Experimental Psychology: Learning, Memory, and Cognition*, vol. 11, pp. 59–69.

Holsti, O.R., 1962. 'The Belief System and National Images: A Case Study', *Journal of Conflict Resolution*, vol. 6, no. 3, pp. 244–252.

Hovland, C.I.; A.A. Lumsdaine & F.D. Sheffield, 1949. *Experiments on Mass Communication.* Princeton, NJ: Princeton University Press.

Jervis, R., 1976. *Perception and Misperception in International Politics.* Princeton, NJ: Princeton University Press.

Jervis, R.; R.N. Lebow & J.F. Stein, 1985. *Psychology and Deterrence.* Baltimore: Johns Hopkins University Press.

Kelly, H.H. & A.J. Stahelski, 1970. 'Social Interaction Basis of Cooperators' and

Competitor's Beliefs about Others', *Journal of Personality and Social Psychology*, vol. 16, pp. 66–91.

Kruglanski, A.W., 1989. *Lay Epistemics and Human Knowledge: Cognitive and Motivational Bases*. New York: Plenum.

Kruglanski, A.W., 1988. 'Knowledge As a Social Psychological Construct', in D. Bar-Tal & Arie W. Kruglanski, eds, 1988.

Kruglanski, A. & T. Freund, 1983. 'The Freezing and Unfreezing of Lay-inferences: Effects on Impressional Primacy, Stereotyping and Numerical Anchoring', *Journal of Experimental Social Psychology*, vol. 19, pp. 448–468.

Mroz, J.E., 1980. *Beyond Security: Private Perceptions Among Arabs & Israelis*. New York: Pergamon.

Sherif, M.; O.J. Harvey; B.J. White, W.R. Hood & C.W. Sherif, 1961. *Intergroup Cooperation & Competition: The Robbers's Cave Experiment*. Norman, OK: University Book Exchange.

Singer, J.J., 1958. 'Threat Perception and the Armament-Tension Dilemma', *Journal of Conflict Resolution*, vol. 2, no. 1 pp. 90–105.

Stroebe, W; A.W. Kruglanski, D. Bar-Tal & M. Hewstone, eds, 1989. *The Social Psychology of Intergroup Conflict*. New York: Springer.

Streufert, S. & H. Fromkin, 1969. 'True Conflict & Complex Decision Making: The Effect of the Three Party Duel and Military and Economic Behavior of Decision Making Groups in Complex Environments'. (ONP Technical Report No. 25). West Lafayette, IN: Purdue University.

Suedfeld, P. & P.E. Tetlock, 1977. 'Integrative Complexity of Communications in International Crises', *Journal of Conflict Resolution*, vol. 21, no. 1, pp. 159–184.

5

Netzah Yisrael, Symbolic Immortality, and the Israeli-Palestinian Conflict

Moshe Hazani

> It was like we were returning to a dream,
> Retying the bonds that had been torn asunder.
> The glory reascended to the roofs of Jerusalem –
> A young sun.
> Whether awake or dreaming
> A ladder firmly planted on which
> An entire nation strived to ascend.
>
> – Amir Gilboa

1. Introduction

Many have observed that Israel clings to uncompromising attitudes in the Israeli-Arab conflict, particularly with regard to questions involving the Palestinians. For example, most Israelis deny the Palestinians' right to self-determination; many claim that there is no such thing as a 'Palestinian people'. A majority of Israelis are vigorously opposed to the establishment of a Palestinian state west of the Jordan River. Most significantly, even those who would agree to a Palestinian state in part of the territories Israel captured in the 1967 Six-Day War are adamantly opposed to any negotiations over the holy city of Jerusalem.[1]

Several attempts have been made to account for this rigidity, one of which involves the Holocaust: 'what do you expect of a post-Auschwitz Jew if you threaten to throw him into the sea?' It would seem only natural for him to entrench himself in his position on hearing Arab vows to throw 'all the Zionists' into the sea. However, this view ignores several crucial aspects of the Arab-Israeli conflict. It disregards the *pre*-Auschwitz Zionist willingness to die for Jerusalem – possession of which is no guarantee against being thrown into the sea. It also fails to explain the Israeli perception that it is the Palestinians, and not the hostile Arab states, that threaten Israel's existence. If anything, it is the far stronger Arab states, such as Syria and Iraq (which amassed an enormous war machine during the Iran-Iraq War and has practiced a quasi-Holocaust against the Kurds), whom Israel should fear. Yet while they deal with the Arab states rationally (by coolly bombing an Iraqi nuclear reactor, for example), Israelis view the Palestinians as their diabolical enemy.

Attempting to account for this view, some Israelis agree that a Palestinian entity west of the Jordan River would be a 'springboard' for the regular Arab armies to invade and annihilate Israel. This theory, however, fails to explain why the Israelis demonize the 'springboard' rather than the Arab states. Nor does it explain why it is the Palestinians who arouse intense anxiety and memories of the Holocaust among Israelis – to the extent that the PLO is often equated with the Nazis. This author is far from being an apologist for Palestinian organizations, which have perpetrated atrocious deeds against Israeli civilians; nevertheless, comparing Arafat to Hitler seems going a bit too far.

All this suggests that the explanation lies not in the realm of man's need for physical existence, but in the realm of symbols. Employing Lifton's paradigm of symbolic immortality (Lifton, 1969, 1979), this chapter argues that the 'rigid' characteristics of the Israeli political mentality are two aspects of a *natural human response to the threat of symbolic extinction*. More specifically, the chapter avers that: (a) Zionism is, in part,[2] an attempt to resurrect the Jewish sense of immortality, shattered repeatedly since the late 19th century; (b) the Palestinians impede this attempt and have consequently come to represent Jewish mortality; (c) this is why it is the Palestinians who symbolically reactivate among Israelis a long-standing death anxiety and its attendant rigidity; (d) and this is why it is the Palestinians who embody for Israelis the Nazi arch-villains who sought to put an end to Jewish history and existence.

2. Symbolic Immortality, Connection to Life, and Historical Dislocations

> Man requires a sense of immortality in the face of inevitable death. This sense of immortality need not be merely a denial of the fact of his death, though man is certainly prone to such a denial. It also represents a compelling, universal urge to maintain an inner sense of continuity, over time and space, with the various elements of life (Lifton, 1969, p. 21).

Lifton enumerates five modes of symbolic immortality, of which two are crucial for our discussion: One is the *biological* mode, i.e., 'the sense of living on through, but in an emotional sense *with* or *in* one's sons and daughters and their sons and daughters'. In varying degrees, this mode extends into the social dimension, into 'the sense of surviving through one's tribe, organization, people, nation or even species'. The second is the *theological* mode, as experienced both in the ideas posited by various religions concerning life after death and in the more general theological principle of the spiritual conquest of death.[3]

The modes of symbolic immortality are not merely problems pondered when one is dying: they are *constantly perceived* (albeit often unconsciously) inner standards by which we evaluate our lives and maintain the feelings of connection, meaning, and movement so necessary to everyday psychological existence. In other words, the modes of symbolic immortality are the same links that bind us to life, whatever our age, health, or state of mind. They serve not only to overcome death, but also to endow life with meaning and protect us from death in life – an agonizing, unbearable existence.

For our discussion, two modes of symbolic immortality should be added to Lifton's five: or rather, two 'submodes' of which Lifton is aware should be elevated to independent status. Lifton refers to social institutions as a specific instance of his third mode ('man's works'); in some historical periods, however, social institutions ought to be singled out as a separate avenue to symbolic immortality. Individuals have often transcended death through the idea that the Church (or the Party, or the Fatherland) will survive them. For example, during World War II, nation and state energized the Japanese soldier to die willingly (and to kill others).

Another possible mode of symbolic immortality is that achieved by being associated with and survived by 'pieces of space' or objects in space. As G.H. Mead (1938) has shown, spatial objects are not 'just there', but are endowed with cultural or individual meaning, and as such bind us to life (see, e.g., Firey, 1947; Fried, 1963; Hazani & Ilan, 1970). 'Pieces of space' charged with cultural meaning are highly conducive to a sense of immortality; this is why people are willing to die (and kill) for holy places and territories.

When an individual faces the prospect of losing his sense of immortality – which is also his sense of continuity and connection to life – he experiences *threatened vitality*, the anxiety associated not only with death but also with death equivalents: separation, stasis, and disintegration (Lifton, 1979, p. 128). The individual's sense of immortality may be impaired for a variety of reasons, one of which should be mentioned here. Since man is a 'cultural animal', individual modes of symbolic immortality are embraced by collective symbolizations; consequently, desymbolization (the breakdown of the collective symbolizations) may engender death anxiety among individual members of a collectivity. The more tightly the individual modes are embraced by collective symbolizations, the more likely individuals are to experience intense death anxiety as a result of desymbolization.

Historical dislocations, regardless of their causes, are accompanied by desymbolization. In such periods, man has special difficulties in finding symbolic forms within which to locate himself; he finds it difficult to believe in larger connections, and experiences psychic numbing, apathy, an absence of trust and faith. At the same time, there is an explosion of symbolizing forays to overcome collective deadness and reassert larger connections. All too easily these can take the form of ideological totalism, asserting an all-or nothing claim to truth, a belief that there is only one valid mode of being, only one authentic avenue to immortality. Yet totalistic systems rarely restore the old security: beneath their surface, death anxiety lurks. This is why they are so rigid and intolerant, while promising salvation: man's response to the impairment of his sense of immortality, then, is a combination of hope and despair, dogmatic faith and fear of extinction. (Lifton, 1969, xi; Lifton, 1979, pp. 293, 296, 298; Lifton, 1980.)

Historical dislocations do not invariably lead to totalism (accompanied by death anxiety). Sometimes people can extricate themselves from their agonizing situation by 'survivors' creativity' (Lifton, 1979, p. 296), i.e., channeling their uneasiness into constructive paths. Significantly, totalism and creativity are not mutually exclusive: responses to a damaged sense of immortality may include *both* alternatives, in different proportions. This, as shall be demonstrated, is the case with Zionism.

3. Netzah Yisrael – the Old, Traditional Version

As noted, individual modes of symbolic immortality are embraced by collective symbolizations; this is particularly true in Judaism, which views the entire Jewish people as a unified, eternal entity with a collective immortalizing system. To understand what befalls the individual Jew in historical dislocations, then, we must acquaint ourselves with the religious Jewish national immortalizing system, that two-millennium-old complex of ideas that will be referred to here as *Netzah Yisrael* (Hebrew for 'the eternity of Israel'). What be presented here is the *popular version of this system*, not the elaborate teachings of the Jewish sages – it is the former, not the latter, that crystallizes into collective symbolizations. Hence this chapter will not draw upon learned philosophical texts to illustrate its points, but on the Jewish prayer book, since this text is the common denominator of the beliefs accepted by all Jews, including the most eminent philosophers.

The first element of the *Netzah Yisrael* conceptual complex is the belief in the biological immortality of the Jewish people *qua* people,[4] reiterated in the daily liturgy: 'The Lord will not forsake His people; He will not abandon His very own' (Ps. 94:14).

The second element of *Netzah Yisrael* is the belief that the Jewish people is God's Chosen People. This belief is inseparable from the belief in the Jewish people as one huge familiy, descending from the Patriarch Abraham. But the Chosen People is not only a biological concept: some theological 'cement' is required to hold the nation-family together. For instance, an apostate is viewed as no longer a member of his own biological familiy, let alone of the Chosen People.[5] For religious Jews, then, 'pure' biological ties hardly exist, and dissolution of the theological 'cement' may engender a disintegration of the family – i.e., undermine the biological mode of immortality.

Finally, *Netzah Yisrael* includes the belief in the ultimate Redemption of the People of Israel by a God-sent Massiah. The Redemption is depicted as encompassing the ingathering of the exiles to the Promised Land, the restoration of the Jewish state under the royal House of David, the reconstruction of the Temple in Jerusalem, and often also the resurrection of the dead. These images are kept alive in the Jewish mind and repeated three times a day in the liturgy. The belief in the Redemption is inseparable from the belief in the eternity of the Jewish people, for the former provides the teleology and meaning of the eternal existence of the Jewish people, just as the eternal existence of the Jewish people is the warrant for the Redemption at the End of Days. It is also inseparable from the concept of the Chosen People, since it is only God's intervention on behalf of His people that leads to their Redemption. Thus all three elements fuse into a logically coherent complex of ideas pervaded by the belief in the national God of Israel.

Two crucial characteristics of the Jewish immortalizing system, alluded to above, should be spelled out. First, Jews make scant distinction between the individual and collective modes of symbolic immortality: For instance, the Jewish belief in an afterlife holds that the individual's soul will reside in heaven *in the company of the souls of the ancestors of the nation-family* until *the collective resurrection of the entire people.*

Second, while immortalizing systems that merge several modes of symbolic immortality are extremely strong, their very source of strength is also a source of weakness: because they absorb and assimilate potentially independent modes of symbolic immortality, their breakdown leaves the individual with no alternative modes on which to fall back. This, coupled with the inseparability of the individual and collective immortalizing vehicles in Judaism, endows *Netzah Yisrael* with an all-or-nothing quality. Normally, the individual Jew enjoys an extraordinarily strong sense of community, continuity, and immortality. But if *Netzah Yisrael* cracks, he is left naked and bare on the stormy heath of the world, suffering acute death anxiety and desperately searching for symbolic salvation. It seems that this all-or-nothing quality accounts both for the Jews' capacity to survive physical calamities, and their well-known over-representation in radical movements in times of historical dislocations.

4. Netzah Yisrael – the New, Zionist Version

The Zionist movement emerged from the valley of the shadow of symbolic Jewish death in late nineteenth-century Eastern Europe. As Arendt (1944) describes this era of Jewish history, modern anti-Semitism, in interaction with the Jewish assimilation and securalization, correspondend to the erosion of the old religious and spiritual values of Judaism. Just at a time when Jews were threatened by physical extinction from without, they were also threatened by dissolution from within. Katz, who analyzes the crisis of European Jewish tradition (1961, 1979), also writes that Zionism was an important factor in the reintegration of symbolically uprooted individuals. It is Gonen (1975), however, who discusses the impact of the desymbolization on individual Jews: employing Laing's term, he describes the inner world of the Jews as 'merely a vacuum', and views Jewish existence as 'death in life' (pp. 30–31).

These accounts are firmly buttressed by the testimony of Jewish poets, novelists, and essayists who personally experienced the Jewish lot in Eastern Europe and gave it trenchant expression. 'The people are plucked grass ...

look in their hearts – behold a dreary waste'; 'There is no way out because there is no God'[6] – these lines underscore the breakdown of the Jewish sense of immortality, resulting from the process of desymbolization that had been occurring among Jews for years, cracking open the immortalizing vehicle of *Netzah Yisrael* and leaving the individual Jew totally unprotected, searching desperately for symbolic salvation. Many Jewish youth embraced Communism; others, however, sought to change Jewish history by restoring the Jewish people to a golden age of security. While they abjured Judaism as a religion, they were still imbued with the belief in the eternity of the Jewish people and were looking for a new, secular version of the old religious immortalizing system: Zionism was to become that new version.

The new, Zionist version of *Netzah Yirsrael* differed from the old one. Gone was the religious 'cement', as well as patently religious elements like the belief in a Redemption by a God-sent Messiah. But the belief in the eternity of the Jewish people and its chosenness remained, as did the conviction that Jewish immortality depends upon the link with the Promised Land and the restoration of a Jewish nation-state (a secular version of the kingdom of the House of David).

This was not merely a shift of emphasis, but a symbolic revolution as well. The core of the old, religious version of *Netzah Yisrael* was the belief in God as ensuring the immortality of His Chosen People. The connections to the Promised Land and the House of David, while contributing to the Jewish sense of timeless immortality by keeping the images of glorious past and future alive and vivid, were of secondary importance. Secular Zionism turned the old system upside down by considering these links to be the core of the new immortalizing vehicle, while rejecting the belief in God. In our terms, while the old version of Netzah Yisrael rested on the theological mode of symbolic immortality, the new version rests on the spatial and institutional ones.[7] Moreover, Zionism sought to establish concrete spatial and institutional connections in place of the old spiritual and religious ones. As Ben-Gurion put it:

> If there is any tangible content to the Zionist idea, it must be the content of the state. Zionism is the desire for a *Jewish state*, the desire for a land and for earthly dominion (1971, pp. 275–276; emphasis in original).

The central pillars of the Zionist version of *Netzah Yisrael* were the concrete *spatial and institutional modes of symbolic immortality*, embodied in the establishment of a Jewish nation-state in the Promised Land.

This might seem to account for Israeli rigidity vis-à-vis the Arabs, who threaten the central pillars of the Zionist immortalizing system. However, it fails to explain why Israelis often cling anxiously to their attitudes, or why there exist images of death and destruction in the Israeli consciousness; most important, it fails to explain the paradox of Israeli apprehension of the Palestinians – in fact, their weakest enemy – and their association of the latter with the Nazis.

5. Halutzi Rebirth and the Graveyard of Kinneret

The young Zionists – the *halutzim* – who emigrated to Palestine in the early twentieth century to realize the Zionist dream,[8] were survivors of the symbolic death that had befallen Eastern European Jewry. As Rachel Yanait-Ben Zvi, wife of the future second president of Israel, wrote: 'I felt ... as if I had not been living ... until just yesterday (when she first visited Jerusalem)' (1959, pp. 22). And Ben-Gurion assured his father that 'the first stirrings of dawn are already breaking in the eastern sky' (1971, p. 30). East, in Jewish symbology, is the Land of Israel, but it also designates rebirth.

Lurking behind these images of rebirth, however, were also images of death and despair (see Almog, 1992, pp. 169–170). Many *halutzi* writings and popular songs associate images of death with belief in the national rebirth. The most telling, though silent, testimony to the state of mind of many *halutzim* is the graveyard of the settlement of Kinneret, near the peaceful Sea of Galilee, where more than a few suicide victims found their last repose.

As befits an attempt to overcome death anxiety, *halutzi* Zionism was a stern and totalistic ideology, an all-or-nothing assertion of truth, incapable of accepting shades other than black and white. One manifestation of this totalism was the bitter clashes between various ideological trends, often within the same camp, that we can hardly understand today. Yet they are comprehensible if we recall the dogmatic nature of totalistic ideologies, which allow no differences of views, however slight. Another manifestation was the paradox of atheists who tenaciously clung to basically religious beliefs,[9] such as the right of the Jewish people to inherit God's Promised Land: this, too, is comprehensible if we recall that when old symbolizations crumble, people salvage whatever they can from the wreckage, rationally or not, in order to overcome death anxiety.

Finally, *halutzi* Zionism made the dichotomy between the worthy and the unworthy typical of totalistic ideologies. The unworthy was the old, 'exilic' Jew, and the worthy – the *halutzi* Jew; in Ben-Gurion's (1971, p. 40) terminology, the 'mummified Jew' and the 'proud and militant' new Jew.

There was an additional aspect, however, to the dichotomization of the Jewish people. The brave, new *halutzim* also viewed themselves as their exilic brothers' keepers. As Ben-Gurion put it (Bar-Zohar, 1977, p. 132), 'the Hebrew community in *Eretz Yisrael* [the Land of Israel] is only a small part of the nation ... but it is the part known as the heart.' While this certainly smacks of totalistic elitism, he and his friends viewed themselves as charged with ensuring the symbolic immortality of the 'body' of the entire Jewish people scattered all over the world.

It follows, then, that Zionism should not be reduced to totalism accompanied by death anxiety. This would ignore the *halutzi* concern for the entire Jewish people, as well as the Zionist creative energy that generated a new Jewish national entity and made it a conspicuous instance of survivors' creativity. As stressed above, survivors' creativity and totalism (plus anxiety) are not mutually exclusive. In the final analysis, Zionism should be viewed as a *complex* response to the impairment of Jewish sense of immortality, a response that includes both collective survivors' creativity and totalism accompanied by anxiety. While the former led ultimately to the creation of the modern state of Israel, the latter spawned *halutzi* rigidity.

6. Thou Hast Chosen Us from among All Peoples

Some historical instances show that people can regenerate themselves through survivors' creativity and gradually extricate themselves from totalism and death anxiety. For the *Yishuv* (the Pre-State Jewish community in Palestine), however, this proved difficult. The Jews contiuned to suffer during and after World War I, and virulent anti-Semitism spread and intensified all over Eastern Europe. Despite their elitism, the *halutzim* perceived themselves as sharing the fate of their exilic brethren, all the more so as practically all the *halutzim* had families in Eastern Europe and Jewish survivors kept arriving in Palestine from abroad (the fourth wave of immigration – 1925 – was triggered by a wave of anti-Semitism in Poland).[10] Thus the *Yishuv* was not given a chance to recover from its death anxiety; in 1933 the Nazis rose to power in Germany, and in 1939 World War II broke out.

The Holocaust was a terrible shock to the Jewish faith in *Netzah Yisrael* – but, as one who did not personally experience the Holocaust, this author feels unable to discuss that blow. Yet one remark must be made: the Holocaust differed from, say, Hiroshima, in one major symbolic aspect: the Nazis used what are *basically Jewish categories*, part and parcel of the idea of *Netzah Yisrael*, to 'justify' their genocide. They, too, defined the Jewish people as a 'chosen' people, singled out from all the other peoples ... for extinction. Thus, they attacked not only Jewish bodies – as the Americans attacked their Japanese enemies – but central Jewish symbols as well. *Netzah Yisrael* was pushed into the Auschwiz gas chambers along with the believers – and almost perished: the fact that most Jews survived the Holocaust, and that their immortalizing system remained, however cracked, was merely a geopolitical accident.

7. Heart, Arm, and God-Equivalent

Far from discouraging the *Yishuv*, the Holocaust served only to enhance the conviction that the exilic version of *Netzah Yisrael* was mortal and that only the Zionist version could ensure Jewish immortality. This enhanced totalism resulted in two tenets: The first was the implicit belief that a Jewish state in the Holy Land is physically immune from destruction, since it rests on the concrete spatial and institutional modes of *Netzah Yisrael*. The second was the conviction that the *Yishuv* (as well as its direct descendant, the State of Israel) ensures not only the symbolic but also the physical existence of world Jewry. Thus, the pre-Auschwitz view of the *Yishuv* as a 'heart' animating the 'body' of the Jewish people was transformed into a post-Auschwitz tenet that a Jewish state is also an 'arm' which ensures the *physical existence* of each and every Jew in the world. This makes Israel, which emerged from the *Yishuv* in 1948, the embodiment of *Netzah Yisrael* – an immortalizing system in the form of a geopolitical reality. In this capacity, many Israelis unconsciously view their state as a God-equivalent – a substitute for the God who protects His people.[11]

Both Israeli beliefs – the link between the Land of Israel and Jewish immortality, and the role of the State of Israel as guarantor of that immortality – are irrational. It was a matter of luck that the *Yishuv* survived the Holocaust: If the British had not halted the Germans at el-Alamein, Palestine would have been overrun and its Zionist population exterminated. Nor is the institutional connection any stronger: even if a Jewish state had existed before World War II it could not have withstood the onslaught of the Nazi war machine. Moreover, when Israel is in trouble today, it often prompts US Jewry to intervene on its behalf with Congress and the Administration – incidentally, a tactic this author sees as normal and legitimate.

The Israeli irrationality becomes understandable, though, if we realize that Zionism – like all totalistic ideologies – shuns agonizing ambiguities and insists upon its own permanence and immutability. In reaction to disconcerting events such as the Holocaust, it entrenched itself deeper in its original conviction and become even more dogmatic, while its underlying death anxiety increased.[12]

Moreover, it must be conceded that the irrational beliefs adumbrated above do have some factual basis. During and after World War II the *Yishuv* made valiant efforts to rescue European Jews and offer them shelter. After the State of Israel was established (1948), the tiny country (600,000 inhabitants) opened its doors to multitudes of Jews from practically all around the world. Among other things, it has fought to free Soviet Jews from that immense gulag, helped 400,000 Romanian Jews settle in Israel, absorbed oppressed Ethiopian Jews, and most recently began to absorb large numbers of Jews from the disintegrating Soviet Union.

As an Israeli, the author is proud of his country's achievements, which demonstrate that Israel is indeed an important cornerstone of Jewish existence. Yet, impressive as these achievements are, they can all be explained rationally – here the role of US Jewry in cooperation with Israel should not be forgotten – and cannot justify the land-state-immortality linkage. They also demonstrate something else: Israel, like the early *halutzim*, responded to the loss of Jewish sense of immortality in a complex manner, applying itself in an intensive survivors' creativity that greatly mitigated its totalism and death anxiety. Israel would seem to be a supreme instance of survivors' creativity.

8. The 'Autochthones' and the Image of Auschwitz

In 1947 the UN resolved to establish a Jewish and an Arab states in Palestine; the territory of the Jewish state was to encompass only that portion of Palestine that had a Jewish majority. Thus, the Jewish state was the embodiment of only the institutional pillar of the Zionist *Netzah Yisrael*, and not of the spatial one, since the bulk of the Holy Land was left in Arab hands. The *Yishuv* greeted the resolution enthusiastically, but it never relinquished its desire to restore concrete links with the entire territory of the Promised Land, especially with Jerusalem – which the UN did not include in the Jewish state. In the 1948 Israeli-Arab war Israel made repeated unsuccessful attemps to capture the Old City of Jerusalem as well as other parts of the Promised Land. The failure created a general feeling among Israelis that the 1948 military victory, although it established the State of Israel, was only partial. Ben-Gurion viewed the territorial outcome of the war as 'a source of grief for the generations' (Bar-Zohar, 1977, pp. 803–804, 815, 825).

This grief ended in the 1967 Six-Day War, when Israel captured the entire territory of the Promised Land, including the Old City of Jerusalem. Yet at this point the problem of the indigenous population, of which the Zionist leadership never seemed to have been unaware (Bar-Zohar, 1977, pp. 355–360), surfaced in the most concrete terms. The new territories proved to be inhabited by the Palestianians, who, much like the autochthones of Greek myth, were created from and therefore inseparable from the earth. They stood between the victorious Israelis and the space of the Promised Land; most importantly, they inhabited the Old City of Jerusalem, with their mosques on the site of the ancient Jewish Temple. Furthermore, their very existence as non-Jews endangered the Jewishness of the Israeli nation-state. Thus the Palestinians came into conflict with the two central pillars of the Zionist immortalizing system – the spatial and institutional bonds to life. Of course, if merely ensuring its Jewishness were the prime requisite, Israel could have returned to its mostly Jewish pre-1967 border. But this would mean cutting itself off from part of the territory of the Promised Land and from the Old City of Jerusalem. This is unacceptable to most Israelis, as it implies that it is impossible to erect both pillars of the Zionist *Netzah Yisrael*.

Whether they wanted to or not, the Palestinians impeded the century-old Zionist attempt to resurrect the shattered *Netzah Yisrael*. Willy-nilly they perpetuated the breakdown of Jewish continuity and the impaired sense of immortality, originally caused by processes that had unfolded far away from the Middle East. Moreover, since for post-Auschwitz Israelis Israel ensures the symbolic immortality as well as the continued individual *bodily* existence of world Jewry, the Palestinians have come to represent the agonizing destiny of Jewish life in the valley of the shadow of death – on *both* the national *and* the individual, on the symbolic and the physical planes.

Thus the Palestinians reactivate death anxiety among Israelis, who respond by clinging more rigidly than ever to their totalistic immortalizing system. *This is a natural human response*, particularly if we recall the *tremendous existential significance* of *Netzah Yisrael for Jews throughout history.*

As for the Israeli equation of the PLO with the Nazis: even though the Holocaust was not the wellspring of Israeli death anxiety – which in fact had accompanied Zionism from its earliest days – it greatly augmented it and *focused it in a single historical episode, symbolized by Auschwitz.* Anything that arouses the Israeli death anxiety conjures up the image of the gas chambers and crematoria; and whoever arouses it, wittingly or unwittingly, is automatically perceived as among the perpetrators of that genocide. Thus the unspeakable guilt of the Nazis becomes transferred to anyone who threatens the Jewish sense of immortality – be this directly or by *impeding the Jews' reunification with their source of vitality.*

This does not imply that all Palestinians are peaceful autochthones who impede the Jewish renascence by passively inhabiting the Promised Land; as the PLO Covenant makes plain, there are Palestinians who dream of annihilating Israel (see Jancu, 1989). The Covenant even contends that there is no such thing as a Jewish people. But in this chapter I am dealing with the Israelis, not the Palestinians; whether the latter are innocent autochthones or virulent enemies, they still pose no serious military threat to Israel. Yet symbolically, it is they who have come to represent Jewish mortality, after more than 3000 years of existence.

9. Conclusion

Thus, this chapter suggests that the Israeli-Palestinian conflict be viewed not as simply an instrumental conflict over territory, on the model of the conflict between the American settlers and the indigenous Indians; nor as an expressive conflict over the possession of sacred space, like the conflict between the Crusaders and the Muslims; nor as simply resulting from an Israeli desire for physical survival (since 1948, more Jews have been killed in Israel than in any other place in the world). While all these elements certainly exist in the conflict, its unique nature and the bitter and extreme emotions it arouses result from a desperate human need to regain a sense of immortality in the face of expiring vitality. Zionism was, in part, a totalistic response to the breakdown of *Netzah Yisrael*, the Jewish traditional immortalizing system. The new Zionist version of *Netzah Yisrael* rested on two pillars, the spatial and institutional modes of symbolic immortality; it sought to create a Jewish nation-state in the Promised Land, and thereby bring forth Jewish revitalization. This, however, has proven hard to attain, since the 'autochthones' impede Jewish re-connection with their life-giving space. The 'autochthones', then, perpetuate the Jewish sojourn in the valley of the shadow of death; in Israeli consciousness, they have come to represent Jewish mortality, symbolically replacing the Nazis.

It would be wrong to end this essay in a pessimistic vein, suggesting that the Israeli-Palestinian conflict is insoluble – all the more so since Palestinian ideology begins to speak of a Palestinian holocaust (in 1948), regarding Israel as an impediment to the restoration of the Palestinian sense of immortality. Determinism is out of place, if we recall that collective survivors' creativity is an alternative to totalism and death anxiety, as demonstrated so strikingly by the Zionist achievement in Palestine. Moreover, it does seem that gradually both parties have come to realize that ensuring symbolic immortality may become too costly – that in seeking to avoid death in life they end up pursuing life in death. Hence it is this author's belief that we may yet see the light at the end of the tunnel.

Notes

1 These data are taken from public opinion polls regularly conducted in Israel during the last 20 years. For instance, Dr. Mina Zemach (1989) of the Dahaf Research Institute has repeatedly found that most Israelis (over 70 %) are opposed to a Palestinian state; she also found that only 5 % of Israelis view Jerusalem as negotiable. Zemach's findings concur with those of others (e.g., Inbar & Yuchtman-Yaar, 1985, who found that Israelis have rigid views about the ideal political order). True, a public opionion poll conducted in December, 1989, found that 50 per cent of the Israelis do not reject negotiations with the PLO; but the pollster (Diskin, 1990) holds that this does not reflect a change in attitude toward the Palestinians (almost 50 per cent of those polled think it justified to deprive *Israeli* Arabs of voting rights). Israeli enmity toward the Palestinians has reached new heights in the wake of the Palestinian *intifada*, as has Israeli support of nationalist parties.

2 The chapter is far from proposing a mono-causal explanation of Zionism. For works dealing with the origins and history of Zionism, see Halpern (1961); Laqueur (1972); Vital (1975, 1982, 1987).

3 The other three modes are: that achieved through man's works (art, thought, institutions, etc.); that represented by the continuity of nature itself, the sense that one will live on in natural elements, which are limitless in time and space; and experiential transcendence, similar to what Freud referred to as the 'oceanic feeling' (Lifton, 1969, pp. 21–23).

4 This can be called '*Netzah Yisrael* proper', and is in fact the source of the term that the author has borrowed to designate the broader Jewish immortalizing system, which includes additional elements.

5 This popular position, held by most Jews, clashes with Jewish law, according to which an apostate remains legally a Jew.

6 Ch. N. Bialik, 'The City of Slaughter'; U.Z. Greenberg, 'Great Dread and a Moon.' Both poets are titans of modern Hebrew literature.

7 The religious Zionists – initially a small minority – did not see Zionism as a substitute for the traditional belief in the Redemption by a God-sent Messiah. However, they too accepted the view that *Netzah Yisrael* (and the coming of the Messiah, in their version of Zionism) depends upon the resumption of concrete spatial and institutional connection.

8 The discussion of practical Zionism in Palestine begins with the Second *Aliya* (the second wave of Zionist immigrants that arrived in 1905–1914) because it was this group that constituted the core of the Zionist endeavor in Palestine and left its imprint on the *Yishuv* (the Jewish community in Palestine) and later on the State of Israel (see Vital, 1982, p. 384).

9 On this paradox, see Almog, 1987, pp. 10–11; Almog, 1992, pp. 169–182.

10 For the complex topic of the relationships between the *Yishuv* and European Jewry, see Weitz (1988, 1989).

11 Even religious Zionist Israelis, who never abandoned their belief in God, implicitly view the old version of Netzah Yisrael as fragile, compared with their version of God plus Land and State. For them the State of Israel, while no substitute for God,

does buttress His power to protect His people – which endows the country with some 'godly' meaning.

12 Today's Israeli mind still harbors images of death and annihilation. For instance, when Israel was attacked by the Egyptians and the Syrians in October 1973, then Defense Minister Moshe Dayan anxiously remarked that 'this is the end of the Third Temple'. Dayan, who epitomized the Israeli sense of reinforced invulnerability, typically reversed himself and exhibited a heightened sense of vulnerability, as is often the case (see Lifton, 1967, p. 481; 1968, p. 14n).

References

Almog, Shmuel, 1987. *Zionism and History*. Jerusalem: The Magnes Press (in Hebrew).

Almog, Shmuel, 1992. *Nationalism, Zionism, Antisemitism*. Jerusalem: Hassifria Haziyonit (in Hebrew).

Arendt, Hanna, 1944. 'The Jew as a Pariah: A Hidden Tradition', *Jewish Social Studies 6*, vol. 1, pp. 99–122.

Bar-Zohar, Michael, 1977. *Ben-Gurion*. Tel Aviv: Am Oved (in Hebrew). The abridged English translation of the book omits important passages.

Ben-Gurion, David, 1971. *Memoirs*. Tel Aviv: Am Oved (in Hebrew).

Diskin, Abraham, 1990. Personal communication.

Firey, Walter, 1947. *Land Use in Central Boston*. Cambridge, MA: Harvard University Press.

Fried, Marc, 1963. 'Grieving for a Lost Home', pp. 151–171 in L.J. Duhl, ed., *The Urban Condition*. New York: Basic Books.

Gonen, Jay T., 1975. *A Psychohistory of Zionism*. New York: Mason and Charter.

Halpern, Ben, 1961. *The Idea of the Jewish State*. Cambridge, MA: Harvard University Press.

Hazani, Moshe & Y. Ilan, 1970. *Social Implications of Urban Renewal*. Haifa: Technion Research and Development Foundation (in Hebrew).

Inbar, Michael & E. Yuchtman-Yaar, 1985. 'Some Cognitive Dimensions of the Israeli-Arab Conflict', *Journal of Conflict Resolution*, vol. 29, no. 4, December, pp. 699– 725.

Jancu, Robert, 1989. 'Wanted by the Arabs – A Holocaust', *Judaism*, vol. 38, no. 2, spring, pp. 135–142.

Katz, Jacob, 1961. *Traditions and Crisis*. New York: Schocken Books.

Katz, Jacob, 1979. 'The Jewish National Movement – a Sociological Analysis', pp. 15–35 in J. Katz, *Jewish Nationalism*. Jerusalem: Hassifria Haziyonit (in Hebrew).

Laqueur, Walter, 1972. *A History of Zionism*. London: Weidenfeld and Nicolson.

Lifton, Robert J., 1967. *Death in Life: Survivors of Hiroshima*. New York: Random House.

Lifton, Robert J., 1968. *Revolutionary Immortality*. New York: Random House.

Lifton, Robert J., 1969. *Boundaries*. New York: Simon & Schuster.

Lifton, Robert J., 1979. *The Broken Connection*. New York: Simon & Schuster.

Lifton, Robert J., 1980. 'On the Consciousness of the Holocaust', *The Psychohistorical Review*, vol. 9, no. 1, pp. 3–22.

Mead, George Herbert, 1938. *The Philosophy of the Act*. Chicago, IL: Chicago University Press.

Vital, David, 1975. *The Origins of Zionism*. Oxford: Oxford University Press.

Vital, David, 1982. *Zionism: The Formative Years*. Oxford: Oxford University Press.

Vital, David, 1987. *Zionism: The Crucial Phase*. Oxford: Oxford University Press.

Weitz, Yechiam, 1988. 'The Yishuv's Self-Image and the Reality of the Holocaust', *The Jerusalem Quarterly*, vol. 48, Fall, pp. 73–83.

Weitz, Yechiam, 1989. 'Yishuv, Gola, and the Shoa – Myth and Reality', paper presented at the Seminar on History and Myth, January 1989, Jerusalem.

Yanait-Ben Zvi, Rachel, 1959. *Anu Olim* [*We Immigrate*]. Tel Aviv: Am Oved (in Hebrew).

Zemach, Mina, 1989. Personal communication. (The findings of the Dahaf Research Institute are regularly published in the Israeli media.)

6

Mirroring and Misperceptions

'Where ignorant armies clash by night'*

A review of misperceptions and mirroring in intergroup relations

Michael Moore

1. Introduction

Some thirty-three centuries ago, on the outskirts of Jericho, Joshua encountered a sword-wielding man. The only recently emerged leader of the Israelites hailed this stranger with the words: 'Are you for us or for our adversaries?' (Joshua 5:13). This prototype of subsequent 'Friend or foe?' expressions[1] illustrates one of the most basic mechanisms responsible for the perception of our social environment, namely its dichotomization into *us vs. them*. This fundamental categorization of others into an in-group and an out-group has, in itself, even deeper-going roots. Hilgard (1957, p. 506) sought its source in the perceptual tendency to structure the environment into figure and ground. Stagner (1961) blamed homeostasis for the demarcation of in-groups from out-groups. Simpson & Yinger (1972, p. 16) related the origin of the out-group to the development of the nation-state system, and suggested that its creation reflected the simultaneous action of two conflicting principles: the tribal vs. the state form of organization. Wilder (1986) saw in categorization the application to social objects of the tendency to organize stimuli into categories.

2. Categorization and Stereotyping

Whatever the driving force behind it, categorization, per se, is a beneficial

---

* The quote in the title is from Matthew Arnold's 'Dover Beach' (1867), here quoted from Arnold (1940). This chapter was written during the author's visiting appointment at the University of California, Davis.

process in that it facilitates both physical and cognitive coping with the environment. A basic principle of categorization is 'that the task of category systems is to provide maximum information with the least cognitive effort' (Rosch, 1978, p. 28). This admirably economical principle, however, has a dangerous shortcoming. While its latter requirement of minimum effort is quite objective, tending to reduce the number of categories formed, the former one (maximum information) is notoriously subject to biases. Instead of optimizing input and output, this minimax principle is more than likely to provide minimum information, and to result in stereotyping. (For a history, see Ashmore & Del Boca, 1981; for its dangers: Snyder, 1981). For once an in-group and an out-group are identified, within-group homogeneity and between-group heterogeneity are overemphasized (e.g. Linville, Salovey & Fischer, 1986; Quattrone, 1986). That this is a misperception rather than a veridical account is demonstrated in a series of studies. Wilder (1986) summed these up as follows: 'Persons often assume similarities within groups and differences between groups to a greater degree and across a broader range of characteristics than is warranted by objective evidence' (p. 307). In much stronger language, but following the same line of thought, did Erikson (1984) describe pseudospeciation, where members of the in-group 'consider themselves ... the only truly human species, and *all* others ... as less than human' (p. 481).

3. Biases and Misperceptions

The inevitable overgeneralization found in the above examples, while in itself rooted in biases, is also the source of further distortions. Two of these - intergroup bias and biased information gathering – have particularly damaging effects on intergroup relations. Intergroup bias refers to the frequent finding that the mere categorization of persons into an in-group and an out-group is sufficient to create in-group favoritism at the out-group's expense (Wilder, 1986, p. 311). Studies by Tajfel (1970; see also Billig & Tajfel, 1973) show that such favoritism occurs even when (a) one's own interests are not involved, and (b) dichotomization is based on extremely trivial grounds. Bias is, of course, far stronger and has potentially catastrophic consequences in real-life situations (as in Burn & Oskamp, 1989). Such intergroup bias is in line with derivations from theories of cognitive consistency, in particular with Heiderian balance principles (Moore, 1978, 1979). Biases in information gathering are similarly related to cognitive consistency approaches, in this case to cognitive dissonance theory.

An often noted manifestation of such biases is *selective exposure* (and selective avoidance): people actively seek information that supports their beliefs and avoid information that contradicts them (e.g. Festinger, 1964; Sweeney & Gruber, 1984; Frey, 1986). A long line of research by Snyder and his associates (e.g. Snyder & Swan, 1978; Snyder, Campbell & Preston, 1982) shows preferential collecting of evidence by individuals, intended to confirm one's hypotheses about another person. (For a different interpretation of their findings see Trope & Bassok, 1982, 1983.) An experiment by Wilder and Allen (1978) demonstrated that the selective exposure hypothesis is applicable to information gathering about in-groups and out-groups, as well. Other forms of information-related bias include the reinterpretation and differentiation of discrepant information (Holsti, 1967), refutation of information incongruent with prior schemata (O'Sullivan & Durso, 1984) and the faster processing of information which confirms a stereotype than one that refutes it (Dovidio, Evans & Tyler, 1986).

A long list of other misperceptions may be derived from the two 'generic' distortions mentioned above, acting either separately or in combination with one another. These include the Devil Shift (opponents are perceived as more powerful and evil than they actually are; see Sabatier, Hunter & McLaughlin, 1987; for the diabolical enemy image see also Finlay, Holsti & Fagen, 1967, pp. 8–9, as well as White, 1970, 1983); the effect of first impressions (preventing the absorption of new and different information; see Campbell & Yarrow, 1961; Gergen, 1968); the related problem of assimilation instead of accommodation (e.g. Kahneman & Tversky, 1973); and the ultimate attributional error (out-group members' negative action is perceived as dispositional and often genetic, while their positive behavior is attributed to situational factors; see Pettigrew, 1979). Numerous examples of such misperceptions at the inter-national level are found in Jervis (1968, 1976), White (1970, 1977), Bolkosky (1975), Deutsch (1983a), and Vertzberger (1984). Lebow's (1981) detailed cognitive analyses of the Korean and Sino-Indian crises are especially noteworthy.

4. Mirroring: Background

Up to this point we have oversimplified matters by disregarding the necessarily bidirectional nature of social perception. Yet, if misperception is as widespread as the above theories suggest, then A's perception of B is as likely to be distorted as B's perception of A is! The often identified cases of such mutual misperception are referred to as examples of *mirroring*.

Before surveying the literature on the mirroring phenomenon, I will briefly consider the underlying metaphor. It is necessary to realize that the metaphoric and allegorical use of mirrors is based on an extremely rich and varied realm of associations. This is primarily caused by the physical characteristics of the tangible object, including reflection, reproduction, focusing of light, clarity, distortion, reversal, and image intangibility (Moore, 1983). A secondary but nonetheless important source of mirror significations is psychological. Whether it is the defense mechanism of projection (Harding, Kutner, Proshansky & Chein, 1954), narcissism (e.g. Roheim, 1919), the 'need to be mirrored' (Kohut, 1966), or the 'looking-glass self' (Cooley, 1902) that is discussed, the mirror metaphor seems to be involved in profound psychological processes.[2] It is against this background that one should

consider the 'mirror images' that appear below, constantly asking oneself:
Is the mirror true or distorting? Is the image real or just a semblance?

5. Mirroring: Empirical Studies

Though complementary stereotypes had been commented upon earlier (Mack,
1954; Bruner, 1956), the first modern application of the 'mirror image' to
intergroup relations was by Bronfenbrenner (1961), in his description of
Soviet–American perceptions in 1960. Having realized that 'the Russians'
distorted picture of us was curiously similar to our view of them – a mirror
image', Bronfenbrenner went further and wrote of 'a mirror image in a twisted
glass.' The difficulty with this metaphor is that A and B are mirror images
of one another, but only in C's eyes (e.g. Bronfenbrenner in a Moscow
restaurant), and only by virtue of their misperception of each other. The
'twisted mirror' is a misnomer: If A misperceives B just as B is wrong
about A, then the mirror shows a true image. The message of the mirror is
exactly this: *Tat twam asi* (a Brahmanic verse, usually translated as 'This is
you!').[3]

Following Bronfenbrenner's description of the mutual misperception
between the USA and the USSR as a mirror image, several additional
instances have been analyzed by social scientists. Some of these continued
to use the two superpowers as the participants in an intergroup conflict[4] (e.g.
Eckhardt & White, 1967; White, 1970, 1983), others found mutual stereotypes
and misperceptions in other trouble spots and between additional nations:
Japanese vs. Americans (Berrien, 1969), the Indo-Pakistan conflict (Haque,
1973), World War II (Jervis, 1976, p. 331), Colombia vs. Venezuela (Salazar
& Marin, 1977) and, most extensively, the Israeli–Arab conflict (Eckhardt,
Young, Azar & Sloan, 1974; Heradstveit, 1974; White, 1977, Haque &
Lawson, 1980; Hareven, 1983; Vallone, Rossi & Lepper, 1985; Shamir &
Sullivan, 1985; Bilu, 1989). Using several different methodologies, such as
historical analysis, content analysis of documents, semantic differential type
questionnaire, and dream analysis, these studies report varying degrees of
mirroring (or 'ethnocentric illusions,' according to Sande et al., 1989), that
is to say, similarities between the stereotypical enemy images held by the
participants of each conflict.

A number of other studies extended their comparisons beyond the traditional A perceives B, B perceives A paradigm. O'Donnell (1977) investigated
both 'real' and 'supposed' stereotypes of Roman Catholics and Protestants in
Northern Ireland, by asking each group not only to describe both themselves
and the other group, but also to guess how the other group describes itself
and how it describes the first one. In addition to some specific mirroring
found in this study (each group thinking, for example, that the other is
'brainwashed') there was also a considerable amount of general intergroup
bias, or 'universal stereotype' (Campbell, 1967; Lindskold, 1986). The latter
contains a self-image which is moral, clean, loyal, honest and peace loving,
along with a diametrically opposed image of the other (Sande et al., 1989).

In a similar vein, Moore and Heskin (1983) and Moore and Tyson (1990) studied four groups at a time: Groups A and B, in conflict, were asked to express their attitudes and reveal their knowledge about groups C and D, also in conflict, and vice versa. In these studies, as in O'Donnell's work, the mirror now tells each group: 'This is how others see you.' Moore and Heskin (1983) applied this paradigm to the Middle Eastern and Northern Irish conflicts; the Moore and Tyson (1990) study compared the Middle East with South Africa. Since respondents in these studies were asked neither about themselves, nor about their local adversaries, the mirroring is of a different kind than observed elsewhere. Thus, both Jews and Arabs in Israel found parallels between their situation and the plight of Protestants and Catholics in Northern Ireland. Mirror images could be detected in attitudes, as well. For example, South African whites' support for Israel was reflected in the Israeli respondents' differential attitudes toward the South African conflict. There was even some universal stereotyping: South African Blacks and whites (especially Jewish ones) regarded the group with which they identified (Israeli Arabs and Jews, respectively) as an in-group which was morally right. (Cf. similar findings vis à vis own and enemy allies in Haque & Lawson, 1980).

A still different type of mirroring present in these studies relates to information or rather to its absence. Though in varying degrees, all groups questioned in both Moore & Heskin (1983) and Moore & Tyson (1990) revealed ignorance about the target conflict. They misidentified the participants and their demands, misdated the conflicts (at times by centuries) and had only vague ideas about their causes. Mutual misperceptions are thus accompanied by mutual misconceptions and ignorance (cf. Silverstein & Flamenbaum, 1989).

6. Conclusion

Having identified the powerful psychological mechanisms underlying mirroring and misperception, we can clearly see the inherent difficulties of intergroup conflict resolution. The abundance of attempts[5] at this crucial task is no proof of their success, for it is largely a matter of the critics' personality whether they regard these attempts with some hope and optimism (Deutsch, 1983b; Erikson, 1984; Gould, 1984), or with a deep sense of pessimism (Kull, 1983; Mack, 1986). This ambiguity is promoted by the relevant social psychological literature, resplendent with exhortations and warnings, prophecies of doom and offerings of solutions, not infrequently voiced by the same author. That there should be such double messages is not surprising: We tend to be skeptical of theoretical analyses and of laboratory simulations (Blight, 1987), disappointed with the unfulfilled promise of social reforms and other large-scale interventions (Stephan, 1986), and yet reluctant to remain passive in view of the escalating danger of annihilation. It is rare to find any allusion to the incontrovertible fact that in spite of mankind's ability to destroy itself, it has not done so, and that some intergroup conflicts do get solved. Among the notable exceptions are Auerbach and Hareven. Auerbach's (1986) analysis of turning-point decisions concluded that occasionally the very mechanisms which cause misperceptions and flaws in the decision-making process induce positive changes and breakthroughs in intergroup relations. Hareven (1983) writes in a similar vein, but places heavier emphasis on the effect of single individuals on the rare breakthroughs: De Gaulle's attitude toward Algeria, Sadat's visit to Jerusalem (and Gorbachev's stance toward the West) have contributed more to intergroup conflict resolution than any amount of social psychological theory could have predicted.

So let me add my own ambiguous conclusion to those of my colleagues and predecessors: Social categorization, misperception and conflict are globally and generally inevitable, yet there is always a possibility for a turn of events and for a courageous individual to solve specific intergroup conflicts.

Notes

1 Actually 'friend or fiend' in two Old English manuscripts dating from 1000 and from 1175; see Grein, 1863, p. 129, l. 954, and Morris, 1868, p. 231, respectively.

2 The following has special significance in the present context: Human understanding is 'a false mirror, which, receiving rays irregularly, distorts and discolors the nature of things by mingling its own nature with it' (Bacon, 1677/1863).

3 There is a similar difficulty in Elms (1972), when he writes of a 'warp in the mirror through which each side misperceives the other' (p. 380). On the other hand, Bolkosky's (1975) *distorted image* is an accurate description of German Jewish perception of Germany between the wars, for there there was no mirroring. Cf White's (1977) reference to the *distorted image* of both the moral self and of the diabolical enemy in the Arab–Israeli conflict.

4 This chapter deals with the role that misperception plays in intergroup conflict. Conflict has another source: only-too-good perception, combined with competition over limited resources. As Crespi (1983) has pointed out, 'an occupational disease among communication professionals ... is a tendency to exaggerate the extent to which international tension derive[s] from faulty communication.' See also Finlay et al. (1967, pp. 8–9), Blight (1987) and Coombs (1987) on the inevitability of social conflict.

5 For example Osgood (1961) and Sherif et al. (1988). See reviews by Amir (1969) and Blight (1986).

References

Amir, Yehuda, 1969. 'Contact Hypothesis in Ethnic Relations', *Psychological Bulletin*, vol. 71, no. 5, pp. 319–342.

Arnold, Matthew, 1940. *The Poems of Matthew Arnold*. London: Oxford University Press.

Ashmore, Richard & Frances K. Del Boca, 1981. 'Conceptual Approaches to Stereotypes and Stereotyping', in D. L. Hamilton, ed. *Cognitive Processes in Stereotyping and Intergroup Behavior*, pp. 1–35. Hillsdale, NJ: Lawrence Erlbaum.

Auerbach, Yehudit, 1986. 'Turning-Point Decisions: A Cognitive Dissonance Analysis of Conflict Reduction in Israel–West German Relations', *Political Psychology*, vol. 7, no. 3, pp. 533–550.

Bacon, Francis 1863. 'Novum Organum', in J. Spedding et al., eds. *Collected Works of Francis Bacon*. Cambridge: Riverside Press. (Original work published in 1677.)

Berrien, F. Kenneth, 1969. 'Familiarity, Mirror Imaging and Social Desirability in Stereotypes: Japanese vs Americans', *International Journal of Psychology*, vol. 4, no. 3, pp. 207–215.

Billig, Michael & Henri Tajfel, 1973. 'Social Categorization and Similarity in Intergroup Behavior', *European Journal of Social Psychology*, vol. 3, pp. 27–52.

Bilu, Yoram, 1989. 'The Other as a Nightmare: The Israeli-Arab Encounter as Reflected in Children's Dreams in Israel and the West Bank', *Political Psychology*, vol. 10, pp. 365–389.

Blight, James G., 1986. 'How Might Psychology Contribute to Reducing the Risk of Nuclear War?', *Political Psychology*, vol. 7, pp. 617–660.

Blight, James G., 1987. 'Toward a Policy-Relevant Psychology of Avoiding Nuclear War', *American Pschologist*, vol. 42, pp. 12–29.

Bolkosky, Sidney M., 1975. *The Distorted Image – German Jewish Perceptions of Germans and Germany, 1918–1935*. New York: Elsevier.

Bronfenbrenner, Urie, 1961. 'The Mirror Image in Soviet-American Relations: A Social Psychologist's Report', *Journal of Social Issues*, vol. 17, no. 3, pp. 45–56.

Bruner, Edward M., 1956. 'Primary Group Experience and the Process of Acculturation', *American Anthropologist*, vol. 58, pp. 605–623.

Burn, Shawn M. & Stuart Oskamp, 1989. 'Ingroup Biases and the U.S.-Soviet Conflict', *Journal of Social Issues*, vol. 45, no. 2, pp. 73–89.

Campbell, Donald T., 1967. 'Stereotypes and the Perception of Group Differences', *American Psychologist*, vol. 22, pp. 817–829.

Campbell, John D. & Marian R. Yarrow, 1961. 'Perceptual and Behavioral Correlates of Social Effectiveness', *Sociometry*, vol. 24, pp. 1–20.

Cooley, Charles H., 1902. *Human Nature and the Social Order*. New York: Scribner.

Coombs, Clyde H., 1987. 'The Structure of Conflict', *American Psychologist*, vol. 42, no. 4, pp. 355–363.

Crespi, Leo P., 1983. 'West European Perceptions of the United States', *Political Psychology*, vol. 4, pp. 717–729.

Deutsch, Morton, 1983a. 'The Prevention of World War III: A Psychological Perspective', *Political Psychology*, vol. 4, pp. 3–31.

Deutsch, Morton, 1983b. 'Conflict Resolution: Theory and Practice', *Political Psychology*, vol. 4, no. 3, pp. 431–453.

Dovidio, John F., N. Evans, & R. Tyler, 1986. 'Racial Stereotypes: The Contents of their Cognitive Representation', *Journal of Experimental Social Psychology*, vol. 22, pp. 22–37.

Eckhardt, William & Ralph K. White, 1967. 'A Test of the Mirror-Image Hypothesis: Kennedy and Khrushchev', *Journal of Conflict Resolution*, vol. 11, pp. 325–332.

Eckhardt, William; Chris Young, Edward Azar, & Thomas Sloan, 1974. 'Arab-Israeli Perceptions of the Middle East Conflict', *Peace Research*, vol. 5, pp. 69–73.

Elms, Alan, 1972. *Social Psychology and Social Relevance*. Boston, MA: Little, Brown.

Erikson, Erik H., 1984. 'Reflections on Ethos and War', *Yale Review*, vol. 73, pp. 481–486.

Festinger, Leon, 1964. *Conflict, Decison and Dissonance*. Stanford University Press.

Finlay, David J.; Ole R. Holsti, & Richard R. Fagen, 1967. *Enemies in Politics*. Chicago, IL: Rand McNally.

Frey, D., 1986. 'Recent Research on Selective Exposure to Information', *Advances in Experimental Social Psychology*, vol. 19, pp. 41–80.

Gergen, Kenneth J., 1968. 'Personal Consistency and the Presentation of Self,' in C. Gordon & K. J. Gergen, eds. *The Self in Social Interaction*, vol. 1. New York: Wiley.

Gould, Stephen J., 1984. 'A Biological Comment on Erikson's Notion of Pseudo-speciation', *Yale Review*, vol. 73, pp. 487–490.

Grein, Christian W. M. 1863. *Dichtungen der Angelsachsen*, vol. 2. Göttingen: Wigand.

Haque, Abdul, 1973. 'Mirror Image Hypothesis in the Context of Indo-Pakistan Conflict', *Pakistan Journal of Psychology*, vol. 6, pp. 13–22.

Haque, Abdul and E. O. Lawson, 1980. 'The Mirror Image in the Context of the Arab-Israeli Conflict', *International Journal of Intercultural Relations*, vol. 4, pp. 107–115.

Harding, John; Bernard Kutner, Harold Proshansky, and Isidor Chein, 1954. 'Prejudice and Ethnic Relations', ch. 27, pp. 1021–1061 in G. Lindzey, ed., *Handbook of Social Psychology*, vol. 2. Cambridge, MA: Addison-Wesley.

Hareven, Alouph, 1983. 'Victimization: Some Comments by an Israeli', *Political Psychology*, vol. 4, pp. 145–155.

Heradstveit, Daniel, 1974. *Arab and Israeli Elite Perceptions*. New York: Humanities Press.

Hilgard, Ernest R., 1957. *Introduction to Psychology*, 2nd ed. New York: Harcourt, Brace.

Holsti, Ole R., 1967. 'Cognitive Dynamics and Images of the Enemy', *Journal of International Affairs*, vol. 21, pp. 16–39.

Jervis, Robert, 1968. 'Hypotheses on Misperception', *World Politics*, vol. 20, pp. 454–479.

Jervis, Robert, 1976. *Perception and Misperception in International Politics*. Princeton, N. J.: Princeton University Press.

Kahneman, Daniel & Amos Tversky, 1973. 'On the Psychology of Prediction', *Psychological Review*, vol. 80, pp. 237–251.

Kohut, Heinz, 1966. *The Analysis of the Self*. New York: International Universities Press.

Kull, Steven, 1983. 'Nuclear Arms and the Desire for World Destruction', *Political Psychology*, vol. 4, pp. 563–591.

Lebow, Richard N., 1981. *Between Peace and War: The Nature of International Crisis*. Baltimore, MD: Johns Hopkins University Press.

Lindskold, Svenn, 1986. 'GRIT: Reducing Distrust through Carefully Introduced Conciliation', in S. Worchel & W. G. Austin, eds. *Psychology of Intergroup Relations*, 2nd ed. Chicago, IL: Nelson-Hall.

Linville, Patricia W.; Peter Salovey, & G. W. Fischer, 1986. 'Stereotyping and Perceived Distributions of Social Characteristics: An Application to Ingroup-Outgroup Perception', in J. F. Dovidio & S. L. Gaertner, eds. *Prejudice, Discrimination, and Racism*. New York: Academic Press.

Mack, John E., 1986. 'Nuclear Weapons and the Dark Side of Humankind', *Political Psychology*, vol. 7, pp. 223–233.

Mack, Raymond W., 1954. 'Ecological Patterns in an Industrial Shop', *Social Forces*, vol. 32, pp. 351–356.

Moore, Michael, 1978. 'An International Application of Heider's Balance Theory', *European Journal of Social Psychology*, vol. 8, pp. 401–405.

Moore, Michael, 1979. 'Structural Balance and International Relations', *European Journal of Social Psychology*, vol. 9, pp. 323–326.

Moore, Michael, 1983. 'Ambivalence in Mirror Significations', *Archivio di Psicologia Neurologia e Psichiatria*, vol. 44, no. 1, pp. 128–138.

Moore, Michael & Ken Heskin, 1983. 'Distortions in the Perceptions of International Conflict', *Journal of Social Psychology*, vol. 120, pp. 13–25.

Moore, Michael & Graham Tyson, 1990. 'Perceptions and Misperceptions: The Middle East and South Africa', *Journal of Social Psychology*, vol. 130, no. 3, pp. 299–308.

Morris, Richard, ed. 1868. *Old English Homilies and Homiletic Treatises*. London: Trubner.

O'Donnell, Edward E., 1977. *Northern Irish Stereotypes*. Dublin, Ireland: College of Industrial Relations.

Osgood, Charles E., 1961. 'An Analysis of the Cold War Mentality', *Journal of Social Issues*, vol. 17, no. 3, pp. 12–19.

O'Sullivan, Chris S. & Francis T. Durso, 1984. 'Effects of Schema-Incongruent Information on Memory for Stereotypical Attributes', *Journal of Personality and Social Psychology*, vol. 47, pp. 55–70.

Pettigrew, Thomas, 1979. 'The Ultimate Attribution Error: Extending Allport's Cognitive Analysis of Prejudice', *Personality and Social Psychology Bulletin*, vol. 5, pp. 461–476.

Quattrone, George A., 1986. 'On the Perception of a Group's Variability', in S. Worchel & W. G. Austin, eds. *Psychology of Intergroup Relations*, 2nd ed. Chicago, IL: Nelson Hall.

Roheim, Geza, 1919. *Spiegelzauber*. Leipzig: Internationaler Psychoanalytischer Verlag.

Rosch, Eleanor, 1978. 'Principles of Categorization', in E. Rosch & B. B. Lloyd, eds. *Cognition and Categorization*. Hillsdale, NJ: Lawrence Erlbaum.

Sabatier, Paul, Susan Hunter, & Susan McLaughlin, 1987. 'The Devil Shift: Perceptions and Misperceptions of Opponents', *Western Political Quarterly*, vol. 40, no. 3, pp. 449–476.

Salazar, Jose M. & Gerardo Marin, 1977. 'National Stereotypes as a Function of Conflict and Territorial Proximity: A Test of the Mirror Image Hypothesis', *Journal of Social Psychology*, vol. 101, pp. 13–19.

Sande, Gerald N.; George R. Goethals, Lisa Ferrari, & Leila T. Worth, 1989. 'Value-Guided Attributions: Maintaining the Moral Self-Image and the Diabolical Enemy-Image', *Journal of Social Issues*, vol. 45, no. 2, pp. 91–118.

Shamir, Michal & John L. Sullivan, 1985. 'Jews and Arabs in Israel: Everybody Hates Somebody, Sometime', *Journal of Conflict Resolution*, vol. 29, no. 2, pp. 283–305.

Sherif, Muzafer; L. J. Harvey, B. J. White, W. R. Hood, & C. W. Sherif, 1988. *The Robbers Cave Experiment: Intergroup Conflict and Cooperation*. Middletown, CT: Wesleyan University Press.

Silverstein, Brett & Catherine Flamenbaum, 1989. 'Biases in the Perception and Cognition of the Actions of Enemies', *Journal of Social Issues*, vol. 45, no. 2, pp. 51–72.

Simpson, George E. & J. Milton Yinger, 1972. *Cultural Minorities*, 4th ed. New York: Harper & Row.

Snyder, Mark, 1981. 'On the Self-Perpetuating Nature of Social Stereotypes', pp. 183–212 in D.L. Hamilton, ed. *Cognitive Processes in Stereotyping and Intergroup Behavior*. Hillsdale, NJ: Lawrence Erlbaum.

Snyder, Mark, Bruce H. Campbell & Elizabeth Preston, 1982. 'Testing Hypotheses about Human Nature: Assessing the Accuracy of Social Stereotypes', *Social Cognition*, vol. 1, pp. 256–272.

Snyder, Mark & William B. Swann, 1978. 'Hypothesis-Testing Processes in Social Interaction', *Journal of Personality and Social Psychology*, vol. 36, pp. 1202–1212.

Stagner, Ross, 1961. 'Personality Dynamics and Social Conflict', *Journal of Social Issues*, vol. 17, no. 3, pp. 28–44.

Stephan, W. G., 1986. 'The Effects of School Desegregation: An Evaluation 30 Years after *Brown*', pp. 181–206 in M. J. Saks & L. Saxe, eds. *Advances in Applied Social Psychology*, vol. 3. Hillsdale, NJ: Lawrence Erlbaum.

Sweeney, Paul D. & Kathy L. Gruber, 1984. 'Selective Exposure: Voter Information Preferences and the Watergate Affair', *Journal of Personality and Social Psychology*, vol. 46, pp. 1208–1221.

Tajfel, Henri, 1970. 'Experiments in Intergroup Discrimination', *Scientific American*, vol. 223, pp. 96–102.

Trope, Yaacov & Miriam Bassok, 1982. 'Confirmatory and Diagnosing Strategies in Social Information Gathering', *Journal of Personality and Social Psychology*, vol. 43, pp. 22–34.

Trope, Yaacov & Miriam Bassok, 1983. 'Information Gathering Strategies in Hypothesis-Testing', *Journal of Experimental Social Psychology*, vol. 19, pp. 560–576.

Vallone, Robert, Lee Rossi, & Mark R. Lepper 1985. 'The Hostile Media Phenomenon: Biased Perception and Perceptions of Media Bias in Coverage of the Beirut Massacre', *Journal of Personality and Social Psychology*, vol. 49, pp. 577–585.

Vertzberger, Yaacov, 1984. *Misperceptions in Foreign Policy Making: The Sino-Indian Conflict, 1959–1962*. Boulder, CO.: Westview.

White, Ralph K., 1970. *Nobody Wanted War: Misperception in Vietnam and Other Wars*. New York: Doubleday.

White, Ralph K., 1977. 'Misperception in the Arab–Israeli Conflict', *Journal of Social Issues*, vol. 33, pp. 190–221.

White, Ralph K., 1983. 'Empathizing with the Rulers of the USSR', *Political Psychology*, vol. 4, no. 1, pp. 121–137.

Wilder, David A., 1986. 'Social Categorization', *Advances in Experimental Social Psychology*, vol. 19, pp. 291–355.

Wilder, David A. and Allen, V. L., 1978. 'Group Membership and Preference for Information about Other Persons', *Personality and Social Psychology Bulletin*, vol. 4, pp. 106–110.

PART 2

Social Psychological Approaches

Introduction to Part 2

Rabbie opens this section with a contribution that makes a conceptual distinction between social groups and social categories. The intention is to clarify the difference in approach between Social Identity Theory (SIT) and an Interdependence Perspective (IP) in explaining how in-group favoritism comes about in the Minimal Group Paradigm (MGP) which provides the main evidence for SIT. After a conceptual critique of SIT, Rabbie shows that the allocation behavior in the standard MGP can be better understood as (instrumental) inter-individual behavior aimed at maximizing one's selfish outcomes than as (relational) inter-group behavior designed to enhance a positive social identity or self-esteem. Finally, a Behavioral Interaction Model is proposed that integrates these seemingly conflicting views.

The chapter by *Fisher* identifies social-psychological contributions to the study of conflict – including work on ethnocentrism, realistic conflict theory, games research, social identity theory, the escalation process, and theories of intergroup relations. Conflict theory in social psychology is fragmentary and often restricted in constructs and levels of analysis, thus indicating a need for an integrative model which is phenomenological, interactive, and multi-level as well.

Systematic strategy of theory construction is used to build an eclectic model of intergroup conflict based on the dimensions of time and level of analysis. Variables are categorized as antecedents, orientations, processes, and outcomes; and are grouped at the individual, group, and intergroup levels. The presentation of the model provides a dynamic description of the causation, escalation, and resolution of conflict through illustrative principles of interaction among variables. A spiral of escalation is graphically indicated to capture the core elements of the process. Two system-states of low and high intensity conflict are described in terms of individual behavior, group processes, the inter-group relationship, the forms of attempted settlement, and the key indicators of intensity. Although the boundaries restrict the model to two groups at a time, it is still seen as a middle-range theory of considerable scope.

This model captures the essence of inter-group conflict in terms of under-lying conditions and dynamic processes, but cannot accurately portray the complexity of collectivities in conflict and the processes of de-escalation and institutionalization of conflict. Nonetheless, it provides a stimulating summarization that may be useful in understanding protracted social conflict between identity groups, a conflict-type common in the world today.

The focus of the study by *Roux et al.* is a group process. In this study the subjects – all of whom had tended towards xenophobia – initially resisted the minority influence and showed clear national favoritism. Later, however, when confronted with resolutions that would benefit foreigners and when allowed to make judgements in the independent mode, they curbed this tendency, particularly when the minority position was highly provocative. Thus, it seems that articulating an independent approach to intergroup rela-tions with a certain intensity of conflict generated by the minority message, may predispose to an attitude of solidarity or equality that could counteract, if not substitute, discrimination.

The chapter by *Criss and Johnson* addresses the use of theory from community psychology and related fields in understanding and promoting world peace. The necessity of a social-systems approach is discussed and com-munity psychology is defined. The concepts of first- and second-order change; and of problem creation and maintenance (including 'more of the same', 'simplification', 'the Utopia syndrome' and 'errors of conceptualization') are defined, discussed, and related to questions of war and peace. Issues of prob-lem exacerbation through the wrong levels of problem definition and inter-vention are highlighted. Finally, the authors apply solution generation through the process of reframing, and the concept of empowerment, to endeavors to promote peace. They make a case for the need for metaperspectives on global 'games' and for an empowerment perspective of reframing the prevention of war towards the active promotion of peace.

The objective of the chapter by *Auerbach and Agid* to apply the conceptual framework of an Attitude in an Existence Conflict (AEC) to the attitudes of Israeli leaders Rabin and Sharon. The AEC framework serves as a criterion according to which the attitudes of the two decision-makers are analyzed and assessed. This framework facilitates a subtle analysis of their attitudes over time and the detection of nuances that distinguish each of them in the complex and highly emotional Palestinian issue.

In inter-group negotiations, the negotiator represents a group. Much work has gone into studying the influence of the constituents in the outcome of bargaining. Generally, the representatives' role obligations tend to check rapid attainment of an agreement. The compromise then awakens an intra-organizational conflict between the negotiator and his constituents. *Louche* summarizes some of this work, and by considering labor negotiations con-ducted in France criticizes the postulates on which they are founded.

Psychological peace research is largely based on a deterministic- mechanistic paradigm which holds that the phenomenon we are attempting to explain is determined by certain factors, not directly but through the mediation of certain mechanisms. These relationships are assumed to reflect scientific laws. In the final chapter of this section, *Eskola* highlights some important limitations in this line of thinking and outlines a broader research paradigm in which laws and rules also have their place. According to this paradigm, in their activity human actors take into account laws and rules of the type 'if X then Y', but on the basis of a certain logic. 'Rules' here refers to constitutive and regulative social rules; 'laws' to empirical regularities. Activity is constituted by the actions of the individual actor, but it is also shaped by society and its process of historical change. The concept of logic is illustrated by a discussion on the behavior of state actors in international relations. Eskola suggests a reconciliation between the traditional methods employed in the search for laws and those concerned with meanings and logics (e.g. ethnogenics, ethnomethodology, discourse analysis). In the application of psychological peace research, both types have a role to play.

7

A Behavioral Interaction Model

Towards an Integrative Framework for Studying Intra- and Intergroup Behavior

Jacob. M. Rabbie*

1. Introduction

There is a pervasive tendency for people to favor their own group over another group. This tendency has been variously labelled as ethnocentrism (Sumner, 1906), intergroup bias (Rabbie & Horwitz, 1969) in-group favoritism (Tajfel, et al. 1971) or in-group/out-group differentiation (Rabbie, 1993). The intergroup bias is reflected in positive attitudes, stereotypes, and behavior toward members of the in-group (and the group as a whole); and in negative attitudes, stereotypes, and discriminatory behavior toward (members of) the out-group. An *attitude* is a readiness to respond in a favorable or an unfavorable manner to a particular object or class of objects (Oskamp, 1977). *Prejudice* is a negative attitude toward a member of a social category or a group as a whole. A *stereotype* is defined here as a set of beliefs about the attributes of members of a group or social category.

There is only one important exception to the tendency for people to prefer their own group to another group: members of minority groups that have a underprivileged position in our society sometimes have more positive attitudes toward the powerful majority groups than toward their own group.[1] This

* This chapter is based on previous publications by Horwitz & Rabbie (1982, 1989), Rabbie & Horwitz (1969, 1988), Rabbie, Schot & Visser (1989), Rabbie & Lodewijkx (1987, 1990), and Lodewijkx, Mlicki, Syroit & Rabbie (1992). Therefore it can be considered as the result of a collective effort of a 'we' group. The author wishes to thank these co-authors for their invaluable contributions. I am particularly grateful to Murray Horwitz, a life-long friend and colleague who died in August of 1991. The author is also indebted to Dr Jeffrey Goldstein, guest professor at the University of Utrecht, for his editorial advice. The Dutch Organization for the Advancement of Research (NWO) funded this project through a PSYCHON-grant to the author (560-270-012).

may lead to low self-esteem or even to self-hatred at times (Lewin, 1948). Members of minority groups may experience a strong conflict between their socio-emotional or relational dependence on their own group to satisfy their belongingness and status needs and an instrumental interdependence for their material outcomes on (often discriminatory) out-groups (Rabbie, 1992b).

Our perceptions about naturally existing in-groups and out-groups are influenced by what we have learned from our parents and other socializing agents about them. To avoid these socialization effects we have mainly worked with 'concocted' groups in the laboratory (McGrath, 1984), instead of using naturally existing groups, to avoid contamination and get at the origins of the in-group/out-group differentiation.

The intergroup bias has been explained at different 'levels of analysis' (Stroebe & Insko, 1989). At the societal level, the origins of positive attitudes toward (privileged) majority groups and negative attitudes toward (under-privileged) minority groups have been described in terms of socialization processes through the mass media, schools, peer groups, and parents. This societal approach stresses the importance of social learning processes in the development of in-group/out-group differentiation. At the intergroup level, the in-group bias has been seen as a result of realistic (instrumental) or symbolic (relational) conflicts between groups (e.g. ethnocentrism, realistic group conflict theory). At the individual level, there are motivational and cognitive approaches that attempt to account for in-group cohesion and out-group hostility in terms of intra-individual motives and personality traits (e.g. scapegoat theory, the theory of the authoritarian personality) or that focus mainly on the limitations of the information-processing or cognitive capabilities of members in a group (e.g. social categorization theory and social identity theory). These different approaches have been reviewed by Condor & Brown (1988), Brown (1988), Stroebe & Insko (1989), and Rabbie (1992a, b, in press).

Over the past twenty years, research in social psychology about stereotyping and prejudice has been guided almost exclusively by a social-cognitive approach that views stereotypes as mental representations or cognitive sche-mas of groups and social categories, and seeks to understand how these cognitive intra-individual structures influence information processing and social perception (Hamilton & Sherman, 1989). This cognitive approach has been reviewed elsewhere, e.g. Stephan, 1985; Brewer & Kramer, 1985; Stroebe, et al., 1989; Messick & Mackie, 1989.

This cognitive intra-individual approach to intergroup relations has been very fruitful in stimulating research, but it is not without its own specific shortcomings, as will be the case in any other one-sided perspective (Schruyer, 1990). For example the cognitive approach has not spelled out in any detail how these intra-individual stereotypes and perceptions influence the actual behavior of individuals toward the out-group targets of these stereotypes, how these stereotypes are supported and maintained by the values and norms expressed by in-group members, how they may change as a function of intra-group processes, or actual intergroup interactions which are inconsistent with these stereotypes and how these in-group and out-group stereotypes are affected by changes in the wider social and cultural context.

In reaction to this exclusively intra-individual cognitive approach, we have developed a Behavioral Interaction Model (BIM) which stresses the importance not only of cognitive but also of emotional, motivational and normative orientations in group formation and intergroup behavior which have to be studied at various levels of analysis (Rabbie, 1978; Rabbie et al., 1989; Rabbie and Lodewijkx, 1991, 1992; Rabbie, 1991a, b, in press; Rabbie et al. 1992). This preliminary model attempts to provide an integrative framework for the study of intra- and intergroup orientations and behavior.

To illustrate the possible usefulness of the model, the main body of this chapter will be devoted to a critical discussion of Social Identity Theory (SIT), which is currently one of the most influential theories in the area of intergroup relations (Messick & Mackie, 1989). The aim of this discussion is to bring out our own specific contribution to this area and to indicate how SIT may fit into the broader theoretical framework of our model.

Recently, a controversy has emerged between the proponents of Social Identity Theory of Tajfel and Turner (1986), and Turner et al. (1987) and our interdependence hypothesis derived from our model. This debate was initiated by Turner (1982) and Turner et al. (1987). They reject the interdependence perspective in favor of their Self-Categorization Theory (SCT), a more cognitive elaboration of Social Identity Theory (SIT). Turner et al. (1987) believe that both perspectives are mutually incompatible. We hold a different view. In our model we have argued that, for a full understanding of the determinants of intra-and intergroup behavior, this behavior should be studied at different levels of analysis and from various approaches, including both the social identity position and the interdependence perspective.

In the second section of this chapter, I make a conceptual distinction between 'social groups' and 'social categories' which may clarify the apparent differences between the two perspectives. In section three I review an early 'minimal group' experiment that forms the basis for the interdependence approach. In the fourth section, the interpretation of the results of the Minimal Group Paradigm (MGP) of Tajfel and Turner (1986) is critically evaluated. My reinterpretation of their data led to the design of several experiments, reported in section five. The sixth section presents a brief sketch of the Behavioral Interaction Model which attempts to integrate the interdependence and SIT perspectives. In the concluding discussion the possible implications of this in-group/out-group research will be related to issues of war and peace.

2. Social Groups and Social Categories

In our research on intergroup relations, a conceptual distinction is made between social groups and social categories (Horwitz & Rabbie, 1982). Following Lewin (1948) we consider a social group as a 'dynamic whole' or social system, ranging from a 'compact unit' to a loose 'mass' whose members are defined not by their similarity to each other but by a perceived 'interdependence of fate' among its members and with the group as a whole (Horwitz & Rabbie, 1989). The group may mediate important symbolic or material outcomes for the individual member and for the group as a whole. Symbolic rewards include self-esteem, status, and a sense of psychological security (Lewin, 1948). The group may also provide opportunities to develop closer interpersonal relations, cohesion and a sense of belongingness and other relational and communal outcomes (Bakan, 1966). In this view not only cognitive but also motivational aspects of groups are emphasized. The main defining characteristic of a social group is the perceived relational and instrumental interdependence between its members.

A social category, on the other hand, is defined as a collection of individuals who have at least one attribute in common – e.g. can be classified at random as members of Blue or Green 'groups' (Rabbie & Horwitz, 1969) or can be divided on the basis of their alleged preferences for paintings by Klee or Kandinski (Tajfel et al., 1971). Existing social categories or 'sociological categories' (Merton, 1957) are based on similarities in attributes like skin color, gender, age, sex and occupation. Individuals in these sociological categories are likely to experience 'an interdependence of fate' (Lewin, 1948) – and hence become a social group in the process – since members in these sociological categories are often treated differentially, by outsiders and themselves, solely as a function of their membership in these types of social categories which may have positive or negative consequences for them (Rabbie, 1992b).

Turner et al. (1987) reject our basic assumption that a common fate or 'interpersonal interdependence' as they call it, can be considered as a basis for the formation of a social group. In characterizing their own position they write: 'The most distinctive feature of the hypothesis is the assertion of the importance of the *perceptual identity* of people in the sense of their forming a *cognitive unit or perceptual category* and the rejection of interpersonal interdependence for need satisfaction as a basis of group formation (and attraction)' (emphasis added, p. 52). Thus, in their view a social group is simply a cognitive unit as any other perceptual category. As a consequence, they use the terms social groups and social categories interchangeably.

In their Social Identity Theory, Tajfel and Turner (1986) define a social group 'as a collection of people who perceive themselves to be members of a social category, share some emotional involvement in this common definition of themselves, and achieve some degree of social consensus about the evaluation of their group and of their membership in it' (p. 15).

There are several problems with this definition. There is no specification how much 'emotional involvement' and how much 'consensus' is needed to characterize a collection of people as a social group. The main evidence for their theory is based on research with the Minimal Group Paradigm (MGP) where no direct social interaction is allowed between the members.[2] It is difficult to imagine how, in the absence of direct social interaction between them, the members of these 'groups' can ever achieve a 'social consensus about their evaluation of their group and their membership in it'. Moreover, in the anonymous, impersonal task-environment of the MGP the emotional involvement of the subjects has been found to be very low indeed (Schot, 1992). Thus, even by Tajfel and Turner's own definition, the 'groups' in the MGP do not qualify as social groups. In their research, particularly in the MGP, the degree of 'in-group' identification is rarely measured. This makes it difficult to ascertain whether we are dealing with interpersonal or intergroup behavior in the standard MGP (Bornewasser & Bober, 1987; Rabbie & Schot, 1990). If that is done subjects indicate they acted much more as individuals than as group members in the standard MGP (Schot, 1992).

Tajfel and Turner (1986) suppose that individuals desire positive self-esteem and that they are therefore motivated to seek positive distinctiveness on some valued dimension for the in-group in comparison with a relevant comparison group. Their hypothesis is, according to Turner (1981) 'that self-evaluative social comparisons directly produce competitive intergroup processes which motivate attitudinal biases and discriminatory actions' (p. 80). Thus, their theory assumes that an intra-individual need – the desire to maintain and enhance one's self-esteem – produces intergroup behavior. This assumption betrays a very self-centered and individualistic approach to intergroup behavior. Intergroup behavior is studied only at an intra-individual and inter-individual but not at a group level of analysis as Sherif (1966) has proposed. In their view intergroup behavior is 'essentially competitive' (Tajfel & Turner, 1986, p. 17). In their theory there is no place for intergroup cooperation. It should be obvious, however, that groups may also cooperate with each other to attain a 'super-ordinate goal' (Sherif, 1966). International alliances and coalitions indicate very clearly, for example during the Gulf War against Iraq, that nations will work together to defeat a common enemy. Experimental research has shown that groups, just as individuals, will cooperate with each other in an effort to maximize their joint outcomes (Rabbie et al., 1982; Rabbie & Lodewijkx, 1991; 1992).

3. Early Research on 'Minimal Groups'

Lewin's (1948) distinction between a social group and a social category was the point of departure for our first minimal intergroup experiments (Rabbie, 1966; Rabbie & Horwitz, 1969; Rabbie & Wilkens, 1971). On the basis of his classic camp studies, Sherif (1966) has argued that intergroup bias occurs only among well-organized groups that have a definite leadership structure, and at least some standards or norms that regulate behavior toward in-group and out-group members. According to Sherif, a situation with two well-organized groups with incompatible or competing group goals (negative goal interdependence) will lead to intergroup hostility, while a common superordinate goal (positive goal interdependence) will lead to intergroup harmony and cooperation.

These classic 'intergroup experiments' of Sherif (1966) have played an important role in the social psychology of intergroup relations. However, from a methodological point of view they leave much to be desired (Rabbie,

1974; 1982). The most important methodological criticism is that intergroup competition and intergroup cooperation were not manipulated independently of each other but *after* each other. In the absence of comparable control groups the results of Sherif (1966) can be attributed to a variety of other factors. In our research we have tried to investigate these factors under more controlled laboratory conditions (Rabbie, 1982; Horwitz & Rabbie, 1989; Rabbie, 1992b).

The aim of the first study in this research program was to isolate the minimal conditions sufficient to generate discriminatory in-group/out-group attitudes (Rabbie & Horwitz, 1969). In this 'minimal group' experiment several treatments were employed that varied the perceived interdependence of fate within and between two groups. Following suggestions of Lewin (1948), strangers, males and females, were classified at random into two 'distinct' Blue or Green groups for alleged 'administrative reasons'. They had no opportunity to interact with each other, either within or between the groups. In the experimental 'common fate' conditions, subjects were either privileged or deprived relative to an out-group solely as a function of their membership in the Blue or Green group (negative intergroup interdependence). Subjects were rewarded or not on the basis of chance (a flip of a coin), an authority figure (the experimenter) or, allegedly, by the actions of one of the two groups. Presenting the experiment as a study of first impressions, we asked subjects to stand up in turn, introduce themselves, and rate each other on a variety of personality traits scaled along a favorable-unfavorable dimension. In addition to the ratings of individual members, subjects also rated the traits of each group as a whole. Thus, the in-group/out-group bias was measured at an individual as well as at an intergroup level of analysis.

As expected, in the experimental 'common fate' conditions a significantly greater in-group/out-group bias was found in favor of the own group and its members, particularly in the chance condition, in comparison with a category (control condition). In the control condition an attempt was made to create minimal or near-zero interdependence between the groups. In that condition, the subjects were classified only as members of Blue or Green groups and were neither privileged nor deprived as a function of their membership in these groups. Our 1969 experiment failed to detect a bias in the control condition, but with an increased N in follow-up experiments, subjects were found to give more favorable ratings to the in-group and its members than to the out-group and its members, especially on social-emotional or relational traits rather than on the instrumental attributes (Horwitz & Rabbie, 1982, pp. 247–248). We assume therefore that there is a minimal degree of perceived (positive) interdependence even among members in social categories since the external designation of individuals into a social category may induce a feeling of 'belongingness' or an 'interdependence of fate' (Lewin, 1948), in spite of the fact that membership in the social category has no direct positive or negative consequences for them (Cartwright & Zander, 1968). Apparently, the experimenter's interests in dividing them into two groups could have suggested to them that differential consequences might befall each group as a whole (Rabbie & Horwitz, 1988, p. 118). For this reason we have proposed an individual-group continuum. At one pole of this continuum there are self-centered individuals in social categories who perceive themselves to be minimally interdependent on each other for attaining their relational and instrumental outcomes. At the other pole, there are group-centered individuals in social groups who perceive themselves as maximally interdependent on each other for attaining their relational and instrumental outcomes, not only for themselves but also for the group as a whole (Lodewijkx & Rabbie, 1992; Rabbie and Lodewijkx, 1992). We will return to the relevance of this individual-group continuum.

4. The Minimal Group Paradigm

Doise (1988) has noted that the experiment designed by Tajfel et al. (1971) was modeled on the category or control condition in our experiment. In the initial modification of our control condition by Tajfel et al. subjects were again classified into groups for 'administrative reasons'. However, this time they were led to believe that they had been divided according to similarities or differences in their individual characteristics, purportedly measured by tests of oesthetic preference (pro-Kandinski versus pro-Klee) or of estimation tendencies (over-estimators versus under-estimators). The dependent measures of bias were a series of matrices by means of which subjects could allocate money to *and receive money from* anonymous members of each group.

Tajfel's modifications had the effect, first, of transforming the experiment from one that manipulated intergroup interdependence as the sole independent variable to one that simultaneously manipulated two independent variables: intergroup interdependence and category differentiation. A second effect was to make explicit and strengthen subjects' perceptions of their interdependence on anonymous members in the own and the other social category for maximizing their own monetary outcomes. Subjects tended to allocate more money to 'in-group' members than to 'out-group' members, but they did not depart too far from fairness, i.e., from equal allocations to both categories (Tajfel et al., pp. 173–174)

Initially, Tajfel et al. interpreted their results as a compromise solution between two conflicting social norms which guided subjects' behavior. A 'generic' social norm of 'groupness' (p. 175) according to which it seems 'appropriate' to favor in-group members and discriminate against out-group members; and a norm of fairness: to give each group an equal share. They wrote: '... the pattern of data can be best understood as showing a strategy in which a compromise between these two norms is achieved' (pp. 173–174).

In the design of the experiment one of the criteria was that the responses requested from the subjects 'should not represent any utilitarian value to the subject making them (p. 154). This criterion is curious in view of instructions to the subjects 'that each would receive the amount of money that the others awarded him' (p. 156). These instructions imply that the subjects may have perceived themselves as dependent for their financial outcomes on the decisions of *both* 'in-group' and 'out-group' members. The assertion that the allocations had no utilitarian value, seems rather odd in the light of Tajfel's report of subjects' spontaneous comments: 'It may be worth mentioning that ... several Ss talked to the E about the obvious thing to do '... to get as much money as possible out of the situation' (p. 172). Apparently, what was obvious to the subjects was not obvious to the researchers.

The assumption that there is no interdependence of interest among groups and their members in the minimal intergroup situation has been a central tenet in the development of Social Identity Theory. The claim is repeatedly made that in the allocation task 'there is neither a conflict of interests ... between the "groups" ... nor is there any rational link between economic self interest and the strategy of in-group favoritism. Thus, these groups are purely cognitive, and can be referred to as "minimal"' (Tajfel & Turner, 1986 p. 14).

It follows that if the cause of behavior cannot be found in the person's perception of the situation, it must be located within the person. The intra-personal cause proposed by Social Identity Theory is the need to maintain or enhance self-esteem The steps in the chain of assumptions by which this need is deemed to produce 'competitive intergroup processes' is described by Turner (1982; p. 16) as follows: '... psychological group membership has primarily a perceptual or cognitive basis .... it considers that individuals structure their perceptions of themselves and others by means of abstract social categories, that they internalize these categories as aspects of their self-concepts, and that social cognitive processes related to these forms of self-conception produce group behaviour.' Thus intergroup competition is said to flow from social comparison processes whereby one seeks superiority for oneself by aggrandizing one's own group or derogating the other group. We have argued elsewhere that social comparison processes are indeed present in the minimal intergroup situation (Horwitz & Rabbie, 1989). However, the first crucial assumption in the chain of arguments (namely that subjects' categorization into, say, a Blue or a Green group is internalized by them to define their identity) has not been adequately tested to our knowledge. Abrams & Hogg (1988) and Schiffmann & Wicklund (1992) have questioned the validity of Turner's assumption and the studies cited in support of it (e.g., Oakes & Turner, 1980; Lemyre & Smith, 1985). Abrams & Hog (1988) have also pointed out that it is unclear whether self-esteem should be considered primarily as a cause or as an effect of discrimination.

5. Experimental Evidence

In recent papers I have argued that the in-group/out-group differentiation is a function of intra-group cooperation and intergroup competition (Rabbie, 1992a, b). In competitive situations, the fates of the parties are negatively linked or correlated with one another: the greater the movement of one party to reach one's goals, the less the likelihood that the other parties will reach their goals (negative or 'contrient' goal interdependence – Deutsch, 1982). In cooperation there is a positive correlation between the goal attainments of the parties: they have to coordinate their efforts since the success of one party contributes to the success of the other(s) (positive or 'promotive' goal interdependence – Deutsch, 1982).

In our Behavioral Interaction Model, two types of competition and cooperation have been distinguished, dependent on the nature of the goals the actors or parties wish to achieve (Rabbie 1987; Rabbie et al., 1989). In instrumental competition the aim is to compete with others in order to achieve more economic or other tangible outcomes. Instrumental cooperation occurs when the interdependence structure between the parties is such that it is better in the long run to strive for mutual cooperation with the other party to obtain tangible and material outcomes than to compete against the other (Pruitt & Kimmel, 1977). In social or relational cooperation the aim is to achieve a mutually satisfying relationship with the other as an end in itself rather than as an instrument to reach an external material goal. The goal is to attain a relational understanding with the other in an attempt to explore whether the relation may grow in depth or will stay at a more superficial level. The goal of social or relational competition is aimed at differentiating one self or one's own group, from comparable others in an effort to achieve more symbolic or intangible rewards like prestige (Sherif 1966), status or self-esteem (Lewin 1948) or a 'positive social identity' (Tajfel & Turner 1986). Social or relational competition between groups may contribute to a positive or a negative group identity depending on the way in which members perceive their own group relative to other comparison groups (Lewin, 1948). We made similar distinctions between instrumental or relational fairness and altruism (Rabbie et al.1992). Instrumental fairness is aimed at maximizing one's own material outcomes through others by giving about as much to members in one's own group as to those in another social group or category. Relational fairness is aimed at preserving a mutually satisfying relationship between the parties. Similarly, instrumental altruism occurs when people make an calculated effort to maximize the outcomes of another interdependent party in the hope and expectation that this action will be reciprocated in the same way. The goal in relational altruism is to maintain or achieve a relationship which meets the socio-emotional needs of single individuals or members of groups (Rabbie et al., 1992).

Our interdependence hypothesis assumes that the development and maintenance of in-group cohesion and out-group discrimination is a function of, respectively, intra-group cooperation and intergroup competition (Rabbie, 1991; 1992a, b). The evolution of in-group cohesion is facilitated by instrumental and relational intra-group cooperation. Out-group discrimination and aggression result from instrumental and relational intergroup competition, particularly when the in-group members assume that the competing (and frustrating) out-group has obtained an unfair advantage over them (Goldenbeld, 1992; Rabbie & Lodewijkx, 1987; 1991).

Instrumental and relational competition (and cooperation) do not exist in pure form but are always mixed in some way. It will depend on particular circumstances whether the instrumental or the relational component of the cooperative or competitive relationship will dominate. For example, when realistic (economic or material) interests are at stake, it is likely that more instrumental competition and cooperation will occur. When symbolic points or intangible rewards are involved the relational component in the cooperation or competition will become more important and salient (Rabbie & Schot, 1989; Schot, 1992).

As we indicated earlier, Tajfel & Turner (1986) are insistent in their belief that in the MGP no utilitarian instrumental competition or cooperation happens between the subjects. Only social competition occurs in their view. We take a different position. In the standard instructions of the MGP, the subjects in the Tajfel et al. (1971) experiment were told that 'They would always be allotting money to others (i.e. always members of the in-group or out-group).' At the end of the task ... each would receive the amount of money that the others had awarded him.' (p. 156). These instructions imply that the individual outcomes of the subjects in the Tajfel et al. (1971) experiment are dependent upon both the allocation decisions of individuals in the own and other social category, but not on their own decisions. Thus, their perceived 'outcome dependence' (Kelley & Thibaut, 1978) is two-sided: on their own 'group' or category and on the *other* 'group' or social category. Although subjects in the standard MGP of Tajfel et al. cannot directly allocate money to themselves, they can do it *indirectly* on the reasonable assumption that the other 'in-group' members will do the same to them. By giving more to their 'in-group' members than to the out-group members, in the expectation that the other 'in-group' members will reciprocate this cooperative action, they will increase the chances of maximizing their own outcomes. In this view, perceived interdependence induces a 'reciprocity' norm (Gouldner, 1960), according to which members in a 'group' expect more from each other than from outsiders to the 'group'. Thus, although subjects in the MGP may be seen as acting independently from each other, they *perceive* themselves to be interdependent with respect to reaching their goal to maximize their individual outcomes. When they act on these perceptions, a 'tacit coordination' (Schelling, 1963) is achieved, which helps them to gain as much as they can in the MGP. Thus, in our view, 'in-group favoritism' should be reinterpreted as a form of instrumental 'intra-group' cooperation with members in the own social category which is aimed at maximizing economic rather than relational outcomes of the subjects. Instrumental fairness i.e. giving the member in the own social category about as many monetary points as members in the other social category serves a very similar function. In the following experiments supportive evidence will be presented for this reinterpretation.

Experiment 1. Perceived interdependence. In a recent experiment we have found strong support for this interdependence hypothesis (Rabbie et al. 1989). Three conditions of interdependence were employed among 'in- and out-group' members. Subjects, categorized as favoring one of two series of paintings, were informed that they would receive monetary points from an anonymous individual in the own social category or 'in-group'. In this In-group Dependence condition (ID) the subjects perceived themselves to be interdependent with members in their own social category. In the 'Out-group' dependence condition (OD), subjects perceived themselves to be dependent for maximizing their own economic outcomes upon an anonymous individual in the other social category or 'out-group'. In the control or IOD condition the standard instructions of Tajfel et al. (1971) were given. Thus in the control condition the perceived interdependence was two-sided: on the 'in-group' and on the 'out-group'. In the two other one-sided conditions, they were informed that they would receive money from someone in the 'in-group' alone or in the 'out-group' alone. The results showed that in the standard control condition they displayed the usual behavior by giving more to 'in-group' members than to 'out-group' members. Where they viewed their outcomes as solely dependent on the actions of in-group members, they gave much more to in-group members than subjects did in the control condition and even less to 'out-group' members. However, where they viewed their outcomes as dependent solely on the actions of the 'out-group', they allocated more money to *'out-group'* members than to 'in-group members'. Thus by altering the perceived interdependence of subjects' outcomes, one can obtain either 'in-group' or 'out-group' favoritism in the MGP, holding category differentiation constant.

Moreover, as predicted by our interdependence hypothesis, more (instrumental) fairness was obtained in the two-sided control condition than in the two one-sided experimental conditions. This finding indicates that the equal distribution of money in the standard MGP does not only reflect a 'norm of fairness' as Tajfel et al. (1971) have suggested but should mainly be viewed as an instrumental strategy to further one's financial outcomes. This result is important since Tajfel & Turner (1986) acknowledge that in the usual MGP research next to 'in-group favoritism', 'fairness is also an influential strategy' (p. 14). However, in developing their theory, they focus exclusively on the strategy of 'in-group favoritism', virtually ignoring the 'influential strategy of fairness' in standard MGP research (Brantwaite, 1979). Such use of the data is understandable since the fairness strategy is in fact incompatible with their theory that intergroup relations are 'essentially competitive' since the aim is 'to maintain or achieve superiority over an out-group on some dimensions' (p. 17). They claim that their theory is consistent with the data from the minimal intergroup experiments which, in their view, show that the 'mere awareness of an out-group is sufficient to stimulate in-group favoritism' (p. 17). In fact, both their results and our data of standard MGP experiments do provide strong evidence that the mere awareness of an out-group is also 'sufficient' to stimulate fairness, a strategy which goes against the tendency of 'in-group favoritism' and 'out-group discrimination'. From this point of view, our interdependence hypothesis provides a more parsimonious explanation of *all* the research findings of the MGP, cited by Tajfel and Turner (1986), than does their own theory.

Thus, the allocation data in the Rabbie et al. (1989) experiment show, in contrast to the assertions by Tajfel & Turner (1986) and Turner et al. (1987), that there *is* an instrumental link between allocation behavior in the MGP and the economic self-interests of the subjects. Moreover, there is clearly a *perceived* or constructed 'form of functional interdependence within or between groups', contrary to what Turner et al. (1987, p. 27) have stated. The allocations do not seem so much guided by social competition in an effort to achieve a positive social identity, as they claim, but more by instrumental cooperation, fairness and altruism with or toward those 'group' members subjects perceive themselves to be the most dependent upon.

Moreover, contrary to Social Identity Theory, the questionnaire data indicate that the operation of important normative orientations, e.g. the norm that one ought to give greater weight to the desires of in-group members than those of out-group members (Horwitz & Rabbie, 1982) cannot be excluded as contributing factor to the allocation behavior in the Minimal Group Paradigm. These data show clear evidence for a normative in-group schema: the learned beliefs and anticipations that more can be expected from in-group members than from 'out-group' members, an idea that is consistent with the earlier 'generic group norm' hypothesis of Tajfel et al. (1971) and our own weight hypothesis (Horwitz and Rabbie, 1982). There is also clear evidence for the operation of the reciprocity norm of Gouldner (1960) that members of in-groups are inclined to expect more of each other than from outsiders to the 'group'.

Experiment 2. Symbolic and economic rewards. It was suggested earlier that the degree of instrumental cooperation and competition will depend on the kind of incentives which are at stake in the MGP. When economic incentives are involved mainly instrumental cooperation and competition will occur. When symbolic incentives are introduced (e.g., points), people will be more motivated to engage in social or relational competition (i.e. to strive more for prestige, status, recognition or for a 'positive social identity' as is assumed by Social Identity Theory.

To obtain information on this issue, the Rabbie et al. (1989) experiment was replicated, but this time not only monetary but also symbolic points had to be allocated (Rabbie & Schot, 1989; Schot, 1992). As expected, more 'in-group' favoritism was obtained in the points than in the money condition. Moreover, in the symbolic points condition there was a greater tendency to differentiate oneself from the other and less willingness to cooperate with others. Thus, when money was at stake, subjects were more interested in maximizing their own (valuable) outcomes than when symbolic points were involved.

Also a significant interaction between the money and point condition was obtained. In the money condition there was strong support for our interdependence hypothesis; subjects allocate the most money to those group members they perceived themselves to be the most dependent upon. For example, in the 'out-group' dependence (OD) condition, the expected '*out-group*' favoritism or (instrumental) outgroup cooperation was obtained. When symbolic points had to be allocated 'out-group' favoritism in the OD condition disappeared. In fact, when points were allocated in the OD condition a significant 'in-group' favoritism was obtained, although the 'in-group' favoritism is smaller in the OD condition than in the control and the in-group dependence (ID) conditions.

Thus, as expected, when money was at stake, support was found for our interdependence hypothesis; when symbolic points were involved support for Social Identity Theory was found. This finding suggests, in accordance with our model, that the two perspectives are not incompatible with each other, as Turner et al. (1987) have asserted, but that both hypotheses may explain the allocation behavior in the Minimal Group Paradigm, dependent on the incentive conditions that stimulate either instrumental or relational cooperation, competition, fairness, and altruism.

Experiment 3. Individual and group oriented behavior. As we have noted earlier, Tajfel & Turner (1986) tend to equate 'social categories' and 'social groups'. To view both concepts as 'purely cognitive' as they do (p. 14), makes it very difficult to ascertain whether the allocation decisions in the MGP can be considered mainly as (inter) individual or as (group) behavior. The experiment reported below is designed to resolve this issue.

Tajfel (1978, pp. 38) and Tajfel & Turner (1986, pp. 8–9) have made a distinction between two extremes of social behavior corresponding to what they label as *interpersonal* versus *intergroup* behavior. At the interpersonal end of the continuum, the behavior of two or more individuals is said to be mainly determined by their personal relationships and individual characteristics. At the intergroup end of the continuum, the interaction of individuals is mainly determined by their membership in groups or social categories which they perceive themselves to belong to.

This distinction is not entirely satisfactory. In their example 'nearing the interpersonal extreme' of the continuum, they refer to the 'relations between husband and wife'. They seem to overlook, however, that many angry encounters and quarrels between spouses can only be understood by referring to their allegiances, attachments, and 'identifications' with their own parents and the original family groups, as the traditional 'mother-in-law' jokes would suggest.

'Near the intergroup extreme', Tajfel & Turner (1986) mention the example of 'the behavior at a negotiation table of members which represent two parties in an intense intergroup conflict' (p. 8). However, as Stephenson (1981) has pointed out intense intergroup conflicts, at the group level of analysis, may often be moderated by strong interpersonal bonds the negotiators may have with each other. These close interpersonal relations may prevent the intergroup conflict from escalating in an uncontrollable way. Stephenson (1981) expresses various misgivings about the 'continuum' hypothesis of Tajfel (1978) as he calls it. One difficulty arises from the hypothesized correspondence between perceived situation and observed behavior. He writes: 'There is obviously a danger of circularity here unless some means is provided of recognizing the position of the situation on the continuum independently of the behaviour it is meant to explain' (p. 192). He also refers another difficulty: 'Tajfel's notion of the continuum suggests that in the case of both situations and actions, the interpersonal and interparty aspects are *alternatives*. This rules out the possibility of *conflict* between the different aspects. The continuum implies that as one factor increases in strength, the other decreases, a situation in mid-continuum being neither one thing nor the other but some mixture of both, and the same for behaviour. In truth, conflict between the two factors is of the essence, and no aspect of our social life can escape the problem of reconciling intergroup and interpersonal objectives' (pp. 193–194).

The problems raised by Stephenson (1981) can be resolved when it is assumed that the individual-group continuum is not based on some unspecified 'individual characteristics' or on 'respective memberships in various social groups or categories' as Tajfel & Turner (1986, p. 8) have proposed but on a continuum of perceived instrumental and relational interdependence between individuals in social categories and members in social groups as we have advanced in our Behavioral Interaction Model. At one pole of this continuum there are egoistic self-centered individuals in social categories who perceive themselves as minimally interdependent on each other for attaining their instrumental or relational outcomes. At the other pole of the individual-group continuum there are group-centered members in social groups who perceive themselves to be maximally interdependent on each other for attaining their instrumental and relational outcomes not only for themselves but also for the group as a whole.

The degree of salience of the individual–group continuum with respect to instrumental outcomes in this experiment was varied in two ways: in the high salience Inter-individual or *Individual condition,* the subjects in a standard MGP were instructed to maximize their economic self-interests. In the high salience intergroup or *Group condition* the subjects were instructed to maximize their monetary group interests. In the low salience or *Control condition* the standard instructions of Tajfel et al. (1971) were given in which individual or group interests were not specifically mentioned. A comparison of these three salience conditions should provide information whether the allocation strategies in the standard MGP can be best characterized as inter-individual or as intergroup behavior.

When individuals are categorized into, say, Blue or Green groups, it may well be that they perceive themselves to belong to the same cognitive social category. As members of a perceptual social category they may pursue their selfish individual goals, almost independent from one another (Rabbie & Horwitz, 1988). It is assumed that the 'groups' in the *Individual* and *Control condition* can be better characterized as 'perceptual social categories' than as social groups as we have defined them. As a consequence, no differences in allocation behavior between the two conditions are to be expected. In the Group condition, however, members perceive themselves as positively interdependent on members in their own group and negatively interdependent on members of the out-group in their efforts to maximize their collective economic outcomes. Therefore, as compared with the two social category conditions, in the Group condition more (instrumental) intra-group cooperation and more (instrumental) intergroup competition are to be expected (Deutsch, 1982; Rabbie, 1991).

These hypotheses received strong support. As expected, no difference in allocation behavior was found between the individual and the control condition in the MGP. These results suggests, contrary to the claims by Turner (1982), that in the standard MGP of Tajfel et al. (1971), we are dealing more with inter-individual than with inter-group behavior. Moreover, more intra-group cooperation and more inter-group competition occurred in the Group than in the Category conditions. Consistent with our expectations, intergroup orientations in the Group condition led to less fairness and more discrimination in favor of the own group than did interindividual orientations in the Category conditions. When subject could directly allocate monetary points to themselves or to the other group members, it was shown that in intergroup relations, members in the Group condition, in comparison with the self-centered individuals in the Social Category conditions, appeared to be more willing to sacrifice a direct economic gain for themselves in favor of their own group as a whole. Thus social groups, in contrast to social categories, encourage personal sacrifices from their members.

5. A Behavioral Interaction Model

Our reinterpretation of the results of the allocation behavior in the Minimal Group Paradigm is guided by our Behavioral Interaction Model as depicted in Figure 1.

Consistent with the interactionist position of Lewin (1936), this model assumes that behavior, including the allocation behavior of subjects in the MGP, is a function of the external environment and of the cognitive, emotional, motivational, and normative orientations which are in part elicited by the external environment and in part acquired by individuals, groups, organizations, and other actors in the course of their development. The main function of these psychological orientations is to reduce uncertainty in the external environment to such a manageable level that the individual or group can achieve desirable outcomes and avoid undesirable ones. The external environment consists of three components: a physical (task) environment, an internal and an external social environment (i.e. the behavior of other people within and external to the social system), and an interdependence structure between the parties which may be positive or negative, loosely or tightly coupled, and symmetrical or asymmetrical with regard to the power relations between the parties. It is assumed that in social groups the members will be more tightly coupled to each other than in social categories. These psychological orientations produce a meaning or interpretative system about the situation which in turn generates various action tendencies in the actor.

Although many types of meaning systems may exist, we have focused on the significance of instrumental and relational orientations which combine with the different cognitive, emotional, motivational, and normative orientations distinguished in the literature (Deutsch, 1982; McClintock, 1988). In line with various value-expectancy models (e.g. Lewin, 1952; Vroom, 1964; Ajzen & Fishbein, 1980), we assume that among competing action tendencies and available strategies, those actions and alternatives will be chosen that promise, with a high probability of success, to attain the most valued goals or profitable

Figure 1   *Behavioral interaction model*

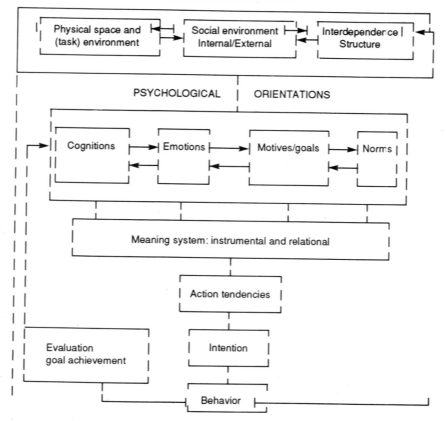

outcomes, whereby the gains seem to exceed the costs of achieving them.

According to our interaction model, the allocation behavior of the subjects in the MGP is a function of the cognitive expectancies and attributions about the behavior of others in the in-group and out-groups, the low emotional involvement with the other people in the anonymous, strategic environment of the MGP, the motivational orientations leading to cooperation, competition, or equal distributions in the allocation task, and normative orientations such as reciprocity, fairness and the normative in-group schema to expect more of in-group members than of out-group members (Rabbie & Lodewijkx, 1992; Lodewijkx & Rabbie, 1992).

These kinds of psychological orientations are mainly elicited by the nature of the perceived interdependence structure of the MGP. The subjects in the MGP perceive a positive goal interdependence with in-group members and a negative goal interdependence with out-group members in their efforts to maximize their own economic self-interests and perhaps those of their fellow in-group members (cf. Bornewasser & Bober, 1987). Through instrumental cooperation with 'in-group' members and some relational but primarily instrumental competition with out-group members subjects in the standard MGP are able to maximize mainly their financial outcomes (Schot, 1992).

As we noted earlier, these instrumental and relational orientations seldom exist in pure form. According to our model, in most of our relationships there is a mix of various these instrumental and relational orientations in which one may dominate the other. Which orientations prevail will depend on various factors – the uncertainties and the kind of physical and social environment one has to cope with; the perceived interdependence structure and consequent power relationships between the parties; the accessible cognitions, attributions and cognitive in-group schemas which are used; the state of emotional arousal and current moods; the kind of goals or outcomes one is striving for; the salience of social norms, entitlements, and obligations; the issues and incentives at stake; the degree of congruence which exists between the dispositional or cultural orientations of individuals and groups and those elicited by the external environment (Rabbie, 1987; 1991a, b; Rabbie, in press).

In the Minimal Group Paradigm, subjects do not receive any feedback about the effects of their actions. They act on the basis of an expected or constructed social world. In most 'real-life' social interaction situations however, people do receive feedback about the effects of their actions on other people and are often influenced by the reactions of the others they have to deal with. According to the theory of planned behavior of Ajzen and Madden (1986), an intention or commitment to perform or not to perform an act is the best predictor of behavior. The action or the behavior may lead to outcomes or a present state which must be evaluated against the desired future state: the goal or standard the party wanted to achieve. When no discrepancy is observed between the present and desired state the action is terminated. If a discrepancy still remains, the party or actor will have to revise or reconsider the psychological orientations which led to the behavior which was not successful in reaching the standards or goals. The mismatch or discrepancy between actual behavioral outcomes and desired goals may induce a change in psychological orientations, symbolized in Figure 1 by an arrow from the 'evaluation-of-goal-attainment' box to the psychological orientations. This may initiate a new cycle of action sequences which will be terminated when the goal is achieved or when different and more reachable goals are substituted for the original ones. The direct arrow at the right hand side of Figure 1, – from the behavior to the external environment at the top of the figure – expresses the notion that acting on the external environment may have the effect of changing it, leading to different psychological orientations and meaning structures of the situation, which in turn may induce different action tendencies, intentions, and behavior until the original or modified goals are achieved. Just like other cybernetic action models – e.g., the control model of Carver and Scheier (1981), the TOTE-concept of Miller et al. (1960) and the information processing model of emotions of Frijda (1986) – our model can be considered as a self-regulating, negative feedback system, modulated by multiple feedback loops that result in a reorganization of meaning structures, action tendencies and the kind of goals the actor wants to achieve in interaction with other parties until some steady state is attained between them.

Although this model is still in its first stage of development it already appears useful as a heuristic device. Its applications may include to guide research on the differences between individual and group aggression (e.g. Rabbie, 1989a; Rabbie & Lodewijkx, 1987, 1990; Rabbie in press), the study of terrorism of insurgent groups (Rabbie, 1989, 1991), research on intra- and intergroup relations (Rabbie, 1982; Rabbie et al., 1989; Rabbie & Schot, 1989; and Rabbie, 1993, in press), the determinants of instrumental intra-group cooperation (Rabbie, 1991), and the study of sex differences in aggression (Goldenbeld, 1992; Rabbie et al., 1992). On the basis of our research reported in this chapter, it appears that the model may serve as a general theory from which testable hypotheses can be derived.

6. Conclusion

The discovery of Tajfel et al. (1971) that the 'mere' categorization of a group of boys into two subgroups seemed sufficient to arouse a significant 'in-group' favoritism appeared to be rather damaging to the basic assumptions of realistic conflict theory of LeVine and Campbell (1972) and Sherif (1966). In a recent review on intergroup relations, Messick and Mackie (1989) have noted that: 'This discovery challenged the idea that intergroup discrimination resulted from a real conflict of interests between the two groups ...' (1990, p. 59). This point of view is shared by many other researchers (e.g. Brewer, 1979; Tajfel & Turner, 1986; Brewer & Kramer, 1985; and Brown, 1988). As I have tried to show in this chapter this common view is incorrect. Realistic (or instrumental) intergroup conflict theory cannot be excluded as a viable explanation of the 'in-group favoritism' and instrumental fairness obtained in the Minimal 'Group' Paradigm.

In our view, social categorization in the MGP does not so much stimulates social competition and discriminatory *intergroup* behavior aimed at achieving a 'positive social identity', as Tajfel & Turner (1986) have asserted, but can be better understood as primarily instrumental and *inter-individual* behavior aimed at cooperating with those individuals in the own and other social categories whom one perceives oneself as the most dependent upon in trying to maximize one's individual self-interests, at least when money has to be allocated (Rabbie & Schot, 1989). This view implies, to put it very bluntly, that there is almost no relational 'in-group bias' or 'in-group favoritism' in the standard MGP: there are mainly self-centered individuals in social categories, who tacitly coordinate their choices with anonymous members of the own and other social category in an effort to maximize their individual self-interests. They may use the category labels not so much as a means for 'self-categorization' or 'self-identification', as Turner et al. (1987) have asserted, but mainly as cues or instruments to attain their own individual interests.

This conclusion does not mean, of course, that Social Identity Theory is incorrect. Since Lewin (1948) emphasized the importance of social groups as a major source of self-esteem and social status, there can be no doubt that people may derive a positive (or a negative) social identity from their perceived membership in the group. In our view it is only too one-sided in its approach to intergroup behavior. The theory needs to be complemented by other approaches including the interdependence perspective we have favored. Our data do show, however, that the empirical evidence for SIT, as far as the research with the Minimal 'Group' Paradigm is concerned, appears to be much weaker than is often assumed (Brown, 1988). In this respect I agree with the verdict of Messick and Mackie (1989) who after an extensive review of the empirical evidence for Social Identity Theory conclude: 'Nearly 20 years after the discovery that mere categorization produced intergroup bias, an adequate theory of the phenomenon has yet to be developed' (p. 62). It is our hope that a further elaboration of our Behavioral Interaction Model may provide the main elements of such a theory.

Implications for War and Peace

What are the possible implications of this in-group and out-group research to the momentous issues of war and peace? A provisional answer to this question is given by Primo Levi (1988) who wondered whether those who returned from Auschwitz were able to understand and make others to understand what they have experienced. He wrote:

> What we commonly mean by 'understand' coincides with 'simplify': without profound simplification the world around us would be an infinite, undefined tangle that would defy our ability to orient ourselves and decide upon our actions. In short, we are compelled to reduce the knowable to a schema: ... perhaps for reasons that go back to our origins as social animals, the need to divide the field into 'we' and 'they' is so strong that this pattern, this bi-partition – friend-enemy – prevails over all others'. (Primo Levi, 1988, p. 22).

In our experimental research we have tried to understand the origins of the 'us'–'them' partition and how this bifurcation affects our fate and behavior. This can indeed be a matter of life or death. When innocent people – men, women or children – were categorized as Jews during the Nazi occupation of great parts of Europe and were forced to wear a yellow star, that fact alone was sufficient to condemn them to death. The same thing happened in Cambodia with people who were unfortunate enough to wear glasses during the Pol-Pot regime. It still occurs in several parts of Africa and elsewhere in the world where people are raped, tortured or slaughtered simply because they are perceived to belong to another group, tribe or religion. Other norms appear to apply to the treatment of people who are considered one of 'us' than one of 'them'. In this chapter I have argued that the more people perceive themselves to be interdependent upon each other for attaining their relational and instrumental outcomes the more they will cooperate with each other to realize their goals in a peaceful fashion. This it is not to say that we necessarily have to belong to the same social group or nation in order to behave cooperatively and peacefully with each other. France and Germany, bitter enemies during two disastrous world wars, have lived peacefully together for more than forty years within the superordinate framework of the European Community. It is simply not true that loyalty and peace in the in-group and hatred and contempt for the out-group *always* go together, as Sumner (1906) has proposed in his ethnocentrism theory. Our research has shown that intra-group cohesion and out-group hostility may vary independently from each other and are not invariably negatively associated as Sumner has assumed (Rabbie, 1982). It will depend on the perceived interdependence structure within and between groups or nations whether they find themselves in peace or in war with each other. Only perceived negative interdependence in intergroup or international relations induces feelings of threat and suspicion (Rabbie, 1992). Larsen (1986) has argued that perceived threat, whether valid or not, is the major dynamism underlying the arms race.

This idea received strong confirmation by an astounding event that happened only recently. On 21 November 1990 at the CSCE conference in Paris, 32 heads of state and government leaders of Europe, the United States, and Canada signed a disarmament treaty marking the end of the Cold War between the NATO alliance and the Warsaw pact. I can only hope that, one day, such agreement between 'them' and 'us' will embrace the whole world.

Notes

1 The terms 'minority' and 'majority' groups are used not in a numerical but in a psychological sense, denoting that one group is more powerful and privileged than another group (Tajfel, 1981).

2 From now on I will use the term 'group', *without* quotes, when referring to a social group as I have defined it. The term 'group', in quotes, is employed when I refer to a social or perceptual category or when direct comparisons are made between social groups and social categories.

References

Abrams, D. & M.A. Hogg, 1988. 'Comments on the motivational status of self-esteem in social identity and intergroup discrimination', *European Journal of Social Psychology*, vol. 18, pp. 317–334.

Ajzen, I. & M. Fishbein, 1980. *Understanding attitudes and predicting social behavior*. Englewood Cliffs, NJ: Prentice-Hall.

Ajzen, I. & T.J. Madden, 1986. 'Prediction of goal directed behavior: attitudes, intentions and perceived behavioral control', *Journal of Experimental Social Psychology*, vol. 22, pp. 453–474

Bakan, D. 1966. *The duality of human existence*. Chicago IL: Rand McNally

Bar-Tal, D; C.F. Graumann; A.W. Kruglanski & W. Stroebe, eds, 1989. *Stereotyping and prejudice: Changing perceptions*. Berlin: Springer.

Björquist, K. & P. Niemellä, 1992, in press. *Of mice and women: aspects of female aggression.* New York: Academic Press.

Bornewasser, M. & J. Bober, 1987. 'Individual, social group and intergroup behaviour: Some conceptual remarks on social identity theory', *European Journal of Social Psychology*, vol. 17, pp. 267–276.

Brandstätter, H; J.H. Davis & G.Stocker-Kreichgauer, eds, 1982. *Group decision-making.* London: Academic Press.

Brantwaite, A.; S. Doyl & N. Lightbown, 1979. 'The balance between fairness and discrimination', *European Journal of Social Psychology*, vol. 9, pp. 149–163.

Brewer, M.B., 1979. 'Ingroup bias in the minimal intergroup situation: cognitive-motivational analysis', *Psychological Bulletin*, vol. 186, pp. 307–24.

Brewer, M.B. & R.M. Kramer, 1985. 'The psychology of intergroup attitudes and behavior', *Annual Review of Psychology*, vol. 36, pp. 219–243.

Brown, Rupert, 1988. *Group processes: dynamics within and between groups.* Oxford: Basil Blackwell.

Cartwright, D. & A. Zander, eds. *Group dynamics*, 3rd edn. London: Tavistock.

Carver, C.S. & M.F. Scheier, 1981. *Attention and self regulation: control theory approach to human behavior.* New York: Springer-Verlag.

Condor, S. & R. Brown, 1988. 'Psychological processes in inter group conflict', pp. 3–26 in W. Stroebe et al.

Derlega, V.J. & J. Grzelak, eds, 1982. *Cooperation and Helping Behavior.* New York: Academic Press.

Deutsch, M., 1982. 'Interdependence and psychological orientation', pp. 15–42 in V.J. Derlega & J. Grzelak.

Doise, W., 1988. 'Individual and social identities in intergroup relations', *European Journal of Social Psychology*, vol. 18, pp. 99–111.

Drenth, P.J.D.; J.A. Sergeant & R.J.Takens, eds, 1990. *European Perspectives in Psychology*, Chichester: Wiley

Frijda, N.H., 1986. *The Emotions.* New York: Cambridge University Press.

Groebel, J & R.H. Hinde, eds, 1989. *Aggression and War: Their Biological and Social Bases.* Cambridge: Cambridge University Press.

Goldenbeld, Ch., 1992. *Aggression after provocation* (in Dutch). Dissertation, University of Utrecht.

Gouldner, A.W. 1960. 'The norm of reciprocity: A preliminary statement', *American Sociological Review*, vol. 25, pp. 161–178.

Hamilton, D.L. & S.J. Sherman, 1989. 'Illusory correlations: implications for stereotype theory research', pp. 59–52 in D. Bar-Tal et al.

Hinde R.A. & J. Groebel, eds, 1991. *Pro-social behaviour, altruism and cooperation.* Cambridge: University of Cambridge Press.

Harcourt & F. de Waal, eds, 1992. *Cooperation in conflict: Coalitions and alliances in animals and humans.* Oxford: Oxford University Press.

Horwitz, M. & J.M. Rabbie, 1982. 'Individuality and membership in the intergroup system', pp. 241–274 in H. Tajfel

Horwitz, M. & J.M. Rabbie, 1989. 'Stereotypes of groups, group members and individuals in categories: A differential analysis of different phenomena', in D. Bar-Tal et al.

Kelley, H.H. & J.W. Thibaut, 1978. *Interpersonal relations: A theory of interdependence.* New York: Wiley.

Larsen, K.S., 1986. 'Social psychological factors in military technology and strategy', *Journal of Peace Research*, vol. 23, no. 4, pp. 391–398.

Lemyre, L. & P.M. Smith, 1985. 'Intergroup discrimination and self-esteem in the minimal group paradigm', *Journal of Personality and Social Psychology*, vol. 49, pp. 660–670.

LeVine, R.A. & D.T. Campbell, 1972. *Ethnocentrism: Theories of conflict, ethnic attitudes and group behavior*. New York: Wiley

Lewin, K., 1936. *Principles of topological psychology*. New York: McGraw Hill.

Lewin, K., 1948. *Resolving Social Conflicts*. New York: Harper and Row.

Lodewijkx, H.F.M., 1989. *Aggression between individuals and groups*. Dissertation, University of Utrecht (in Dutch).

Lodewijkx, H.F.M. & J.M. Rabbie, 1992. 'Group-centred and self-centred behaviour in intergroup relations'. Paper to presented at the XXV *International Congress of Psychology*, Brussels, 19–24 July 1992, Belgium.

Lindzey G. & E. Aronson, eds, 1985. *The handbook of social psychology*, vol. 3. New York: Random House.

Markovski, B; E.J. Lawler; J. O'Brien & K. Heimer, eds. *Advances in group processes*, vol. 11. Greenwich, CT: JAI Press.

McClintock, C.G., 1988. 'Evolution, systems of interdependence, and social values', *Behavioral Science*, vol. 33, pp. 59–76.

Merton, R.K. 1957. *Social Theory and Social Structure* (rev. edn). New York: Free Press.

Messick, D.M. & D.M. Mackie, 1989. 'Intergroup relations', *Annual Review of Psychology*, vol. 40, pp. 45–81.

McGrath, J.E., 1984. *Groups: Interaction and performance*. Englewood Cliffs, NJ: Prentice-Hall.

Miller, G.A; Galanter, E. & K.H. Pribram, 1960. *Plans and the structure of behavior*. New York: Holt, Rinehart & Winston.

Oakes, P.J. & J.C. Turner, 1980. 'Social categorization and intergroup behaviour: Does minimal intergroup discrimination make social identity more positive?', *European Journal of Social Psychology*, vol. 10, pp. 295–301.

Oskamp, S., 1977. *Attitudes and opinions*. Englewood Cliffs, NJ: Prentice-Hall.

Pruitt, D.G. & M.J. Kimmel, 1977. 'Twenty years of experimental gaming: critique, synthesis, and suggestions for the future', *Annual Review of Psychology* vol. 28, pp. 363–392.

Rabbie, J.M., 1966. 'Ingroup-outgroup differentiation under minimal social conditions'. Second European Conference of Experimental Social Psychology. December, 1966, Sorrento, Italy.

Rabbie, J.M., 1982. 'The effects of intergroup competition on intragroup and intergroup relationships', pp. 123–149 in V.J. Derlega & J. Grzelak.

Rabbie, J.M., 1987. 'Armed conflicts: Toward a Behavioural Inter action Model', pp. 47–76 in J. von Wright et al.

Rabbie, J.M., 1989. 'Group Processes as Stimulants of Aggression', in J. Groebel and R.H. Hinde.

Rabbie, J.M., 1991a. 'Determinants of instrumental intra-group cooperation', pp. 238–262 in R.A. Hinde & J. Groebel.

Rabbie, J.M., 1991b. 'A Behavioral Interaction Model: A theoretical frame work for studying terrorism', *Terrorism and Political Violence* vol. 3, no. 4, pp. 133–162.

Rabbie, J.M., 1992a. 'Effects of intra-group cooperation and intergroup competition on ingroup-outgroup differentiation', pp. 175–205 in A. Harcourt and F. de Waal.

Rabbie, J.M., 1993, in press. 'Determinants of ingroup cohesion and outgroup hostility', *The International Journal of Group Tensions*.

Rabbie, J.M. & M. Horwitz, 1969. 'The arousal of ingroup-outgroup bias by a chance win or loss'. *Journal of Personality and Social Psychology*, vol. 69, pp. 223–228.

Rabbie, J.M; Goldenbeld, Ch. & H.F.M. Lodewijkx, 1992, in press. 'Sex differences in conflict and aggression in individual and group settings', in Björquist & Niemellä.

Rabbie, J.M. & M. Horwitz, 1988. 'Categories versus groups as explanatory concepts in intergroup relations', *European Journal of Social Psychology*, vol. 18, pp. 117–123.

Rabbie, J.M. & H.F.M. Lodewijkx, 1987. 'Individual and group aggression', *Current Research on Peace and Violence*, no. 2–3, pp. 91–101.

. Rabbie, J.M. & H.F.M. Lodewijkx, 1991. 'Aggressive reactions to social injustice by individuals and groups: Toward a Behavioral Interaction Model', pp. 280–309 in R. Vermunt & H. Steensma.

Rabbie, J.M. & H.F.M. Lodewijkx, in press. 'The study of conflict and aggression between individuals and groups using a behavioral interaction model', in B. Markovski et al.

Rabbie, J.M. & J.C. Schot, 1989a. 'Instrumental and relational behavior in the Minimal Group Paradigm'. Paper presented to the 1st Congress of Psychology, Amsterdam, 2–7 July 1989.

Rabbie, J.M. & J.C. Schot, 1990. 'Group behavior in the minimal group paradigm: Fact or fiction?', pp. 251–263 in P.J.D. Drenth et al.

Rabbie, J.M; J.C. Schot & L. Visser, 1989. 'Social identity theory: a conceptual and empirical critique from the perspective of a Behavioural Interaction Model', *European Journal of Social Psychology*, vol. 19, pp. 171–202.

Rabbie, J.M; L. Visser & J. van Oostrum, 1982. 'Conflict behaviour of individuals, dyads and triads in mixed-motive games', pp. 315–343 in H. Brandstätter et al. London: Academic Press.

Schelling, T.C., 1963. *The strategy of conflict*. Cambridge, MA: Harvard University Press.

Schiffmann, R. & Wicklund, R.A., 1992. 'The Minimal Group Paradigm and its minimal psychology: on equating social identity with arbitrary group membership', *Theory & Psychology*, vol. 2, no. 1, pp. 29–50.

Schot J.C., 1992. *Allocations in the Minimal Group Paradigm: Consequences of social identity pressures and perceived interdependence*. (In Dutch). Dissertation, University of Utrecht.

Schruijer, Sandra, G.L., 1990. *Norm violation, Attribution and attitudes in intergroup relations*. Doctoral Dissertation University of Brabant, Tilburg: University Press.

Sherif, M., 1966. *In common predicament: social psychology of intergroup conflict and cooperation*. Boston, MA: Houghton Miffin.

Stephan, W.G., 1985. 'Intergroup relations', pp. 599–650 in G. Lindzey & E. Aronson.

Stephenson, G.M., 1981. 'Intergroup bargaining and negotiation', pp. 168–198 in J. Turner & H. Giles.

Stroebe, W; A.W. Kruglanski, D. Bar-Tal & M. Hewstone, eds, 1988. *The social psychology of intergroup conflict: Theory, research and application*. Berlin: Springer.

Stroebe, W. & Ch.A. Insko, 1989. 'Stereotype, prejudice, and discrimination: Changing conceptions in theory and research', in D.Bar-Tal, et al., eds.

Summer, W.G., 1906. *Folkways*, New York: Ginn & Co.

Tajfel, H.; M.G. Billig; R.P. Bundy & C.I. Flament, 1971. 'Social categorization and intergroup behaviour', *European Journal of Social Psychology*, vol. 1, pp. 149–178.

Tajfel, H., ed., 1982. *Social identity and intergroup relations*. Cambridge: Cambridge University Press and Paris: Editions de la Maison des Sciences de l'Homme.

Tajfel, H. & J.C. Turner, 1986. 'The social identity theory of intergroup behavior', pp. 7–24 in S. Worchel and W.G. Austin, eds.

Turner, J.C. & H. Giles, eds, 1981. *Intergroup Behaviour*. Oxford: Blackwell.

Turner, J.C., 1981. 'The experimental social psychology of inter group behaviour', pp. 66–101 in J.C.Turner and H. Giles.

Turner, J.C., 1982. 'Towards a cognitive redefinition of the social group', pp. 15–40 in H. Tajfel, 1982.

Turner, J.C; M.A. Hogg; P.J. Oakes; S.D. Reicher & M.S. Wetherell, 1987. *Rediscovering the social group: A self-categorization theory*. Oxford: Basil Blackwell.

Vermunt, R. & H. Steensma, eds, 1991. *Social injustice in human relations*, vol. 1: *Societal and psychological origins of justice (Critical issues in social justice)*, New York: Plenum.

Vroom, W.H., 1964. *Work and Motivation*. New York: Wiley.

Wright, J. von; K. Helkama & A.M. Pirtilla-Backman, eds, 1986. 'European Psychologists for Peace', Proceedings of the Congress in Helsinki, 1986.

Worchel, S. & W.G. Austin, eds, 1986. *Psychology of intergroup relations*. Chicago, IL: Nelson-Hall.

8

Towards a Social-Psychological Model of Intergroup Conflict

Ronald J. Fisher*

1. Introduction: Social-Psychological Contributions to the Study of Conflict

The discipline of social psychology has evidenced a long-term interest in the understanding and resolution of intergroup conflict within the broader study of intergroup relations. From early work on attitude measurement, to theories of attitude formation and change, to studies of ethnic stereotyping, to research on social perception, cognition, and communication, social psychology has produced concepts and methods relevant to the study of conflict. Unfortunately, most of these contributions have focused on the individual level of analysis (e.g., attitudes, attributions) in an attempt to explain group and intergroup phenomena (e.g., discrimination, injustice), and have not been integrated into a multi-level perspective. Moreover, the amount of theory and research directly devoted to intergroup conflict has been surprisingly sparse. The purpose of this chapter is briefly to review classic and contemporary contributions to the study of intergroup conflict and to integrate these into an initial, eclectic model.

In 1906, Sumner coined the term *ethnocentrism* to denote a cultural narrowness in which the 'ethnically centered' individual rigidly accepted those of the ingroup while rejecting those of the outgroup. This influential

* Many of the ideas expressed in this chapter were first presented in the initial lecture in a series on Social-Psychological Contributions to the Understanding and Resolution of Conflict sponsored by the Canadian Institute for International Peace and Security and the Faculty of Social Sciences, Carleton University, Ottawa, Canada, October, 1987. This chapter was prepared while the author was Visiting Professor in Social Sciences at Carleton University. Certain portions of the chapter, particularly the adaptation of Figure 1 and Figure 2 are taken from R. J. Fisher, *The Social Psychology of Intergroup and International Conflict Resolution*, Springer-Verlag Publishers, 1990. The author would like to thank Pierre Cadrin and Ruth Kinzel for helpful suggestons and comments on the revision of the eclectic model.

concept was extended by Adorno and his colleagues (1950) who portrayed ethnocentrism as a generalized prejudice rooted in the dynamics of the *authoritarian personality*. This individual-level explanation was countered by the research and theorizing of Sherif and his colleagues (1961), who saw prejudice and discrimination as rooted in the functional relations between groups. These investigators carried out a series of field experiments in which intergroup conflict and many of its manifestations were induced through competitive interactions and then reduced through the imposition of a series of superordinate goals. Sherif's studies with pre-adolescent US males were later replicated by Blake and Mouton (1961) with US adults in management training sessions, and have also been extended cross-culturally (e.g., Diab, 1970).

The work of Sherif was integrated with sociological and anthropological evidence to produce Campbell's (1965) statement of *realistic group conflict theory* (RCT): fundamentally, this asserts that real conflicts of interest – incompatible goals and competition for scarce resources – cause intergroup conflict. The real conflict of interest in combination with the presence of a hostile, competitive outgroup and a history or current expression of conflictual behavior results in real threat which drives the psychological elements of ethnocentrism. That is, real threat causes hostility to the outgroup, ingroup solidarity or cohesion, and awareness of ingroup identity. Ethnocentrism is thus a reaction to real conflict of interest, rather than an expression of psychodynamic processes within the individual. In this way, RCT parallels the functional approach to conflict brought forward primarily by sociologists such as Coser (1956) and Dahrendorf (1959).

A great deal of effort, particularly by social psychologists in the United States, has been expended in *games research* as a means of understanding conflict. The most frequent methodology is a mixed-motive game known as the Prisoner's Dilemma, in which each of two players makes a choice between competing or cooperating in ignorance of the other's choice. The design of the payoff matrix determines that competing while the other cooperates maximizes one's own gain, mutual competition incurs small losses, and mutual cooperation yields small gains. The game thus represents a real conflict of interest; and not surprisingly, general results indicate that competition tends to predominate. In addition, the norm of reciprocity strongly affects game behavior, and a 'tit-for-tat' strategy is generally most effective in maximizing outcomes in the long run. Games provide for a precise definition of the interdependence between the parties, and an efficient method for looking at relationships among variables. However, the external validity of games research has been severely questioned, and the method has been used only to test scattered hypotheses (Pruitt & Kimmel, 1977); thus, the results do not cumulate in any useful way toward developing a comprehensive theory on intergroup conflict.

The propositions of RCT have been in part contradicted but also complemented by the development of *social identity theory* (SIT), which grew out of research on *social categorization*. The assumption of this line of investigation is that people use the same cognitive processes in making social judgements used in dealing with physical stimuli (e.g., Bruner, 1957; Tajfel & Wilkes, 1963). In both cases, research has demonstrated that we tend to exaggerate similarities within categories and differences between categories. With respect to intergroup relations, the effects are that ingroup members are assumed to be similar; outgroup members are seen as different (e.g., Stephan, 1985; Wilder, 1986). Grant (1990) reviews research and theorizing on social categorization in the areas of stereotyping, causal (mis)attribution, and ingroup bias. The overall theme is that social categorization links to a variety of cognitive processes that accentuate group differences and ethnocentrism, and thereby cause and/or escalate intergroup conflict.

The surprising aspect of the initial work on SIT by Tajfel et al. (1970) was that the mere perception of belonging to a group, even an artificially created one, was sufficient to produce intergroup discrimination, that is, ingroup favoritism. Following on this finding and building on the process of social categorization, theorists turned to a combination of the concepts of social identity and self-esteem with social comparison theory to produce their statement of SIT (Tajfel & Turner, 1986). The basic propositions of the theory are that individuals strive to maintain a positive self-concept and therefore social identity; membership in groups contributes to social identity; the evaluation of one's own group is based on social comparison with outgroups; and a positive social identity is based on favorable comparisons. Tajfel and Turner (1986) have also proposed that when social comparison leads to a negative social identity, dissatis-faction will occur, and if the intergroup situation is perceived as unstable or unjust, action will be taken to improve social identity. Ethnocentrism and related biases are driven by a need for enhanced self-esteem based on group distinctiveness and invidious comparisons with other groups. Thus, in contrast to RCT, the SIT research demonstrates that real conflicts of interest are not always necessary to create an initial element of intergroup conflict, that is, intergroup discrimination. However, this discrimination is expressed as ingroup favoritism rather than outgroup hostility and rejection (Brewer, 1979), thus attenuating the scope of SIT. Nonetheless, the potency of social categorization and social identity as important contributors to intergroup conflict has been demonstrated.

Much of the social-psychological contribution to the study of conflict comes from the work of Deutsch (1973) which emphasizes the processes of intergroup conflict, particularly escalation. Deutsch (1990) himself has provided a contemporary overview of what he sees as the major contributions of social psychology to the study of conflict over the past 60 years. Deutsch (1973) has defined conflict as existing whenever incompatible activities occur between parties – that is, actions that prevent, obstruct, or interfere with the other's activity. One early and major specification is the difference between a cooperative and competitive social interaction in terms of the perceptions, attitudes, communication, and task orientation of the parties. In a cooperative interaction, parties perceive that they have positively related goals, are sensitive to similarities, and hold friendly, trusting and helpful attitudes to each other. Communication is open, accurate, and relevant; and task orientation addresses conflict as a mutual problem to be solved. In a competitive interaction, parties perceive negatively related goals, are sensitive to differences, and hold suspicious, hostile, and exploitative attitudes. Communication is limited or non-existent, misleading or used for propaganda and espionage, while task orientation involves each party attempting to impose its solution on the other through coercion and escalation.

Given that most relationships and conflicts are mixed-motive situations, it is extremely important which approach parties take, since this will come to determine the predominant nature and outcome of their interaction. Deutsch (1973) has expressed this through his *crude law of social interaction*, which states that the characteristic processes and effects elicited by a type of social relationship (cooperative or competitive) tend also to elicit that type of social relationship. In intergroup conflict, this leads to a very powerful and destructive dynamic in which parties attempt to protect their interests by taking a competitive orientation; this simply begets a competitive response which in turn leads to an escalating spiral of ultimately destructive interaction. At high levels of escalation, the interaction becomes a *malignant social process* which is increasingly dangerous and costly but from which the parties seen no way of extricating themselves without unacceptable losses – material and/or psychological. (See Deutsch, 1983.)

The malignant social process demonstrates cognitive rigidity, partly in the form of stereotypes, misperceptions and misjudgements – such as actor/perceiver differences in attributions, unwitting commitments in which post-decision dissonance reduction strengthens prior beliefs, and self-fulfilling prophecies. These distortions feed into escalating spirals in which increasing risks are required to justify past investments, and lead to a gamesmanship orientation divorced from the awesome reality that violent confrontation would bring. Thus, Deutsch's theorizing provides a descriptive integration of a good deal of the social-psychological work on intergroup conflict, and is especially useful in linking individual cognitive processes to intergroup interaction.

Intergroup conflict lies at the center of the broader field of intergroup relations, which involves any form of interaction between individuals behaving in terms of their group identities. In a recent comprehensive analysis of the major theories of intergroup relations, Taylor and Moghaddam (1987) cover all models which 'claim to deal with the fundamental issues associated with intergroup relations: How intergroup conflicts arise, what course they take, and how they become resolved' (p. 14). In addition to RCT and SIT, Taylor and Moghaddam discuss equity theory, relative deprivation theory, and elite theory, before presenting Taylor and McKirnan's (1984) *five-stage model of intergroup relations*. This model is especially appealing since it incorporates concepts from the other major theories as well as employing central concepts from social psychology, including social comparison and causal attribution.

The five-stage model focuses primarily on groups of unequal status and on the responses of disadvantaged groups to perceived injustice. In stage one, clearly stratified intergroup relations are based on inherent (e.g., race) or ascribed (e.g., religion) characteristics and are not questioned by members of either group. In stage two, group membership comes to be seen as a matter of individual achievement rather than group characteristics; this leads in stage three to social mobility – that is, attempts by disadvantaged group members to pass into the advantaged group. Some may be successful and thus legitimate the system, but others will not be, and their perception of unjust treatment in stage four leads to consciousness-raising activities within the disadvantaged group. This leads to the final stage of competitive intergroup relations, where members of the disadvantaged group engage in collective action to improve their position. This can result in a win-lose outcome for either group or in a healthy state of competition. Thus, the five-stage model can explain how unequal groups in a society come to a point of open conflict. In that way it complements other theoretical contributions which deal only with equal groups or do not specify the etiology of the conflict prior to the confrontation point.

This brief and selective overview of social-psychological contributions to the study of conflict demonstrates that theoretical work has been fragmentary and largely unconnected. Each theory or model has attempted to explain some part of intergroup conflict with its own primary constructs and with a concentration at only one or two levels of analysis. RCT concentrates on the group and intergroup levels, but tends to ignore the individual level. SIT integrates the individual level nicely into the group level through the primary construct of social identity, but is relatively weak at the intergroup level, in that it downplays the significance of real conflict of interest.

There is clearly a need for an eclectic, integrative model of intergroup conflict that captures the essential variables and key processes of the phenomenon. This model should be built on a combination of classic and contemporary contributions and be inclusive of variables at multiple levels of analysis. The model should be constructed following the social-psychological approach that is more or less evident in all of the above contributions and displays the following characteristics. First, it is *phenomenological* in that the subjective reality of the parties – their perceptions, cognitions, attitudes, needs, and values – are seen as critical influences on their behavior toward each other. Second, it is *interactive* in that it emphasizes the centrality of behavioral interaction between the parties in conflict escalation and maintenance as well as in de-escalation and resolution. Third, it stresses the need for considering *multiple levels of analysis* within a systems orientation in order to understand the complexity of intergroup conflict. The social-psychological perspective leads to a definition of conflict that stresses the subjective side of the phenomenon but also accepts real conflict of interest: 'a social situation involving perceived incompatibilities in goals or values between two or more parties, attempts by the parties to control each other, and antagonistic feelings by the parties toward each other' (Fisher, 1990, p. 6). The following sections will outline a model which is compatible with this definition and with the characteristics of the social-psychological perspective.

2. Constructing an Integrated, Eclectic Model

A systematic and comprehensive strategy of theory construction applicable to intergroup conflict has been provided by Dubin (1969, 1976) who includes both inductive and deductive processes for developing applied models with immediate relevance to the real world. His approach is expressed in seven features or building blocks of a theoretical model, which also indicate the steps that a scientist goes through in constructing the model. The process moves from specifying the *units* or basic *variables* of interest to formulating the *laws of interaction* or *principles* that indicate how the variables relate to each other. *Boundaries* define the domain within which the variables interact lawfully, while *system states* portray conditions of the theoretical system in which the variables take on characteristic values that persist for some period of time. At this point, the modeling process shifts from induction to deduction, and *propositions* are derived that represent logical statements about the system. The terms in the propositions are then converted into *empirical indicators* or operational definitions which connect the variables to observations or measurements in the real world and from which *hypotheses* are formed for testing predicted relationships.

The social-psychological contributions reviewed above and elsewhere yield a large number and range of variables associated with the causation, escalation, and resolution of intergroup conflict. Thus, the choice of variables for inclusion must combine range with selectivity by including those that have been consistently identified in research or theory construction. In addition, the process of model building must place some order on this variety – for this purpose, the dimensions utilized are level of analysis, and time or point of primary influence. Three levels are required for the minimal specification of a social-psychological model of intergroup conflict: individual, group, and intergroup. On the temporal dimension, four categories of variables are identified: (1) *antecedent variables*, which exist prior to the manifest expression of the conflict and are characteristics of individuals, groups or the intergroup relationship; (2) *orientations*, which are motives, predispositions, perceptions, attitudes, and approaches that are expressed in the early stages of conflict development and escalation and have a critical bearing on the ultimate form and intensity; (3) *processes*, which refer to individual styles, group behaviors, and intergroup interactions that both express and feed into the escalating conflict; and (4) *outcomes,* which are the products and effects of the conflict.

Figure 1 presents an overview of the model with the variables organized by level of analysis and time, and the principles indicated by the connecting lines and arrows. Some principles are based on restatements and combinations from previous work, while others have been developed to fill in gaps in the theoretical logic of the model. The present model is an extension of one developed by Fisher (1990) in that social categorization has been given direct prominence, and antecedents and orientations from the five-stage

Figure 1   *The eclectic model of intergroup conflict*

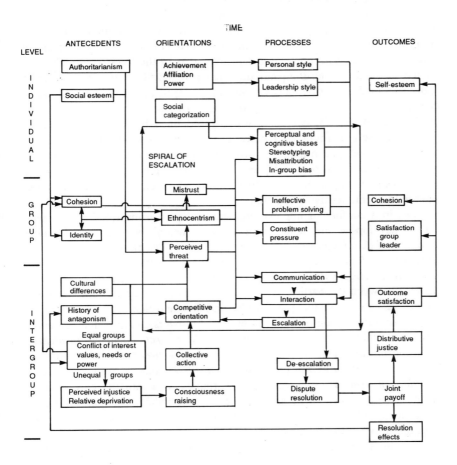

Source: Adapted with revisions from R.J. Fisher, *The Social Psychology of Intergroup and International Conflict Resolution*, Springer-Verlag Publishers, 1990. Reprinted with permission.

model of Taylor and McKirnan (1984) have been added. This expands the boundaries of the original model to include unequal groups which move toward confrontation and power parity over time. An exhaustive discussion of variables and principles will not be included here, but is available in Fisher (1990). What will be provided is a dynamic description of the development, escalation, re-cycling and resolution of intergroup conflict as captured by the variables and certain selected principles of the model. Illustrative principles from the individual, group and intergroup levels of analyses will be indicated with italics. The theoretical and empirical bases for the principles will not be cited here, but are available in Fisher (1990).

In terms of causation, the model follows RCT in positing that *real conflict of interests, values, needs, or power causes intergroup conflict*. With groups that are relatively equal and thus capable of mutual confrontation, *the conflict of interest in combination with a history of antagonism and cultural differences leads to a competitive orientation, all of which cause perceived threat*. With unequal groups, elements of the five-stage model and related theories of intergroup relations are invoked. The conflict of interest under specified conditions leads to perceived injustice (as defined by equity theory and by social exchange theory) and a sense of relative deprivation on the part of the disadvantaged group (as defined by relative deprivation theory). These conditions eventually lead to consciousness-raising activities by disadvantaged group members who have been prevented from achieving, by discrimination and oppression on the part of the advantaged group. These activities build support for collective actions which challenge the status quo and feed the competitive orientation.

Thus, in a conflict of interest situation, unequal group relationships ultimately develop to the same point as relationships between equal power groups: *real conflict causes a mutually competitive orientation and reciprocal competitive interaction*. The resulting *perceived threat causes ethnocentrism, including ingroup solidarity and outgroup hostility, which in turn causes mistrust* between the parties. At this point, antecedents at the individual and group levels also come into play. Authoritarian or anti-democratic trends in the personality functioning of both leaders and followers can heighten perceived threat and ethnocentrism. *Self-esteem is positively related to group identity and cohesion and negatively related to perceived threat and ethnocentrism.* In turn, *group identity and cohesion are positively and reciprocally related to ethnocentrism*. Thus, a variety of variables feed into the core concept of ethnocentrism, which in turn *increases perceptual and cognitive biases, decreases problem-solving competence*, and *increases constituent pressure on representatives*, all of which escalate conflict.

Orientations and processes at the individual level may also operate to escalate the conflict. The primary motives of group members and leaders, in terms of the needs for achievement, affiliation, and power, can affect both personal styles for managing conflict and leadership styles which affect group functioning, and thus intergroup interaction. Social categorization is a fundamental orientation in cognitive functioning which can induce or exaggerate perceptual and cognitive biases in stereotyping, misattribution, and ingroup favoritism. Group level variables also play a role. For example, *group cohesion is positively related to constituent pressure*; *it results in overestimation of ingroup achievements and underestimation of outgroup achievments*, and *fosters concurrence seeking which leads to ineffective problem solving*, which *results in ineffective intergroup interaction*.

All of these factors therefore operate in ways that fuel escalation. However, the primary variables which relate to escalation are to be found in mutual and reciprocal group orientations: that is, *competitive orientation, perceived threat, ethnocentrism, and mistrust escalate conflict through ineffective communication, inadequate coordination, contentious tactics, and reduced productivity.* Effects of the escalating conflict also flow back to the group level; for example, *intergroup conflict initially increases group cohesion and affects the social organization of the group in competitive directions.* The overall trend is a strong predisposition for intergroup conflicts to escalate, unless the groups have a strong cooperative, respectful relationship and related institutional structures to manage differences effectively. Escalation further feeds competitive interactions and recycles the conflict to higher and higher levels of intensity through the same orientations and processes that initially escalated the conflict. Thus, there is a built-in tendency for intergroup conflicts to become more intense and intractable, with each destructive interaction or episode adding to the costs and the commitment to win unilaterally rather than to resolve mutually. In the revised model this is captured by the *Spiral of Escalation* indicated by the box of arrows which surround the core processes of interaction (see Figure 1).

If de-escalation is brought about through mutually cooperative interaction, then resolution of the conflict and/or settlement of the current dispute is possible. This results in joint payoffs to both groups and a mutual sense of distributive justice. In addition, positive resolution-effects flow back to moderate the history of antagonism and help manage the conflict in the longer term. In addition, each group experiences outcome satisfaction, which is *positively related to group cohesion, satisfaction with the group and leader(s), and self-esteem of group members.* Thus, positive effects of resolution flow back to all three levels of variables. Overall, the principles of the model provide for linkages among the levels of analysis and yield an explanatory flow from antecedents through orientations and processes to outcomes.

3. System States and Boundaries of the Model

In Dubin's approach to theory construction (1969), system states are identifiable conditions of the theoretical system in which all of the variables take on distinctive values or ranges of values for some period of time. Thus, a model may exhibit a number of conditions that are related but not identical, and the transitions from one such state to another provide for a dynamic flow that captures crucial aspects of social reality and provides for the asking of important analytical questions. Certain variables are identified as *state coordinates* that identify and determine the characteristics of the system state and provide its distinctive name.

In the model, two system states of low- and high-intensity conflict are specified. The pivotal variable or state coordinate of *intensity* is defined following Deutsch (1973) as the objective difference between winning and losing combined with the psychological investment of the parties. Intensity usually varies also with the magnitude of coercive attempts by the parties to control each other and the level of hostility between them. Figure 2 presents

Figure 2   *System states of the eclectic model*

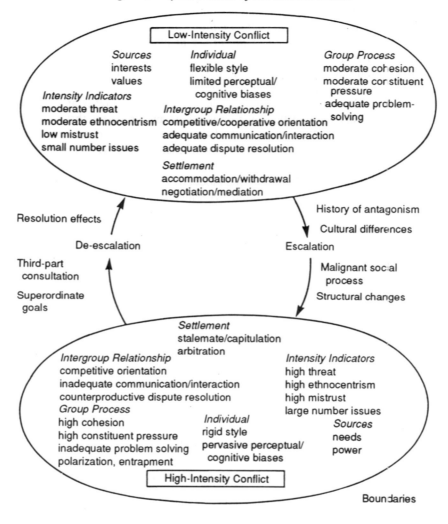

Source: R.J. Fisher, *The Social Psychology of Intergroup and International Conflict Resolution*, Springer-Verlag Publishers, 1990. Reprinted with permission.

the two system states described in terms of the primary sources of conflict, individual behavior, group processes, the intergroup relationship, the key indicators of intensity, and the typical forms of dispute settlement that are common to each state.

Low-intensity intergroup conflict is characterized by conflict of interests (resource or position scarcity) and/or values, a small number of issues, adequate individual and group functioning, a mixed competitive/cooperative orientation, and a reliance on traditional methods of dispute settlement. Although low-intensity conflict is not destructive, integrative solutions of high mutual benefit are not obtained and the situation can easily be escalated toward high intensity. The tendency to escalate is increased by the antecedents identified in the eclectic model; this process has been further described by the work of Deutsch (1983) and Pruitt and Rubin (1986) which combines elements of the conflict spiral and structural change models of escalation.

The high-intensity system state is characterized by a large number of issues and other indicators, ineffective individual and group behaviors, competitive and counter-productive intergroup interaction, and a continuing stalemate or win-lose outcome by capitulation or arbitration. However, the most important aspect of the high-intensity state is that the sources of the conflict have now shifted to the denial or frustration of basic needs and/or a struggle for power. Thus, the groups are primarily battling not for scarce resources or to propagate their values, but for their very survival in terms of identity, security, freedom and recognition. Thus, high-intensity conflict is extremely resistant to de-escalation; and only transcendent or external influences in forms such as superordinate goals (Sherif, 1966) or third-party consultation to induce mutual problem solving (Fisher, 1972, 1983) will be effective in transforming the system back to the low-intensity state.

Boundaries specify the limits within which the model is purported to hold, and are primarily established logically in relation to the characteristics of the variables and the limits of the principles. General boundaries restrict the model to the study of intergroup relations, that is, the attitudes and behaviors of members of one group in relation to members of another group, and to situations in which the above definition of intergroup conflict is met. Specific boundaries relate to each level of analysis – to individuals, groups, and the intergroup relationship. The individuals engaged in conflict covered by the model are seen as normal and well-adjusted rather than pathological; they may come from different cultural, political, and economic backgrounds, although the actual breadth of cross-cultural applicability requires empirical specification. The groups in conflict are assumed to meet the usual definitions of a group, and to have developed adequate identity, cohesion and decision-making capacity. The groups may be small or large, ranging from artificially created laboratory groups, to departments in organizations, to ethnic groups in community settings, to nations in the global context. However, the larger the groups and the more complex their relationship and environment, the more variables and principles will need to be added to the model to capture social reality. At the intergroup level, the boundaries specify that the groups exist in adequate proximity, that they engage in significant interaction and are interdependent, that is, exist in a mixed-motive relationship. The current revision of the model is applicable to groups of equal or unequal power, but it is limited to considering only two groups at a time. This is a significant limitation given the multiple interdependence and interaction that exists among groups in many social systems. Nontheless, the boundaries in total do not place severe restrictions on the domain of the model, and it is therefore deemed to be a middle-range theory of considerable scope.

4. Conclusion: Understanding Protracted Social Conflict

The overview of social-psychological contributions demonstrates that a multi-level, interactive, and phenomenological approach can contribute to inter-disciplinary understanding of the causation, escalation and resolution of intergroup conflict. The model presented is seen as both eclectic and essential in that it integrates information from a variety of sources and captures the essence of intergroup conflict in terms of dynamic processes and underlying conditions. However, the model is clearly limited in complexity at the top end, that is, beyond the simplest elements of group structure and intergroup interaction. The organizational realities of collectivities and the multitude of relations between collectivities are not represented in either structural or behavioral terms. Similarly, the complex processes of de-escalation, institutionalization, and regulation of conflict are more or less ignored. The model is a social-psychological one in the purest sense, and needs to be complemented by models developed in other disciplines in order to represent adequately the reality of intergroup conflict in real-world settings.

Nontheless, the model provides a useful summarization of the basic elements of intergroup conflict that may have utility in understanding and dealing with the most pervasive and intractable form of conflict in the world today – intense and destructive conflict between identity groups. Rupesinghe (1987) has pointed out that ethnic conflict is the major current source of manifest and direct violence, but that its study has been neglected by all relevant disciplines. Azar (1983) has coined the term 'protracted social conflict' to denote deep-seated hatred and hostile interaction between racial, religious, cultural, or ethnic groups that extends over a long period of time with sporadic outbreaks of violence. Burton (1987) speaks of 'deep-rooted conflict' that involves issues of cultural and ethnic identity, the denial of recognition and participation of minorities, and the importance of security and other essentials that are non-negotiable. The source of such conflict is not to be found in the traditional areas of economics or power, but in the denial of the developmental requirements of all people – the pursuit of which is therefore a compelling need.

A number of attempts have been made to identify a core list of basic human needs, and some consensus is emerging (Azar, 1990; Burton, 1979, 1990; Lederer, 1980). Included are needs for personal and collective security, distinct social identity, social recognition of identity, freedom, participation in decision-making, distributive justice to overcome inequity, and valued relationships with others. Distributive injustice or structural inequality combined with historically significant ethnic cleavages provides a particular focus for the frustration of basic needs and the development of protracted social conflict. Identity groups perceive that they are being victimized through a denial of their identity, an absence of security and participation, and a lack of distributive justice. Cultural differences and a history of antagonism further predispose identity groups toward protracted social conflict.

Thus, Azar and Burton have taken an inherently social-psychological approach, since they link the basic needs of the individual through the identity group to intergroup and international conflict. The eclectic model identifies basic needs as an important source of intergroup conflict, particularly in high-intensity, protracted conflict. More importantly, the model supplements the needs analysis by providing a context of conditions and processes that provides for a more comprehensive explanation of the etiology and escalation of intergroup conflict. In that way, the model can provide a stimulating juncture for further theorizing and research.

References

Adorno, T.W.; Else Frenkel-Brunswik, Daniel J. Levinson & R. Nevitt Sanford, 1950. *The Authoritarian Personality*. New York: Harper & Row.

Azar, Edward E., 1983. 'The Theory of Protracted Social Conflict and the Challenge of Transforming Conflict Situations', *Monograph Series in World Affairs*, vol. 20, no. 2, pp. 81–99.

Azar, Edward E., 1990. *The Management of Protracted Social Conflict*. Brookfield, VT: Gower Publishing.

Blake, Robert R. & Jane S. Mouton, 1961. *Group Dynamics: Key to Decision-Making*. Houston, TX: Gulf.

Brewer, Marilyn B., 1979. 'In-group Bias in the Minimal Intergroup Situation: A Cognitive-Motivational Analysis', *Psychological Bulletin*, vol. 86, no. 2., pp. 307–324.

Bruner, Jerome S., 1957. 'On Perceptual Readiness', *Psychological Review*, vol. 64, no. 1, pp. 123–152.

Burton, John W., 1979. *Deviance, Terrorism & War: The Process of Solving Unsolved Social and Political Problems*. New York: St. Martin's Press.

Burton, John W., 1987. *Resolving Deep-Rooted Conflict: A Handbook*. Lanham, MD: University Press of America.

Burton, John W., ed., 1990. *Conflict: Human Needs Theory*. New York: St. Martin's Press.

Campbell, Donald T., 1965. 'Ethnocentrism and Other Altruistic Motives', pp. 283–311 in David Levine, ed., *Nebraska Symposium on Motivation*, vol. 13. Lincoln, NB: University of Nebraska Press.

Coser, Lewis A., 1956. *The Functions of Social Conflict*. Glencoe, IL: Free Press.

Dahrendorf, Ralf, 1959. *Class and Class Conflict in Industrial Society*. Stanford, CA: Stanford University Press.

Deutsch, Morton, 1973. *The Resolution of Conflict: Constructive and Destructive Processes*. New Haven, CT: Yale University Press.

Deutsch, Morton, 1983. 'The Prevention of World War III: A Psychological Perspective', *Political Psychology*, vol. 4, no. 1, March, pp. 3–32.

Deutsch, Morton, 1990. 'Sixty Years of Conflict', *International Journal of Conflict Management*, vol. 1, no. 3, July, pp. 237–263.

Diab, Lutfy N., 1970. 'A Study of Intragroup and Intergroup Relations Among Experimentally Produced Small Groups', *Genetic Psychology Monographs*, vol. 82, no. 1, 49–82.

Dubin, Robert V., 1969. *Theory Building*. New York: The Free Press.

Dubin, Robert, 1976. 'Theory Building in Applied Areas', pp. 17–39 in Marvin D.

Dunnette, ed., *Handbook of Industrial and Organizational Psychology*. Chicago, IL: Rand-McNally.

Fisher, Ronald J., 1972. 'Third Party Consultation: A Method for the Study and Resolution of Conflict', *Journal of Conflict Resolution*, vol. 16, no. 1, March, pp. 67–94.

Fisher, Ronald J., 1983. 'Third Party Consultation as a Method of Intergroup Conflict Resolution: A Review of Studies', *Journal of Conflict Resolution*, vol. 27, no. 2, June, pp. 301–334.

Fisher, Ronald J., 1990. *The Social Psychology of Intergroup and International Conflict Resolution*. New York: Springer-Verlag.

Grant, Peter R., 1990. 'Cognitive Theories Applied to Intergroup Conflict', pp. 39–57 in Ronald J. Fisher, 1990.

Lederer, Katrin, 1980. *Human Needs*. Cambridge, MA: Oelgeschlager, Gunn & Hain.

Pruitt, Dean G. & Melvin J. Kimmel, 1977. 'Twenty Years of Experimental Gaming: Critique, Synthesis and Suggestions for the Future', *Annual Review of Psychology*, vol. 28, pp. 363–392.

Pruitt, Dean G. & Jeffrey Z. Rubin, 1986. *Social Conflict: Escalation, Stalemate, and Resolution*. New York: Random House.

Rupesinghe, Kumar, 1987. 'Theories of Conflict Resolution and Their Applicability to Protracted Ethnic Conflict', *Bulletin of Peace Proposals*, vol. 18, no. 4, pp. 527–539.

Sherif, Muzafer, 1966. *In Common Predicament: Social Psychology of Intergroup Conflict and Cooperation*. Boston, MA: Houghton Mifflin.

Sherif, Muzafer, O.J. Harvey, B. Jack White, William R. Hood & Carolyn W. Sherif, 1961. *Intergroup Conflict and Cooperation: The Robber's Cave Experiment*. Norman, OK: University of Oklahoma Book Exchange.

Stephan, Walter G., 1985. 'Intergroup Relations', pp. 599–658 in Gardner Lindzey & Elliot Aronson, eds, *Handbook of Social Psychology*, vol. 3. New York: Random House.

Sumner, William G., 1906. *Folkways*. Boston, MA: Ginn & Co.

Tajfel, Henri, 1970. 'Experiments in Intergroup Discrimination', *Scientific American*, vol. 223, no. 5, pp. 96–102.

Tajfel, Henri & John C. Turner, 1986. 'The Social Identity Theory of Intergroup Behavior', pp. 7–24 in Stephen Worchel & William G. Austin, eds, *Psychology of Intergroup Relations*, 2nd ed. Chicago, IL: Nelson-Hall.

Tajfel, Henri & Alan L. Wilkes, 1963. 'Classification and Quantitative Judgement', *British Journal of Psychology*, vol. 54, pp. 101–114.

Taylor, Donald M. & David J. McKirnan, 1984. 'A Five-Stage Model of Intergroup Relations', *British Journal of Social Psychology*, vol. 23, pp. 291–300.

Taylor, Donald M. & Fathali M. Moghaddam, 1987. *Theories of Intergroup Relations: International Social Psychological Perspectives*. New York: Praeger.

Wilder, David A., 1986. 'Social Categorization: Implications for Creation and Reduction of Intergroup Bias', pp. 291–355 in Leonard Berkowitz, ed., *Advances in Experimental Social Psychology*, vol. 19. New York: Academic Press.

9

Minority Influence and the Psycho-Social Mechanisms of Discrimination

Patricia Roux
Margarita Sanchez-Mazas
Gabriel Mugny
Juan Antonio Pérez

1. Introduction

Relations between foreigners and a particular country's nationals are frequently difficult, tense and marred by conflict. Social psychology can contribute to an understanding of such intergroup phenomena by describing the processes that underlie them. It was first demonstrated that social competition may depend upon the fact that members of discrete groups perceive an incompatibility between their particular goals. That is, social rivalry arises when the members of group A feel that the goals of group B will be achieved only at the expense of the goals of group A (Sherif, 1966). It has also been shown that intergroup tensions have deeper psychological roots. In particular, when groups evaluate and compare each other on the basis of criteria that they consider to be especially important (Brewer, 1979), discrimination against the outgroup may be employed as the means of preserving self-esteem. In this way, group members can maintain a sense of positive identity, since the group to which they belong has been rated higher than the outgroup and this superiority can be assumed by each individual member (Tajfel, 1978, 1982; Turner, 1981, 1987). Social psychologists have been interested not only in describing the dynamics that characterize intergroup relationships but also in determining the circumstances in which ingroup favoritism and outgroup discrimination do not appear. Thus, Sherif's studies have shown that the incompatibility of group goals may be overridden when there is a 'superordinate goal', i.e. when some more significant common cause can be espoused by both groups, bringing them together. Mummendey and Schreiber

* These researches are part of a joint project with members of the Laboratoire Européen de Psychologie Sociale and were carried out with the assistance of the Fonds National Suisse de la Recherche Scientifique and the French Centre National de la Recherche Scientifique.

(1983) established that discrimination against the outgroup is not observed when members of a group are allowed to reach independent judgements on their own group and on another; that is, they can place a value on their own group without the need to depreciate the other. The search for a positive social identity, which is ensured by the superiority of their own group, does not necessarily lead to ingroup favoritism. This is particularly true when group members can judge their own group favorably on the basis of certain attributes or characteristics, while recognizing the value of a different set of attributes in another group. This process of 'mutual social validation' (Rijsman, 1984; van Knippenberg & Ellemers, 1990) is fair to both groups.

2. Xenophobia and Ways of Considering Intergroup Relations

In this chapter, we are interested specifically in the determinants of xeno-phobia (negative attitude towards foreign people). Xenophobia is manifest as an unfavourable and discriminatory attitude towards people of a different nationality and is rooted partially in the social status of individuals. In the various studies we undertook of relations between Swiss nationals and foreigners, we asked a number of young nationals to quantify the extent of their agreement with various propositions that would be favorable to foreigners (such as rights to freedom of expression, certain political rights and rights to equal salaries; cf. Mugny & Pérez, 1991). Our experimental subjects were mainly apprentices and high school students; we chose these two distinct groups of young people because of the differences between them, in terms both of socio-economic and cultural backgrounds and of the nature of their education. Comparison of the results from the two groups revealed the existence of more negative attitudes towards foreigners among apprentices than among high school students (Mugny, Sanchez-Mazas, Roux & Pérez, 1991).

Similar results were obtained in response to the question of reducing the percentage of the foreign population in Switzerland (currently about 16%). The majority of apprentices are in favour of reducing this percentage, while most students wanted to maintain it at its present level or even increase it. The nature of apprenticeship is such that apprentices will enter the labor market earlier than high school students, and will therefore be exposed sooner to the pressures of productivity, particularly those linked to competition for jobs. Immigrant workers are thus more likely to be seen as a potential threat and as a group who may benefit at the expense of apprentices. Apprentices fear the diminishing of the rights they claim for themselves (such as the right to a job). This negative interdependence of the interests of nationals and foreigners would have more influence on the reasoning of apprentices than on that of the students: benefits for the outgroup would be seen as representing probable losses for the nationals. In contrast, more positive attitudes towards foreigners are often shown by those whose background tends to favor extended formal education, i.e. the high school students. The social status of these individuals is such as to give less prominence to negative interdependence as a factor in their relationships with foreigners and even to promote a feeling of solidarity with people of other national communities.

We aimed to establish whether xenophobic attitudes are function of the way in which intergroup relationships are perceived and not merely of relative social status. We were testing the hypothesis that xenophobia goes hand in hand with a perception of intergroup relationships based on *negative interdependence* ('what the other group gains, my group loses'), and that more xenophilic attitudes (positive attitudes towards foreign people) are linked to a perception of *independence*, if not solidarity or positive interdependence, between groups.

In testing this hypothesis, we studied preferences for two systems of allocating a variety of resources to Swiss nationals and foreigners (Mugny et al., 1991). The subjects had to decide on the extent to which members of the two national groups should benefit from the implementation of various resolutions, such as subsidised accommodation and minimum salary levels. Half the subjects – all Swiss nationals – were asked to apportion a total of 100 points between Swiss and foreigners for each of the resolutions. This first experimental condition produced a negative interdependence in intergroup judgements, since advantages granted to one group necessarily reduced those granted to the other. The other half of the subjects were able to award up to 100 points to Swiss nationals and, separately, up to 100 points to the foreigners. This allowed them to make quite independent judgements of the benefits that should be granted, since awards to foreigners did not detract from those that could be made to nationals.

On the basis of their responses to an initial question concerning whether or not the number of foreign residents in Switzerland should be reduced, it was possible to distinguish three types of subjects. Those who thought the number should be reduced were classed as 'xenophobes', those who wanted to maintain the status quo were classed as 'intermediates', and those who considered that the number of foreigners permitted to live and work in Switzerland should be increased were classed as 'xenophiles'.

Let us consider the principal results. First, subjects were asked a number of questions to determine their opinion of the design of the study. With regard to the experimental condition (having a 100 points to share between Swiss and foreigners or 100 points for each national category), they were asked to say whether this type of question was a fair way of presenting the problem and whether it accorded with their way of thinking. The answers they gave reflected the categories described above: the xenophobes favored a design which allowed them to respond in terms based on negative interdependence and which was more familiar to them; as for the xenophiles, they showed a preference for reasoning in independent terms and identified themselves most with the 'independent design'. Thus, we were able to verify the hypothesis that attitudes towards an outgroup are related to the way in which the individual thinks about intergroup relationships.

The second set of results that we shall consider concerns ingroup favoritism, which was measured by calculating the difference in the number of points awarded to the Swiss and to foreigners for the proposed resolutions (a positive sign indicates the allocation of more points to the ingroup). The xenophobic subjects favored their own group, i.e. the Swiss, in both the independent (m= +30) and the interdependent (m= +33) condition. The xenophilic subjects systematically applied a principle of solidarity, which was equally apparent in the independent (m= +01) and the interdependent (m= +03) condition, no difference was established in the allocation of advantages to both national categories.

The intermediate subjects, who favored maintaining the status quo, were particularly sensitive to the experimental condition. When questions were posed in interdependent terms (100 points to be shared between the two groups),there was evident ingroup favoritism (m= +15); for many resolutions, intermediate subjects clearly favored their fellow citizens. However, when questions were posed in independent terms (up to 100 points could be awarded to each group), this bias disappears (m= +05) and differences in the benefits awarded to Swiss nationals and to foreigners lost all statistical significance. Thus, given the opportunity to make separate judgements on the ingroup and the outgroup, moderate individuals (those in favor neither of reducing nor of increasing the foreign population residing in Switzerland) abandon discrimination in favor of an attitude of solidarity.

Assuming that an important proportion of a population, like that of Switzerland, may be regarded as moderate in their attitudes towards foreigners, it is easy to imagine the importance of social policies favoring one or the other sociocognitive mode. Campaigns that highlight an independent or solidary attitude towards relations between different national groups could result in a significant number of people adopting a more egalitarian stance. One might hope that children could be educated in international relations in a way that would promote this. Even so, xenophobic individuals would remain a problem: they continue to discriminate against foreigners even when given the opportunity to make independent judgements that run contrary to their usual way of considering relations between groups. The question must be asked, what psychosocial processes can prevent such individuals, whose social origins and ways of thinking are so firmly entrenched, from becoming locked in their exclusive and sociocentric attitudes? We looked for a possible solution among the processes of social influence.

3. Xenophobia and Minority Influence

Our model of influence offers certain analogies with the social reality in which such discrimination phenomena occur. Indeed, during the past 20 years, the presence of foreigners in Switzerland has been regularly challenged. Swiss citizens are periodically polled in national referenda which propose a liberalization or a restriction of the rights of immigrant workers (mainly European) or – more recently – of political refugees (mostly colored). The results of these polls have shown quite consistently that the Swiss have reservations about the foreign presence in their country, and that xenophilic attitudes are to be found only among a minority. Whatever the status of those promoting the interests of foreigners (Christians, a left-wing group or any other social movement), their position appears to be diametrically opposed to majority opinion. To persuade xenophobic (or, at least non-xenophilic) individuals to adopt a more tolerant attitude and more open-mindedness towards intergroup relations implies a minority influence on a majority attitude and way of thinking.

It therefore seems wise to turn to the model of minority influence, according to which, changes in norms, in popular opinion, mentality and values are frequently the result of intervention by active minorities (Moscovici, 1976). From the research done in this field (cf. Moscovici, Mugny & Van Avermaet, 1985; Mugny & Peréz, 1991; Paicheler, 1988), we are now interested only in the fact that the effectiveness of minority pressure for change seems to be induced by the *conflict* that it generates rather than by the approval it receives (Moscovici, 1980). A source may be rejected initially because of its minority status or the minority nature of its ideas, but ultimately succeeds in its objectives despite, or perhaps because of, the conflict it has engendered (Peréz & Mugny, 1990).

In the area of intergroup relations it is possible to advance the hypothesis that the conflict aroused by minorities may be a means of challenging the xenophobes, of attracting their attention and persuading them to reflect on the minority alternative (Mugny & Peréz, 1988). Such a reflexion would not have been reached without the minority's intervention. Even if xenophobes do not openly adopt the minority's positions, they may be sufficiently inspired to modify their attitudes and behavior in consequence (Nemeth, 1986).

Looking at the problem from this point of view (i.e. that of the conflict aroused by minorities) is a new approach and one of which no account has been taken in current social practices. Indeed, the usual observation is that people do their best to avoid ideological confrontation. Even those groups who intervene in society in attempts to attract their audience to more xenophilic positions sometimes, if not frequently, employ strategies designed to avoid conflict (Peréz, Mugny & Roux, 1989). Thus, the Christian communities who campaigned in the early 1980s to increase the rights of foreigners in Switzerland did not attempt to prescribe how their fellow citizens should vote, but rather invoked humanitarian principles and biblical rules of conduct. In this way, they systematically avoided provoking conflict – but, the campaign was a total failure. It may therefore be concluded that a minority group that, through inconsistent (in other words, insufficiently coherent) behavior (Moscovici, 1976) or over-conciliatory dialogue, generates too little conflict has scant chance of altering public attitude (in this case xenophobia) or even of persuading the public to consider its proposal.

An experiment by Mugny & Peréz (1985), directly inspired by this anti-xenophobic campaign, illustrates the efficacy of minority persuasion where greater conflict is provoked. We compared the effects on a Christian-derived population of various pro-foreigner messages, designed to be more or less provocative. Eight messages were composed in an effort to simulate both the strategies adopted by the Christian communities described above and more provocative campaigns. The messages were similar to one another but differed in three parameters so as to produce different levels of conflict (weak or strong). Each experimental subject was exposed to only one of the messages, and the intention was to measure the impact of the messages by comparing the reactions of those who read them.

Half of the subjects were exposed to messages advancing accepted humanitarian claims, such as the rights for foreigners to freedom to speech and to social security, and half to more radical messages that advanced claims more usually rejected, in particular the right of foreigners to vote in Switzerland. Moreover, half the messages advanced these claims on the basis of religious principles and, since the experimental population was Christian, induced only weak conflict. The other half based their argument on political principles, which produced greater conflict in these subjects. Finally, half the messages were formulated in conciliatory terms ('It is to be hoped that ...') and half in a more rigid and constraining manner ('It is absolutely necessary that ...').

To reiterate, one of the messages effectively reproduced, in tone and content, that used by the Christian communities in their appeal: widespread humanitarian claims were proposed in a conciliant manner, in the name of biblical principles that subjects could recognize as their own in view of their Christian identity. The other messages were more conflictual, as they introduced more radical claims, they used a more rigid tone and/or they used a more political argumentation difficult for our experimental population to accept.

After subjects had been exposed to one of the messages, they were questioned about their attitudes to foreigners and about whether they approved or disapproved of the various proposals that would benefit foreigners. The results showed that attitudes differed according to the nature of the message presented. Least favorable attitudes were recorded among those subjects exposed to the least provocative message, that is a message based on biblical and humanitarian principles and framed in conciliatory terms. Conversely, and as predicted by the minority influence model, the messages designed to provoke the greatest conflict were those that produced the least discrimination against foreigners. Thus, ideological confrontation with minority ideas has potential innovatory power.

4. Minority Influence and In(ter)dependence of Judgements

As shown above, a relationship exists between people's attitudes to foreigners and the independence or negative interdependence of their thinking with respect to intergroup relations. But what happens to the thinking of the xenophobe who is confronted with a minority argument that provokes conflict? Can minorities influence an attitude of discrimination by persuading the xenophobe to think in independent terms, that is to consider the interests of two groups as no longer being mutually exclusive? In another experiment (Mugny et al., 1991, expt 2), we combined minority influence with both judgement modalities – independence and interdependence. Half of the experimental subjects were presented with a highly xenophilic message couched in conciliatory terms as before ('It is to be hoped that ...'). The other half were given a more rigid message ('It is absolutely necessary that ...'). Subjects were then asked to express themselves as being in favor of Swiss nationals on the one hand or foreigners on the other with respect to five separate issues (rights to social security, minimum wage, training assistance, unemployment benefits, and subsidised accomodation). As in the earlier experiment, half of the subjects had to apportion a total of 100 points between Swiss nationals and foreigners, and the other half could award up to 100 points to each group. Lastly, subjects were asked to complete a questionnaire relating to their attitudes to foreigners, expressing their approval or disapproval for a number of resolutions that would benefit foreigners. Analysis of the results concentrated on those subjects classified as xenophobic on the basis of their initially expressed desire to reduce the number of foreigners living and working in Switzerland.

The results of this study confirmed our earlier observations, that xeno-phobic individuals favor their fellow nationals regardless of the style of the message (conciliatory or rigid) or the mode of judgement (independent or interdependent). Thus, confrontation with the minority viewpoint is not in itself sufficient to counteract the typical discriminatory attitude adopted by xenophobic individuals. Nevertheless, it is important to emphasize that subjects granted more points (and hence more advantages), not only to Swiss, but also to foreigners, in the independent than in the interdependent condi-tions. Moreover, in allowing subjects to be more generous, the independent conditions of judgements also promote a line of reasoning that is opposed to intergroup competition. Indeed, the correlation between points allocated to the ingroup and to the outgroup is close to -1 in the interdependent conditions but approaches 0 and loses all statistical significance in the conditions of independence, i.e. when benefits for the Swiss are not granted at the expense of foreign nationals.

At the end of the experiment, subjects were asked for their opinions on the pro-foreigner resolutions. At this level, the influence of the minority message becomes evident. Subjects who were led to reason in independent terms, i.e. were allowed to award up to 100 points to both groups, clearly displayed less unfavorable attitudes toward foreigners than subjects who had to make interdependent judgements. Freed of the constraint of a competitive relationship between the two groups, which was seen as threatening their own interests, subjects were able to espouse the more egalitarian approach of the minority cause. The more firmly the minority message was expressed, the more pronounced was this effect, which confirms the conclusions drawn in the earlier study.

Subjects of the present study, all of whom had tended towards xenophobia, initially resisted the minority influence and showed clear national favoritism in the first allocation of points to the two groups. Later, however, when confronted with resolutions that would benefit foreigners and allowed to make judgements in the independent mode, they curbed this tendency, particularly when the minority position was highly provocative. It therefore seems that the articulation of an independent approach to intergroup relations with a certain intensity of conflict generated by the minority message, predisposes to an attitude of solidarity or equality that could counteract, if not substitute, discrimination.

5. Conclusions

The foregoing observations open various avenues of thought on counteracting discrimination. On a superficial level, assessing the importance of relative social status as a determinant of xenophobia suggests that the integration of foreigners into society would be less fraught with conflict if nationals did not perceive this process as threatening their own access to certain rights. In other words, a lessening of social injustice and of inequity of rights would do much to reduce conflict between national groups. Many of the xenophobic objections raised about the presence of foreigners in Switzerland are expressed in terms of rising unemployment, housing shortages, budgetary cuts, inadequacy of pensions, tax increases, etc., all of which cause greater problems for the most disadvantaged sections of the society. Categories such as apprentices are highly susceptible to this type of argument, which finds expression as a belief in the negative interdependence of the interests of Swiss nationals and the interests of foreigners.

Of course, it may seem very idealistic to count upon the introduction of a global policy that could help install the conditions for the development of a feeling of equity and social justice that would favor pleasant relations between Swiss and foreigners. The current situation shows that for the time being only minorities nourish such a project and are trying to involve part of the public opinion, thereby creating psychosocial conditions that would favor concrete changes. Social psychology's approach of the processes linked to minority impact can suggest a certain number of considerations to take into account while planning campaigns in favor of foreigners.

A first idea is that minorities could attempt to counter the logic of the negative interdependence of group interests. Anti-racist and anti-xenophobic movements should stress that the interests of the Swiss and those of foreigners can be complementary and a source of mutual enrichment. In doing so, they would demonstrate that these interests are not exclusive and source of social decline. This seems to be the message conveyed by recent campaigns in favor of full citizenship of foreigners in the adoptive land: the joint study of problems equally shared by nationals and foreigners (housing, environment, education, etc.) with the aim of improving the standards of living of the less-favored residents. For a principle of solidarity to substitute discriminatory behavior, one must promote the idea that the answer to the social and economic problems as experienced by Swiss citizens does not imply a strong defense of their interests against those of foreigners. Such an approach would help go beyond an interdependent vision of the world that nowadays is still very common, particularly in certain groups or organizations that give precedence to the defense of social and economical positions for their nationals and thereby encourage the reasoning characteristic of xenophobia and the discriminatory attitudes that go along with it.

A second idea relates to the notion of conflict. A large number of groups defending the interests of foreigners, immigrants and refugees, most often develop a strategy of minimal conflict, using humanitarian ideals as their main argumentation and are reluctant to adventure themselves in a socio-political field that socially proves to be more conflictual. This fear of conflict (that is perhaps overdeveloped in Switzerland, as it is a country used to a certain level of 'social peace'), brings us to one last conclusion in the light of the results of the researches we presented in this chapter. It was indeed shown that conflict could generate personal questioning and innovation. Whereas majorities may call upon the power of consensus to convey their ideas (as is widely done in this country), minorities have another type of argumentation at their disposal: conflict. But, in the case of relations between Swiss and foreigners for instance, the minorities advocating this cause ultimately aim at the establishment of a more equitable and tolerant world, or in other words a more pacific one. Would there then be a certain contradiction between ends and means? between a pacific world and a strategy of conflict?

A positive answer to this question would be contrary to the processes we have analyzed. Confrontation is a mediation that brings individuals to de-center themselves by considering referents other than their own, to set their vision of the world aside and realize the existence of other points of view. Given the opportunity to recognize different points of view, it is then possible for individuals to integrate them in one way or another, at least partly, to their modes of thinking and in their attitudes. The refusal of confrontation too often implies a reproduction of social relations in terms of hierarchy of power, interests and rights. By contrast, the conflict induced by active minorities can bring individuals into the process of redefining these relations.

References

Brewer, M.B., 1979. 'Ingroup bias in the minimal intergroup situation: a cognitive-motivational analysis', *Psychological Bulletin*, vol. 86, pp. 307–324.

Moscovici, S., 1976. *Social Influence and Social Change*. London: Academic Press.

Moscovici, S., 1980. 'Toward a theory of conversion behavior', pp. 209–239, vol. 13 in L. Berkowitz, ed., *Advances in experimental social psychology*. New York: Academic Press.

Moscovici, S.; G. Mugny & E. Van Avermaet, eds, 1985. *Perspectives on minority influence*. Cambridge, Paris: Cambridge University Press, Editions de la Maison des Sciences de l'Homme.

Mugny, G. & J.A. Peréz, 1985. 'Influence sociale, conflit et identification: étude expérimentale autour d'une persuasion "manquée" lors d'une votation', *Cahiers de Psychologie Sociale*, vol. 26, pp. 1–13.

Mugny, G. & J.A. Peréz, 1988. 'Minority influence and constructivism in social psychology', *Newsletter British Psychological Society*, Social Psychology Section, vol. 19, pp. 56–77.

Mugny, G. & J.A. Peréz, 1991. *The social psychology of minority influence*. Cambridge: Cambridge University Press, 1991.

Mugny, G.; M. Sanchez-Mazas, P. Roux & J.A. Peréz, 1991. 'Independence and interdependence of group judgments: xenophobia and minority influence', *European Journal of Social Psychology*, vol. 21, pp. 213–223.

Mummendey, A. & H.J. Schreiber, 1983. 'Better or just different? Positive social identity by discrimination against, or by differentiation from outgroups', *European Journal of Social Psychology*, vol. 13, pp. 389–397.

Nemeth, C., 1986. 'Differential contributions of majority and minority influence', *Psychological Review*, vol. 93, pp. 23–32.

Paicheler, G., 1988. *The psychology of social influence*. Cambridge: Cambridge University Press.

Peréz, J.A. & G. Mugny, 1990. 'Minority influence, manifest discrimination and latent influence', pp. 152–168 in D. Abrams and M. Hogg, eds, *Social identity theory: constructive and critical advances*. Hertfordshire: Harvester-Wheatsheaf.

Peréz, J.A.; G. Mugny & P. Roux, 1989. 'Evitement de la confrontation idéologique: quelques déterminants psychosociaux des stratégies persuasives', *Revue Internationale de Psychologie Sociale*, vol. 2, pp. 151–163.

Rijsman, J.B., 1984. 'Group characteristics and individual behavior', pp. 451–479 in P.J.D. Drenth, H. Thierry, P.J. Willems & C.J. de Wolff, eds, *Handbook of work and organizational psychology*. New York: Wiley.

Sherif, M., 1966. *In common predicament. Social psychology of intergroup conflict and cooperation*. Boston, MA: Houghton Mifflin.

Tajfel, H., ed., 1978. *Differentiation between social groups: studies in the social psychology of intergroup relations*. London: Academic Press.

Tajfel, H., 1982. *Social identity and intergroup relations*. Cambridge: Cambridge University Press.

Turner, J.C., 1981. 'Towards a cognitive redefinition of the social group', *Cahiers de Psychologie Cognitive*, vol. 1, pp. 93–118.

Turner, J.C.; M. Hogg, P.J. Oakes, S.D. Reicher & M.S. Wetherell, 1987. *Rediscovering the social group. A self-categorization theory*. Oxford: Basil Blackwell.

Van Knippenberg, A. & N. Ellemers, 1990. 'Social identity and intergroup differentiation processes', in M. Hewstone & W. Stroebe, eds, *European Review of Social Psychology*, vol. 1. Chichester: Wiley.

10

Community Psychology Applied to Peace Studies*

Julie E. Criss
Paula B. Johnson

1. Introduction

This chapter addresses several ways in which theory from community psychology can be applied to peace studies and to the generation of non-violent solutions to international conflict.

Since the end of World War II, the field of psychology has gradually increased its focus on the study of the causes and prevention of war. Across various areas of the field (e.g., social, biological, cognitive, development, humanistic, experimental, and clinical), psychology has investigated such topics as public opinion towards nuclear war; the psycho-social consequences of the arms race; psycho-biological explanations of war; paranoid attitudes toward the enemy; dehumanization of the enemy; perceptions of risk or threat; conflict resolution; nationalism and ethnocentrism; and gender issues, to name a few (Jacobs, 1989). The area of *community psychology*, however, is noticeably absent from the above mentioned research. Community psychology models have much to offer the growing field of peace studies. Community psychology has at its basis an ecological/interactional model, values of cultural relativity and diversity, a focus on searching for new paradigms, theory that enables examination of social issues at multiple levels, and an openness to multidisciplinary approaches (Rappaport, 1977). It is also more applied than most other areas of psychology.

Community psychology was born during the 1960s, a time of awakening social conscience and activism. It had and still has close ties with clinical psychology. However, social and economic injustices were recognized as contributing to psycho-social distress. As such, the locus of intervention

* A preliminary version of this chapter was presented at the annual convention of the Rocky Mountain Psychological Association and the Western Psychological Association, Reno, Nevada, April 1989.

shifted from the individual to larger social contexts, or systems (i.e., the family, school, neighborhood, organizations, institutions, social structures, and the economy). This 'ecological' view of human issues focuses on the interaction between persons and their environment: not only do environments influence persons, but persons also have the capacity to influence their environment (Rappaport, 1977; 1986). In order to understand human behavior, and how to change it, it is important to understand the systems within which people function. The understanding of systems and how change occurs within systems is particularly relevant to the prevention of war. Viewing war and its prevention and peace and its promotion from a systems perspective is not necessarily a new idea (e.g., Holt, 1984, 1987; Macy, 1983), but community psychology models can help articulate how it might be done.

In this chapter, three major theoretical concepts from community psychology are applied to the psychological study of war and peace, as well as to the interventions taken by the populace and policy-makers. First, the concepts of first and second-order change will be described (Watzlawick, Weakland, & Fisch, 1974). Next, the concepts of problem selection, definition, and formation are discussed (Seidman, 1986; Rappaport, 1986; Watzlawick et al., 1974). Finally, suggestions for community psychology's participation in peace studies are made with regard to the concepts of second-order change, metasystems, reframing, and empowerment (Rappaport, 1986; Seidman, 1986; Watzlawick et al., 1974). The purpose is to raise questions about how people in general, and psychologists, social scientists, and policy-makers in particular, are approaching war and peace, and to lay a framework of thought that may increase their effectiveness in promoting peace.

Other areas of community psychology and how they might be related to peace studies will not be covered here, but it should be noted that they are of great potential value in promoting peace. For example, Sarason's work on the creation of settings (1972) and his work on the psychological sense of community (1974) might be applied to some of the solutions that are being proposed by the peace movement.

However, before interventions can be planned, the concept of how change occurs and how problems are defined needs to be re-evaluated. Thus, as a first step, this chapter includes only a small part of community psychology models, and an initial conceptualization of how theory from community psychology may be useful in the future.

2. First- and Second-Order Change

Watzlawick et al. (1974) have contributed a great deal towards the understanding of both persistence and change within human systems. Watzlawick and colleagues distinguish between two forms of change: first- and second-order change. First-order change is an extension of Group Theory which postulates that a group is made up of members who share some common characteristic. One can change or substitute the members of a group, but little has changed with regard to the way members interact with each other. No matter how many different combinations of behaviors are enacted, the outcome will still be the same. The group has not changed (though individuals within the group may have changed), until the rules of interaction change. Ultimately, a system can exhaust all possible internal changes without systemic change occurring. While Group Theory is useful for understanding persistence and change within a system, the Theory of Logical Types is relevant to understanding how change occurs from outside a system or group.

The Theory of Logical Types regards a collection of similar 'things' as a class, rather than a group. A class is both quantitatively and qualitatively different from a member. For instance, it would not make sense to describe a population in terms of one individual: an individual is part of the population, but the entire population is not an individual (Watzlawick et al., 1974). Thus, the level of change one can attempt with an individual and with a population is very different. Unfortunately, research and theory in psychology have often mistakenly viewed a population as having the same dynamics as individuals.

According to Watzlawick et al. a member of the class may change his or her particular behavior, but this does little to influence the way the class operates as a whole. In order to change the behavior of the entire class, change must occur on a level higher than the individual level, on a 'metalevel'. The class can be defined by the 'rules of the game' that direct the interaction among its members. Watzlawick et al. use the analogy of what a person might do within a nightmare (for example, scream, jump off a cliff). The person can change his/her behavior within a nightmare (first-order change), but cannot stop the nightmare itself. Waking is a way out of the nightmare, a change to a different state, or different rules. The latter would then be second-order change. It is interesting to note that the 'waking up' analogy is used in peace movements to express the recognition of the unacceptability of war (e.g., Glendinning, 1987). Perhaps this sort of 'quantum leap' from one set of rules of the game to another could be part of what Einstein meant by 'a new way of thinking'. Holt (1981, 1987) has suggested social systems analysis as a move in this direction. Watzlawick et al. (1974) explicitly described second-order change as 'systemic change' (p. 22), or change that makes it impossible to follow the old 'rules of the game.' Once change has occurred at a systems level, members can no longer interact in the old ways.

In peace studies, there may be a tendency to focus the problem definition at an individual level, thus perpetuating first-order change. For instance, many studies focus on the individual dynamics of a policy-maker. One example of how second-order change might be achieved is to work with values and assumptions ('rules of the game') about how policy-makers in various cultures interact with each other. This follows the Watzlawick et al. (1974) description of second-order change as operating on the interactions between member elements and thereby defining a new set of rules. Second-order change involves 'metalevel' change, or change that creates systematic change: Such change involves the transformation of the 'rules' which reflect the values and structure of the group. According to Watzlawick et al. (1974), second-order change always comes from outside the system. This is because a 'system cannot generate from itself the conditions for its own change; it cannot produce the rules for the change of its own rules' (p. 22). However, others (e.g., Schaef, 1981; Weick, 1984) show how within system change can have ripple effects that help redefine the system. Such change may be initiated by those 'dissidents' who refuse to play the game the old way; those who are not real stakeholders in the system, but members of a different 'class'. Such may have been the process of change emerging in the Soviet Union in 1989. This example highlights the important role of dissidence in healthy adaptive change within societies. Watzlawick et al. consider second-order change the only 'real' change, and change that is necessary for the healthly functioning of systems.

The concepts of first- and second-order apply well to the problem of war and to how it has been studied by psychologists. Throughout this chapter, it will be argued that many of the interventions proposed by researchers and by policy-makers may be characterized as applying first-order change when second-order change is needed. The issue of problem formation is essential to the level of change attempted. This is addressed in the next section along with a discussion of how problems are maintained.

3. Problem Formation

The issue of problem selection, definition, and formation is central to the change process because what is done about a problem is based on the assumptions one makes about the problem (Caplan & Nelson, 1973; Seidman, 1986;). In this section, three ways of creating and maintaining problems are discussed in terms of first-order change solutions (Watzlawick et al., 1974), followed by a discussion of what Seidman (1986) refers to as errors of conceptualization.

3.1 More of the Same

Problems are often not seen as problems until deviance from some norm is noticed. The most obvious solution for combating deviance is to meet the unwanted behavior with its opposite. While this approach appears simple and logical, it has the unintended effect of exacerbating the problem because action it taken at the wrong level. (Watzlawick et al., 1974)

First-order change can lead to 'no way out' impasses that make second-order change difficult because the system that needs changing is being reinforced. Watzlawick et al. (1974) state that a policy like deterrence is an example of first-order change because it includes no provisions for its own resolution. In the case of military build-up, the difficulty- was initially seen as threat from another country. In order to remedy the difficulty, a nation increases its military arsenal. The opposing nation, in turn, increases their arsenal. What has happened is that 'more of the same' is assumed to 'fix' the problem. This is a real example of how a solution actually becomes the problem. Such 'solutions' of more (or less) of the same are examples of applying first-order change when second-order change was needed; ultimately preventing lasting system change. Watzlawick et al. specifically indicate that responding to force with counter force is an example of more of the same which often leads to a stand-off. Instances of more of the same seem to abound in history. The potential of second-order change for resolving such 'solutions' will be discussed below.

3.2 Simplification

According to Watzlawick et al. (1974), simplification is a form of denial wherein problems are ignored, minimized or seen in unidimensional terms so that although action is necessary, none is taken. The longer the problem is ignored, the more serious it actually becomes. Such denial has been found to be dangerous on an individual and collective level in a nuclear world (Lehnert, 1990).

Watzlawick et al. (1974) state that the process of simplification occurs because although people may be aware of a problem, they are socialized to keep this observation to themselves. When the majority of people agree to pretend that a problem does not exist, those who acknowledge the existence of the problem are regarded as deviant. If they see a problem, then the problem must be theirs. This has been a common experience among minority groups and feminists, who are either blamed for seeing, or for causing the problem (Ryan, 1971). Similarly, Gilbert (1988) and Macy (1983) report that lack of support for nuclear arms may be seen as unpatriotic. Macy (1983) indicates that many people avoid questioning armament issues for fear of appearing stupid, too emotional, causing distress, or sowing panic. Peace researchers have also been criticized by the defense community as being 'naive' or unrealistic by looking for non-violent alternatives to international conflict. Weick (1984) shows how it is quite common for those who don't accept dominant belief systems to be labeled as 'naive'. Thus, the denial is maintained by finding fault with those who bring up the issue.

A major example of simplification can be seen in the common definition of peace as the 'absence of war' (Brock-Utne, 1985; Milbrath, 1988; Wagner, 1988). This oversimplification allows public and policy-makers alike to ignore the complexity of the concept of peace, namely, its connection to other social problems. For instance, peace, environmental, multicultural, feminist researchers have recently begun to view the problems of war, violence, racism, sexism, and environmental exploitation as sharing common roots in dominant cultural attitudes and beliefs (Brock-Utne, 1985; Capra, 1982; Eisler, 1988; Galtung, 1985; Johnson & Friedman, 1989; Milbrath, 1988; Miller-Kustek, 1989; Reardon, 1985).

3.3 The Utopia Syndrome

Watzlawick and colleagues (1974) state that for centuries, humans have sought an ideal society where there is perfection and greatness. When people become aware of the discrepancy between the way things are and the way they think things 'should be', they begin to look for 'an ultimate, all embracing solution'

(p. 48). When people fail to achieve their goal, they become immobilized, angry, frustrated and tend to quit. It is not difficult to become overwhelmed with the growing problems of our time such as the threat of conventional and nuclear war, the progressive destruction of the environment and the growing disparity between those that 'have' and those that 'have not'.

This belief that a panacea, or *the* solution, exists discourages new thinking and action, because if a particular intervention does not work, one either believes that one has not tried hard enough, or that the problem cannot be solved. The chance that it may not be the 'right' solution (or that there can be more than one solution), is not considered (Seidman, 1986; Watzlawick et al., 1974) . In this way, one misses the goals one could realize.

Weick (1984) addresses such utopian thinking by promoting an approach of 'small wins' in which we can: ' recast larger problems into smaller, less arousing problems, so that people can identify a series of controllable opportunities of modest size that can be gathered into synoptic solutions. This strategy of small wins addresses social problems by working directly on their construction and indirectly on their solution' (p. 40). For example, if one's long-term goals are for peace, encompassing justice, equality, and a healthy environment, it may be helpful to approach these in terms of 'small win' projects that can be successful.

3.4 Errors of Conceptualization and Level of Intervention

The concepts of 'more of the same', 'simplification', and the 'Utopia Syndrome', are examples of what Seidman (1986) refers to as 'errors of conceptualization' in which the 'wrong' problem is the focus of interventions applied at the 'wrong' level. Inevitably, any solution that is based on the 'wrong' problem definition will lead to first-order change, creating no change, and /or exacerbating the problem.

Caplan and Nelson (1973) discussed the importance of how problems are defined, because any action or inaction will be based on whether the cause of the problem is seen as residing within the individual or within the external environment. The Western values of autonomous individualism, competition, and success tend to lead to a 'victim-blaming', or a 'causal attributional bias' in which the individual is blamed for his/her problems (Caplan & Nelson, 1973; Ryan, 1971). Despite ample evidence pointing to social, or situational influences on behavior, the individual still remains the locus of change.

Once the problem has been defined and acted upon (i.e., an intervention has been designed and implemented) there is an investment in maintaining the established definition. Institutions are built and maintained based on popular conceptions of problems and solutions, making alternative problem definitions difficult to consider (Caplan & Nelson, 1973).

The dominant Western societal value of individualism has strongly influenced the way psychologists have approached the study of war and peace, as well as most other issues (Ryan, 1983). According to Jacobs (1989) and Wagner (1988), psychology has tended to focus on individualistic explanations of the causes of war such as motivation as drive reduction or the avoidance of pain. Although potentially valuable information has been produced, conceptualizing problems in terms of individuals may prevent us from seeing the complexity of the total picture (Caplan & Nelson, 1973). Interventions at levels other than the individual are needed; examples of which will be presented in the next section.

4. Problem Solution

In this section, problem resolution will be discussed in terms of concepts of second-order change and reframing, and examples of metachange. Finally, the distinction between 'negative' and 'positive' approaches to peace will be discussed in terms of empowerment.

4.1 Second-order Change

Watzlawick et al. (1974) have formulated three postulates regarding second-order change. First, some decisive action should always be applied to the so-called 'solution', not the 'problem' as it is defined. According to Watzlawick and colleagues, it is this ' solution' that has created the problem in the first place . This may seem to be a radical thought, but in the case of war, war was the solution to some initial difficulty (e.g., getting what someone else had or keeping what you have got [Dyer, 1985]).

Second, Watzlawick et al. tell us that the second-order change solution is likely to appear unexpected. This is because such a solution requires people to challenge their faulty assumptions about what the problem is, and how it is maintained. For example, the concept of deterrence is based on a competitive, defensive view of a designated enemy. A novel, or second-order change solution to this adversarial approach might be one in which two countries collaborate to share their resources for peaceful projects such as toxic cleanup, or the exploration of space (Wagner, 1988). Another example of an 'unexpected' solution is that environmental distress has become a catalyst to peaceful conflict resolution across national boundaries. Similarly, a striking example of creating change occurred when the Aquino government took over from Marcos in the Philippines. Demonstrators approached troops, not with force, but in terms of their common status as citizens. As a result, the rules of the game were changed from adversarial to co-operative relationships, a second-order solution.

Third, it is important to apply the second-order solution to the problem in the 'here and now'. The goal is to understand what is being done to perpetuate the problem at this moment, to understand the present assumptions and structures.

4.2 International Metasystem Change

In the case of international conflict, what needs to be addressed may include deep-seated millennia-old beliefs and values associated with social systems that support violence as a way of resolving conflict. Such values may be so entrenched that they are largely non-conscious: even an erudite fish could not define water. Watzlawick et al. describe second-order change as metachange which requires moving to new levels of analysis. The present authors suggest the possibility that such 'meta' level conceptualizations are particularly useful in understanding international dynamics. Metasystems of 'rules of the game' in multinational and multicultural conflict may represent significant global paradigms that are beginning to be defined. Attempts to identify paradigms or 'metagames' have included, variously, the 'dominant social paradigm' (Milbrath, 1988); the dominator model (Eisler, 1988); patriarchal structure (Brock-Utne, 1985; Criss, 1990; Johnson, Handler & Criss, 1993; Reardon, 1985; Spretnak, 1983); lack of balance in Western values (Capra, 1982; Johnson & Friedman, 1989); ritualized ideology (Larsen, 1986); and H-type mindscapes (Maruyama, 1983). Fortunately, these authors have also suggested alternatives. This 'game', as it now stands, refers to a set of interrelated beliefs, values, attitudes, and behaviors that perpetuate war and structural violence.

Rappaport (1977) refers to values as integral to the functions of social systems, while Holt (1987) writes of war and peace systems in terms of values, beliefs, and myths. Defining problems in terms of values and related concepts may lead to useful reframing of the rules of the game (Johnson et al., 1993).

4.3 Reframing

According to Watzlawick et al. (1974), reframing is the act of changing one's 'conceptual and/or emotional' experience of a situation. The situation is placed in another framework which can equally (or even better) explain the facts of the situation. The real change occurs on the level of conceptualization; it is not the facts about the situation that are changed, but the meaning that has been attributed to those facts. The change is in beliefs and values concerning a particular reality.

Reframing is considered second-order change because it requires that underlying values, beliefs, and attitudes (i.e., the rules of the game) be questioned. When an interpretation of reality is challenged and changed, people cannot return to old ways of playing the game. In effect, a new game has been developed.

According to Watzlawick et al., successful problem resolution by reframing requires that the problem or 'symptom' be taken out of the existing reality and be placed in a new reality, 'frame' or 'class'. This new frame does not promote a view of unchangeability; rather, the new frame offers a 'way out'. Furthermore, the new framework respects the views, opinions, expectations, and assumptions of the people who are currently experiencing the problem. If the reframing is to work, the problem must be redefined in a way that makes sense to people; it must be 'translated' into their language. Thus, cultural variations of the metagame described above would need to be taken into account. For example, concepts of compromise and retaliation have different meanings in different cultures (Kimmel et al., 1989). Community psychologists can help to reframe the problems of war and peace by suggesting alternative ways of arriving at scenarios that do not accept some of the current definitions of the dominant world order. One such alternative is discussed in the next, final, section.

4.4 Conclusion: Reframing War

Wagner (1988) distinguishes between 'negative' and 'positive' approaches to the problem of war. He points out that the 'negative' goal of avoidance of war has been a priority because of the increasing nuclear threat posed by both superpowers. Avoiding war is a reactive, concrete and short-term approach to a serious problem. However, focusing only on the prevention of war precludes us from conceptualizing concrete 'positive' goals in the promotion of peace (Wagner, 1988).

Rappaport (1986) called for a social policy of empowerment over prevention. He discussed how the concept of prevention is grounded in the belief that people are 'dependent children' who need to be helped, or protected from the harmful effects of society. This belief leads to interventions that perpetuate the 'expert-helper' stance, in which professionals decide what is best for others.

Empowerment, however, has to do with 'enhancing the possibilities for people to control their own lives' and views people as 'full human beings with both needs and rights' (Rappaport, 1986, p. 154). Whereas prevention suggests the use of professional 'experts', empowerment suggests collaboration between people, regardless of professional level.

The concept of empowerment is useful as a means of moving away from the negative goal of 'preventing war' to a positive goal of 'promoting peace.' Problems of war can be reframed into solutions of peace. This is a major undertaking within peace research at present, and one in which psychology and many other disciplines as well as ordinary citizens are playing a role. Wagner (1988) believes that the goals of creating peace may be more difficult to reach, but once attained, they are much more easily maintained than the goals aimed at preventing war.

As mentioned earlier, peace is more than simply the absence of war (Brock-Utne, 1985; Galtung, 1984). Peace might be defined in terms of 'social justice', or increased access to social, political, and economic resources for those who have been traditionally-denied equality – such as minorities and women (Brock-Utne, 1985). Peace might also be defined as an increased international awareness of, and commitment to, protecting the environment that we share (Milbrath, 1988).

All of these possibilities have to do with the empowerment of the populace, and in particular of disenfranchised groups and cultures that can offer new frameworks. Empowerment, far from being utopian in nature, can involve small, concrete actions towards specific problems, as Watzlawick et al. (1974) and Weick (1984) have encouraged. Empowerment in a post-modern world (Sampson, 1989) also requires new views of individuals in relation to society, and social issues in relation to each other. Community psychology applied to peace studies can help provide for this empowerment by assisting in the questioning of assumptions and the reframing of war systems to peace systems.

References

Brock-Utne, Birgit, 1985. *Educating for Peace : A Feminist Perspective*, New York: Pergamon.

Caplan, Nathan & Stephen Nelson, 1973, March. 'On Being Useful', *American Psychologist*, vol. 28, no. 3, pp. 199–211.

Capra, Fritjof, 1982. *The Turning Point. Science, Society and the Rising Culture*. New York: Bantam.

Criss, Julie E., 1990. 'Patriarchal Structures in Acceptance of War and Peace: Values of Dominance. Competitive Hierarchy. Instrumentalism, and Masculinity'. Unpublished doctoral dissertation, California School of Professional Psychology, Los Angeles.

Dyer, Gwynne, 1985. *War*. New York: Crown.

Eisler, Riane, 1988. *The Chalice and the Blade*. San Francisco: Harper and Row.

Galtung, John, 1985. 'Twenty-five Years of Peace Research: Ten Challenges and Some Responses', *Journal of Peace Research*, vol. 22, no. 2, pp. 141–158.

Gilbert, Richard K., 1988. 'The Dynamics of Inaction. Psychological Factors Inhibiting Arms Control Activism', *American Psychologist*, vol. 43, no. 10, pp. 755–764.

Glendinning, Chellis, 1987. *Waking Up in the Nuclear Age. The Book of Nuclear Therapy*. New York: Beach Tree Books.

Holt, Robert R., 1984. 'Can Psychology Meet Einstein's Challenge?', *Political Psychology*, vol. 5, no. 2, pp. 199–225.

Holt, Robert R., 1987. 'Converting the War System to a Peace System: Some Contributions from Psychology and Other Social Sciences'. Paper presented at the Exploratory Project on the Conditions for Peace, Cohasset, MA.

Jacobs, Marilyn, 1989. *American Psychology and The Quest For Nuclear Peace*. New York: Praeger.

Johnson, Paula B. & Dana Friedman, 1989. 'Western Values and War'. Paper presented at the annual meeting of the Western Psychological Association and the Rocky Mountain Psychological Association, Reno, Nevada.

Johnson, Paula B., Andy Handler & Julie E. Criss, 1993. 'Beliefs Related to Acceptance of War: A Social Systems Approach', in Knud Larsen (ed.) *Conflict and Social Psychology*. London: Sage.

Kimmel, Paul, Raymond Cohen & Glen Fisher, 1989. 'The Influence of Inter Cultural Factors on the International Negotiations'. Paper presented at the annual meeting of the International Society for Inter Cultural Education and Research (SIETAR), Boston, MA.

Larsen, Knud, 1986. 'Social Psychological Factors in Military Technology and Strategy', *Journal of Peace Research*, vol. 23, no. 4, pp. 391–398.

Lehnert, Bettina, 1990. 'Nuclear Denial. Individual and Systemic Denial of Nuclear Threat'. Unpublished doctoral dissertation, California School of Professional Psychology, Los Angeles.

Macy, Joanna R., 1983. *Despair and Personal Empowerment in the Nuclear Age*. Philadelphia: New Society Publishers.

Maruyama, Magoroh, 1983. 'Cross-Cultural Perspectives on Social and Community Change', in Edward Seidman, ed., *Handbook of Social Intervention*, pp. 33–47, Beverly Hills, CA: Sage Publications.

Milbrath, Lester W., 1988, July. 'Making Connections: The Common Roots Giving Rise to the Environmental, Feminist and Peace Movements'. A paper presented at the annual meeting of the International Society for Political Psychology.

Miller-Kustek, Alane M., 1989. 'The Relationship Between We/ They Attitudes and the Acceptance of War and Planned Violence Against Groups'. Unpublished doctoral dissertation, California School of Professional Psychology, Los Angeles.

Rappaport, Julian, 1977. *Community Psychology: Values, Research and Action*. New York: Holt, Rinehart and Winston.

Rappaport, Julian, 1986. 'In Praise of Paradox: A Social Policy of Empowerment over Prevention', in Edward Seidman & Julian Rappaport, eds., *Redefining Social Issues* pp. 141–164, New York: Plenum Press.

Reardon, Betty A., 1985. *Sexism and the War System*. New York: Teacher's College Press.

Ryan, William, 1971. *Blaming the Victim*. New York: Random House.

Ryan, William, 1983. 'Waking from the American Dream'. Paper presented at the annual meeting of the American Psychological Association, Anaheim, CA.

Sampson, Edward E., 1989. 'The Challenge of Social Change for Psychology: Globalization and Psychologists' Theory of the Person', *American Psychologist*, vol. 44, no. 6, pp. 914–921.

Sarason, Seymour B., 1972. *The Creation of Settings and the Future Societies*. San Francisco: Jossey-Bass.

Sarason, Seymour B., 1974. *The Psychological Sense of Community-: Prospects for a Community Psychology*. San Francisco: Jossey-Bass.

Schaef, Anne W., 1981. *Womens Reality: An Emerging Female System in the White Male Society*. Minneapolis, MN: Winston Press.

Seidman, Edward, 1986. 'Justice, Values, and Social Science: Unexamined Premises', in Edward Seidman & Julian Rappaport, eds, *Redefining social problems*, pp. 235–257. New York: Plenum Press.

Spretnak, Charlene, 1983. 'Naming the Cultural Forces that Push Us towards War', *Journal of Humanistic Psychology*, vol. 23, no. 3, pp. 104–1 14 .

Wagner, Richard V., 1988. 'Distinguishing between Positive and Negative Approaches to Peace', *Journal of Social Issues*, vol. 44, pp. 1–15.

Watzlawick , Paul, John H. Weakland & Richard Fisch, 1974. *Change: Principles of Problem Formation and Problem Resolution*. New York: Norton.

Weick, Karl E., 1984. 'Small Wins: Redefining the Scale of Social Problems', *American Psychologist*, vol. 39, no. 1, pp. 40–49.

11

Attitudes to an Existence Conflict

Rabin and Sharon on the Palestinian Issue, 1967–87

Yehudit Auerbach
Hemda BenYehuda Agid

1. Introduction

This chapter applies a theoretical framework of an Attitude in an Existence Conflict (AEC) to the attitudes of Yitzhak Rabin and Ariel Sharon towards the Palestinian issue. The chapter is part of a larger 'Israeli Attitudes to the Palestinian Issue' project (IAPI) which examined the attitudes of six Israeli decision-makers: Yigal Allon, Menachem Begin, Moshe Dayan, Shimon Peres, Yitzhak Rabin, and Ariel Sharon. Each of these leaders held one or more of the three most prominent positions in the Israeli political system, namely, Prime Minister, Foreign Minister, Defense Minister. The time span chosen for the project was 1967–1987.

The AEC framework was presented in two earlier papers: Auerbach & BenYehuda, 1987; Agid BenYehuda & Auerbach, 1991. We will begin this study with a short summary of the basic concepts and propositions of the framework and proceed with an empirical analysis.

2. The AEC Framework: Concepts and Propositions

An Existence Conflict is one in which each adversary demands recognition as a distinct national entity and claims the same stretch of land as its legitimate and exclusive territory. In addition to the Israel-Palestine case, some examples of existence conflicts are France and Algeria, Iraq and the Kurds, Spain and the Basques, as well as India and the Sikhs. In each of these cases at least one of the adversaries denies the opponent's claim for a distinct national identity and rejects its demand for sovereignty. In the Israel-Palestine case, the mutual denial of the opponents' claims and demands increases the intensity of the conflict and makes an interesting 'critical case' for the study of processes involved in existence conflicts. The essence of such processes is a mutual delegitimation and denial of national identity between the adversaries (Kelman, 1987, 1982).

The purpose of this chapter is to examine patterns of continuity and change in attitudes within the context of an Existence Conflict. We follow the tradition of applying psychological frameworks to political research. Other studies have suggested the usefulness of concepts such as images, perceptions, belief systems, and schemata (e.g. George, 1979; Hermann, 1988; Holsti, 1967; Jervis, 1970, 1976; Stein & Brecher, 1976; Zinnes, 1972). In our study we focus on political attitudes formerly addressed by several studies such as Harkabi (1972), Hermann & Milburn (1977), Kelman (1980), and Suleiman (1973).

To probe the question of conflict reduction or escalation we therefore propose a hypothetical model of an Attitude in an Existence Conflict, termed here AEC. An AEC, like other attitudes, consists of three components: cognitive, affective, and behavioral (for a review of the discussion on attitude components, see Breckler, 1984; Pratkanis & Greenwald, 1989; Zanna & Rempel, 1988). However, an AEC is a special type of attitude which has specific characteristics. It is an ideal type attitude shaped by the existence conflict setting from which it emerges thereby manifesting unique attributes. The following section will suggest several propositions regarding the cognitive, affective and behavioral components of an AEC.

The *Cognitive component* of an AEC serves as a conceptual base for the decision-makers' approach towards the adversary. The cognitive component of any attitude consists of two types of beliefs: existential and evaluative (Rokeach, 1968). Existential beliefs in an AEC relate to the authenticity of the adversary and to the legitimacy of his claims.

Proposition 1: In an Existence Conflict the decision-makers tend to deny the adversary's claim to national identity.

Proposition 2: In an Existence conflict the decision-makers tend to deny the relationship between the adversary and the contested territory.

An AEC expresses total denial of the adversary's claims regarding both its national identity and its relationship to the disputed territory: since the adversary is deprived of national distinctiveness, his claim to nationhood and demand for an independent state are also nullified. At best, the relationship of the adversary to the disputed territory may be acknowledged in religious or cultural terms but never as national-historical links. By contrast, the decision-maker holding an AEC tends to highlight his nation's own legitimacy and to emphasize the multifaceted links between his people and the territory which he claims to be his exclusive homeland. Evaluative beliefs in an AEC describe the opponent along two dimensions: power and hostility.

Proposition 3: In an Existence Conflict the decision-makers tend to evaluate the adversary as (a) strong in the short run; and (b) bound to lose in the long run.

Proposition 4: In an Existence Conflict the decision-makers tend to evaluate the adversary as (a) hostile; (b) harboring politicidal/genocidal aspirations; and (c) making no distinction between aspirations and goals.

When evaluating the adversary's capability and sources of support, decision-makers vacillate between two opposing trends. The first projects the opponent as weak and incapable of enduring a long struggle. The other trend describes the adversary as supported by mighty and evil powers and therefore overwhelmingly strong. The decision-maker will tend to reconcile these conflicting trends claiming: we are fundamentally stronger and will therefore win in the long run; the adversary is strong at present but will ultimately be the loser. Such a dual description serves a double purpose: to motivate strong devotion to the struggle and to justify setbacks in the context of the conflict when these occur. As for the hostility dimension, the adversary is presented as inimical and aggressive, with the goals of complete destruction of the decision-makers' state. No differentiation is made between the enemy's long and short term goals. His genocidal/politicidal aspirations are manifested in operational plans pursued resolutely at present. This negative view is transformed into a mirror image cycle. The opponent's nature and intentions are seen as totally negative. So too, in response, are those of the decision-makers, as will be reflected in the affective and behavioral components of attitude.

The *Affective component* of an AEC refers to feelings towards the adversary.

Proposition 5: In an Existence Conflict the decision-makers tend to (a) express hostility towards the adversary; and (b) associate negative traits with the adversary.

The AEC will be marked by strong negative feelings leading to a categorical denunciation of the enemy. In moral terms the adversary will be viewed as dishonest, deceitful, and untrustworthy. In some cases the adversary will be associated with and described by demonic terms. These negative dispositions will be reflected in a total rejection of the idea of *rapprochement* between the adversaries. The hostile feelings will, in turn, have a strong impact on the behavioral component of the decision-makers' attitude.

The *behavioral component* of an AEC has two dimensions: ideology and policy.

Proposition 6: In an Existence Conflict the decision-makers tend to forward an ideology which is (a) self-centered; (b) possessive; (c) predominated by fundamental principles; and (d) marked by high correspondence between fundamental and operational principles.

The existence conflict environment encourages a self-centered ideology which focuses on the values and needs of one's own party and emphasizes their pre-eminence in shaping policy towards the adversary. Moreover, the ideology is possessive, namely, claiming the entire contested territory as one's own with no regard to adversary's demands. Regarding the organization of the ideology a distinction is made between fundamental and operational principles (Seliger, 1976). Fundamental principles in an AEC regard the core issues of the conflict and serve as a set of prescriptions and proscriptions for policy formation and behavior towards the enemy. Operational principles serve as instrumental guidelines which preserve the fundamental premises while forwarding flexible solutions to specific issues of contention. In an AEC, fundamental principles predominate the ideology and are tightly linked to the operational principles. As a result the ideology is rigid and inflexible thereby paving the way to consistency and continuity in the policy toward the enemy.

Proposition 7: In an Existence Conflict the decision-makers tend to formulate a policy that involves: (a) a zero sum conflict resolution; (b) a comprehensive solution; (c) direct strategy; and (d) military means.

The rigid and inflexible ideology leads to a policy which aims at maximizing one's own gains and inflicting total loss on the adversary. Such a zero sum policy calls for a comprehensive solution involving the use of military means in direct confrontation with the enemy.

A summary of the cognitive, affective and behavioral components of an AEC is presented in Table 1. The AEC framework defines an ideal type of an attitude and serves as a criterion according to which attitudes in a conflictual setting can be analyzed. The framework facilitates the subtle analysis of attitude over time and the detection of nuances that distinguish each of the decision-makers in a complex and highly emotional issue.

3. Sources and Research Methods

This study is based on primary and secondary sources. The first group includes the following: *Divrei HaKnesset* – the Official Records of Israel's Parliament – during the 1967–1988 period; autobiographies (Rabin, 1974; Rabin with Goldstein 1979; Sharon with Chanoff, 1989); electronic and printed media and English translations of interviews with decision-makers from *Daily Report* (Foreign Broadcasting Information Service); secondary sources include biographies (Benziman, 1985; Slater, 1977), and other publications such as Carter (1982), Cobban (1984), Cohen (1972), Elazar (1983), Gazit (1985), Haber, et al. (1979), Haig (1984), Inbari (1982), Marcus (1979), Melman & Raviv (1987), Quandt (1986, 1977), Sadat (1978), Touval (1982), Vance (1983) and Weizman (1982).

We based our analysis on a content analysis of public pronouncements, assuming that public rather than private political statements are geared to the mobilization of internal as well as external legitimation. Moreover,

Table 1   *An ideal type attitude in an existence conflict*

COGNITIVE COMPONENT
  Existential
    Identity
          – denial of claimed national identity
    Links
          – denial of relationship between the adversary and
            the contested territory while highlighting one's
            own links to that territory
  Evaluative
    Adversary's Approach
          – hostile
          – genocidal/politicidal aspirations
          – no distinction between aspirations and goals

    Adversary's Power
          – strong on short run
          – will lose in long run

AFFECTIVE COMPONENT
    Decision-Makers' Approach
          – hostile
          – negative traits associated with the adversary

BEHAVIORAL COMPONENT
    Ideology
          – self-centered
          – possessive
          – predominance of fundamental principles
          – correspondence between fundamental and
            operational principles

    Policy
          – zero sum conflict resolution
          – comprehensive solution
          – direct strategy
          – military means

---

public attitudes create strong commitments which define the boundaries of the decision-makers' policy thereby limiting their maneuverability (for a description of the IAPI methodology see Auerbach & Ben Yehuda, 1987).

4. Rabin and Sharon on the Palestinian Issue

The attitudes of Rabin and Sharon toward the Palestinian issue are of special interest since both played a central role in Israel's politics, serving in turn as defense ministers during the last decade. Sharon held this position during Begin's second term as Prime Minister from August 1981 to February 1983, when he resigned following the Kahn commission report on the Sabra and Shatilla massacre.

Rabin took over the defense portfolio when a national unity government was set up in 1984 and has held the position continuously thereafter. Rabin also served as Prime Minister during 1974–1977.

4.1 The Cognitive Component of Attitude: Existential Beliefs

The essential issue of Palestinian identity was almost entirely sidestepped by Rabin. For him the Palestinian problem was part of the conflict between Israel and Jordan. He regarded the Palestinians as a distinct group with a 'special identity' but did not recognize them as a separate national entity (*Daily Report*, Hamburg DPA, July 9, 1975 and Government Press Office, January 11, 1976). Although Rabin eventually spoke about the national aspect of Palestinian identity, he persisted in his belief that the conflict was between the Arab States and Israel and not between the Jewish people and the Palestinian nation (*Divrei HaKnesset*, October 21, 1985, p. 75).

Rabin repeatedly used the expression 'the so-called PLO', denying the organization its claim to be a genuine national liberation organization representing the Palestinians (*Daily Report*, BBCTV, February 25, 1977 and JDS, March, 1977).

Unlike Rabin, Sharon was aware of the political aspect of the Palestinian issue. He acknowledged the separate national identity of the Palestinians residing on both banks of the Jordan River (*Daily Report*, JDTV, April 9, 1976; Paris AFP, June 26, 1977; and JDS, April 5, 1982). While Sharon, like Rabin, did not regard the PLO as a liberation organization, he was willing, at an early stage in his political career, to recognize it as a genuine representative of the Palestinian people, contending that 'we[Israel] are not the ones to determine who represents the Palestinians (*Daily Report*, JDS, January 17, 1977).

Rabin believed that Palestinians from all over the Arab world were part of the same entity, that a solution should therefore be found for all the Palestinians within one sovereign political framework, namely Jordan: 'The Palestinian issue must be inseparably bound up with the territory and the population east of the Jordan'(*Daily Report*, Jerusalem Post, June 11, 1976 p. 12; see also Hamburg DPA, July 9, 1975; JDS, August 22, 1985; and *Divrei HaKnesset*, October 18, 1982, p. 42).

Rabin highlighted the deep and strong links between the Jews and the Land of Israel. These ties were 'the source of Jewish uniqueness and of Jewish existence' (*Daily Report*, JDS, July 23, 1975; see also JDTV September 4, 1985). Nevertheless, Rabin believed that means other than settlements should be found to express the connection between people and land: 'it makes much more sense to invest efforts in archeological excavations and rebuilding the sites [of ancient Hebron] ... than to move trailers there' (*Daily Report*, Yediot Aharonot, October 26, 1984, pp. 3, 4). Moreover Rabin argued that historical ties should not be translated into political commitments and stated: 'For peace however I am willing to compromise over my rights' (*Daily Report*, Ha'aretz, November 21, 1985, p. 3).

Sharon emphatically stressed the links between the people of Israel and the Land of Israel. He urged the 'tightening [of] the ties between the Jewish people and Eretz Yisrael ... [since] Eretz Yisrael belongs to the people of Israel' (*Daily Report*, JDTV, April 6, 1976; see also JDS, October 26, 1979; Itim, April 28, 1982; and Jerusalem Post, April 8, 1985 p. 2). These historical links legitimized the Israeli claim for sovereignty over Judea and Samaria and should therefore be expressed politically through extensive settlements and eventual annexation. He stated: 'The territories are part of the Land of Israel. I am sure it will be very soon also part of the State of Israel' (*Daily Report*, JDS, May 19, 1986). Sharon's aspirations extended to 'areas east of the Jordan River [which] are also part of Eretz Yisrael. They are not in our hands, but they are ours' (*Daily Report*, JDS, September 25, 1983; JDS, September 4, 1982; and *Der Spiegel*, April 5, 1982, pp. 138–152).

Sharon maintained a clear position on the relationship between the Palestinians and Jordan: 'Jordan is to all intents and purposes a Palestinian state'. In his view Palestinians in 'Jenin, in Nabulus, in Ramallah, in East Jerusalem, even in Nazareth' are 'the same as' the Palestinians in Jordan. Sharon contended that Jordan 'today happens to have a King who is not a Palestinian Arab' and insisted that Jordan was the only state where Palestinian identity could find political expression (*Daily Report*, JDS, April 25, 1979; see also Paris AFP, June 26, 1977; and JDS, September 4, 1982).

When we compare the attitudes of Rabin and Sharon on identity and links we find more similarity than difference. Both Rabin and Sharon acknowledged Palestinian political links to Jordan. However, whereas Sharon regarded Jordan as a genuine Palestinian state, Rabin saw it as a joint Jordanian-Palestinian state in which both identities would express themselves. As to the ties between the people and the land, both attributed great significance to the historical links between the Jews and Eretz Yisrael. However, Rabin dissociated historical and political rights, maintaining that security needs only should determine Israel's future borders, while Sharon refused to separate historical and security borders.

In relation to the AEC framework, the findings are crosscutting. On identity Sharon was further from the ideal type than Rabin since he recognized the Palestinians' political distinctiveness and their right for a state of their own. However on links Sharon was closer to the AEC since he claimed a total Israeli right to the disputed territory.

4.2 The Cognitive Component of Attitude: Evaluative Beliefs

Both Rabin and Sharon drew a sharp distinction between the PLO and the Palestinian population. Both considered the PLO an antagonistic organization whose 'very essence of ... existence and outlook run counter the existence of Israel '(Rabin in *Daily Report*, JDTV, April 26, 1987). Rabin regarded the PLO as a terrorist organization that could not change over time, since 'the desire for terrorism [was] inherent in [its] very existence (*Divrei HaKnesset*, October 21, 1985, p. 75; *Daily Report*, IDF Radio, April 14, 1987).

Rabin pointed to a predominant theme in the PLO's policy: an 'ambition to destroy and totally annihilate Israel' (Rabin in *Daily Report*, Ma'ariv, March 18, 1977, p. 13; and *Divrei HaKnesset*, June 10, 1987, p. 2985). The destruction of Israel was not only a long range aspiration, but a core political goal to which all other goals were harnessed. All of its specific goals were part of a 'program of stages' to establish a democratic secular Palestinian state replacing Israel. Rabin concluded that the PLO was totally pledged to the secular state and that it could not 'cut loose from that commitment without undermining their whole *raison d'être*' (*Daily Report*, Jerusalem Post, June 11, 1976, p. 12).

Regarding the Palestinian population, Rabin noticed signs of moderation and readiness for compromise and coexistence: 'most of the population ... wants to go on living in peace with us regardless of their political views' (*Daily Report*, JDTV, September 4, 1985, and *Divrei HaKnesset*, October 21, 1985, p. 77, June 10, 1987, p. 2985).

Sharon also distinguished between the PLO and the local population. Like Rabin, he regarded the PLO as 'a political threat to the very existence of the state of Israel' (*Daily Report*, Government Press Office, December 15, 1981). During and following the 1982 Lebanon War, Sharon intensified his negative evaluation of the PLO and portrayed it as 'a cruel and merciless enemy' (*Daily Report*, Ma'ariv, August 22, 1982, p. 1) whose 'basic and deep seated' desire [was] to annihilate the physical existence of the State of Israel' (*Daily Report*, Yediot Aharonot. June 18, 1982, p. 2).

The Palestinian population, which had not received much of Sharon's attention until his nomination as Defense Minister in August 1981, gradually became the object of a favorable and embellished evaluation. Sharon presented the Palestinians as moderate and reasonable and claimed that: 'there are more and more people everyday in Judea and Samaria who say: we do not regard the PLO as our sole representatives' (*Daily Report*, JDTV, February 17, 1982; IDF Radio, March 23, 1982; BBC, June 21, 1982).

In sum, both Rabin and Sharon regarded the PLO as extremely hostile towards Israel and attributed to the organization politicidal aspirations. This view corresponds with the AEC. Yet their assessment of the Palestinian population's approach to Israel deviated somewhat from the ideal type. Both detected signs of moderation in the Palestinian camp, particularly Sharon who in the post-1981 period repeatedly stressed the distinction between the belligerent PLO and the peace-seeking Palestinian population.

Turning to the question of the adversary's strength both Rabin and Sharon related only to the PLO. Rabin viewed the organization as a strong and threatening enemy whose power was on the rise (*Daily Report*, Ha'aretz, May 3, 1976, pp. 5, 6, 7, 29). He painted a picture of broad state support for the organization, with the most hostile states using it in their struggle to annihilate Israel (*Daily Report*, Ma'ariv, November 3, 1976, p. 4; and Al-Hamishmar, June 3, 1982, p. 2). Rabin regarded the PLO as a pawn in the global

Table 2 *Rabin and Sharon on the Palestinian issue*
Cognitive and affective attributes

Component	Rabin	Sharon	Conclusions	
			Rabin vs. Sharon	Rabin & Sharon vs. AEC
Cognitive				
Existential Identity	Acknowledgement of a Palestinian distinct identity. Shift to national identity. Term: Palestinians. Rejection of PLO authenticity. Term: 'so-called PLO'	Acknowledgement of a Palestinian nation. Denial of a Jordanian nation. Term: Palestinians. Rejection of PLO authenticity as a genuine liberation organization. Shift from acceptance to rejection of PLO as the representative of the Palestinians. Term: PLO	Difference Similarity	Both deviate from AEC. Rabin closer than Sharon Both close to AEC
Links	Emphasis on historical links between Jews and the Land of Israel, with no political significance. Emphasis on multiple (including political) links between Palestinians and Jordan	Emphasis on deep-rooted and multifaceted links between the Jews and the Land of Israel, with political significance. Inseparable links between Palestinians on both banks of the Jordan. Jordan is Palestine	Difference Similarity	Rabin deviates from AEC. Sharon close to AEC Sharon closer than Rabin to AEC
Evaluative Adversary's approach	Emphasis on PLO's hostility. Long & short-term goal: destruction of the State of Israel (politicide)	Emphasis on PLO's hostility. Long- and short-term goal: destruction of the State of Israel (politicide). Post-1981: intensification of negative evaluation	Similarity	Both close to AEC

	Recognition of Palestinian's readiness to compromise	Up to 1981 Palestinian approach overlooked, thereafter recognition of a peaceful trend within the Palestinian population	Similarity	Both deviate from AEC
Adversary's power	Recognition of major support from most hostile Arab states and the USSR. Post-1982: realization that the PLO cannot be destroyed.	Recognition of major support from most hostile Arab states and the USSR. Pre-1982: emphasis on PLO's military strength Post-1981: emphasis on total collapse of PLO's power	Shift from similarity to difference	Sharon closer than Rabin to AEC
Affective	Extreme hostility to the PLO.	Hostility to the PLO, intensified post-1981	Similarity	Both close to AEC
	Formal obligation to Palestinian standard of living and well-being.	Benevolent approach towards the Palestinians. Peaceful coexistance between Jews and Palestinians under Israeli rule.	Difference	Both deviate from the AEC

superpower confrontation, used by the Soviet Union to undermine American diplomatic efforts in the Middle East (*Daily Report*, Davar, September 5, 1975, p. 11). Rabin argued that the PLO had emerged from the 1982 Lebanon War weakened but not fully destroyed: 'Israel has not managed to totally liquidate the PLO's military power and it is doubtful if it will be able to do so' (*Daily Report*, IDF Radio, July 15, 1982; *Divrei HaKnesset*, July 3, 1985, p. 3279, October 31, 1985, p. 76, June 1, 1987, p. 2864).

Like Rabin, Sharon saw the PLO as supported by Arab states which used it 'to carry out terrorist activities' (*Daily Report*, Government Press Office, December 15, 1981). Sharon attributed to the USSR a much greater role, as a source of PLO support, than did Rabin (*Daily Report*, JDTV, June 16, 1982; Yoman Hasavua, March 30, 1982; Ma'ariv, June 18, 1982, p. 13–14).

Throughout the 1982 Lebanon War, Sharon repeatedly expressed his amazement at the PLO's huge military infrastructure in Lebanon (*Daily Report*, JDTV, June 14, 1982; Ma'ariv, June 18, 1982, pp. 13–14). In Sharon's view the Lebanon War brought about an 'absolute downfall, military and political' of the PLO (*Daily Report*, Ma'ariv, December 17, 1982, p. 13).

On the whole Rabin viewed the PLO's strength as an irksome problem which could not be solved by military means, therefore requiring patience and enduring determination on Israel's part. This assessment deviates slightly from the ideal type which foresees the likelihood of overcoming the enemy. Sharon regarded the PLO as a virulent enemy against which Israel should wage a total war. This evaluation along with the belief that the PLO could be defeated conforms closely with the AEC.

4.3 The Affective Component of Attitude

The decision-makers' affective attitude towards the enemy is conveyed in both direct and indirect ways: the former, expressions of the extent of compromise; the latter, characterization of the adversary.

Throughout 1967–1987, Rabin depicted the PLO as a terrorist organization and characterized the organization as deceptive and ruthless. The PLO's leader was in Rabin's eyes 'just a murderer' (*Daily Report*, Guardian, October 22, 1975, p, 3) who presented himself as 'an angel of peace' (*Daily Report* Hadashot, October 18, 1985).

Sharon's approach to the PLO underwent change: during the early 1970s he straightforwardly proclaimed his readiness to talk with the PLO: 'Israel must talk with the PLO representatives if they represent the Palestinians (*Daily Report*, JDS, January 17, 1977). When Sharon became Defense Minister an adamant rejection of the PLO as a negotiation partner replaced his rather lenient approach: 'We are not prepared to talk to the PLO or people who speak for it' (*Daily Report*, Jerusalem Post, January 12, 1983, p. 1; see also *Daily Report*, Ma'ariv, November 5, 1985, p. 2).

Similarly Sharon characterized the PLO as an organization of murderers which concealed its true nature from the world through 'terrorist games of deception' and shrewd use of 'false propaganda ... following precepts of the communist and Goebbels tradition' (*Daily Report*, IDF radio, August 3, 1982; and IDF radio, July 13, 1982, respectively).

Both Sharon and Rabin were more forthcoming towards the Palestinian population. Rabin regarded the Palestinians living in the territories as a social community with the right to live in peace and prosperity, claiming: 'we should offer those who want to make peace with us the opportunity to prosper and to develop ....' (*Daily Report*, Jerusalem Post, August 23, 1985; JDS October 7, 1984; JDS, April 22, 1986). Since 1984, this has been Rabin's response to the continuous unrest in the territories under his direct jurisdiction. The escalation of violence did not discourage him: 'There are difficulties, terror has to be dealt with and standard of living and quality of life must be improved' (*Daily Report*, JDS, March 5, 1986). Rabin's well-intentioned plans, however, were confined to the economic domain and did not extend to the political sphere.

Sharon, in a way, was more forthcoming towards the Palestinians by recognizing their identity as a people who could and should live in harmony with the Jewish people. Accordingly he defined the goal of his 'carrot and stick' policy in the territories as 'creating an atmosphere that will lead ... to peaceful coexistence of Jews and Arabs, one people alongside the other' (*Daily Report*, JDS April 5, 1982). He repeatedly expressed his belief that the Jews and the Palestinians 'can find a solution of communal living' (*Daily Report*, Ma'ariv, September 9, 1977; JDTV, February 17, 1982; Yoman Hasavua March 30, 1982). This position was intensified following the 1982 Lebanon war when Sharon highlighted the difference between the PLO and the Palestinian population. Sharon's response to the PLO threat was total war; his offer to the Palestinian moderates, goodwill and cooperation (*Daily Report*, IDF Radio, August 21, 1982; see also BBC, June 21, 1982; JDS, July 27, 1982).

In sum, both Rabin and Sharon viewed the PLO and the Palestinian population in radically different ways. For both the PLO was a tenacious enemy that should be resolutely confronted. Both displayed a far more positive approach towards the population. Rabin focused on Israel's responsibility towards the Palestinians in the short term until a permanent solution to the Arab-Israeli conflict could be found. Sharon believed that harmonious coexistence was not only desirable but also possible in the immediate as well as future terms.

The affective component in both leaders' attitudes towards the PLO closely corresponded to the AEC while both deviated significantly from the model in their attitude towards the Palestinian population. Yet, Rabin appears closer to the ideal type than Sharon since he was totally opposed to the PLO and only partly responsive to the Palestinian population's demands. Table 2 presents a summary of the cognitive and affective components in the attitudes of Rabin and Sharon.

4.4 The Behavioral Component of Attitude: Ideology and Policy

The behavioral component of an attitude consists of two subcomponents: ideology and policy.

Rabin's approach to the Palestinian problem emanated from a state-centric world view which emphasized the role of the Arab states and belittled the Palestinian issue. He expressed his belief that 'the Palestinian issue is not the heart of the problem, ... there is a need to solve the Palestinian issue but in the context of a decision by the Arab countries to reconcile with Israel to make peace' (*Daily Report*, Government Press Office, January 11, 1976).

Following this Weltanschauung, Rabin advocated a policy based on several ideological precepts:

1 No independent Palestinian state.
2 No negotiations between Israel and the PLO.
3 Defensible borders as prerequisite for withdrawal.
4 United Jerusalem to remain the Capital of Israel.
5 Israeli settlements in security regions only.
6 Preservation of the Jewish democratic character of Israel.
7 Maintenance of Law and Order in the territories and provision of means for an adequate standard of living for the local inhabitants.

Rabin saw a Palestinian state as the most serious threat to the state of Israel. The PLO, with its official aim of a Palestinian state, was 'totally unacceptable as a political partner for negotiation' (*Daily Report*, Guardian, October 22, 1975, p. 3,). This precept remained unchanged despite the PLO's improved status in the international arena and of Hussein's demand that the PLO join the negotiating table (*Daily Report*, Davar, February 27, 1976, p. 11, 18; BBCTV, February 25, 1977; JDTV, September 23, 1977; JDS, October 12, 1979; Davar, July 26, 1985, p. 1; JDS, March 12, 1986; and JDS, December 22, 1987).

Rabin's readiness to trade territory for peace stemmed mainly from his concern for the Jewish and democratic character of the State of Israel which would be jeopardized if Israel kept one and a half million Palestinians under its rule (*Divrei HaKnesset*, October 18, 1982, p. 41; *Daily Report*, JDS, July 25, 1979; Ma'ariv, December 17, 1982, p. 13; Hadashot, April 9, 1986, p. 11; JDTV, April 26, 1987). To facilitate compromise without dismantling settlements, Rabin contended that the future map of Israel should shape the location and spread of settlement rather than the reverse. He opposed all efforts to settle in densely populated areas and called for settlements in regions which were necessary for Israel's security, particularly the Jordan Valley and around Jerusalem. He felt that Jerusalem should never be divided again (*Daily Report* JDTV, April 26, 1987). Though Rabin considered Israel's future borders negotiable, he ruled out withdrawal to the June 4, 1967 lines and insisted on defensible borders as a prerequisite for territorial compromise (*Daily Report*; BBCTV, February 25, 1977; JDS, March 15, 1973; JDTV, April 26, 1987).

On the whole, Rabin's ideology regarding the Palestinian issue appears highly self-centered and moderately possessive. It focuses on values and needs that were in his eyes crucial for the security of Israel, while disregarding the Palestinian side. Moreover these fundamental principles are closely tied to operational guidelines thereby creating an ideology consistent with the ideal type AEC. Yet Rabin's ideology is not entirely predominated by fundamental precepts, thereby permitting some flexibility. However these prospects of change did not find expression in Rabin's policy vis-à-vis the Palestinian issue from 1967–1987.

Inasmuch as changes appeared in Rabin's view regarding various peace proposals, they were tactical in nature and related to form and procedure only. Notable among the matters on which Rabin's view changed were: the participants in the diplomatic process (Jordan, the Palestinians, or the PLO); the negotiation framework (bilateral, multilateral, or international conference), and the pace and nature of the future settlement (step-by-step, interim, or comprehensive). Jordan was Rabin's chosen partner for bilateral negotiations, which should lead to a comprehensive settlement. It was only under the pressure of unfolding events inside and outside the region that Rabin accepted other partners, agreed to the introduction of interim agreements in the eastern border, and became gradually less opposed to an international rather than bilateral negotiation framework. During the 1967–1973 period, Rabin's approach was primarily shaped by his roles as IDF (Israeli Defense Force) Chief of Staff and later as Israeli Ambassador to the USA. He believed that Israel was strong enough to repel Arab demands for territorial concessions that fell short of formal and comprehensive peace.

Even after the 1973 War when Jordan's status was on decline and the PLO gained increasing international recognition Rabin clung to his previous view that Jordan remained the one and only partner. While Rabin was Prime Minister during 1974–1977 he acknowledged the difficulty of reaching a comprehensive agreement with Jordan and suggested a more limited end-of-war arrangement (Melman & Raviv, 1987).

The unexpected change in role from Prime Minister to opposition member that followed the Likud's 1977 rise to power temporarily relieved Rabin of the need to offer practical responses to the rapidly changing environment. Consequently Rabin displayed little enthusiasm for the efforts to convene a Geneva Conference and vehemently rejected the participation of a separate Palestinian delegation in the negotiation process.

The remarkable developments in the region, peaking with Egyptian President Sadat's visit to Jerusalem and the signing of the Camp David Accords, caused a thorough reconsideration of former positions. Rabin thought that peace with Egypt would lead to agreement with other Arab states, starting with Jordan. He supported the Autonomy Plan as part of the overall Camp David Agreements without letting party politics bias his stand. Rabin suggested that Autonomy take the form of an interim and not a final agreement. During the five-year Autonomy phase, a joint Israeli-Jordanian rule over the territories would be established with both countries cooperating to prevent terrorism, and Jordan responsible for administering the daily affairs of the local inhabitants. Rabin believed this arrangement would prevent a Palestinian political infrastructure in the area and block the creation of an independent Palestinian state. Eventually this transition phase would pave the road towards a comprehensive peace agreement with Jordan based on territorial compromise (*Divrei HaKnesset*, March 21, 1979, p. 2067). The central role granted Jordan left little room for any genuine Palestinian participation in the actual Autonomy scenario. Yet Rabin agreed to a separate Palestinian delegation in the negotiations, realizing it was the price Israel would have to pay for the peace treaty with Egypt in particular and the continuation of the peace process in general.

As the Israel-Egypt Autonomy talks met increasing difficulties Rabin backed down from his original support of the Autonomy Plan. He then presented the Autonomy Plan as a 'political mongoloid' which would lead to the creation of an 'Arafatist Palestinian state', and proposed Territorial Compromise as the only real political alternative (*Daily Report*, Hatzofeh, February 5, 1979, p. 6). To induce Jordan into the peace agreement Rabin was willing to concede 'large parts of the West Bank' (*Daily Report*, Ha'aretz, May 23, 1980, p. 5). Meanwhile, he suggested that Israel make a supreme effort to reach an Autonomy Agreement before April 1982, so as to add momentum to the peace process with Egypt. The source of authority, the participation of East Jerusalem residents in elections to the Autonomy council, and control over water and land were major stumbling blocks that Rabin was willing to remove by introducing a more flexible Israeli position.

Rabin supported the harsh measures carried out against the PLO in the 1982 Lebanon War, but was extremely alarmed by the 'Sharon Plan' which allegedly sought the establishment of a new order in Lebanon, to be followed by the Palestinians' retreat to Jordan and the establishment of a Palestinian state there. Rabin repeatedly expressed his conviction that the Palestinian problem could not be solved by military means and that the Camp David process was the route to be followed.

When Rabin became Defense Minister in the 1984 National Unity Government, the Palestinian issue fell once again under his direct authority. He aimed at driving a wedge between the PLO and the local inhabitants through a 'carrot and stick' policy. Rabin proposed economic measures, such as establishing an Arab bank, that would promote a decent standard of living in the territories, but objected to any change that would transfer political power to the Palestinians (*Divrei HaKnesset*, October 31, 1984, p. 298, July 28, 1987, p. 3890), and opposed general elections in the territories which he assumed would be held under the threatening shadow of PLO terror and lead to the rise to power of PLO supporters (*Divrei HaKnesset*, March 5, 1986, p. 2043). In the wake of terrorism and civil unrest in Judea, Samaria and Gaza, Rabin reiterated his strong belief that: 'we are not experiencing a distinct wave of incidents and for all its gravity it should be viewed in world proportions ... law and order must be established and terrorist elements should be fought with all due severity' (*Daily Report*, JDS, February 4, 1985). The unsuccessful efforts to transfer authority to the local inhabitants and Israel's failure to quell the increasingly intense upheavals did not sway Rabin from his approach. Despite the escalating violence, leading to the 'Intifada' in December 1987, Rabin did not lose his calm posture: 'we [should] not despair and arm ourselves with patience. We can go on holding Judea, Samaria and Gaza without any particular problems ... Israel has the breathing space to stand up to all these challenges' (*Daily Report*, JDS, March 5, 1986). He directed all his efforts and concessions towards the Hashemite regime, accepting Jordanian demands for an international conference but insisting that the conference would have no real authority and opposing Soviet participation (*Daily Report*, JDS, February 15, 1987). Jordan's demand for Palestinian representation in the conference forced Rabin to seek further formulas acceptable to both parties. In April 1985, he accepted the participation of Palestinians who were not PLO followers in a joint delegation with Jordan. Then, in February 1986, he agreed to PLO supporters from the territories, but not from the Palestinian diaspora (*Daily Report*, IDF Radio, April 18, 1985; *Jerusalem Post*, February 26, 1986, pp. 1, 19). By the end of 1987 Rabin seemed disappointed in Jordan's refusal to reciprocate and restated his long-held rejection of any PLO presence in a Joint Jordanian-Palestinian delegation (*Daily Report*, JDS, December 22, 1987).

Sharon's core belief was that Eretz Yisrael belongs to the People of Israel. The relationship between the land and the people epitomized for Sharon the real essence of Zionism, and was viewed through and expressed by two interrelated prisms: security and settlement. Sharon described these ties in passionate terms: 'Security springs from a willingness to defend something which belongs to you ... Security is a link between the people and their country' (*Daily Report*, Ma'ariv, January 4, 1979, p. 3).

Sharon advocated a political platform based on several guidelines emanating from this world view:

1 The entire Land of Israel is neither divisible nor negotiable.
2 Jordan is Palestine. No Palestinian state should be created west of the Jordan River.
3 Israeli settlement should be established throughout the entire Land of Israel.

For Sharon, settlement was not only a prerequisite for security, but 'Zionism's true banner' (*Daily Report*, JDTV, April 6, 1976; JDS, December 14, 1982). Unlike Rabin, Sharon believed that the location and spread of settlements should determine Israel's borders. He called for the surrounding of Jerusalem with settlements to ensure that 'Jerusalem remains the capital of Israel forever' (*Daily Report*, JDS January 29, 1982). On the whole, Sharon's ideology seems highly self-centered and possessive. It places high value on needs that were considered not only crucial to Israel security but also sanctified by Zionist dicta, and therefore demanding immediate implementation. These fundamental beliefs predominate the ideology and are translated to operational guidelines, thereby forming a rigid structure immune to change. As such Sharon's ideology conforms with the stipulations of the AEC and reduces the prospects of change.

Sharon's ideology remained unchanged throughout the period under review. While political exigencies prevented the immediate realization of his plans, Sharon did not concede on these matters and formulated his responses to current issues in ways that preserved his fundamental positions.

Table 3   *Rabin and Sharon on the Palestinian issue*
Behavioural attributes

Component Behavioural	Rabin	Sharon	Rabin vs. Sharon	Conclusions Rabin & Sharon vs. AEC
Ideology				
No independent Palestinian State	Fundamental Self-centered	Not an ideological principle	Rabin only	Rabin close to AEC
No negotiations with the PLO	Pre-1982: fundamental Post-1982: operational Self-centered	Not an ideological principle Post-1981: fundamental Self-centered	Difference	Pre-1981–2: Rabin close to AEC Sharon deviates from AEC Post-1981–2: Sharon close to AEC Rabin deviates from AEC
United Jerusalem capital of Israel	Fundamental Self-centered Possessive	Fundamental Self-centered Possessive	Similarity	Both close to AEC
Israeli settlements in security regions only	Operational Moderately self-centered	Not an ideological principle Moderately possessive	Rabin only	Rabin deviates from AEC
Settlements throughout Israel	Not an ideological principle	Fundamental and operational Self-centered Possessive	Sharon only	Sharon close to AEC
Defensible borders – a prerequisite for peace	Operational Moderately self-centered Moderately possessive	Not an ideological principle	Rabin only	Rabin deviates from AEC
Entire Israel not divisible	Not an ideological principle	Fundamental Moderately self centered Moderately possessive	Sharon only	Sharon close to AEC
Preservation of Jewish democratic character	Fundamental Self-centered	Not an ideological principle	Rabin only	Rabin close to AEC

Jordan is Palestine	Not an ideological principle	Operational Moderately self-centered	Sharon only	Sharon deviates from AEC
Obligation for standard of living	Operational Not self-centered	Moderately possessive	Rabin only	Rabin deviates from AEC
Summary	Prevalence of operational principles High correspondence between fundamental and operational principles	Prevalence of fundamental principles Post-1981: some discrepancy regarding PLO and a Palestinian State in Jordan	Difference Difference	Rabin deviates from AEC Sharon close to AEC Both close to AEC Pre-1981: Sharon deviates from AEC
Policy				
Territorial compromise	Support	Rejection	Difference	Rabin deviates from AEC Sharon close to AEC
Annexation	Rejection	Support	Difference	Rabin deviates from AEC Sharon close to AEC
Palestinian state	Rejection	Rejection	Similarity	Both close to AEC
Autonomy	Conditional support	Conditional support	Similarity	Both deviate from AEC
Unilateral withdrawal	Rejection	Rejection	Similarity	Both close to AEC
Federation–Confederation Israeli–Palestinian	Rejection	Support	Difference	Rabin closer than Sharon to AEC
Israeli–Jordanian–Palestinian	Support	Rejection	Difference	Sharon closer than Rabin to AEC
Settlements within Alon Plan lines	Support	Rejection	Difference	Sharon closer than Rabin to AEC
with governmental approval only	Support	Rejection	Difference	Sharon closer than Rabin to AEC
International conference	Pre-1985: rejection Post-1985: conditional support	Rejection	Similarity	Both close to AEC

Major partner to negotiations				
Jordan	Support	Rejection	Difference	Rabin close to AEC / Sharon deviates from AEC
Palestinian	Rejection	Support	Difference	Rabin close to AEC / Sharon deviates from AEC
PLO	Rejection	Pre-1977: support / Post-1977: rejection	Difference	Rabin closer than Sharon to AEC
Elections	Rejection	Rejection	Similarity	Both close to AEC
Summary	Palestinians Pre-1978: not considered as a central issue. post-1978: mixed motive; non-comprehensive; indirect political and economic means / PLO Zero sum; comprehensive Pre-1982: military direct Post-1982: military direct and political indirect	Pre-1977: Palestinians and PLO Mixed motive; comprehensive; direct political means. / Post-1977: PLO zero sum; comprehensive; direct military means / Palestinians Mixed motive: comprehensive; direct political means	Similarity in short term policy / Difference in long term policy	Both deviated from AEC regarding Palestinians / Both close to AEC regarding PLO / Both close to AEC

The 1967–1976 period, when Sharon was in military service and later served as a special adviser to Prime Minister Rabin, was a gestation period for his future political career. While in the opposition, Sharon worked mainly to introduce and promote his plan: Israel must establish settlements in the territories; encourage a Palestinian regime in Jordan; and strive towards comprehensive peace with a Jordanian-Palestinian State involving 'open bridges ... taking advantage of the resources in the dead sea ... [and] free access to the ports of Haifa and Ashdod' (*Daily Report*, JDTV, April 6, 1976). Sharon suggested a harmonious relationship in which 'the people in Judea and Samaria, if they wish, will retain Palestinian citizenship ... [and] we can also grant Palestinian citizenship to the Israeli Arabs who do not wish to serve in the IDF'(*Daily Report* Ma'ariv, August 16, 1976).

As member of newly elected Likud government, Sharon advanced a proposal of his own, an antecedent to Begin's Autonomy Plan. It combined earlier ideas with new elements: the Palestinians were offered a choice between Israeli or Palestinian citizenship. Those who opted for Israeli status would be granted cultural autonomy while the political aspirations of the others would find full expression in the 'country east of the Jordan River'. Cooperation between Israel and the 'Palestinian state' could take the form of a Federation or Confederation, with Jerusalem as the joint capital of the Federation (*Daily Report*, Ma'ariv, September 9, 1977, p. 24).

As Minister of Agriculture and chairman of the Ministerial committee for settlement affairs, Sharon held a position which enabled him to actualize his plans. Again he stressed the importance of building Jewish towns and villages in the territories but still warned against placing them 'in areas with high Arab population density' (*Daily Report, Jerusalem Post*, September 9, 1977, p. 14). In 1980 Sharon advocated Israeli presence within Arab towns, urging the government to rebuild the Jewish Quarter in Hebron (*Daily Report*, JDS, February 25, 1980).

Sharon regarded the Autonomy Plan as a major Israeli concession, and warned against turning it into 'a Balfour Declaration for the Palestinians' (*Divrei HaKnesset*, October 15, 1979, p. 4095). Sharon called on Jordan to join the peace process, proposed cooperation in maintaining security, and suggested the demilitarization of the Jordan Valley as well as joint Israeli-Jordanian patrols in the area (*Daily Report*, JDTV, June 1, 1979; JDS, September 8, 1980). Sharon also strove to remove the PLO from the diplomatic process and ruled out negotiations with the organization.

When he became Defense Minister Sharon directed his efforts towards separating the Palestinians and the PLO. He adopted a moderate stance towards the local residents: the civil administration was established indicating Israel's serious intention to implement Autonomy, and the Village Leagues were supported fostering substitute leadership in the territories. The harsh posture against the PLO supporters was epitomized by the order to outlaw and dissolve the National Guidance Committee, which was considered 'a PLO branch in theory and practice' (*Daily Report*, Itim, March 11, 1982).

This hard-handed policy climaxed with the 1982 Lebanon War, officially aimed at pushing the PLO beyond a forty kilometer security zone, but unofficially geared to destroying the organization's infrastructure. These moves were actually part of Sharon's 'grand design' which envisioned the retreat of the PLO to Jordan and the establishment of a Palestinian state replacing the Hashemite regime. During and after the war Sharon persisted in his efforts to liquidate the PLO, while offering reconciliatory gestures to the Palestinians in the territories. This duality is well illustrated in his readiness to grant 'a temporary shelter [to Palestinians] whose hands are not stained with blood and who will declare that they will leave the terrorist organizations' (*Daily Report*, JDS, July 19, 1982). By contrast Sharon rejected any suggestion 'to negotiate, bargain, court, or hold discussions with a den of terrorists like the PLO' *Daily Report*, *Le Figaro*, September 30, 1983).

As Minister Without Portfolio in Begin's government, following his forced resignation from the Defense Ministry, Sharon forcefully professed that Israel's borders would be determined by the presence of Israeli settlements 'On no account must there be any place left without Jews living there ... not one place must be left' (*Daily Report*, JDS, March 4, 1984). Given Jordan's reluctance to participate in the Autonomy Plan, Sharon called 'to implement Israeli law on the territories' (*Daily Report*, Ma'ariv, November 5, 1985 and JDS, May 19, 1986).

Table 3 presents the main findings regarding the behavioral component in the attitudes of Rabin and Sharon.

5. Conclusions

The objective of this chapter has been to apply the conceptual framework of an Attitude in an Existence Conflict to Rabin and Sharon. The AEC framework served as a criterion according to which the attitudes of the two decision-makers were analyzed and assessed. The framework facilitated the subtle analysis of their attitudes over time and the detection of nuances that distinguish each of them in a complex and highly emotional issue.

Though Sharon and Rabin represent polarized strands in the Israeli political system, their short-range policies towards the Palestinians were quite similar. This similarity stemmed from a common perception that the Palestinian issue though important was not the core of the Arab-Israeli conflict. Also, their long military career helped to bring issues of security into central focus. Their main concern was Israel's existence and defense, and it was the Arab states and not the Palestinians that were seen as threatening.

Yet when one examines the basic designs Rabin and Sharon proposed for resolving the conflict, the discrepancy between the two cannot be overlooked. Sharon believed that the entire Land of Israel belongs to the People of Israel. In effect Sharon was suggesting his own version of territorial compromise: recognition of the Palestinian right to a state east of the Jordan in an area to which Israel had legitimate claims, but concession of no further Israeli territory west of the Jordan.

Paradoxically, Rabin, who promoted the 'official' territorial compromise, was less forthcoming towards the Palestinians. He bypassed the issue of Palestinian identity and self-determination, concentrating solely on the Jordanian option. Rabin accepted Palestinian participation in the peace process only to lure Hussein to join the negotiation. By the late 1980s Rabin felt that Israel had done its utmost to set negotiations with Jordan in motion and believed that it was Hussein's turn to come up with new initiatives. Consequently, Rabin's sensitivity to the rapidly unfolding events in the territories was diminished, and he missed the radical transformations that took place in the Palestinian mood.

On the whole the attitude of both Rabin and Sharon towards the PLO conformed closely to the ideal type AEC. In their approach to the Palestinian population, however, both deviated from the ideal type in their readiness to meet this group's social and economic needs. Sharon went beyond Rabin in recognizing the Palestinians' political aspirations, while insisting that these aspirations be fulfilled at Hussein's, rather than Israel's, expense.

During the crucial 1981–1987 period the Israeli policy on the Palestinian issue reflected a convergence of Rabin's and Sharon's short-range proposals, rather than their differences regarding the desirable final arrangements. This policy involved tough measures against the PLO and its supporters along with a rather indulgent approach to the local residents. While Rabin pleaded for patience and Sharon urged intensified settlement efforts, both believed that Israel had the necessary breathing space to overcome the rising tides of unrest in the territories.

Unfortunately, the convergence of the two leaders' short-range policies contributed to a political stalemate at a time when bold breakthroughs were essential for all parties to the conflict.

References

Agid BenYehuda, H. & Y. Auerbach, 1991. 'Attitudes to an Existence Conflict: Allon and Peres on the Palestinian Issue 1967–1987', *Journal of Conflict Resolution*, vol. 35, no. 3, pp. 519–546.

Auerbach, Y. & H. BenYehuda, 1987. 'Attitudes Towards an Existence Conflict: Begin and Dayan on the Palestinian Issue', *International Interactions*, vol. 13, no. 4, pp. 323–351.

Benziman, U., 1985. *Sharon: An Israeli Caesar*. Tel-Aviv: Adam (in Hebrew).

Breckler, S., J., 1984. 'Empirical Validation of Affect, Behavior and Cognition as Distinct Components of Attitudes', *Journal of Personality and Social Psychology*, vol. 47, pp. 1191–1205.

Carter, J.D., 1982. *Keeping Faith: Memoirs of a President*. New York: Bantam Books.

Cobban, H., 1984. *The Palestine Liberation Organization: People, Power and Politics*. Cambridge: Cambridge University Press.

Cohen, Y., 1972. *The Allon Plan* , Tel-Aviv: Hakibbutz Hameuchad, (In Hebrew).

Daily Report. Foreign Broadcasting Information Service (FBIS), 1967–1980.

Divrei HaKnesset (Official Records of rhe Israeli Parliament). Jerusalem and Tel-Aviv: Government Printer, 1967–1980.

Elazar, D.J., ed., 1983. *From Autonomy to Shared Rule: Options for Judea Samaria and Gaza*. Jerusalem: Jerusalem Center for Public Affairs.

Gazit, S., 1985. *The Stick and the Carrot: Israeli Administration in Judaea and Samaria*. Tel-Aviv: Zmora Bitan, (In Hebrew).

George, A.L., 1979. 'The Causal Nexus Between Cognitive Beliefs and Decision-Making Behavior: The Operational Code Belief System', pp. 95–124 in Falkowski, L., ed. *Psychological Models in International Politics*. Boulder, CO: Westview.

Haber, E.Z. Schiff & E. Yaari, 1979. *The Year of the Dove*. New York: Bantam Books.

Haig, A., 1984. *Caveat: Realism, Reagan and Foreign Policy*. New York: Macmillan.

Harkabi, Y., 1972. *Arab Attitudes to Israel*. Jerusalem: Keter.

Harkabi, Y., 1974. *Arab and Israel Elite Perceptions*. Oslo: Norwegian University Press.

Hermann, M.C. & T.W. Milburn, eds, 1977. *A Psychological Examination of Political Leaders*. New York:Free Press.

Hermann, R., 1988. 'The Empirical Challenge of the Cognitive Revolution: A Strategy for Drawing Inferences about Perceptions', *International Studies Quarterly*, vol 32, pp. 175–203.

Holsti, O.R., 1967. 'Cognitive Dynamics and Images of the Enemy: Dulles and Russia', pp. 25–96 in Finlay, D., O.R. Holsti & R.R. Fagan, eds. *Enemies in Politics*, Chicago, IL: Rand McNally.

Inbari, P., 1982. *Triangle on the Jordan: The Secret Contacts Among USA, Jordan and the PLO*. Jerusalem:Cana.

Jervis, R., 1976. *Perception and Misperception in International Politics*. Princeton, NJ: Princeton University Press.

Jervis, R., 1970. *The Logic of Images in International Relations*. Princeton: Princeton University Press.

Kelman, H.C., 1987. 'The Political Psychology of the Israel-Palestinian Conflict: How Can We Overcome the Barriers to a Negotiated Solution?', *Political Psychology*, vol, 8, no. 3, pp. 347–363.

Kelman, H.C., 1982. 'Creating the Conditions for Israeli-Palestinian Negotiations', *Journal of Conflict Resolution*, vol. 26, pp. 39–75.

Kelman, H.C., 1980. 'The Role of Action in Attitude Change', pp. 117–194 in Howe, Jr. & M.M. Page, eds. *Nebraska Symposium on Motivation: Beliefs, Attitudes and Values*. Lincoln, NE.: University of Nebraska Press.

Marcus, Y., 1979. *Camp-David: An Opening to Peace*. Tel-Aviv: Schocken, (In Hebrew).

Melman, Y. & D. Raviv, 1987. *A Hostile Partnership: The Secret Relations Between Israel and Jordan*. Tel-Aviv: Yedi'ot Aharonot, (In Hebrew).

Pratkanis, A.R. & A.G. Greenwald, 1989. 'A Sociocognitive Model of Attitude Structure and Function' pp. 245–285 in Berkowitz, L., ed. *Advances in Experimental Social Psychology*, vol. 22. San Diego, CA: Academic Press.

Quandt, W.B., 1986. *Camp David: Peacemaking and Politics*. Washington D.C.: The Brookings Institute.

Quandt, W.B., 1977. *Decade of Decisions: American Foreign Policy Towards the Arab-Israeli Conflict 1967–1976*. Berkeley, CA: University of California Press.

Rabin, Y., with D. Goldstein, 1979. *Pinkes Sherut – An Autobiography*. Tel-Aviv: Ma'ariv, (in Hebrew).

Rabin, Y., 1974. *My Father's Home*. Tel-Aviv: Hakibbutz Hameuchad, (In Hebrew).

Rokeach, M., 1968. *Beliefs, Attitudes and Values*. San Francisco, CA: Jossey-Bass.

Sadat, A., 1978. *In Search of Identity: An Autobiography*. New York: Collins.

Seliger, M., 1976. *Ideology and Politics*. London: George Allen and Unwin.

Sharon, A., with D. Chanoff, 1989. *Warrior – An Autobiography*. New York: Simon and Schuster.

Slater, R., 1977. *Rabin of Israel*. London: Robson Books.

Stein, J.B. & M. Brecher, 1976. 'Image, Advocacy and the Analysis of Conflict: An Israeli Case Study', *The Jerusalem Journal of International Relations*, vol.1, no. 3, pp. 33–58.

Suleiman, M.W., 1973. 'Attitudes of the Arab Elite Toward Palestine and Israel', *American Political Science Review*, vol. 67, pp. 482–489.

Touval, S., 1982. *The Peace Brokers*. Princeton, NJ: Princeton University Press.

Vance, C., 1983. *Hard Choices: Critical Years in America's Foreign Policy*. New York: Simon and Schuster.

Weizman, E., 1982. *The Battle for Peace*. Jerusalem: Edanim, (in Hebrew).

Zanna, M.P. & J.K. Rempel, 1988. 'Attitudes: A New Look at an Old Concept', pp. 315–334 in Bar-Tal, D. & A.W. Kruglanski, eds. *The Social Psychology of Knowledge*, Cambridge: Cambridge University Press.

Zinnes, D., 1972. 'Hostility in Diplomatic Communication: A Study of the 1914 Crisis', in Hermann, C.F., ed. *International Crisis: Insights From Behavioral Research*. New York: Free Press.

12

Delegation in Labor Negotiation

Claude Louche

1. Introduction

In the nineteenth century, clashes between wage-earners and company management were at times resolved through violence. Since then, negotiation processes have gradually superseded violent confrontation. Such peaceful solutions were made possible only because changes occurred in intergroup conflicts and, above all, in the relationships between the parties involved in the conflict.

Negotiation implies that two requirements should be met: Firstly, each party must acknowledge the other as a valid representative. Secondly, violence must give way to exchanges and must be channeled, even though pressures may still be extant in the background of the discussions. For this reason, negotiation has become instrumental in bringing groups closer together while also enabling social change.

Since the 1960s, psychosociologists have been involved in experimental research aimed at analyzing the negotiation processes. This research work can be illustrated by Vidmar and McGrath's (1970) definition:

> Negotiation, then, may be defined as a situation in which representatives from two (or more) reference groups within an involved social community come together with the intent of setting forth a mutually acceptable solution to one or more issues about which the reference groups are in conflict. (p. 154)

This definition grants a major role to the delegation process and to the negotiator as representative in discussions. We will first expound on some of the research carried out on this subject before criticizing it in the light of our own experience of labor negotiations. Finally we turn to the implications of the results on the resolution of intergroup conflict.

2. Works on Delegation

In conducting discussions with their opponent, negotiators do not speak on their own behalf, but represent a group whose interests they have to defend. Since the negotiator plays the role of representative, psychosociologists have been interested in studying the influence that the group in the bargaining background exerts on their representative. Klimoski (1978) has presented the various methodologies that have been designed to study delegation.

This laboratory research work has been induced from the idea that the negotiator is subject to pressures from his group. These pressures would check a quick solution of the conflict. They would be all the heavier when a short distance between negotiator and group might allow the latter to control its representative. In the concept of distance, the components of both status-induced distance and physical distance can be analyzed.

2.1 Status-induced Distance

The status level of the negotiator within his group may afford him more or less freedom towards the latter. In labor negotiations, workers or employers may have their interests defended by negotiators with different status levels.

The first distinction might be between elected negotiators and those who are officials within their organization. Elected negotiators have no real power and are dependent on their electors, whereas officials enjoy greater autonomy. Lamm (1973) has shown in an experiment that elected representatives took longer to conclude negotiations than did the non-representatives. The position of the negotiator may also be of relevance. Several writers think that negotiators who have leader status in the group will more easily leave the prior positions of their group and will exercise greater latitude than those inferior in rank.

Experiments carried out on this aspect of status-induced distance bear out the checking influence of the group on the representative. Herman and Kogan (1968) state that higher-ranking negotiators will bargain more easily, tending to stray from the group's position more freely than negotiators with lower rank. They are more flexible in discussions and reach agreement more readily. This result is confirmed by Lamm and Kogan (1970), who claim that representatives with inferior status in their organization show a greater toughness and rigidity than the leaders. Settlement is reached more often when negotiations are conducted by leaders. A more recent work by Jackson and King (1983) comes to similar conclusions: 'This study suggests that when quick settlement is desired, organizations. should send higher ranking officials to negotiate'. (p. 183)

2.2 Physical Distance

In France, labor negotiations take place at several levels: they can be held within a company but also at the national level. In company negotiations, the negotiator is closely linked to his constituents, and thus greatly sensitive to their influence. Such delegation will be less clear-out at the national level. In company negotiations, the role of the constituents will be greater, as Druckman et al., (1972) have shown. These experimentators made up dyads of negotiators who had to deal with the distribution of resources and conflicting interests concerning this distribution.

Negotiators may represent a group which is physically present during the negotiation; in the other experimental situation, the negotiator upholds his own interests. It has been established that the exchanges were harsher and competition keener when the negotiator was near the group. From same research perspective we can mention Gruder and Rosen (1971). They conclude that delegates who have to account for their negotiations behavior to the group they represent are less liable to make concessions, and take longer to negotiate than negotiators free from their group's control.

3. Follow-up: Intra-organizational Conflict

The works referred to above show that the stronger the influence of the group on the negotiator (short distance), the more difficult the settlement will be; all the literature indicates that the group would prove to be a check to the quick settlement of the conflicts, for it exerts pressures on the negotiator and exercises control over its representative (Figure 1).

If group pressures urge the negotiator to show firmness, other pressures may prompt the negotiator to make concessions and strive for an agreement. Thus the negotiator's position has often been described as resting on contradictory requirements which put the negotiator in a role-conflict situation (Touzard, 1987). Indeed, the negotiator must, on the one hand, reach a settlement, but on the other hand bring the group's views to a successful conclusion.

These contradictory pressures have been described as follows by Walton and McKersie (1965):

> Thus, the boundary role occupied by the chief negotiator is the target of two sets of prescriptions about what the negotiator ought to do and how he should behave. That role expectations should originate from within his own organization should be obvious. In addition, a negotiator is often expected to behave with understanding and to act in a way that accommodates the needs of his opponent. (p. 284)

Thus, these researchers consider that the settlement of the intergroup conflict puts the negotiator in a situation of intraorganizational conflict. The group's expectations may not be in keeping with the concessions the negotiator is led to make to reach a compromise.

Figure 1   *Factors affecting group control on negotiators*

Walton and McKersie put forward a model for resolution of the intra-organizational conflict. They rule out the possibility that the negotiator might avoid the intra-organizational conflict by complying totally with his constituents' expectations, as that would be at the expense of the failure of the intergroup negotiation. According to these authors, negotiators are presumed to be eager to reach a settlement.

4. Critical Analysis of the Works on Delegation

The research work on delegation we have presented in all above sections rests on the following postulates.
- The group determines the negotiation positions that the representative will have to bring to a successful conclusion: throughout the discussion, the group does not depart from its prior positions and does not change.
- It is assumed that, a priori, the negotiator is eager to reach a settlement. This is the very essence of his role.
- As the only one aware of the necessity of an agreement, the negotiator finds himself in a deviant position from his group. The greater the group's influence, the more difficult will reaching agreement be. Furthermore, this agreement will be accompanied by an intra-organizational conflict between the negotiator and his constituents.

These three assumptions are based on the autonomy of negotiation with regard to the intergroup conflict. On one hand there is an intergroup conflict with clear-cut, uncompromising positions, and on the other hand, negotiators who have been commissioned to reach agreement and who have to modify the group's positions. The weakness of these assumptions is that they analyze delegation from the single viewpoint of conformity-deviance: the delegate would deviate from his group's positions and would be therefore subject to pressures towards conformity, from his constituents. The research work on delegation summarized above brings out factors (status level) which make the delegate more autonomous and likely to act independently of his group's views. This is the transposition on the delegation level of an approach already developed in psychosociology about social influences, described and discussed by Moscovici (1979). More particularly, he has shown that research on the evolution of positions rests on the following propositions, which concern the influence processes but which apply also to the 'majority approach' of delegation:

> Pressures which lead to innovation originate from outside the group. This pressure towards innovation is exerted only on the leader, since he is the only member of the group to be in touch with the outside world. (Moscovici, 1979, p. 61)

Observation of conflicts and negotiations as well as surveys we have carried out on this subject show the limits of this analysis, however. We have found:
- There is no dividing line between negotiation and constituents;
- constituents seldom check agreement;

– conflict processes remain at the heart of negotiation: it is not absolutely essential to reach an agreement (see Louche, 1981a, b).

Let us take up these different points.

4.1 Dividing Line Between Negotiation and Constituents

Looking at society, it is obvious that at least in France the constituents have been less and less cut off from negotiations which affect their interests since the 1970s. Indeed, the whole French system of labor relations has swung over towards the company. Thus, in the face of an upsurge of labor conflicts, the legislative power was compelled in 1971 to set up a legal framework which made negotiation possible at this level. A 1982 law made labor negotiations compulsory every year. This shift towards the company has brought about a new role for the constituents. Previously, the unions alone could conduct conflicts, but since 1970, labor unions and negotiators have been supervised throughout strikes and negotiations by a general meeting. This evolution has been emphasized by Clerc (1973, quoted by Caire, 1978):

> We cannot say, as four years ago we could, that the unions alone conduct the negotiations. This leads labor unions to alter their behavior: they ceaselessly turn to the constituents, throughout the conflict, negotiating in the presence of or even with the participation of the constituents. (p. 29)

There has thus been a thorough break with the former pattern where the constituents are on strike while, somewhere else, the delegates are negotiating. This outdated pattern, however, forms the basis of a lot of research work on delegation.

4.2 The Constituents Check Agreement

If the constituents are nearer the negotiators, does it mean they check or hinder agreement, as works on delegation imply? This would mean the negotiator would reach an agreement only at the expense of an intra-organizational conflict.

The survey data we have collected and our own observations do not bear out this analysis, however. We studied (Louche, 1981) labor negotiations in which the negotiator is in direct touch with the group he represents and therefore more strongly under its control. It became obvious that the constituents in these negotiations do exercise a very strong influence in setting negotiation strategies and in the final decisions which elicit either the acceptance or refusal of a compromise. But this does not necessarily mean that pressure from the constituents is exerted to check the pursuit or the settlement of a compromise.

As regards the pursuit of a compromise, for example, our studies have established that it was not the electors' influence that prevented the negotiator from making concessions. We found that delegation plays a less important role than the laboratory work, emphasizing this variable, might lead one to suppose. Between social reality and laboratory work, there is major difference, one which might account for the differences in the results: *the cost of conflict.*

In laboratory work, groups are requested to define negotiation positions. Then, on behalf of the group, a delegate starts up the negotiation. If it becomes clear that in these situations the group is acting as a brake to agreement, this is because in the laboratory, the group does not have to sustain the cost of continuation of the conflict. In real life, however, the workers will have to bear the costs brought about by the failure to compromise – for example, if they are on strike. As we have pointed out in a fieldwork survey designed to test Walton & McKersie's model, the workers are then as much aware of the necessity to put an end to a costly situation as their delegate is. If on the other hand, the conflict does not cost money, then it may be that constituents and their representives will refuse a compromise. This challenges the idea that negotiators are a priori supposed to reach an agreement (Louche, 1981).

4.3 The Will to Reach Agreement

As noted above research and patterns about negotiation processes are generally based on the assumption that the negotiator is a priori willing to reach agreement. However, this does not stand up to a close analysis of facts. It can be questioned by two kinds of arguments:

1. The first one is supported by observation of the social situation in France. As Morel (1981) has emphasized, two concepts of negotiation are current in France: on one hand, there is a concept of negotiation based on contract. Negotiation is here considered as a relation of exchange with the opponent. This idea is in keeping with the models put forward by Vidmar & McGrath and by Walton & McKersie. Unions, on the other hand, have a *non-contractual* conception of negotiation. From this point of view (which is widespread in French practice) negotiation is not regarded as leading to an agreement. The sole purpose of negotiation is to obtain concessions from the opponent, without affording him any counter-concessions.

Negotiation is only a means of pressure. In real life, we are far removed from the a priori will to reach agreement which would be characteristic of the role of negotiator. But whatever concept of negotiation the contenders adopt, fieldwork shows that negotiation is an *element* of conflict rather than a process distinct from it and designed to solve it. It is carried out against a background of power struggle.

2. Field surveys: studies carried out in the United States have shown that the development of negotiation depends more on the cost of the conflict and the lack of compromise than on the will to cooperate. Peterson & Tracy (1977) reach the following conclusion: 'Power, probability and the cost of workstoppage are major factors in the behavior in negotiation' (p. 50). In a study released in 1981, Driscoll shows through the analysis of 26 negotiations that there is a correlation between, on the one hand, negotiators adopting a behavior that makes the development of negotiation easier, and on

the other hand the cost of the conflict over the negotiation. We reached similar results in France (Louche, 1981, 1982). It thus seems clear that whatever the sociological context, negotiation is conducted through a conflictual dynamics and not through the mere fact of the negotiator's good will. It is to this end that Merle (1980) writes:

> Negotiation cannot amount to mild muffled discussions round the green baize of conference tables; it remains a confrontation between antagonistic forces and for this reason, it cannot rule out the event of a possible resort to force. Setting the flexibility of negotiation against the tough injunctions of power betrays a simplistic and too idealised a view of what negotiations actually are. (p. 26)

If negotiation avoids the destructive conflict and implies some consensus between competitors, that indicates it is conducted against a backdrop of power-relations, and not on the a priori will to reach agreement.

5. Conclusion

Psychosociological research on negotiation has defined the latter as a situation in which delegates meet with a view to reaching an agreement which would solve the conflict between the groups these delegates belong to. This definition focuses attention on the negotiation group as functioning behind closed doors. The model is then of groups set on unshakable positions which exert pressures on their delegate, who in turn tries to reach an agreement through discussion. This agreement will lead to an intra-organizational conflict. That is what the problem of delegation is all about.

Actual observation of labor negotiations has led us to criticize this approach. Our work has shown that discussions cannot be separated from all the intergroup conflictual dynamics. Negotiation is an element of the intergroup conflict and not a separate process designed to solve it; as such, negotiation comes under intergroup phenomena (Louche, 1992). This is the scope within which we are now studying it.

These results would involve several practical consequences. In various countries, training schemes are being set up with the aim of preparing negotiators to perform their role efficiently. This approach seems to us to be essential but not sufficient.

As our analyses show, negotiation cannot be set apart from intergroup conflict dynamics. It is therefore on the intergroup context that the progress and outcome of negotiations depend. Thus it is up to the managers to ensure within the company the right intergroup relationships likely to promote the efficient development of the negotiation group.

References

Caire, G., 1978. *La Greve Ouvrière*, Ed. ouvriere, Paris.
Clerc, J.M., 1973. 'Les Conflits Sociaux en France en 1970 et 1971', *Droit Social*, January, pp. 16–25.

Driscoll, J., 1981. 'Problem Solving Between Adversaries: Predicting Behavior in Labor-Management Committees', *International Review of Applied Psychology*, vol. 30, no. 2, pp. 277–291.

Druckman, D.; D. Solomon & K. Zechmeister, 1972. 'Effects of Representational Role Obligations on the Process of Children's Distribution of Resources', *Sociometry*, vol. 35, no. 3, pp. 387–410.

Gruder, C., 1971. 'Relations with Opponent and Partner in a Mixed Motive Bargaining', *Journal of Conflict Resolution*, vol. 15, no. 3, pp. 403–446.

Gruder, C. & N. Rosen, 1971. 'Effects of Intragroup Relations on Intergroup Bargaining', *International Journal of Group Tensions*, no. 1, pp. 301–317.

Jackson, C. & D. King, 1983. 'The Effects of Representatives' Power within their Own Organizations on the Outcome of a Negotiation', *Academy of Management Journal*, vol. 26, no. 1, pp. 178–185.

Klimoski, R.J., 1978. 'Simulation Methodologies in Experimental Research on Negotiations by Representatives', *Journal of Conflict Resolution*, vol. 22, no. 1, pp. 161–177.

Lamm, H., 1973. 'Intragroup Effects on Intergroup Negotiation', *European Journal of Social Psychology*, vol. 3, no. 2, pp. 170–192.

Lamm, H. & N. Kogan, 1970. 'Risk Taking in the Context of Intergroup Negotiation', *Journal of Experimental and Social Psychology*, no. 6, pp. 351–353.

Louche, C., 1981a. 'Approche Psychosociologique de la Négociation Professionnelle', Thèse d'Etat. Université de Paris X.

Louche, C., 1981b. 'La Résolution du Conflit Intra-Organisationnel dans des Négociations d'Entreprises', *International Review of Applied Psychology*, vol. 30, no. 2, pp. 235–244.

Louche, C., 1982. 'Open Conflict and Dynamics of Intergroup Negotiations', in H. Tajfel, ed., *Social Identity and Intergroup Relations*, Cambridge University Press.

Louche, C., 1992. 'Relations sociales et Dynamique de la Négociation d'Entreprise', in C. Dupont, *Regards Français sur la négociation*, Actes du Colloque Groupe Sup de Co, Lille.

Merle, M., 1980. 'De la Negociation', *Pouvoirs*, vol. 15, pp. 5–30.

Morel, C., 1981. 'La Grève Froide', Ed. d'Organisation, Paris.

Moscovici, S., 1979. *Psychologie des Minorites Actives*. Paris: PUF.

Peterson, R. & L. Tracy, 1977. 'Testing a Behavioral Theory Model of Labor Negotiations', *Industrial Relations*, vol. 16, no. 1, pp. 35–51.

Touzard, H., 1987. 'La Rigidité Flexible, un Exemple de Processus Integratifs', *Connexions*, vol. 50, pp. 29–42.

Vidmar, N. & J.E. McGrath, 1970. 'Forces Affecting Success in Negotiation Groups', *Behavioral Science*, vol. 15, pp. 154–163.

Walton, R. & R. McKersie, 1965. *A Behavioral Theory of Labor Negotiation*. New York: Academic Press.

13

On the Methodological Paradigms of Psychological Peace Research

Antti Eskola*

1. The Problem

Two recent articles in the *Journal of Peace Research* provide an interesting setting for a methodological comparison within the field of psychology and peace research. Lamare (1989) uses a causal model to explain the connections of gender and age to certain attitudes and behavioural tendencies. Using the traditional jargon of causal analysis, he describes gender as a 'variable' which 'affects' or has a certain 'impact' on some other variable. This analysis is based upon the paradigm (see Figure 1) where the phenomenon being explained (e.g. vote preference) is *determined* by certain factors (e.g. gender), not directly, but through the mediation of certain *mechanisms*. It is assumed that these relationships reflect some sort of general *laws* – biological, psychological, or social.[1]

Brock-Utne (1989), on the other hand, examines results concerning the behaviour of men and women in the Prisoner's Dilemma game. A radical feminist perspective suggests an interesting interpretation for the emergence of gender differences: they may arise from the fact that, for women, the context-stripped laboratory experiment is uninteresting and the operationalization of cooperation by means of the PD game unsatisfactory or false. However, it would be equally unsatisfactory to say that the views of women on the experiment constitute a 'mechanism' which mediates the 'determining' influence of gender on women's behaviour in the experimental setting. This line of argumentation, as indeed the entire paradigm represented by Figure 1, reflects what Brock-Utne describes as 'physics envy' and can certainly not produce the kind of methods best suited for the study of human action. Perhaps there does not exist a specific feminist social science methodology: but it is quite clear that there are at least *two* radically different paradigms.

* This chapter was written as part of the Academy of Finland research project no. 12/098, in which my research assistant was David Kivinen.

Figure 1   *The mechanistic-deterministic research paradigm*

Factors $X_1, X_2 \ldots X_k$, etc.	determine $\longrightarrow$	action (Y) of individual and society

Scientific law

The skeleton of the former is described in Figure 1. The latter derives from the critique of that paradigm and from alternative solutions which have been proposed not only by critical feminist scholars but also by writers such as Harré and Secord (1972) or Israel and Tajfel (1972).

In another connection the editor of the *Journal of Peace Research* (Gleditsch, 1989) said he felt there is a trend in peace research towards specialization. This would also seem to be the case with regard to research methodology. There are researchers who specialize in the methodology represented by Figure 1, and others who specialize in methodologies based on an alternative paradigm (e.g. ethnomethodology, ethogenics, discourse analysis). Insofar as the choice of methodological approach is made on the basis of the characteristics of the research object in question, there should be no reason for concern. But peaceful coexistence among researchers, each with their own methodological niches, is not always possible. If we all shared the same object of research – say, cooperative action – then sooner or later we would have to settle the question of the appropriateness of different methodologies to studying this particular object. For instance, should all the work that has used PD experiments to resolve the problem of cooperative behaviour be denounced as useless because – if we are to believe the radical feminist critique – the methodology does not fit that object?

The purpose of this chapter is to look into the possibility of integrating different paradigms in psychological peace research. As far as I can see, the approach described in Figure 1 is far too narrow. However, this line is so strongly entrenched in modern psychology that discarding it altogether would be impossible. Our entire arsenal of statistical methods, from correlation coefficients to path analysis, is based on the conviction that by organizing empirical observations we can discover psychological laws which identify the factors determining the phenomenon under study. The psychologist's laboratory has been built on the strength of this conviction, which has been handed down from generation to generation through university courses on psychometrics and test theory. Moreover, most psychological journals seem to have a preference for papers using this type of methodology.

Fortunately, there is no need to discard this kind of research. Traditional laboratory experiments and survey studies aiming to discover laws do have their own legitimate function in psychology – but only within the context of a broader paradigm. These methods provide us with practical information that may be used in day-to-day activity, but the structure of that activity is not given a truthful representation by the approach shown in Figure 1.

2. The Place of Laws in Human Activity

Anyone wanting to say something good about warfare, might point out that wars have always boosted scientific and technological development. This argument from a psychologist or a sociologist might refer to the impetus given by World War I to the study of human aptitudes. Or perhaps they would take a more recent example, such as 'The American Soldier' studies conducted during World War II by the US army.[2] In addition to their intentions of producing information for applied purposes, these studies also had the explicit scientific aim of formulating hypotheses of the type 'If X, given specified conditions, then Y', and to verify those hypotheses – that is, to detect the kind of 'laws' depicted in Figure 1. The ideal of verification was better attained in experiments rather than in survey analyses (cf. Stouffer et al., 1949a, pp. 44–46).

A decade or so later, criticism against these methods started to gather momentum: attention focused on the ethical problems of laboratory experiments, the obvious shallowness of survey studies, and the assumptions of 'constant traits' upon which scaling techniques were based. This attack was no doubt at least partly motivated by the discovery that the methods originally developed in and for army conditions were less successful outside those restricted conditions. Major General Osborn, Director of the Information and Education Division of the War Department, is here referring to those special conditions:

> Not only did the Army contain all the diverse elements of young American men, in numbers adequate for valid statistical results, but each of these men was indexed for various items of personal background of a kind important in drawing samples. Further, the organization of the Army was such that at the word of command groups of men could be drawn out for study with a minimum of effort, provided only that the Army authorities were willing that such studies should be made. (Stouffer et al., 1949a, p. vii)

The first point mentioned by Osborn is quite plainly an invitation to conduct studies where a few simple tests or a short questionnaire can be administered to a large sample of people. Although this kind of setting lends itself to elegant statistical analysis, our conclusions from that analysis would have to be based on pure conjecture because we would know nothing about the thought processes leading from question to answer. And this problem is always there, no matter how large the sample.[3] On the other hand, the conditions under which 'at the word of command groups of men could be drawn out for study with a minimum of effort' – these conditions serve to maintain and reinforce false images of the human being as a machine whose reactions are mechanically determined on the basis of certain laws. Maintaining those images is even easier if the subjects are men who will not criticize the method and if the experimenter is exempted from all ethical responsibility, which lies instead with the army authorities. So the technical advantages which facilitate the practical implementation of the study may in fact prove a major drawback as far as scientific relevance is concerned.

As a matter of fact, even under the technically ideal army conditions these men did not respond as deterministically as had been assumed. By the mid-1950s there were already some critical commentators (see e.g. Katz & Lazarsfeld, 1955, pp. 36–37) who pointed out that the target met by orders and other stimuli is never an isolated individual, even though this is how one easily sees the solitary soldier who is completing his questionnaire. In reality he will be intricately bound up with his own primary groups and in close interaction with those groups. It is important to realize that those groups do not constitute a 'mechanism' through which the impact of factors $X_1, X_2, ... X_k$ is mediated onto the individual's behaviour Y, but rather a source of freedom and unpredictability. The group introduces into the system what has been described as 'complex interactions' and 'loose couplings' (on these concepts, see Perrow, 1984, pp. 72–97).

The psychologist who does not have access to large numbers of men who at the word of command can be transformed into experimental subjects, should be able more readily to see that human individuals always enjoy some measure of freedom in their actions. To be sure, there are certain laws and rules which we cannot escape, but our activity is not determined by them; instead, we take them into account on the basis of a certain logic (Figure 2). This line of reasoning does not divide phenomena into 'stimuli', 'reactions' and 'mediating mechanisms'. Rather, it draws our attention to (1) the meanings of activity to different actors; (2) the laws and rules that actors take into account in this activity; and (3) the logic on the basis of which they do so. We do not reject the concept of law (or the related methodology) so central in Figure 1, but integrate it into the broader and more realistic concept of human activity.

Looking more closely at Figure 2, let us begin with those laws and rules. There are, first, *social rules* of the type 'If X, then Y', which either constitute a certain activity or only regulate it. For instance, there is a rule which specifies the acts (X) which are required of the Parliament or Cabinet Ministers or President of a certain country before that country can be considered officially to have 'declared war' (Y) against some other nation. In this case, the acts of those individuals 'institutionally constitute' the nation's action, as Tuomela (1989) puts it. Regulative rules, then, are those that states normally observe in their international relations but the violation of which does not yet mean they have 'declared war', 'broken off diplomatic relations', etc.[4] It is quite obvious that the behaviour of states is not restricted to just one alternative

Figure 2   *Realistic paradigm for the study of human action*

In activity the actor	takes into account, according to a certain logic, that	if X, then Y ⎵ law, rule

determined by rules of this kind. Rather, state actors take very close account of these rules in their attempts to create such outcomes as 'security', 'deterrence', 'threat', etc.

All this is possible because acts not only produce meanings but also have consequences which can be expressed in the form of *empirical laws* or regularities.[5] So when an actor breaks a given rule, this serves not only to constitute a certain act (e.g. 'show hostility') but also to provoke aggressiveness in other actors. Perhaps it is even possible to discover an empirical law which says that 'when actor A behaves in a hostile manner towards actor B, then B is very likely to respond by some hostile act'. It is this type of law that researchers applying the paradigm shown in Figure 1 have been looking for; and that attempt is fully legitimate insofar as we bear in mind that laws do not determine our activity in any given way, that we always have more than one alternative because we can take those laws into account in our activity on the basis of either this logic or that logic. If, for instance, I adopt the aim of 'remaining on friendly terms' with my neighbours, I will *not* respond to their aggressiveness by hostility but attempt to act according to the logic which says that 'If you are provoked, don't be'. The law that was discovered on the basis of Figure 1 does not seem to apply to my behaviour; but when we leave that line of thought aside and insert the law in Figure 2, then it makes sense.

In the context of peace and security a particularly important kind of empirical proposition is that which concerns the probability of extremely dangerous outcomes (for instance, the probability of a nuclear power plant exploding, or of nuclear war breaking out by accident). Even these laws do not deterministically force us into acting in a certain manner (into shutting down nuclear power plants or dismantling nuclear weapons, for example), but they do involve one important necessity which we cannot escape. Although the probability of a nuclear power plant blowing up is extremely small, the *possibility* of this happening will be always there as long as there are nuclear power plants. It is also absolutely certain that the possibility of nuclear war breaking out by accident will always be there as long as nuclear weapons systems are poised on their launching pads. All this has very real consequences. The world which is aware of these threats is in psychological terms very different from the world in which such threats did not exist; just as the world which knows AIDS differs from the world that did not – even for an individual who may be at no real risk of ever contracting the disease.

3. Logics and Activities

The psychologist who takes an interest in the differences mentioned above will soon notice that potential threats do not engender just one, predetermined type of behaviour. These threats and eventualities can also be taken into account on the basis of this or that logic. For instance, a young man or woman could take them into account by not wanting to set up a family and have children in a world fraught with threats; someone else might feel that in this world the only refuge and source of personal happiness is provided by the family and children (see Eskola et al. 1988, pp. 298–300).

In the attempt to uncover the underlying logic of an individual actor's choices or decisions, it is useful to know what meanings are attached to that actor's activity. If a person has climbed to the roof of a high building in order to fix the roof, we may assume that that person will take into account the physical law of gravity by having a safety rope attached. If, on the other hand, that person is planning to commit suicide, then he or she might want take account of that law by making sure there are no obstacles on the way down. The logic of the circus artist is more complicated in that here the law serves to create excitement in the audience: while the outer appearance must be one of a would-be suicide, there must at the same time be the safety of the repairman.

In a more theoretical analysis, too, the concept of activity implies the existence of an object towards which that activity is oriented.[6] This refers both to the individual actor's subjective object and to the societal object of the same activity (see Leont'ev, 1978, pp. 50–54). In other words, in my own activity as a university professor I have a different object than my brother in his activity as a farmer; but so too are the objects of universities in society different from the societal objects of agriculture. The internal constitution and logic of an activity derive, at least to a certain degree, from its object. I perform different types of acts in my activity as a university professor than my brother does in his activity as a farmer. Where he has to take account of the laws of nature and the foodstuffs market, there I have to take account of the laws of the academic marketplace. The constitution and logic of my activity also differ to some extent from those of the professor who lived at the beginning of the century, as of course do the constitution and logic of my brother's activity from those of our father, who toiled on that same farm during the inter-war period. This follows by necessity from the objective links of our activities to society and the process of historical change.

The concept of logic is not completely alien to discussions of the psychology of war and peace. Hoffman (1986), for instance, says that 'there seems to be something implacably constant about the logic of behavior of sovereign actors in the international state of nature'. Modern empires and nations, he feels, seem to be performing the same ballet as former ones: 'the music may be different; the choreography hasn't changed' (Hoffman, 1986, p. 3).

Nevertheless Hoffman identifies two state choreographies, two different logics of action. One of these is suggested by 'traditionalists' (with whom Hoffman is associated) and the other by 'radicals'. He says the division is first and foremost 'a split about *what is possible*, which is tied to a different reading of reality' (ibid., p. 3). The basis for the distinction does not lie in these groups having different objects (or 'values', to use Hoffman's own word): 'The concern for survival, the anxiety about black-and-white thinking, cognitive closure, and deadly miscalculations are the same in both group (ibid., p. 3).

However, upon closer inspection it seems that we are in fact talking about the logics of two actors with at least partly different objectivess. Let us begin with the traditionalists, because Hoffman is more straightforward in his description of them than he is in his caricature of the radicals. In my opinion this logic distinctly represents the logic of a superpower which is concerned not only to maintain its power position but also to strengthen that position, to play the role of world police and to impose its moral views as well as its economic system on other nations. Out of these objectivess there grows the logic according to which 'it is of the very essence of international politics that the two biggest actors must be rivals, that the growth of the power of one must cause fear in the other, that each one shall see the other as malignant, itself as benign; (...)' (ibid., p. 5).

It is much harder to see what Hoffman means by radicals because his account of their thinking is packaged in ready interpretations. If he is trying to say that the radicalist logic represents an alternative to the traditionalist view, then surely there should be contained in that logic a way of reading the world and its prospects which is opposite to the traditionalist view. For example, although in inter-state relations 'there is always a *risk* that weakness might tempt a rival or foe' (which, according to Hoffman, is what the traditionalists believe), the 'logic of deterrence' is not the only way that this can be taken into account (ibid., p. 4). It is also possible to try the 'logic of mutual trust'. Or, even though it may seem that a nation living between East and West is subject to the law that if they bow to the West they will necessarily be turning their backs to the East and vice versa, it may well be possible, in reality, to maintain good and friendly relations in both directions: all this nation has to do is find the right logic.

The reason why all this makes sense to me is not because I approach these questions from a therapeutic angle or on the basis of a simplistic model of individual psychology, which is how Hoffman describes his radicals. It makes sense to me because that logic grows out of the objectives that a small neutral country between East and West – my own country Finland – has pursued in the post-war international ballet. Let us take just one example: in the words of Dr Kekkonen, the late President of Finland, the 'Finnish paradox'. First, he described a law which could just as well fit the logic of Hoffman's traditionalists: 'Normally it would seem that when in a border country between West and East the influence of the Western world is on the increase, the influence of the East would correspondingly diminish. And in reverse, if the influence of the Eastern world grows, the West must retreat.' Finland is a border country between East and West, Kekkonen wrote, 'but in our case, the better we succeed in maintaining the confidence of the Soviet Union in Finland as a peaceful neighbour, the better are our possibilities for close cooperation with the countries of the Western world ...' (quoted in Jakobson, 1987, p. 120).

In 1985, when Hoffman presented his paper as a Presidential Address to the International Society of Political Psychology, it was easy to believe that rivalry between Moscow and Washington or East–West confrontation had become an eternal law of international politics. But even the action of a superpower has not only an internal constitution and logic; it, too, is bound up with historical changes within the world system at large. Events since 1985 lend strong support to the above arguments. The changes we have seen within the former socialist bloc during these last few years could never have been predicted from Hoffman's traditional logic, which petrifies the choreography of the international ballet. I admit that the final verdict as to who is right and who is wrong can only be passed by history; but the important thing is precisely that it is *history* which will do that. The fact that action is bound up with historical change must be incorporated in the methodological paradigm of psychological peace research.

4. The Applicability of Knowledge

Psychologists and social scientists who operate on the basis of the paradigm represented by Figure 1 have always been spurred on by the hope that their results will be of some practical use. 'The scientific method has hitherto been used chiefly as a way of getting what we want from the physical world', said a sociology textbook in the 1950s, promising its students that there is 'every reason to believe that it will become equally important in attaining what we want in the way of harmonious social relations. With knowledge gained through this method, social workers, 'social engineers', administrators, or other persons can take intelligent action with some assurance that it will have the effects they seek' (Lundberg, Schrag and Larsen, 1954, p. 5). Above I have attempted to explain why these expectations have been largely disappointed. The explanation is contained in the freedom of the actor, in the key phrase of Figure 2: 'take into account'. Can we now, on this basis, give any promises that the knowledge produced by this methodological approach can be applied to the practical purposes that the peace researcher has in mind?

I think we can. The phrase 'take into account' does not mean that we continually observe our own activity, consciously weigh different rules and laws, or consistently follow different logics in different situations. Most of what we do happens on the basis of what Giddens (1984, p. xxiii) describes as practical consciousness, which he defines as follows: 'Practical consciousness consists of all the things which actors know tacitly about how to "go on" in the context of social life without being able to give them direct discursive expression.' But if there appear unexpected difficulties which impede the fluency of action, then the actor may stop to look at those difficulties and at his own activity and strive towards a 'discursive consciousness'. At both stages the researcher's knowledge about the constitution and logic of action as well as of its historical changes can be applied to practical purposes.

It is a known fact that at low levels of reflection, when we are doing something of a routine nature, verbal representations tend to guide our activity as if suggesting a certain logic. To quote a classical example: 'Thus, around a storage of what are called "gasoline drums", behavior will tend to a certain type, that is, great care will be exercised; while around a storage of what are called "empty gasoline drums", it will tend to be different – careless, with little repression of smoking or of tossing cigarette stubs about' (Whorf, 1956,

p. 135). However, if we point out that also the 'empty' drums may contain explosive vapour, the person in the storage area will have no difficulty in switching back to carefulness again; there was no power in the word 'empty' that would have forced the person to a certain type of behaviour.

Whorf's idea really works, as we can observe in Mikula's (1989) experiments. Here the experimenter was able to exert some influence on children's food preferences by giving them food A and food B and saying: 'If you eat A, you can have B'. This increased the desirability of B, especially if B was something that the children had never had before. There was also some indication that the desirability of A may have declined. Apparently the children were familiar with the logic which says that good food is used as a reward for eating something that is not so good. Especially in those cases where the children had never tasted the food before, the offer 'If you eat A, you can have B' meant that B acquired the meaning 'good' and A the meaning 'not so good'. However, the place of 'food' in the sentence (that is, whether it is 'if-food A' or 'then-food B'), is not a 'variable' which in accordance with some mechanical law 'determines' whether or not there is an increased preference for that food. The most important thing is the logic of the sentence. 'Eat your cookies and then you can have some vegetables' did not make 'then-food' any more desirable: to this the children reacted with surprise and laughter. In the light of what the children knew about the food they were being offered, the logic implied by the sentence was completely meaningless or more like a joke.

5. Conclusion

The basic idea of this chapter was to suggest a reconciliation between the traditional laboratory experiment and survey analysis on the one hand, and such methods as ethogenics, ethnomethodology or discourse analysis on the other. It should be quite obvious that if we want to understand the meanings which actors attach to their activities, the laws and rules which they take into account, and the logics on the basis of which they do this, it is useful to listen to their own accounts – which is what 'ethogenic' techniques do (see Harré, 1979, pp. 124–128). By bending or breaking rules, which has been the trademark of ethnomethodological research techniques, we will be able to uncover elements of that practical consciousness which the actor cannot express discursively (e.g. Garfinkel, 1967, pp. 35–75). If we want to find out how communicative action produces such realities as 'security', 'confidence' or 'threat' through the application of different logics, the techniques of discourse analysis (e.g. Potter and Wetherell, 1987) will prove particularly useful. All these methods are anchored to the paradigm represented by Figure 2, but it is important to remember that in this paradigm there is also a place for laws or regularities so central to traditional methods.

Psychological peace research is one of the areas where these two methodological paradigms could well enter into a fruitful cooperation. Take the various results and prognoses we have of the consequences of nuclear war. Some of these prognoses have been produced by psychologists, and written in the form 'If X, then Y', as for instance the following conclusions by Thompson (1985, p. 42):

> A nuclear attack on the United Kingdom at the expected level of roughly 200 megatons will leave the 15 million or so immediate survivors severely and permanently impaired, and will destroy their capacity for productive social interaction. Given the further consequences which will follow upon the destruction of the economy, the capacity of the survivors to reconstruct any form of functioning society without a massive and sustained outside help will be negligible. It is highly unlikely that a civilized society will survive.

This kind of information – provided it is reliable – is extremely important; and the model described in Figure 1 is fully adequate for purposes of producing it. However, it is also important to carry this effort further and to supplement these results by the kind of information generated by the paradigm of Figure 2. It is clear that Thompson's 'If X, then Y' laws completely knock the bottom out of the traditional logic that has been contained in such representations as 'winning a war', 'civil defence' or 'reconstruction'. How, for example, can anyone say that war provides an important impetus to scientific development if it is highly unlikely that a civilized society will survive a nuclear war?

It is a different matter how people actually take these laws into account in their private life, on political arenas, etc. No doubt a common conclusion is to turn against war and nuclear weapons even more sharply than before, but for many people there must be some logic that allows them to ignore that information. The researcher who wishes to put his results to practical use must also be familar with this proximal area of attitude-formation. Although peace researchers may be chiefly interested, in the same way as the repairman on the roof, in developing new security devices, they must also be prepared to say something to those people who look at their results with the logic of the would-be suicide or the circus artist.

Notes

1 Lundberg, Schrag and Larsen (1954, p. 9), among others, are very plain in expressing their faith in this type of scientific law: 'A statement asserting that certain conditions are related to some phenomenon is called a *hypothesis*. When a hypothesis has been tested *and verified*, we call the statement a *scientific law*.'

2 The first reports published on these studies (Stouffer et al., 1949a and 1949b) were very influential, providing as they did a model for what was to become a popular method of social research: the survey method with its questionnaires and interviews. The third volume in the series (Hovland, Lumsdaine & Sheffield, 1949) provided an authoritative model for the social-psychological laboratory experiment. And the fourth volume (Stouffer et al., 1950), in turn, was a major influence in the use of scale techniques.

3 A typical example of this type of study is the work of Zajonc and Markus (1976), which involved about 400,000 people; all we know about these people is their birth order, familiy size and Raven Progressive Matrices score.

4 Giddens (1984, p. 20) argues in favour of the position that instead of two types of rules, we should speak of the constitutive and regulative aspects of rules.
5 We refer to 'empirical law' in a rather loose sense here, without taking any stand on the question of whether there can exist certain empirical knowledge about social or psychological phenomena, or whether Brown (1984, p. 262) is right in arguing that 'there are not, and cannot be, scientific laws of society as there are scientific laws of nature.'
6 We are here employing the distinctions and terminology proposed by A.N. Leont'ev (1978), who holds that human activities are realized by separate actions. Activities have objects, which in turn are the motives of activity. Actions, then, are directed towards goals, which represent the purpose of actions.

References

Brock-Utne, Birgit, 1989. 'Gender and Cooperation in the Laboratory', *Journal of Peace Research*, vol. 26, no. 1, pp. 47–56.

Brown, Robert, 1984. *The Nature of Social Laws*. Cambridge: Cambridge University Press.

Eskola, Antti, in collaboration with Anna Kihlström, David Kivinen, Klaus Weckroth and Oili–Helena Ylijoki, 1988. *Blind Alleys in Social Psychology: A Search for Ways Out*. Amsterdam: North-Holland.

Garfinkel, Harold, 1967. *Studies in Ethnomethodology*. Englewood Cliffs, NJ: Prentice-Hall.

Giddens, Anthony, 1984. *The Constitution of Society*. Cambridge: Polity Press.

Gleditsch, Nils Petter, 1989. 'Journal of Peace Research', *Journal of Peace Research*, vol. 26, no. 1, pp. 1–5.

Harré, Rom, 1979. *Social Being*. Oxford: Basil Blackwell.

Harré, Rom & Paul F. Secord, 1972. *The Explanation of Social Behaviour*. Oxford: Basil Blackwell.

Hoffman, Stanley, 1986. 'On the Political Psychology of Peace and War: A Critique and an Agenda', *Political Psychology*, vol. 7, no. 1, pp. 1–21.

Hovland, Carl I., Arthur A. Lumsdaine & Fred D. Sheffield, 1949. *Experiments on Mass Communication*. Princeton, NJ: Princeton University Press.

Israel, Joachim & Henri Tajfel, eds, 1972. *The Context of Social Psychology*. London: Academic Press.

Jakobson, Max, 1987. *Finland: Myth and Reality*. Helsinki: Otava.

Katz, Elihu & Paul F. Lazarsfeld, 1955. *Personal Influence*. Glencoe, IL.: The Free Press.

Lamare, James W., 1989. 'Gender and Public Opinion: Defence and Nuclear Issues in New Zealand', *Journal of Peace Research*, vol. 26, no. 3, pp. 285–296.

Leont'ev, Alexei N., 1978. *Activity, Consciousness, and Personality*. Englewood Cliffs, NJ: Prentice-Hall.

Lundberg, George A., Clarence C. Schrag & Otto N. Larsen, 1954. *Sociology*. New York: Harper & Brothers.

Mikula, Gerold, 1989. 'Influencing Food Preferences of Children by "If–Then" Type Instructions', *European Journal of Social Psychology*, vol. 19, no. 3, pp. 225-241.

Perrow, Charles, 1984. *Normal Accidents*. New York: Basic Books.

Potter, Jonathan & Margaret Wetherell, 1987. *Discourse and Social Psychology*. London: Sage.

Stouffer, Samuel A.; Edward A. Suchman, Leland C. DeVinney, Shirley A. Star & Robin M. Williams, Jr., 1949a. *The American Soldier: Adjustment During Army Life.* Princeton, NJ: Princeton University Press.

Stouffer, Samuel A.; Arthur A. Lumsdaine, Marion Harper Lumsdaine, Robin M. Williams, Jr., M. Brewster Smith, Irving L. Janis, Shirley A. Star & Leonard S. Cottrell, Jr., 1949b. *The American Soldier: Combat and Its Aftermath.* Princeton, NJ: Princeton University Press.

Stouffer, Samuel A.; Louis Guttman, Edward A. Suchman, Paul F. Lazarsfeld, Shirley A. Star & John A. Clausen, 1955. *Measurement and Prediction.* Princeton, NJ: Princeton University Press.

Thompson, James, 1985. *Psychological Aspects of Nuclear War.* Leicester: The British Psychological Society.

Tuomela, Raimo, 1989. 'Collective Action, Supervenience, and Constitution', *Synthese*, vol. 80, no. 2, pp. 243–266.

Whorf, Benjamin Lee, 1956. *Language, Thought and Reality.* New York: Wiley.

Zajonc, Robert B. & Gregory B. Markus, 1976. 'Birth Order and Intellectual Development', pp. 157–177 in Lloyd H. Strickland, Frances E. Aboud & Kenneth J. Gergen, eds, *Social Psychology in Transition.* New York: Plenum Press.

PART 3:

Empirical Studies

Introduction to Part 3

In the chapter by *Olsen*, theories from cognitive psychology, and the theory of attribution in particular, are applied to an analysis of the ethnic conflict in Sri Lanka. In interviews, representatives of the Sinhalese and Tamils as well as of the Muslim elites disclose their perceptions concerning the origin and cause of the conflict, its actors, and the possibilities for a durable solution. The focus is on how the image of self and the image of the opponent are sustained and reinforced through the attributional process. In comparison with the respondents in Heradstveit's Arab-Israeli study, the Sri Lankan interviewees display a more moderate and balanced view of the opponent. This would seem to offer hope for a future reconciliation between the ethnic groups.

A pioneering study on national identity is reported in Chapter 15 in which *Larsen and Killifer et al.* report on investigations of national identity. Two thousand twenty-seven respondents representing nine distinct domestic groups and foreign students responded to the survey. Results show consistency in the placement of responses into ten major identity components. Concordance is also apparent between foreign students' and domestic groups' perception of US national identity. Finally, some remarkable concordance is observed in the rankings of the identity components across all participating groups, suggesting a common national identity which transcends socio-political differences. In addition, investigations of Hungarian, Bulgarian,and Greek student samples yield unique national identity components, as well as some concordance, again suggesting the presence of universal values.

Johnson, Handler and Criss employ a social systems perspective where relationships are examined across a range of patriarchal, moral, and nationalistic beliefs, attitudes and values, and acceptance of war. Such a belief system is proposed to be part of 'the rules of the game' that perpetuate war. Eleven components of the system are identified, as well as three variables for acceptance of war. These 14 variables are measured with a survey sample of 162 adults and then subjected to statistical analysis of their interrelationships using a covariance structure model. Four factors underlying the variables are initially identified and labeled as (1) the war system, (2) patriarchy, (3) connectedness, and (4) patriotism/nationalism. These factors remain largely intact as latent variables in the converged covariance structure. This model reveals a complex interrelationship in which acceptance of the war system is positively predicted by patriotism/nationalism, and negatively predicted by connectedness. In turn, 'patriarchy' emerges as a positive predictor of patriotism/nationalism, and a negative predictor of connectedness. The war-system latent variable consists of the three war acceptance variables, plus masculinity; belief in abstract, absolute rules; and negative relationship to internationalism. *Johnson et al.* conclude with suggestions for future research and speculations on potentials for changing the war system, highlighting the value of a multivariate systems approach.

The purpose of the final chapter by *Gould* is to explore gender differences in attitudes to the stress of living under the threat of war. This study inquires into the attitudes of young people aged 15–18, looking at their reactions to growing up in the nuclear age, in terms of sexual identification. Prior to glasnost, contemporary studies of children in the United States and other countries had indicated concern about war as one of the top three worries mentioned spontaneously by youth. Although some studies report sex differences, this important issue has received little systematic attention. The study of sex differences in relationship to war can be of great help in understanding the psychology of today's youth, a group that has grown up in a nuclear world.

14

The Sri Lanka Conflict as Mirrored through Attributions Applied by the Elites

Bendigt Olsen

1. Introduction

Following severe riots and persecutions of the Tamils, the present Sri Lanka conflict escalated in 1983 into outright civil war between the Sri Lankan security forces and the Tamil militant groups. Since then, numerous studies by Sri Lankan and other scholars have been published, analysing the conflict from various perspectives. The revival of Sinhalese and Tamil nationalism and identity is the central theme of some authors (Jayawardena, 1985, 1987; Tambiah, 1986), while others focus on how constitution-making and enactment of laws have hindered nation building (Coomaraswamy, 1984; de Silva, 1986; Wilson, 1988). The general underdevelopment and dependency of the country, the competition for scarce resources, and the change to an open economy have been treated i.a. by Gunasinghe (1984), Nithiyanandan (1987), Sivanandan (1984), and Tiruchelvam (1984); the authoritarian state, the violence and the abuses of the human rights, by Sanmugathasan (1984) and Sieghart (1984), among others.

The need for more research on ideological and psychological variables conducive to the polarization of the communities has been emphasized by Jayawardena (1985) and Tambiah (1986). While perceptions of Buddhist monks were studied by Katz (1988) and those of Sinhala workers by Perera (1984), cognitive theories were not applied by these authors.

This chapter reviews the main findings of a study focusing on the Sri Lanka conflict from a cognitive perspective (Olsen, 1989). The reason for this approach was to bring in a new aspect to the many and well-documented studies of the ethnic conflict in Sri Lanka. Open-ended interviews were applied to encourage representatives of the elites to unfold their perceptions with regard to the cause of the conflict, the main actors, and the possibilities for a political solution and reconciliation. How do they explain the conflict? What are their images of the opponent and of self? Who is to be blamed and who is charged with responsibility for a change to take place?

'The fundamental attribution error' – the main hypothesis of the theory of attribution – postulates the tendency among actors to explain their own action

as caused by requirements of the situation, whereas the same behaviour is by
the observer attributed to stable characteristics of the actor. This hypothesis
was tested, in addition to the four sub-hypotheses formulated by Heradstveit
(1981), incorporating the evaluative dimension of action. The interviews and
the subsequent analysis were organized to facilitate direct comparison with
Heradstveit's study of the Arab-Israeli conflict, and especially his testing of
attributions.

2. Selection of Interviewees and Representativeness

In selecting persons from the elites for interviews, as broad as possible
representativeness of the main ethnic and religious communities, as well as of
different political opinions, was endeavoured. They included representatives
of the main parties to the conflict, i.e. the government and the militants.
Save a few persons approached in advance by letter, contact with respondents
was made by telephone upon arrival in Colombo.[1] In addition to the list
of preferred respondents prepared beforehand, others were suggested and
recommended during the interviews or in private discussions. The interviews
took place in January–February 1987, mainly in Colombo, but also in Kandy;
however, security restrictions prohibited any visit to the Northern and Eastern
Provinces. Tamil politicians in exile and leaders of Tamil militant groups were
interviewed in Madras, India.

The data-base consists of interviews with altogether 50 persons – namely 26
Sinhalese, 19 Tamils and 5 Muslims. Among the respondents are four women,
representing all three communities. The major criterion for selection of these
particular elite representatives was their importance as opinion leaders. Sri
Lanka's long tradition of having a great number of political parties is also
mirrored in the formation during the 1980s of several different militant groups
on the Tamil side. The majority of the interviewees are leaders of political
parties, militant groups, and trade unions, some of them nestors in the political
life of Sri Lanka. Religious leaders, particularly the Buddhist clergy, have
also played an important role over the years in influencing the politics of the
country. The participation of pre-eminent Buddhist priests in the interviews is
therefore of relevance, as well as that of spokespersons for Hindu, Muslim
and Christian organizations. A third category of elites included in this
study are so-called neutral opinion leaders. They represent non-government
organizations working for peace and harmony among the ethnic communities.
In this group of respondents are also researchers, academics, journalists, and
some other intellectuals taking part in the official debate.

The interviews clearly confirmed that the respondents are indeed highly
knowledgeable persons. Moreover, as they are elites with a presumed complex
and consistent belief system (Putnam 1976), answers given in the interview
can consequently be assumed to reflect their beliefs, and would be the same
as if given to someone else. The set of persons interviewed thus represents
a cross-section of different elite groups in Sri Lanka. They mirror the
whole range of the political spectrum of all three communities, although not

proportionally to the political strengths of the different parties. This is not a random sample of the elites, and even less so of the population. However, it provides the qualitative latitude required in this type of exploratory research.

3. The Conflict and its Main Actors

The Sri Lanka conflict is a conflict of interests. The confrontation is an inter-ethnic struggle between the Sinhalese, who form the majority (74 % of the population), and the Tamils, the largest minority community (18.2 %). The most important differences between the two groups refer to language and religion. Both communities can trace their roots back to the ancient history of Sri Lanka. The Tamils have for many centuries inhabited the Northern and Eastern parts of the country. A third party to the conflict are the Muslims, the third largest ethnic group (7 %), of whom one third are since long settled in the Eastern Province.

While relatively peaceful coexistence has characterized community relations over the centuries, interrupted by occasional strifes, the present conflict is a twentieth-century phenomenon, particularly of the post-independence era. Sinhalese-dominated governments have since 1948 pursued policies of ethnic preferential treatment, which by the Tamils are perceived as deliberate attempts to erode their political base, as well as denying them equal access to employment and economic opportunities. Efforts made by the same government to accommodate some Tamil demands and to reach a negotiated settlement have been obstructed by the main Sinhalese party in opposition. In cooperation with Sinhalese-Buddhist champions, the opposition has protested that such proposals would betray the Sinhalese cause, the land, race and faith. By alluding to old myths and history, the Tamils have been exposed as the perpetual opponent, withholding from the Sinhalese their due rights. Eruptions of anti-Tamil riots have followed, forcing the government to withdraw negotiated agreements. The policies carried through and the sufferings experienced have caused deep grievances and frustration among the Tamils, especially the youth. Out of this distress have arisen a demand for a separate Tamil state, and military resistance.

From 1983 and up to the time of the interviews, i.e. January–February 1987, a civil war was being fought in the Northern and Eastern Provinces, between the armed forces and Tamil militant groups. The Liberation Tigers of Tamil Eelam (LTTE) emerged as the dominant militant group. Simultaneously with the ongoing war, peace negotiations were being carried out under the auspices of India. Proposals for a devolution of powers to provincial units, however, provoked the Muslim community, which feared that it would become a minority within a Tamil-ruled Eastern Province.

4. Theoretical Approach

According to cognitive psychology, the human mind is 'an information-processing system' and man an interpreting being, who acquaints himself with the physical and social environment by obtaining, accumulating, estimating and utilizing information (George, 1980). Cognitive beliefs refer to a set of fundamental beliefs which constitute the ideology of a person and his understanding of the world through which new information is filtered. Among the central, fundamental beliefs are the image of self and the image of the opponent. Both are strong and stable, not easily changed, and there is an interdependence between the image of the opponent and the image of oneself: the one is very negative, the other is most likely equally positive. There is a common tendency to resort to selective perception and generalization, e.g. through the application of ethnic stereotypes. This supports the overriding aim of keeping the cognitive beliefs intact, as consistency-seeking is the principal phenomenon in the information process.

The attribution process is one of the psychological mechanisms applied to maintain cognitive consistency and to reinforce fundamental beliefs. The theory of attribution describes the way human beings explain and interpret the surrounding world. 'In particular, attribution theory deals with the causal explanations that individuals construct for their own behaviour and the actions of others' (Monson & Snyder, 1977, p. 89).

What causal explanations do Sri Lanka elites offer concerning past events, and the behaviour of the parties to the conflict? Will their beliefs be reinforced by attributions, and possibly block a reconciliation?

The main hypothesis derived from the theory of attribution, originally formulated by Jones and Nisbett (1972), has subsequently been referred to as the 'fundamental attribution error' (Ross, 1977). This states that 'there is a pervasive tendency for actors to attribute their actions to situational requirements, whereas observers tend to attribute the same actions to stable personal dispositions' (Jones & Nisbett, 1972, p. 80). Strong cognitive forces induce the actor to explain his behaviour by reference to environmental conditions and the observer to emphasize the role of stable dispositional characteristics of the actor. This tendency is due to differences in information accessible to the actor and observer, as well as in information-processing. However, Jones and Nisbett also recognize that motivational factors – the need to maintain and enlarge one's self-esteem being the most prevalent – may often serve to exaggerate or even mute the tendencies described by them.

Attribution theory, originated in the study of individuals, has also been applied to groups, as well as in the analysis of international relations – e.g. that of the Cold War (Jervis, 1976; Larson, 1985).

Heradstveit and Bonham (1986), analysing the attributions made by Norwegian and US policy-makers in connection with the 1978 Soviet boat incidents in Northern Norway, found support for the biases predicted in the hypothesis of 'the fundamental attribution error'. Rosenberg and Wolfsfeld (1977) focused on the distorted attributions of students, and showed that group affiliation, indicating degrees of emotional involvement, is an important factor when explaining the behaviour and actions of the parties to the Arab-Israeli conflict. In Heradstveit's (1981) research on the Arab-Israeli conflict, attribution theory was applied for analysing the causal statements made by elites representing both parties to the conflict. Heradstveit found, however, the hypothesis of the 'fundamental attribution error' insufficient to explain the results obtained through the interviews, and therefore embarked upon a more discriminative analysis which took the motivational factors into account. It appeared that whether the behaviour was considered positive or negative was decisive for the causal explanation presented by the respondent. Heradstveit then formulated this evaluative dimension into four sub-hypotheses as follows (1981, p. 55):

1 There is a tendency to make situational attributions when observing one's own bad behaviour.
2 There is a tendency to make situational attributions when observing the opponent's good behaviour.
3 There is a tendency to make dispositional attributions when observing the opponent's bad behaviour.
4 There is a tendency to make dispositional attributions when observing one's own good behaviour.

These tendencies imply denying own responsibility – i.e., the situation did not allow any choice (1), but taking credit for one's own good behaviour (4). The opponent, however, is seen as having freedom of choice: he is thus blamed for his bad actions (3), whereas his good behaviour is belittled and considered only temporary (2). All these biases work to support cognitive consistency.

Making attributions along the lines formulated in the four sub-hypotheses can have considerable negative impact by impeding conflict resolution. The actor is never willing to take the full responsibility and blame for his behaviour, and any move made by the opponent is interpreted and received in a suspicious and negative way. The result is status quo.

5. Attributions of Sri Lankan Elites

The present analysis attempts to elucidate the attributions made by representatives of the Sri Lankan elites. Six questions, almost identical to those of Heradstveit's Arab-Israeli study, were chosen to elicit causal statements and to permit comparison of the findings. To detect whether the respondents resort to 'the fundamental attribution error', a discriminative analysis showing the locus of causation is made with regard to the first and the sixth question. Since the conflict is just the opposite of an evaluatively neutral situation, which is the point of departure for Jones and Nisbett's hypothesis, the data can be further analysed along the sub-hypotheses developed by Heradstveit.

5.1 Identification of Attributions

In causal statements, respondent directly or indirectly explains why an action has happened, is taking place or fails. While interpreting the behaviour of one's own ethnic group or that of the opponent, attributions are inferred, following a basic dichotomy. Dispositional attributions are those explaining

Table 1   *List of cues*

	ATTRIBUTIONS	
	DISPOSITIONAL	SITUATIONAL
Locus of causation and inference	characteristics, qualities, traits of the person	characteristics of the environment, the context
	lasting	changing
	for a long period of time	short period
	purpose, motives, intentions	pressure and restraints in the environment
	freedom of choice	no choice, reflexive
	non-representative	representative
	abnormal behaviour	normal, common behaviour
	special, unique, atypical, distinguishing, personal disposition	typical, outward external factors and logical points sufficient to explain the behaviour
	narrow	wide spectrum
	irrational	rational

the behaviour as originating from the characteristics or traits of a person or a group. Situational attributions explain behaviour and actions as caused by environmental constraints or stimuli and characteristics of the context. Table 1 shows the cues, giving the qualities of the dispositional vis à vis the situational attributions, that guided the discriminative analysis.

Of special relevance for this study are the two pairs of attributions referring to purposes, motives and intentions (dispositional) as contrasted to those relating to pressure and restraint in the environment (situational) and the freedom of choice (dispositional) and no choice, reflexive (situational). Dispositional attributions explain the behaviour as intentional and initiated of free choice, whereas the situational attributions interpret the behaviour as caused by the circumstances, as reactive, with the actor having no choice but to behave as he did.

Despite the guidance provided by the list of cues, the identification of a dispositional as opposed to a situational attribution can be difficult. The dichotomy is not always evident, as a causal statement may sometimes be interpreted either way. In addition, the formulation of the statement can be misguiding. The context, therefore, must also be evaluated.

The following examples may illustrate the coding dilemma. While statements directly ascribing to the character and traits of a community are easily identified as dispositional attributions, statements referring to groups and their behaviour are somewhat more ambiguous. The question arises: is the group a social force and the behaviour of its members to be considered

Table 2   *Locus of causation*
Attributions made in answers to the question: 'If you should point out one single factor as the main cause of the conflict, which would you mention?'

Respondents	Caused by our side		Caused by other side		Caused by both sides	
	No. of dispositional attributions	No. of situational attributions	No. of dispositional attributions	No. of situational attributions	No. of dispositional attributions	No. of situational attributions
Sinhalese	3	12	4	2	7	3
Tamil	–	1	10	6	3	5
Muslim			S 3	S 1	–	1

S – Sinhalese

only as reactive, a response to stimuli? In this case, it ought to be coded situational. Or do the members represent something unique and irrational, or pursue bad motives? In that case, they should get the value 'dispositional'. Political decisions with major repercussions can be even more intricate to code. Should they be seen as merely events forced by the political situation or socio-economic conditions of the country, or can they be understood as evil intentions and a purposely chosen decision aimed at, say, suppressing the minorities?

Any coding procedure certainly involves a risk of subjectivity. Therefore the coding reliability was tested by three independent coders, one of whom is a native of a South Asian country. The results, analysed according to standard statistical methods, showed that the ratios of coding agreement were within an acceptable range, bearing in mind that the coders were not experienced in this type of coding (Olsen, 1989).

The application of the methodology is displayed below, with examples taken from the coding manual and referring to attributions summarized in Table 2.

'Caused by our side' – dispositional attribution
  Sinhalese: 'The absence of democratic attitude of the rulers'
'Caused by our side' – situational attribution
  Sinhalese: 'Unsuitable economic policy of this government'
  Tamil: 'Our violence is against the violence of the oppressor'
'Caused by other side' – dispositional attribution
  Sinhalese: 'Their objective is to establish a Tamil racial state by definition'
  Tamil: 'The reluctance of the Sinhalese to share power with the Tamils'
  Muslim: 'The unwillingness to accept the minority as an equal'

'Caused by other side' – situational attribution
Sinhalese: 'There is no ethnic conflict but an insurgency using terrorist and guerrilla methods'
Tamil: 'Citizenship act, standardization, land-policy'
Muslim: 'The Sinhalese argued that along with the independence the former status should also come with regard to language'

5.2 Cause of the Conflict

The question: 'If you should point out one single factor as the main cause of the conflict, which would you mention?' was chosen to generate attributions explaining the reason(s) to the conflict. With a few exceptions, the Sinhalese respondents refrained from taking the full blame by applying mainly situational attributions (12 out of 15) when the locus of causation was their own community. This then corroborates the relevant sub-hypothesis by Heradstveit. These attributions refer to various political decisions taken previously or by the present government. However, three persons do impute dispositional attributions, alluding to the absence of a democratic attitude of the Sinhalese rulers, as well as their denying the Tamils the right to exist as a community. Most likely these Sinhalese respondents consider themselves as either neutrals in the conflict, or in opposition to the UNP government, and thus do not feel any personal guilt for what has taken place.

An opposite bias can be traced when the Tamils are seen as the locus of causation. By imputing dispositional attributions, the Tamils are considered responsible for their behaviour. However, these biases are smaller than could be expected. More inferences are made to neutral forces, i.e. the Western countries and both sides, than to the Tamils.

The Tamils almost totally reject referring to, as well as blaming, their own side. Instead, the responses may indicate that they are inclined to make more dispositional attributions (10 out of 16) when ascribing the cause of the conflict to 'the other side'. A majority believe that the conflict is caused by factors such as failure to uphold the principle of equality, reluctance to share power, chauvinism and 'national oppression' by the Sinhalese. The bias is hence in accordance with the 'fundamental attribution error' and Heradstveit's sub-hypothesis.

The number of Muslim interviewees is admittedly very small. Their replies indicate that also they see the conflict as being caused by the Sinhalese, who are accused of favouring the Sinhala man and refusing to accept the minority as an equal. The attributions inferred by the Muslims mainly support Heradstveit's hypotheses in as much as they do not take any guilt upon themselves, but blame the other side or a neutral. This is, however, rather self-evident, as the Muslims are a third party to the conflict.

The Arab-Israeli study by Heradstveit (1981) disclosed an overall tendency to make situational attributions by both parties when ascribing the cause of the conflict. This was explained as an inclination to be more 'detached' when looking back to the distant past than when observing today's behaviour. In the Sri Lankan case, a forbearing attitude increased by time is apparently not pertinent, however, and especially not to the Tamils and the Muslims. In Heradstveit's material very few respondents referred the locus of causation of the conflict to own side. Such responses were made only by a couple of the Israelis, and their attributions were all situational. By contrast, the Sri Lanka data show that about half of the attributions made by the Sinhalese ascribe the cause of the conflict to own side, and most of these are situational. The fact that some of the attributions made when alluding to own side are dispositional, is, therefore, outstanding compared to Heradstveit's findings.

5.3 Image of Self and Image of the Opponent

The image of the opponent is directly exposed in answers to the question: 'What do you think are the basic good and bad aspects of the other side in the conflict?' However, many replies also produced causal statements and attributions relating to the respondent's own community. The outcome of the more elaborated analysis is presented in Table 3.

The Sinhalese answers focusing on the good aspects of the opponent have no marked overweight of situational attributions (7 out of 12), and therefore do not support Heradstveit's sub-hypothesis. Good behaviour may equally emanate from the opponent's own character and free will, as from circumstances in the environment. The Tamils are here described as very able, efficient, hardworking and dedicated people, having contributed a great deal to the professional life and development of Sri Lanka. Most of the situtional attributions made by the Sinhalese refer to the militant movement as a social force, which is considered a positive phenomenon when seen by some leftist

Table 3 *Image of opponent*
Attributions made in answers to the questions: 'What do you think are the basic good and bad aspects of the other side in the conflict?'

Respondents	Other side is good		Other side is bad		Both/all sides are good		Both/all sides are bad	
	No. of dispositional attributions	No. of situational attributions	No. of dispositional attributions	No. of situational attributions	No. of dispositional attributions	No. of situational attributions	No. of dispositional attributions	No. of situational attributions
Sinhalese	5	7	10	4	6	1	6	3
Tamil	12	1	14	5	1	–	2	–
S	2	–	2	1				
Muslim					1	–	1	–
T	1	–	1	–				

S, T – Sinhalese or Tamil, respectively.

eyes. Other interviewees refer to the Tamils returning from asylum in India, and those opposing the 'terrorism'. In all these cases, Tamil behaviour is seen as positive and rational. The Tamil and the Muslim answers, on the other hand, show a clear prevalence of dispositional attributions (Tamil: 12 out of 13, Muslim: 3 out of 3). The result therefore deviates from what could be expected according to the sub-hypothesis. The good behaviour of the opponent – here the Sinhalese – is seen as a reflection of the character and moral values of his community, and less as reactive responses to forces in the environment.

In contrast, all three communities show a tendency to make dispositional attributions when referring to the bad aspects of the opponent (Sinhalese: 10 out of 14, Tamil: 14 out of 19, Muslim: 3 out of 4). This would support the sub-hypothesis predicting the bias of making dispositional attributions when observing the opponent's bad behaviour. Such bad behaviour is not as much ascribed, though, to the character of the opponent itself, as to his bad motives, intentions and irrational fears and ideas. An exception is the reference to Tamil clannishness and their exaggerated preoccupation with education.

Mainly Sinhalese respondents answered that both or all sides are good and/or bad. They tend to make dispositional attributions, not only when pointing at bad behaviour (6 out of 9), but even more so when alluding to the good conduct (6 out of 7). It is of course easier to be generous or condemning when the credit and blame are shared by all communities. The statement is then perceived as neutral. Here one can note the so-called 'black-top' tendency: that the ordinary man is declared innocent and good, while the politician is deemed the guilty. Attributions made in this category, therefore, only partly support the biases predicted by the sub-hypotheses.

The answers to this question thus suggest that the representatives of the main communities in Sri Lanka do not have a completely rigid and locked image of the opponent, as there is no systematic bias in the attribution process. Rather they justly admit the good as well as the bad traits and behaviour of the other side. One may ascribe this inclination to the supposed complex cognitive system and the common background and interest of the elites (Putnam, 1976).

In contrast, the Arab-Israeli study disclosed a tendency, especially among the Arab respondents, to make situational attributions when observing good behaviour on the part of the opponent. The decent demeanour of the adversary is thus perceived as resulting from environmental constraints. The opponent is not given credit for his good behaviour, since it does not arise of free choice, but is forced upon him; such commendable conduct is therefore expected to be only temporary. Thus, the Sri Lanka material does not confirm Heradstveit's findings with regard to the good aspects of the opponent.

The tendency to make dispositional attributions when observing the opponent's bad behaviour was apparent among both the Israelis and the Arabs. The 'devil-image' already established is confirmed by recent behaviour of the adversary, and consistency in the beliefs of the respondents is thereby secured. Also, the Sri Lanka material validates the bias predicted in this sub-hypothesis. Respondents from all three communities make more or less similar proportions of dispositional attributions when alluding to the bad aspects of the opponent.

In certain answers one finds a similarity in the arguments of the respondents in the two studies. The unity of the opponent is referred to by the Arabs as well as by the Sinhalese – thus indirectly admitting the division on one's own side. On the other hand, the contradictory forces within the opponent's camp are also referred to as a hope for change. In the Sri Lankan case, the militants have taken up this role, according to some Sinhalese respondents, whereas more conservative Sinhalese find the return of Tamil refugees promising. In the Arab-Israeli study, the Jews are characterized as 'special' with regard to traits, behaviour and policy followed. The present study shows that the Tamils are considered 'clannish', while the Sinhalese are perceived as sustaining irrational ideas and fears. The idea of being God's own people, chosen to live in a particular country, is common to both the Jews and the Sinhalese, and alluded to in the interviews. However, a parallel between the Tamils and the Jews can also be drawn: both perceive their fight as a defence for their existence as a separate people and for their 'homelands'. In both studies some respondents blame the politicians, whose motives and behaviour are contrasted to those of ordinary people.

Causal statements were also derived from the question: 'Do you think that the other side is threatening you?'. In Table 4, the answers have been coded into the categories 'yes', 'no' and 'both/all sides feel threatened'.

Generally, there is a noticeable similarity in the attributional patterns of the Sinhalese and Tamils. Several of the Sinhalese interviewees acknowledge the irrational feeling of threat pertaining among their own community, due not to the opponent, but to themselves. The ordinary Sinhalese dreads an invasion by

Table 4

Attributions made in answers to the question: 'Do you think that the other side is threatening you?'

Respondents	Yes		No		Both/all sides feel threatened	
	No. of dispositional attributions	No. of situational attributions	No. of dispositional attributions	No. of situational attributions	No. of dispositional attributions	No. of situational attributions
Sinhalese	8	12	5	5	4	4
Tamil	3	12	2	2	4	1
Muslim S	–	3				
					1	2
T	–	3				

S, T, refer to threats by Sinhalese and Tamils, respectively.

the over 50 million Tamils of South India. Most of the attributions made under this category are situational, though, relating to the actual and physical threat felt through the activities of the militants on the one side, and of the security forces, the police and the mobs on the other. The Muslims feel concrete threats from both the other communities, stressing that despite particular sufferings caused through Sinhalese colonization, the Muslims of the East would no more than the Sinhalese like to become part of the Northern Province.

Evidently, those Sinhalese respondents who stress that the threat is coming from the authoritarian and repressive state, represent the political Left. Their Tamil counterparts also use similar language in their explanations of the Sri Lanka government. Some respondents, Sinhalese as well as Tamils, while confirming the feeling of threat by the 'terrorist' or the state, simultaneously stress that they do not feel threatened by the Sinhalese or Tamil people. Once more one can note the phenomenon of contrasting ordinary people against the 'black-top', with some respondents accusing the latter of purposely instilling fear in the minds of people.

The tendency in these confirmative answers to make situational attributions (Sinhalese: 12 out of 20, Tamil: 12 out of 15, Muslim: 6 out of 6), thus goes against the hypothesis of the fundamental attribution error, as well as Heradstveit's 3rd sub-hypothesis, i.e. that there is a bias to make dispositional attributions when observing the opponent's bad behaviour. The threat is felt as real and present, not so much irrational or related to the character of the opponent. At the same time the violence exercised by their own side is fully perceived as reactive by the Tamil respondents, and as well as by a few Sinhalese.

The question: 'Do you think that the other side is threatening you?' did not elucidate enough causal statements by the Arab-Israeli respondents to warrant a quantification. Those who did make more elaborate answers emphasized the bad intentions of the opponent – what he was going to do, more than the bad things he had done. This was a common feature of both Israelis and Arabs in Heradstveit's study.

The Sri Lanka study has, however, revealed a propensity to make causal statements with a bias for situational attributions. Representatives of all three communities point to the threat either already experienced or actually felt. Such a bias is certainly understandable against a background of a violent ethnic conflict.

Those respondents in the Arab-Israeli study who declared that they did not feel threatened alluded to the opponent's scant prospects to do so, not to his good will. Some Arabs envisaged themselves becoming stronger as a reality, and therefore said they did not fear the opponent. The power component, according to Heradstveit, is thus a strong variable in the causal analysis made by his respondents. The Sri Lanka study discloses more references to 'the people as such' when renouncing any threat.

Causal statements, some identical to those disclosed through the previous question, were also evoked by the question : 'Do you think that the other side believes that you are threatening them?'. Although the question does

Table 5
Attributions made in answers to the question: 'Do you think that
the other side believes that you are threatening them?'

Respondents		Yes		No		Both/all sides feel threatened	
		No. of dispositional attributions	No. of situational attributions	No. of dispositional attributions	No. of situational attributions	No. of dispositional attributions	No. of situational attributions
Sinhalese		1	13	1	9	2	2
Tamil		12	1	1	3	3	2
	S	1	–	–	1		
Muslim						1	2
	T	–	1				

S, T – threatened by Sinhalese and Tamils, respectively.

not really apply to the Muslim respondents, they answered the question all
the same, referring not to their own community, but to the Sinhalese and the
Tamils. Table 5 presents attributions under the same categories of answers as
in Table 4.

The answers given by the Sinhalese are divided almost equally between
'yes' and 'no', with an overweight of situational attributions. The Sinhalese
answering 'yes', while inferring situational attributions, recognize the feeling
of threat and insecurity among the Tamils. The respondents confirm that the
fear is caused by years of rioting and harassing by their own community.
A clear majority of the Tamil interviewees, however, impute dispositional
attributions when recognizing that the other side feels threatened by them. The
respondents point to the sense of insecurity felt by the Sinhalese as a minority
within a larger South Indian context. All such fears, though, are considered
hypothetical, baseless and irrational.

Those respondents – Sinhalese, Tamil and Muslim – who deny that the other
side feels threatened give almost similar answers as to the previous question,
alluding to the good character of both peoples, etc.

Answers found under the category 'both/all sides feel threatened', as well,
are also practically identical with those given to the last question. Mutual
discord, mistrust and physical threat are alluded to.

The hypothesis of 'the fundamental attribution error', as well as Heradstveit's sub-hypothesis about a tendency to make situational attributions when
explaining one's own bad behaviour, find support only in the Sinhalese
answers (13 out of 14). The hypothesis further implies that the actors – in
this case the Sinhalese – while making situational attributions do not take
the full blame for the bad actions performed by their community. However, it

should be kept in mind that both the Tamils and the Muslims made situational attributions in reply to the previous question, when declaring that they felt threatened by the Sinhalese – as well as by the Tamils, in the case of the Muslims. The real events, thus, seem to be 'engulfing' the scene, from the point of view not only of the actors, but also of the observers. Those Sinhalese who declare that the Tamils are not threatened, and who make situational attributions by pointing to evidence in daily life, are apparently resorting to ego-defensive mechanisms, such as selective perception and denial of certain facts inconsistent with their belief system and the image of self.

By referring to the irrational fear pertaining to the Sinhalese the Tamil answers comply with the bias explained by the fundamental attribution error. The locus of causation is seen as being with the opponent himself, and not in the situation created by the respondent and his side, which would be expected. Ego-defensive mechanisms seem once more to be working. These dispositional attributions made by the Tamil respondents correspond, though, to those made by several Sinhalese respondents in replies to the previous question (Table 3. Yes. Number of dispositional attributions: Sinhalese: 8 out of 20). Both groups regard the fears as unfounded, irrational and part of the Sinhala myth. Also some of the Muslim respondents refer to these irrational fears held by the Sinhalese, as contrasted with the real threats experienced by the Tamils.

In Heradstveit's study also the answers to the question: 'Do you think that the other side believes that you are threatening them?' did not justify a quantitative analysis. However, in both studies this question brought out analogous attributional biases. Certain similarities are found between the Arab and the Sinhalese answers, both groups referring to events and characteristics of the situation. The opponent's fear is recognized as real, due among other things to physical harassment in the case of the Tamils, and the Arab strength, as demonstrated in the October War, giving grounds for a rational fear among the Israelis.

The Tamils, like the Israelis, on the other hand, tend to infer dispositional attributions in their causal explanations. Several of these respondents are inclined to impute the locus of causation to the opponent himself, thus making use of ego-defensive mechanisms. The fear is considered irrational, e.g. ascribed by the Israelis to the religious and cultural traits of the Arabs, and as part of the Sinhala myth by the Tamils. As in the Arab-Israeli study, also some of the Sinhalese and Tamil respondents differentiate between the elites, 'the black-top' instigating fear, and the ordinary people who are normal and do not feel any threat.

To extract more precise perceptions about the situation of the Mulims, the following question was included: 'What do you think are the main fears among the Muslims?'. The locus of causation, divided into the three categories is unfolded in the discriminative analysis given in Table 6.

The bias as predicted in one of Heradstveit's sub-hypotheses – namely, the tendency to explain the bad behaviour of the opponent by referring to his personal traits, bad motives or irrationality – has been tested. The results

Table 6

Attributions made in answers to the question: 'What do you think are the main fears among the Muslims?'

Respondents		Threatened by one side only		Threatened by both the Sinhalese and the Tamils		No reason for fears	
		No. of dispositional attributions	No. of situational attributions	No. of dispositional attributions	No. of situational attributions	No. of dispositional attributions	No. of situational attributions
Sinhalese	S	1	1				
				–	8	6	–
	T	1	13				
Tamil	S	–	9				
					6	3	2
	T	–	2				
Muslim					5		

T, S – threatened by Sinhalese and Tamils, respectively.

derived from this question do not support the hypothesis, however. Instead there is a tendency to make situational attributions, even when the locus of causation is the opponent: e.g. the Sinhalese respondents accusing the Tamils of causing the threat (13 out of 14) or vice versa (9 out of 9). When explaining the reasons for their fear – which they consider real – Muslim respondents as well refer to actual political and economic constraints. The majority of the Sinhalese respondents point to the conflict between the Tamils and the Muslims in the Eastern Province, alluding to the feeling of fear among the Muslims of becoming a 'minority within a minority' in case of a merger of the Northern and Eastern Provinces into a Tamil Eelam. The Tamil version reveals an almost reverse picture, namely the notion among the Muslims, that they will be suffering the same oppression once the Tamil problem is 'solved'. Other Tamils point to the discrimination against the Muslims, which has already taken place, especially in the Eastern Province, where they are the biggest losers territorially through the policy of colonization.

Several respondents, both Sinhalese and Tamils, stress how accommodatingly and peacefully the Muslims live together with the other communities. The impression is that the Sinhalese, as well as the Tamils, both think that they are closest to the Muslims. Any discrimination of the Muslims, as perceived by themselves, is clearly admitted only by a few Sinhalese and Tamil respondents. The lack of real understanding of the Muslim cause is apparent. Once more we see the propensity to resort to self-defensive mechanisms, by denying certain facts. This is especially noticeable among some of the Tamil respondents, who are sure that the Muslim people of the East would say yes

Table 7   *Image of change*
Attributions made in answers to the question: 'Do you bel.eve that a political solution is still possible?'

| | Locus of causation | | | | | |
| Respondents | Change to be caused by our side | | Change to be caused by other side | | Change to be caused by both sides | |
	No. of disposi-tional attribu-tions	No. of situa-tional attribu-tions	No. of disposi-tional attribu-tions	No. of situa-tional attribu-tions	No. of disposi-tional attribu-tions	No. of situa-tional attribu-tions
Sinhalese	1	6	7	3	4	8
Tamil		1	10	1	–	6
Muslim					4	1

to a merger, or that at least quite a few of them are prepared to 'throw in their lot' with the Tamils. The statements admitting shared responsibility embody only situational attributions, and thus lend some support to the sub-hypothesis of a tendency to make situational attributions when observing one's own bad behaviour.

5.4 Image of Change

Answers to the question: 'Do you believe that a political solution is still possible?' elucidate the image of change. Through a discriminative analysis the locus of causation for a political solution is established, as set out in Table 7.

The analysis discloses certain biases in the attributional inferences made by all the three groups. The Sinhalese respondents who admit that change must originate from their own side make mainly situational attributions (6 out of 7) by referring to necessary changes in the current politics. Personal responsibility is thereby avoided. These results are in line with Heradtveit's postulate of the tendency to make situational attributions when change is seen as caused by one's own side.

The analysis has also detected an aptitude to charge the opponent with the responsibility for a political solution to take place. One notes the predomi-nance of dispositional attributions. This tendency is most evident among the Tamils, where only one person refers the causal candidate of change to own side. A political solution is possible, according to these respondents, provided the government is fair and prepared to realize the just aspirations of the Tamil people. Several of the Sinhalese interviewees, on the other hand, refer to the intransigence of the Tamil militant groups as not being willing to accept the government's latest proposals. As there were more dispositional attributions

(Sinhalese: 7 out of 10, Tamil: 10 out of 11) when referring to the other side, these results support Heradstveit's predictions that there will be a tendency to make dispositional attributions when change is perceived as caused by the opponent.

Most of the Sinhalese who argue that change must emanate from both sides, stress the characteristics of the context, pointing at the exhaustion prevailing in the government camp, as well as in that of the LTTE. Similar arguments are presented by the Tamil interviewees. All the Muslim respondents are convinced that a change must be initiated from both sides. The characters and intentions of the Sinhalese government and the Tamil militant groups are referred to. It is e.g. doubted whether a political solution is possible with the present set-up of people involved in the talks.

Although the Arab-Israeli study detected an attributional bias related to the causal candidate of change, the majority of the respondents alluded to a neutral force, especially the UN, as the initiator of change while making situational attributions. Heradstveit's findings indicated an overall emphasis on situational attributions by both Arab and Israeli respondents, the same pattern as found with regard to what caused the conflict. His results, therefore, gave rise to two additional hypotheses, namely 'an attributional bias related to bias as a function of time, and a bias as a function of pre- or post-decision' (Heradstveit, 1981, p. 71).

As discussed above, the Sri Lankan respondents, especially the Tamils and the Muslims, do not seem to be more detached when considering future change than when observing the past. This does not necessarily imply, however, that the motive of sustaining self-esteem is more predominant among the Sri Lankan respondents than among the Arabs and Israelis. On the contrary, the tendency to make dispositional attributions may equally well be a sign of realism.

One possible interpretation is that the cause of the conflict is felt very close in time. In particular, several of the Tamil respondents living as refugees in Madras carry with them personal and painful memories. They tend to explain the conflict as caused by the opponent's bad intentions. With regard to the image of change the Muslims feel special uncertainty about their future, and therefore stress that the character and intentions of the main parties have to change. Hence, the Sri Lanka material does not warrant any distinction with regard to attributional bias in a post-decision or a pre-decision stage, and the two additional hypotheses put forward by Heradstveit are therefore not supported.

5.5 Discussion

The comparative analysis has revealed many similarities between the two studies. However, on the whole, a somewhat less strong bias is noticed among the Sri Lankan elites. The tendency to blame the opponent by imputing dispositional attributions is less evident. Responses show that all three groups infer situational attributions when explaining the threat felt by the Muslims.

There is also a tendency to make dispositional attributions when describing the good aspects of the opponent.

One possible explanation of the difference is that the Sinhalese and Tamils, in contrast to the Arabs and Israelis, have lived reasonably peacefully together for centuries, except for occasional eruptions of ethnic strife, especially after Independence. Despite 'the Sinhala myth' and Tamil clannishness the ordinary Sinhalese and Tamil seem to have tolerated each other. The reason is most likely that they – and even the Muslims – by and large share a common cultural and historical heritage. This is particularly so with regard to the Sri Lankan elites, who at least up to now have been recruited from strata with a common social background. A good number are graduates from European universities, and many of them 'fought' together for an independent Ceylon. Several have also been living as colleagues and friends in Colombo, and their personal relationships have deteriorated only after 1983.

The parties in the Arab-Israeli conflict were, and still are, much further apart than in Sri Lanka. The conflict, being international, has involved the big powers since the creation of the state of Israel. At the time of Heradstveit's study – 1970–1976 – conflict had remained at a much higher level for a longer period than was the case of the Sri Lanka conflict in early 1987. Mistrust seems to have deeper roots among the Arabs and Israelis, who have never really lived together. Furthermore, their cultural, social, and political background is – at least was – very different. These circumstances have most likely contributed to their strong and generally negative image of the opponent. Propaganda on both sides has presumably also done much to create and sustain such images. Differences in the level of escalation of the conflict, as well as in the level of tolerance, may thus explain the rather stronger attributional bias detected in the Arab-Israeli study.

The hypotheses deduced from the theory of attribution have been the starting point for the analysis presented in this chapter. The results indicate that the Sri Lankan elites make attributions which largely comply with the hypotheses. The attributional biases differ with the observer and the actor, and hence with the locus of causation, quite in accordance with 'the fundamental attribution error', postulated by Jones and Nisbett. The evaluative and motivational forces, as stated in Heradstveit's sub-hypotheses, are in most cases found reinforcing the attributional tendencies, but not always.

The analysis has elicited an attributional pattern among the respondents, which is not fully symmetrical. The Tamil and Muslim respondents deviate from the Sinhalese in making some more dispositional attributions. This can most likely be explained by their far higher degree of involvement in the conflict. Motivational factors seem to work more strongly among these groups of respondents. Their emotional memories of the past make them also suspicious about the future. A real 'change of heart' has to take place among the Sinhalese; both Tamil and Muslim rights will have to be acknowledged for a political solution to be realized.

On the other hand, the Tamils' own violence, experienced as threat by several of the Sinhalese respondents, is explained as being reactive, forced through the violence of the security forces. The Tamils consider themselves as having no choice, but have to fight back, whereas the opponent – the government – has voluntarily chosen a military solution.

The Sinhalese respondents are in general more divided in their attributional tendency. The reason is probably the composition of these respondents, which comprises politicians and associates representing the whole Left-Right scale including pro-Sinhalese/Buddhists and also several neutral respondents. Several of these respondents acknowledge the injustices committed against the Tamils, as well as their own irrational fears of an invasion from South India. The present government, though accused of brutality and anti-democracy, still finds support among some of the respondents in its latest efforts to reach a political solution.

This analysis has not confirmed the sub-hypothesis that there is a tendency to make situational attributions when explaining the opponent's good behaviour. The consequences of such attributional bias would be a refusal to accept good behaviour as a sign of good will, seeing it instead as only forced by the circumstances or perhaps by a third party. The attributional process thereby functions as one of the means to maintain the consistency of the cognitive belief system, including the image of the opponent. However, genuine positive behaviour of either side in the Sri Lanka conflict would probably be understood and interpreted as emanating from good intentions. The tendency to make dispositional attributions when observing the good aspects of the other side seems particularly promising.

6. Conclusion

Subsequent events as revealed by Sri Lankan and Indian press (e.g. *Lanka Guardian* and *India Today*), however, would seem to discourage the hopes for peace and reconciliation. The Indo-Sri Lanka Accord of 1987 provoked political parties and organizations championing the Sinhalese-Buddhist cause, calling it a sell-out to the Tamils. They regarded the Indian Peace Keeping Force (IPKF), provided for under the Accord, as an invasion army threatening the independence of Sri Lanka. Protests and violence largely instigated and staged by the JVP (People's Liberation Front) developed into a brutal war in the South with the equally ruthless security forces and pro-government vigilante groups (*Race & Class*, 30, 3, 1989).

Tamils as well were highly critical of the IPKF and its mandate. The LTTE in particular obstructed the peace-process by turning against the Indian forces, and refrained from participating in the 1988 election of Provincial Councils for the temporary merger of the Northern and Eastern Provinces. Ranasinghe Premadasa, after being elected President in December 1988, fulfilled his vow for withdrawal of the Indian troops from Sri Lanka. A negotiated agreement was reached with the Indian government, stipulating the exit of the IPKF by 1 January 1990. The departure was finally accomplished in March 1990.

Although a ceasefire was signed in June 1989 between the security forces and the LTTE, war was being waged on two fronts at the end of the year. In the

South the counter-offensive launched by the security forces against the JVP raged even after the capture and death in November of most of its leadership. In the North-Eastern Province the LTTE fought to replace their main Tamil rivals, the 'stooges of India', who, backed by the Indian troops, had formed the provisional government of the Province.

The guerrilla war thus continued despite the December 1989 transformation of the political wing of the LTTE into a democratic socialist political party, the People's Front of Liberation Tigers (PFLT), which declared itself ready to participate in Provincial Council elections. By mid-June 1990 serious fighting had broken out in the North-Eastern Province after LTTE attacks on several police stations. The military contest escalated towards the end of the month with a series of air attacks on LTTE positions in Jaffna town and other places on the peninsula. August 1990 brought news of frightful massacres of Muslim civilians in the East. The LTTE, charged with responsibility by the government, refuted the accusation, saying that the government had carefully planned and carried out the killings while blaming the LTTE coincidently with its efforts to buy weapons from Muslim countries in the Middle East.

Jaffna Fort, besieged by the Tigers since June, was stormed in September during a full-scale operation by the army, but was shortly after abandoned as militarily futile. The event was looked upon as a glorious and symbolic victory by the government, as well as by the Tigers. The indiscriminate bombings by the government have, however, further alienated many Tamils from the government. In the South there is a noticeable weariness and waning support for the war among the ordinary Sinhalese, who bear the burden of warfare, high inflation, and recent deterioration of the economy following the sanctions against Iraq. The government, while trying to rectify the economy, has simultaneously been buying new weapons and aircraft (*The Economist*, 3 November, 1990).

The Indo-Sri Lanka Accord and the subsequent involvement of the Indian Peace Keeping Force have certainly confirmed for many people the old beliefs – nurtured through the years by Sinhalese-Buddhist chauvinists – of a threat of invasion from South India. The image of the Tamils as the opponent or the enemy has been reinforced by these recent events, demonstrated especially through the intransigence of the LTTE. It is also evident from the news reports in 1990 that the parties to the conflict continue to put the blame on each other for causing the renewed fighting. Actors apparently make situational attributions when explaining their own role, and thereby avoid bearing any blame themselves.

Psychological processes sustaining fundamental beliefs have most likely contributed to the obstruction of negotiations and rejection of the Indo-Sri Lanka Accord that was demonstrated by important groups on both sides. Since the transformation of beliefs is a long process, change can preferably be initiated first with regard to situational constraints. One should not forget that the Sri Lanka conflict is a conflict of interests, which actually boils down to the recognition of the Tamils as a community. Therefore the concrete grievances and main issues of conflict need to be tackled and solved. Introducing changes in the situation usually also leads to modified opinions, and gradually to changed cognitive beliefs. It is conceivable, therefore, that regional autonomy, if well designed, may work better than hitherto experienced, and finally be looked upon as a legitimate and normal form of government for Sri Lanka.

This study has disclosed a tendency for the Sri Lankan respondents to follow the attributional pattern that differs with observer and actor in accordance with 'the fundamental attribution error'. To a certain extent also the biases predicted in Heradstveit's four sub-hypotheses have been supported, though less in comparison with the results reached in the Arab-Israeli study. The tendency to blame the opponent himself for causing the conflict by imputing dispositional attributions is not as pronounced as could be expected. The inclination among Sri Lankan interviewees to make dispositional attributions when describing the good aspects of the opponent is in fact quite remarkable and contrary to the hypothesis. The analysis has further revealed a somewhat stronger tendency among the Tamils and Muslims to make dispositional attributions when discussing future change, which most likely can be explained by their greater personal and emotional involvement in the conflict. The Sinhalese respondents on the other hand display a more diverse attributional pattern, several of them acknowledging their own irrational fears as well as injustices and violence directed against the Tamils in particular.

While the small size of this sample does not permit very firm conclusions, the study indicates a disposition for reciprocal acceptance of each other by the elites of the two main parties to the conflict. Hence, from such a platform of tolerance, there would be scope for reconciliation in spite of all the sad developments in Sri Lanka.

Notes

1 A grant by the Norwegian Council for Social Science and Humanities, partially financing the travel to Sri Lanka and India, is gratefully acknowledged.

References

Abeysekera, C. & N. Gunasinghe, eds, 1987. *Facets of Ethnicity in Sri Lanka*. Social Scientists Association, Colombo.

Coomaraswamy, R., 1984. *Sri Lanka The Crisis of the Anglo-American Constitutional Traditions in a Developing Society*. Vikas Publishing House, New Delhi.

George, A.L., 1980. *Presidential Decisionmaking in Foreign Policy. The Effective Use of Information and Advice*. Westview Press/Boulder, Co.

Gunasinghe, N., 1984. 'Open Economy and its Impact on Ethnic Relations in Sri Lanka', pp. 197–214, in *Sri Lanka, the Ethnic Conflict, Myths, Realities and Perspectives*. Committee for Rational Development, Navrang, New Delhi.

Heradstveit, D., 1981. *The Arab-Israeli Conflict. Psychological Obstacles to Peace*. Oslo: Universitetsforlaget.

Heradstveit, D. & G.M. Bonham, 1986. 'Decision-Making in the Face of Uncertainty: Attributions of Norwegian and American Officials', *Journal of Peace Research*, vol. 23, no. 4, pp. 340–356.

Jayawardena, K., 1985. *Ethnic and Class Conflicts in Sri Lanka*. Centre for Social Analysis, Dehiwala, Sri Lanka.

Jayawardena, K., 1987. 'The National Question and the Left Movement in Sri Lanka', pp. 226–271, in Abeysekera, C. & N. Gunasinghe, eds, 1987.

Jervis, R., 1976. *Perception and Misperception in International Politics*. Princeton University Press, New Jersey.

Jones, E.E. & R.E. Nisbett, 1972. 'The Actor and the Observer: Divergent Perception of the Causes of Behavior', pp. 79–94, in Jones, E.E. et al., eds, *Attribution: Perceiving the Causes of Behavior*. General Learning Press, New Jersey.

Katz, N., 1988. 'Sri Lankan Monks on Ethnicity and Nationalism', pp. 138–152, in de Silva, K.M, P. Duhe, E.S Goldberg & N. Katz, eds, *Ethnic Conflict in Buddhist Societies: Sri Lanka, Thailand and Burma*. Pinter Publishers, London.

Larson, D.W., 1985. *Origin of Containments, A Psychological Explanation*. Princeton University Press, New Jersey.

Monson, T.C. & M. Snyder, 1977. 'Actors, Observers and the Attribution Process', *Journal of Experimental Social Psychology*, 13, pp. 89–111.

Nithiyanandan, V., 1987. 'An Analysis of Economic Factors Behind the Origin & Development of Tamil Nationalism in Sri Lanka', pp. 100–170, in Abeysekera, C. & N. Gunasinghe, eds, 1987.

Olsen, B., 1989. *The Sri Lanka Conflict. A Study of Elite Perceptions*. Derap Publications No. 251, Chr. Michelsen Institute, Derap, Bergen, Norway.

Perera, J., 1984. 'Glimpses of Sinhala Perception'. *Lanka Guardian*, vol. 7, no. 4, 15 June, pp. 11–16; no. 5, 1 July, pp. 13–15; no. 6, 15 July, pp. 15–17.

Putnam, R.D., 1976. *The Comparative Study of Political Elites*. Prentice-Hall, Englewood Cliffs NJ.

Rosenberg, S. and E. Wolfsfeld, 1977. 'International Conflict and the Problem of Attribution'. *Journal of Conflict Resolution*, Vol. 21, no.1, pp. 75–103.

Ross, L., 1977. 'The Intuitive Psychologist and his Shortcomings. Distortions in the Attribution Process', pp. 173–220, in Leonard Berkovitz, ed., *Advances in Experimental Social Psychology*, vol. 10. Academic Press, New York.

Sanmugathasan, N., 1984. 'Sri Lanka: the story of the holocaust', *Race and Class*, Vol. 26, no. 1, pp. 63–82.

Sieghart, P., 1984. *Sri Lanka: A Mounting Tragedy of Errors*. International Commission of Jurists and Justice, Dorset Press, London.

de Silva, K.M., 1986. *Managing Ethnic Tensions in Multi-Ethnic Societies, Sri Lanka 1880–1985*. University Press of America, Lanham, New York and London.

Sivanandan, A., 1984. 'Sri Lanka: racism and the politics of underdevelopment', *Race and Class*, vol. 26, no. 1, pp. 1–38.

'Sri Lanka. If they get bored with the war', *The Economist*, 3 November 1990, p. 66.

'Sri Lanka: the choice of two terrors', *Race & Class*, vol. 30, no. 3, 1989, pp. 57–71.

Tambiah, S.J., 1986. *Sri Lanka. Ethnic Fratricide and the Dismantling of Democracy*. University of Chicago Press, Chicago and London.

Tiruchelvam, N., 1984. 'Ethnicity and Resource Allocation', pp. 185–196 in Goldman, R.B. & A.J. Wilson, eds, *From Independence to Statehood. Managing Ethnic Conflict in Five African and Asian States*. St. Martins Press, New York.

Wilson, A.J., 1988. *The Break-up of Sri Lanka. The Sinhalese–Tamil Conflict*. C. Hurst & Co., London.

15

National Identity:
Group-specific or Common Stereotypes

Knud S. Larsen
Carolyn Killifer
Gyorgy Csepeli
Krum Krumov
Ludmilla Andrejeva
Nadia Kashlakeva
Zlatka Russinova
Laszlo Pordany

1. Introduction

Sherif, Harvey, White, Hood & Sherif (1961) studied the nature of conflict in producing prejudicial responses among boys at a summer camp. During the initial phase the boys developed strong attachments to their own group. After two weeks of competition the groups had developed strong prejudice toward members of the other group. When the conflictual groups worked together to reach superordinate goals that were desired by both parties, however, a dramatic reduction in competitive group identity occurred.

In competitive societies there are strong tendencies to divide the social world into in-groups and out-groups (Tajfel et al., 1987). In these studies participants expressed more negative attitudes toward members of out-groups and treated them less favorably. Doise (1969) has shown that these biases occur even before any intergroup decision, suggesting that biased perceptions serve to justify anticipated interaction. These biased anticipations remain even when the group categorization is nonsensical (Doise et al., 1971).

National identity serves this in-group/out-group function. Tajfel (1982) suggested that individuals enhance self-esteem through identification with specific social groups. When nations are in conflict, or experience a threat to coherence and integration, national identity is especially strong, and may serve to enhance conflict. The origins of nationalism and national identity have been of interest to scholars for some time (Lambert & Klineberg, 1959; Klineberg, 1962). While nationalism refers to loyalty to a nation, and in more extreme cases to ethnocentrism, national identity is a belief or attitudinal-based component (Lambert, 1962). In short, national identity encompasses the beliefs, stereotypes, and attitudes characterized by a sense of national consciousness. Haas (1986) has suggested that nationalism can be seen as the convergence of political or territorial loyalty manifested in feelings of kinship but also based on religion and language.

Thus, nationalism is a major integrating force which appears to transcend international ideologies. That national identity is important can be observed in the recent experience of Eastern Europe: once the ice began to melt. we saw an immediate return to national, tribal, and indeed ethnocentric loyalties.

National identity is the way an individual views his country. From where did the concept of being an American – or a Spaniard, or a Swede, or any other nationality – derive? Here we can note both historical and contemporary influences, including the importance of national symbols. In the USA, especially after the Civil War, heightened levels of nationalism led the flag – the 'Stars and Stripes'- to symbolize everything worthy of reverence. National symbols have often taken on a pseudo-religious character, reinforcing the emotional basis of national identity (White, 1965).

National identity is also formed by social institutions. Mediating national stereotypes are such institutions as the family, peer relationships, school systems, churches, and government. In the process of developing national identity, people will often exaggerate the virtues of their own nation and depreciate the accomplishments of others (Katz, 1965). This belief in the superiority of the in-group (nation) is the essential trait of ethnocentrism. Hayes (1960) has suggested that nationalism may be defined as 'a notion of patriotism with a consciousness of nationality' (p. 2). In other words, we would not observe nationalism unless people also possessed an awareness based on common stereotypes – national identity. Since there are obvious benefits associated with distinguishing between in-groups and out-groups, national identity has its foundation in group categorization processes. An in-group forms when people perceive that they hold things in common (Forbes, 1985). Over time, society has evolved from tribal or clan loyalties to ever larger national units (Shafer, 1977).

This chapter addresses two questions: What are the components of national identity; and is there a discernible pattern or are responses primarily individualized? If a common national identity is present, we could expect responses to be clustered around central dimensions. Also, if society reflects a common national identity, we would expect consistency in responses across a variety of social groups. The studies which follow examine national identity in a large sample of US groups, foreign students living in the US, and among Hungarian, Bulgarian, and Greek students. The survey required respondents to list three words describing national identity.

2. Part 1: The US-based samples

2.1 Method

Respondents. A total of 2077 US students, foreign students, and other US roups participated. 812 were male and 1265 were female; mean age was 25.10. Foreign students were Japanese, Taiwanese, Danish, Dutch, Korean, and Australians (n = 217, $\bar{x}$ age = 23.59). US groups were composed of: US students (n = 533, $\bar{x}$ age = 20.54); members of university sororities and fraternities (n = 148, $\bar{x}$ age = 19.60); individual community member samples (n = 353, $\bar{x}$ age = 21.13); members of religious groups (n = 171, $\bar{x}$ age = 34.01); military-related groups (n = 133, $\bar{x}$ age = 27.24); prison inmates (n = 73, $\bar{x}$ age = 35.5); members of the Republican Party (n = 97, $\bar{x}$ age = 36.48); and high school students (n = 142, $\bar{x}$ age = 16.12).

Survey. Respondents were asked, 'On this page list three words which you think best describe being an American.' This was followed by three spaces labeled 1, 2, and 3.

2.2. Results and Discussion

This study is based on 2,027 respondents each offering three words to specify 'American national identity'. These 6,081 responses were then subjected to a content analysis. Table 1 summarizes the national identity categories, percentage of responses, overall percentage, and rank, for the nine groups.

The content analysis reveals ten major categories. *Freedom* as a category is summarized by such words as free, choice, liberty, pursuit, diversity, free elections. This is clearly seen as a dominant component in national identity. *Social development* refers to the achievements of US society based on components like opportunity, innovative, abundant, industrious, productive, advanced, education, hope, perseverance, prosperity, work ethic, achievement, capitalism, comfort, development, and enterprise. The third component, *political values*, is summarized by words like democracy, constitution, equality, justice, liberal, rights, unity, law, vote, fair, and participation. These words refer to the perceived political underpinnings of society. *Ethnocentrism* is self-described in-group preference, and includes words such as strength, fidelity, patriotic, powerful, allegiance, duty, flag, honor, loyalty, chauvinistic. *Materialism* includes the more hedonistic components of US culture based on self-descriptions such as: greed, pleasure, variety, baseball, Chevy, money, apple pie, stocks, and fun. *Arrogance* is somewhat related to ethnocentrism, but more specific in expressing superiority through words like: proud, pride, cutthroat, dominant, loud, Rambo, and rude. *Positive character* traits are personal laudatory comments including: honest, open, unique, flexible, carefree, friendly, and patient. The US tradition of *rugged individualism* is represented in the independent component described by words like: independence, individualist, and self-governing. *Family values* like happiness, health, community, responsibility, love, religion, provider, moral, integrity and responsibility, represent a distinct component. Finally, relatively few responses reflected outright *negative character* traits such as: lazy, ignorant, self-centered, selfish, and impulsive.

Thus, in a technique analogous to sentence completion we may observe ten major components of US national identity. Were these responses also

Table 1　Content analysis: percentages and rank of national identity for US-based sample (rank in parenthesis)

Identity Components	Foreign students	US students	Sororities & fraternities	Community samples	Religious	Military related groups	Prisoners	Republicans	High school students	Totals	Overall rank
Freedom	14.00 (2)	26.30 (1)	24.75 (1)	21.50 (1)	34.97 (1)	27.60 (1)	26.83 (1)	31.34 (1)	28.08 (1)	235.87	(1)
Social development	13.70 (3.5)	16.27 (2)	14.22 (3)	14.62 (2)	12.44 (3)	9.38 (5)	12.20 (2)	18.28 (2)	10.96 (3)	122.07	(2)
Political values	4.00 (9.5)	12.12 (3)	14.36 (2)	13.49 (3)	18.65 (2)	11.20 (4)	10.24 (3)	10.82 (3.5)	6.62 (6.5)	101.50	(3)
Positive national sentiment	5.70 (7)	6.25 (7)	11.03 (4)	6.53 (7)	2.85 (8)	15.36 (2)	9.27 (5)	10.82 (3.5)	8.68 (4)	76.49	(4)
Materialism	13.70 (3.5)	9.26 (4)	8.82 (5)	11.31 (4)	1.30 (10.5)	7.03 (6)	8.78 (6)	3.36 (10)	6.62 (6.5)	70.18	(5)
Arrogance	8.30 (5)	6.48 (6)	6.86 (6)	7.40 (6)	4.66 (6)	11.46 (3)	9.76 (4)	7.76 (7)	67.53 (5)		(6)
Other	4.00 (9.5)	7.87 (5)	2.21 (10)	8.61 (5)	8.07 (5)	3.13 (9)	3.89 (10)	4.12 (8)	13.24 (2)	55.14	(7)
Positive character traits	22.30 (1)	2.26 (11)	2.45 (5)	2.35 (11)	1.81 (9)	2.34 (10)	7.32 (7)	3.73 (9)	5.94 (8.5)	50.50	(8)
Independent	4.90 (8)	5.50 (8)	4.41 (7)	6.18 (8)	3.89 (7)	3.94 (8)	5.37 (7)	5.22 (6)	5.94 (8.5)	45.31	(9)
Family values	0.00 (11)	3.84 (9.5)	4.17 (8)	4.79 (9)	10.36 (4)	7.03 (7)	3.90 (9)	6.34 (5)	3.88 (10)	44.31	(10)
Negative character traits	6.60 (6)	3.84 (9.5)	1.72 (11)	3.22 (10)	1.30 (10.5)	1.56 (11)	2.44 (11)	1.12 (11)	2.28 (11)	24.08	(11)

consistently placed? A major finding is the consistency with which the responses fall into these categories. A number of words were idiosyncratic, or of such low frequency to preclude categorical distinction. These were placed in the 'other' category, and ranged from a low 2.21 per cent for sororities and fraternities to 13.24 per cent for high school students. In nearly all cases, therefore, responses fall into one of ten categories of national identity.

A second interesting finding is the concordance between foreign students' perception of US national identity and that of domestic groups. The only relative difference is the larger percentage of positive character traits with 'freedom' in second place. That foreign students perceive US national identity in much the same way as domestic groups adds a dimension of validity to the prevalence of these cultural-dimensions. Even foreigners after relative short stays (all were students) clearly identify certain fundamental values of US national character.

Further, a concordance between the rankings of percentages for the ten identity components may be observed across all groups, despite obvious social differences. It might seem that religious groups and prisoners would have little in common. Yet we find a high concordance, as we do for groups such as foreign and US students, community (older) adults and high school students. This would then suggest a common 'national' identity which transcends socio-political differences.

Finally, Table 1 also summarizes the overall percentage across groups and resulting rank of the identity components. Freedom-related concepts constitute the dominant category for all domestic groups, with percentages ranging from 21.5 per cent for community groups to 34.97 per cent for religious groups. Here both historical factors (like the war for national independence) and stereotypical references in the media reinforce this dominant component. America is also seen as the land of opportunity and social well-being, as summarized in the social development components (range = 9.38–16.27 per cent). Political values (range = 6.62–18.65 per cent) refer for example to law and the constitutional underpinnings of government. These are the third most frequently mentioned components. Ethnocentric remarks (range = 2.85–15.36 per cent) refer to material aspects of culture including objects like the 'Chevy', baseball, apple pie – things that make for the 'good life'. Interestingly, foreign students see a much higher level of materialism in US society than do domestic groups.

The sixth component, arrogance (range = 4.66–11.46 per cent) often refers to power and indifference toward others. Positive character traits are next (range = 1.81–7.32 per cent). Here foreign students had more nice things to say about personal character of Americans (22.30 per cent) than any domestic group. The US tradition of rugged individualism is summarized in the 'independent' component (range = 3.89–5.94 per cent). Family values (range = 3.84–7.03 per cent) rank number ten, and finally, negative character traits (range = 1.12–3.84 per cent) rank last among the identity components. (The 'other' category is not taken into account.) Here the foreign students have most negative personal assessments. In fact, the positive and negative character traits of foreign students account for more than a quarter of their total responses. This would suggest that personal encounters with Americans strongly influence their impressions of American national identity, for better or for worse. Alternately, perhaps national identity is perceived in more personal terms by a variety of other cultures.

3. Part 2: The Hungarian Sample

We are all aware of the transition in societies of Eastern Europe. National identity has played, and is playing, a significant role in this process. The first free elections in Hungary, held 25 March and 4 April 1990, were a time of heightened awareness of national identity. The comparative sample reported here was obtained between the two elections.

3.1 Method

Respondents. A total of 155 undergraduate social science students responded: from Attila Joszef University and the University of Budapest, 45 male and 110 female, with a mean age of 21.59.

The *Survey.* Respondents were asked to list 'three words which you think best describe being a Hungarian'. This was then followed by three spaces labeled 1, 2, and 3.

3.2 Results and Discussion

Content analysis yielded six identity components, as shown in Table 2. Here we can observe both some overlap and some drastic differences from the results obtained in the US sample. Similarities can be found in the overlap of categories such as positive and negative character traits, ethnocentrism, and materialism. There is, however, also much in Hungarian national identity which reveals its unique heritage and negative experiences under the Stalinist dictatorship.

Negative character traits dominate, accounting for nearly half of all responses. This suggests a pervading pessimism which is further supported by the responses on negative national sentiment. We can break down the negative

Table 2   *Content analysis, national identity components among Hungarian university students*

	Per cent	Rank
Negative characteristics	49	(1)
Positive characteristics	33	(2)
Ethnocentrism (positive national sentiment)	9	(3)
Materialism	5	(4)
Negative national sentiment	3	(5)
Ironical responses	2	(6)

character traits into cognitive (e.g., waiting for the miracle; oscillating between extremes); affective (e.g., against, indifferent, pessimist, sense of inferiority); and behavioral (e.g. eating too much, drinking too much, irresponsibility, frustration, aggression, intolerance, and laziness).

Likewise, positive character traits can be broken down into cognitive (e.g., intelligent, clever, good sense of humor, creative, cunning); affective (e.g., friendly, proud, peaceful, hoping, loving family); and behavioral (e.g., hospitable, persistence, good works).

Thus, in contrast to the US sample, a large proportion of Hungarian identity responses focus on the individual and personality. While these elements are also present in the US samples, the latter also yield a large number of socio-political components related to freedom, social development, and political values. Lacking data from earlier years, we can nevertheless speculate that the pessimism is a function of the despair of the Hungarian nation, and the loss of national sovereignty and stagnation under succeeding Stalinist regimes.

The ethnocentric component (positive national sentiment) was reflected by concepts such as love of homeland, and national pride in national history. These reflect the positive attributes of nationalism, as contrasted to the chauvinism apparent in the US responses of ethnocentrism (intolerance, powerful, duty, flag, etc.), and arrogance (proud, pride, cutthroat, dominant, loud, Rambo, etc). Even the negative national sentiment in Hungary reflects no arrogance but refers to national misfortune and ill-fate.

The responses for materialism are similar to the US sample, reflecting a desire for material values, and love of money. Finally, there are 'ironic' responses, referring to the existential dilemmas of death, birth, and life. Hungarian society appears especially attuned to these broad philosophical questions that touch on the meaning of life.

Lack of political, social, and economic values, as well as the dominance of psychological-behavioral traits, seems to characterize Hungarian respondents. This may well be due to the dominant pattern of Hungarian (and East European) national ideology which emphasizes the moral, psychological, and cultural components of national attachment. The reason for this emphasis can be found in the characteristics of the development of these national ideologies. Under specific historical circumstances (absence of an independent state, absence of full-fledged class society, permanent sense of insecurity) Eastern European national ideologies were forced to seek 'soft' criteria of national identification – such as the mother tongue, the adherence to cultural norms and values, national character, national literature, national art.

But what is the reason for the frequency of negative responses among the Hungarian sample? Theories of nationalism emphasizing the ethnocentric roots of national affiliation assume that members of every nation are proud of their national belongingness and that they generally maintain a balanced positive pattern of national identity. Empirical studies carried out in the 1970s and 1980s in Hungary show that this general tendency can be observed as a function of the level of education (Csepeli, 1989). Those who have attended

only elementary school or vocational school (which form the majority of the
Hungarian population) are prone to express their national identity in terms of
positive affective terms. But graduates of high schools and especial y college
and university graduates are more critical toward their national group; as
a result of their ambiguity, the weight of the negative affective elements
in the national attitude is increasing. Another factor is age. The younger
generations have not been exposed to the overt cultivation of nationalism
and therefore tend to be generally more critical toward their nation. Our
Hungarian respondents came from the young and educated, and therefore
were more negative.

4. Part 3: The Bulgarian Samples

In November 1989, the regime of Tudor Zhivkov fell; Bulgaria has since seen
the dissolution of its Communist Party, negotiations with the opposition, and
free elections where the Reformed Socialist Party won a majority. As in other
East European countries, national and ethnic identity is of crucial importance
in the transition process. Before the transition, the all-powerful Party defined
identity – usually in ritualized form. Now Bulgarians must look within to
decide the nature of their national identity.

4.1 Method

Respondents. A total of 128 Bulgarian social science students at the University
of Sofia responded to the same survey during the academic year 1990: 39 male
and 89 female, with a mean age of 22.52.

4.2 Results and Discussion

Table 3 shows the results of the content analysis, and percentage of responses
for the identity components.

   Again we can see an overlap with both the US and the Hungarian samples,
as well as a rather unique Bulgarian characteristic. Positive character traits
(hospitality, humor, cordiality, merry nature) account for nearly a fifth of all
responses, as against approximately a third for the Hungarian sample. (For the
US samples, percentages ranged from 1.89 per cent to 7.32 per cent.) Negative
character traits (sly, submissive, naive, narrow-minded) account for 6.87 per
cent compared to 45.0 per cent among the Hungarian respondents, and a range
of 1.12 per cent to 3.84 per cent for the US samples. As with the Hungarian
sample, a large proportion of Bulgarian national identity seems to focus on
personality-related components, whereas in the US samples socio-political
dimensions occur more frequently. Perhaps a personality-based national
identity has also emerged in part as a response to the state and mass-based
identity promoted by the former Stalinist regimes.

   The cultural values category includes items such as lack of education,
Christianity, and cultural heroes and places. Industriousness and social development (struggle, labor, vitality, hope for better life) components together

Table 3   *Content analysis, national identity components among Bulgarian university students*

	Per cent	Rank
Positive character traits	24.23	(1)
Negative character traits	16.87	(2)
Cultural values	11.96	(3)
Industriousness	8.59	(4)
Social development	6.44	(5)
Fatalism	6.13	(6)
Political values	5.21	(7)
Uncle Ganyo (vulgarity)	3.68	(8.5)
Ethnocentrism (patriotism)	3.68	(8.5)
Arrogance (pride)	3.37	(10)
Family values	3.06	(11)
Freedom	1.84	(12)
Independence	1.53	(13.5)
Materialism	1.53	(13.5)
Democracy	0.31	(15)

account for 15.03 per cent of all responses. This would seem an interesting response in view of the low productivity of Bulgarian industry: it may suggest a strong reservoir of will to work for Bulgarian development.

The reverse side of that coin is a component labeled fatalism (uncertainty, having no orientation, depressed, tired, inaction, slave). This suggests the presence of a 'learned helplessness' (Seligman, 1975) where at least some Bulgarians see no linkage between behaviors and outcomes. Fatalism would be a logical result of a totalitarian society. Political values are represented by concepts such as conservative, internationalism, citizen, politics, and state. Patriotic responses account for 3.68 per cent, as do family values (spirituality, health, honesty, love). At the end of the scale freedom, and materialism (money), independence, and democracy account for only small percentages of total responses.

5. Part 5: The Greek Sample

To examine to what extent this projective technique could be applied to a variety of national groups, the survey was also extended to a small sample of Greek students attending the University of Sofia, Bulgaria. The survey again provides an opportunity to examine that which is unique to national identity, and that which is more universal.

5.1 Method

Respondents. A total of 24 Greek students, 7 males and 17 females, participated in the study. The mean age was 21.63.

Table 4   *Content analysis, national identity among Greek university students*

	Per cent	Rank
Positive character traits	20.00	(1)
Negative character traits	16.67	(2)
Hospitality	11.63	(3.5)
Industrious	11.63	(3.5)
Democracy	10.00	(5)
Freedom	8.33	(6)
Ethnocentrism (patriotism)	5.00	(7.25)
Political values	5.00	(7.25)
Arrogance (pride)	5.00	(7.25)
Other	5.00	(7.25)
Cultural values	3.33	(9)
Materialism	1.67	(10)

5.2 Results and Discussion

As with the Hungarian and Bulgarian samples, Greek national identity appears skewed in the direction of a personality-based component. Positive character traits (smart, sincere, happy, humorous), and negative character traits (sly, noisy, egoist, and restless) together account for 36.67 per cent of the responses. If we add hospitality to positive character traits (as we did for the Bulgarian sample), the positive traits would account for 31.63 per cent (close to the Hungarian result), and personality-based traits would reflect 48.30 per cent of the total number of responses. (See Table 4.)

Again, as with the Bulgarian sample, industriousness receives a fair number of responses, as do democracy and freedom. Since some reference, however small, is made to democracy and freedom in all national samples, these probably come closest to what we could term 'universal' values of national identity. Other overlapping components include ethnocentrism (patriotism); political values, arrogance (pride), and cultural values. The latter is similar to that found in the Bulgarian sample, with references to culture, intelligence, self-knowledge, and heroes.

6. Summary

This large-scale study employed the simple technique of asking respondents to list three components of national identity. The results for the US-based samples yielded a remarkable concordance between a variety of social groups, thus indicating the presence of a common national identity. Further, foreign students living in the USA had very similar views of US national identity, adding a dimension of validity to the identity components. In comparison with other samples, the US national identity emerges as 'outer' directed, based largely on socio-political values and norms.

By contrast, the foreign students living in the USA, and the Hungarian,

Bulgarian, and Greek samples, attribute more responses to 'personality' and individually-based components.

The results yield some unique national dimensions. The Hungarian sample reflects a deeply pessimistic outlook; also in Bulgaria we can note a fatalistic component. The Greeks see hospitality as a primary identity component. Industriousness was mentioned relatively frequently by the both the Greek and Bulgarian samples.

This research represents an initial step in the study of national identity. Katz (1965) noted that national identity served the function of internal integration, and protection against enemies. In examining the ideology of the nation-state, he noted that national identity is composed of statism (doctrine of national sovereignty), institutionalized nationalism (e.g. the political institutions of democracy), and cultural identity (the character of the people). The research reported here shows that spontaneous representations of national identity reflect primarily institutionalized nationalism and cultural identity. Further research must address the question of why national sovereignty is not an overt trait of national identity. Research will also need to examine the question of the formation of national identity in the very young, and what changes occur across the lifespan. The rapid social change of Eastern Europe provides an opportunity to see the role of national identity in the socio-political process, and the effects on national communities and multi-cultural societies.

References

Csepeli, G., 1989. *National Identity*. Amsterdam: Peter Lang.

Doise, W., 1969. 'Intergroup Relations and Polarization of Individual and Collective Judgements', *Journal of Personality and Social Psychology*, vol. 12, pp. 136–143.

Doise, W.; G. Csepeli, D. Dann, C. Gorge, K. Larsen, & A. Ostell, 1972. 'An Experimental Investigation into the Formation of Intergroup Representations', *European Journal of Social Psychology*, vol. 1, pp. 203–204.

Forbes, H.D., 1985. *Nationalism, Ethnocentrism, and Personality*. Chicago, IL: University of Chicago Press.

Haas, E.B., 1986. 'What is Nationalism and Why Should We Study it?' *International Organization*, vol. 40, pp. 707–744.

Hayes, C., 1960. *Nationalism: A Religion*. New York: MacMillan Co.

Katz, D., 1965. 'Nationalism and Strategies of International Conflict Resolution', in H.C. Kelman, ed., *International Behavior*. New York: Holt, Rinehart and Winston.

Klineberg, O.A., 1962. 'A Cross-national Comparison of Peoples Considered "Like Us" and "Not Like Us" by Children', *Proceedings of the Sixteenth International Congress of Psychology*. Amsterdam: North-Holland Publishing Co.

Lambert, W.E., 1962. 'A Cross-national Comparison of Ethnocentrism, Perception of Similars, and Affection vis-à-vis Other Peoples', *Proceedings of the Sixteenth International Congress of Psychology*. Amsterdam: North-Holland Publishing Co.

Lambert, W.E., & O. Klineberg, 1959. 'A Pilot Study of the Origin and Development of National Stereotypes', *International Social Science Journal*, vol. 11, pp. 221–238.

Seligman, M.E.P., 1975. *Helplessness*. San Francisco CA: W.H. Freedman.

Shafer, B., 1977. *Faces of Nationalism*. New York: Harcourt Brace Jovanovich.

Sherif, M.; O.J. Harvey, B.J. White, W.E. Hood, & L.W. Sherif, 1961. *Intergroup Conflict and Cooperation: The Robbers Cave Experiment*, Norman, OK: Institute of Group Relations.

Tajfel, H., 1982. *Social Identity and Intergroup Relations*, Cambridge, UK: Cambridge University Press.

Turner, J.C.; M.A. Hogg, P.J. Oakes, S.D. Reicher, & M.S. Wetherell, 1987. *Rediscovering the Social Group: A Self-Categorization Theory*. Oxford, UK: Blackwell.

White, R.K. 1965. 'Images in the Context of International Conflict', in H.C. Kelman, ed., *International Behavior*, New York: Holt, Rinehart and Winston.

16

Beliefs Related to Acceptance of War

A Social Systems Perspective

Paula B. Johnson*
Andy Handler
Julie E. Criss

1. Introduction

This chapter presents a theoretical model relating structures of beliefs, attitudes and values to the acceptance of war, and an empirical test of the model. The theoretical perspective proposes that our social system is supported by widely held cultural beliefs, attitudes and values that constitute the 'rules of the game' (Watzlawick, et al., 1974) and perpetuate war (Holt, 1987). Such a systemic structure can be seen as a web of interrelated beliefs. In order to change this system, this set of beliefs will need to be identified and reframed. Holt (1987) indicates that in order to understand the war system and move toward a peace system, we need to explore 'values, concepts, laws, traditions, belief systems religious and secular, conceptions of the universe, and humanity's underlying conscious attitudes and values.' (Holt, 1987, p. 2). A number of authors have begun to describe such systems: Capra (1982) has focused on an overemphasis of mechanistic western values; Eisler (1987) describes a dominator model based on hierarchies; Milbrath (1988) identifies a dominant social paradigm based on an ideology of control; Reardon (1985), Brock-Utne (1985), Spretnak (1983) and Criss (1990) have named the system in terms of patriarchy and sexism and have focused specifically on its links

* An initial version of this chapter was presented as a paper at the 95th Annual Meeting of the American Psychological Association, New York, New York, August 1987.

We wish to thank Esther Cadavid-Hannon, Lisa Allen, Alane Miller-Kustek, Jonathan Sack, Steve Silverman, Brian Grossman, Terry Gates, Christina De Zan and Mathew Schall for their help in questionnaire development, data collection and data analysis.

with war. This chapter will explore the nature of such a system of beliefs and to provide an empirical test relevant to the extensive theoretical work on such belief systems.

This research presents a theory of belief systems that draws on the work of Rokeach (1968), as well as that of more recent authors who present a systems perspective (e.g., Macy, 1983). This perspective is somewhat different than that of Rokeach (1968), in that the system proposed is a non-hierarchical web of mutually supportive beliefs.[1] Furthermore, it is suggested that the web to be investigated forms a part of a paradigm in that it acts a a model for individuals and society. Another divergence from traditional methods of studying beliefs and values that will be taken in this chapter, is that the concern here is with the relationships between beliefs, rather than group differences in beliefs and values. This research is seen as largely exploratory, hypothesis generating research that integrates ideas in terms of a non-linear, multivariate, multidimensional whole rather than focusing on hierarchies and differences (Wallston, 1981; McGuire, 1973).

The broader motivation behind this research is to help prevent war from occurring by finding what processes are linked to acceptance of war – and which promote or block peaceful pursuits. War does not exist in a vacuum, but is part of a larger system of how the world is understood and what we think it should be like (Holt, 1984, 1987). In order to make changes in culture's war acceptance, better understanding of its roots are needed to make appropriate interventions.

An important theoretical grounding of this research based on the work of Watzlawick et al. (1974), described elsewhere in this volume (Criss and Johnson, 1992), is that war is part of a social system that is self perpetuating, making it difficult to move away from its set of assumptions. It is not enough to simply find 'alternatives' to war. Rather, before true systemic change occurs, we must change the 'rules' which reflect the structure of the system (Watzlawick, et al., 1974). This research will ask *what* is the pattern that constitutes the rules of the game and *how* does it operate (Watzlawick, et al., 1974). By focusing on the rules of the game, as Watzlawick et al., maintain, the covert is made overt, and the game cannot be played in the same way. Hopefully, this research will help identify the problematic rules and their underlying assumptions, and bring to light how some beliefs support war. Once we understand the values and processes that perpetuate war acceptance, we can begin to generate concrete change strategies and appropriate levels (Watzlawick, et al., 1974; Weick, 1984; Criss & Johnson, 1992).

2. Beliefs Related to Acceptance of War

The beliefs described below are all considered to represent parts of major social paradigms such as those described by Capra (1982), Macy (1983) and Eisler (1987). Most of these beliefs are those which are seen as supportive of war and detrimental to peace. However, an attempt will be made to also begin to examine positive beliefs condusive to creating peace.

2.1 Patriarchal Beliefs

Many of the dynamics linked to war have been named in terms of the values many cultures hold for traditional roles for men (Schaef, 1985; Capra, 1982; Eisler, 1987; Spretnak, 1983; Reardon, 1985; Brock-Utne, 1985; Milbrath, 1988). David and Brannon (1976) identified dimensions of stereotypical male roles that were later translated into a measure (Brannon & Juni, 1983). These roles included the desirability of always being in control, of avoiding anything that looks feminine, of looking tough, of always being looked up to by others, of controlling money, and of valuing violence and adventure. However, the valuing of these roles goes beyond an individual enactment level to one of a broader cultural belief set. This belief set has been identified by many as patriarchal beliefs and values (e.g., Capra, 1982; Reardon, 1985; Spretnak, 1983; Brock-Utne, 1985), of which traditional male roles are a part.

Whether one wishes to call this system by another name than patriarchy, as have Schaef (1987), Eisler (1987) and Milbrath (1988), the system that this research will explore is one of dominance, submission, hierarchies, and inequalities between people. It is the intention of this research to describe the 'play' and be backstage mechanisms set up to support the play, as it were, and not to focus on the individual 'players'. In other words, it is not appropriate to place blame for the way the system works on one particular group, be it men in general, or a specific set of politicians. Rather the approach taken in this chapter attempts to avoid individual blame (Caplan and Nelson, 1973), and thus empowers everyone to take responsibility to initiate system change.

Other beliefs related to patriarchal, dominance and submission are the *need for power* and, in Western societies, the accumulation of *material goods* as an indicator of such power. Thus patriarchal structure includes a struggle to be powerful and to climb to the top: Control of material goods are a way one's place in this struggle is marked in some cultures. Roberts (1985), Dyer (1985), and Macy (1983) are among those who have suggested a link between striving for power over others and war; furthermore, Dyer (1985) has related materialism to war.

2.2 Interconnectedness vs. Individual Rights and Absolute Rules

A second set of beliefs proposed to be related to to patriarchal systems and to war come largely from the ideas expressed by Gilligan (1982). Gilligan (1982) reframed a system of moral reasoning based on earlier work of Kohlberg (1964) that had defined the highest levels of moral reasoning in terms of autonomous individual rights and abstract, absolute rules. Gilligan suggested that concepts of interconnectedness, responsibility to others, caring and valuing all people, need to also be considered as the highest levels. This chapter extends the work of Gilligan and others from the realm of moral reasoning to a belief system around the value of interconnectedness with others as an underlying mode of behavior. The perspective taken in this chapter is that the more one values interconnectedness with others, the less likely one is to accept violent actions toward other people, including war. In addition the exclusive reliance on autonomy, abstract rights and absolute rules, are seen as part of a system supportive of war.

Previous work has focused on gender differences in these values (Gilligan, 1982). There are major difficulties with a gender difference approach: It blames victims of a social system by regarding differences between the sexes as evidence of an inferior social and psychological development of one gender or the other (Wallston, 1981). Because gender differences are confounded with so many life experience variables (e.g., income, education), they give very little information. Rather, it is proposed that gender *role* belief systems are strongly related to interconnectedness and rights beliefs in both men and women. That is, the valuing of individual rights and abstract rules is much more consistent with patriarchal structure and traditional male roles than is interconnectedness. This is an attempt to frame the issue in a systems context of societal beliefs concerning appropriate action. Initial study of this set of beliefs has found them related to gender role and acceptance of war, with little relationship to gender (Johnson, 1987).

Another more specific way one can be connected to others is through one's *family*. Feshbach, Kandel and Haist (1985) found that one's valuing of children was related to lack of support for nuclear buildup, unless one valued children for their instrumental usefulness. Thus, in most cases, being connected to a family and wanting to preserve this connectedness, should be related to opposition to war.

2.3 Nationalism, Patriotism, and Internationalism

Kosterman and Feshbach (1989) have identified relationships of the evaluative beliefs about nationalism, patriotism, and internationalism to positive war related attitudes, as positive, neutral and negative, respectively. Briefly, internationalism is defined as cooperation between countries; nationalism is a competitive need to be the best; and patriotism is simply love of country. Theoretically, then, nationalism seems most related to patriarchy, while internationalism may be an extension of some interconnectedness beliefs.

2.4 War

Finally, there are many ways of conceptualizing beliefs towards war, nuclear buildup, and use of nuclear weapons. The present work proposes to measure the 'good/bad' evaluative dimension of such beliefs Thus, the focus was on how acceptable war, nuclear buildup, and nuclear use were to people. Other beliefs about these issues such as those concerning appropriate actions in specific situations, or issues of personal activism are not included, as the focus is on the structure of basic evaluative beliefs around war.

In summary, the proposed model holds that patriarchal beliefs – including the valuing of power, materialism, and traditional male roles – lack of interconnectedness, belief in autonomy and absolute rules, lack of family closeness, belief in nationalism and low acceptance of internationalism are all parts of the cultural value system that supports war.

3. Methods

The methodology of the present empirical exploration of the web of beliefs related to acceptance of war is correlational, utilizing a population survey and covariance structure analysis. (Bentler, 1985).

3.1 Subjects

Subjects were 162 adult volunteers in the Southern California area. 79 were women, and 83 were men. The ages ranged from 18 to 78, with a mean of 36. 63 percent listed themselves as Caucasian, and 9 per cent were African-American, 7 per cent Asian, 14 per cent Latino, and 7 per cent other ethnic minority. Slightly more than half of the sample (53 per cent) had completed at least a B.A. degree. Thus, on the average, the sample was highly educated. 32 percent were currently married; 42 per cent had children. Approximately 46 per cent of the sample were either professionals or managers. The median income fell into the 21 to 25 thousand dollars per year category, very close to the national median. Those in the sample who listed a religion were divided fairly equally between Protestant, Jewish, and Catholic. In terms of political affiliation, 40 per cent indicated that they were Democrats, 28 per cent indicated Republican, 12 per cent Independent, and 18 per cent said they had none. Politically, however, 31 per cent indicated that they were liberal, 21 per cent answered that they were 'neither Liberal or Conservative,' and 41 per cent indicated that there were conservative. 77 percent of the sample were born in the United States. Because the study explores relationships between beliefs that are proposed to hold across populations (Hilsberg, 1989), a random sample was not crucial to the exploration.

3.2 Instruments

Scale construction. Instruments were developed to measure the evaluative beliefs described above. A literature search was undertaken to find measures of these beliefs or related concepts. With the exception of measures of traditional male roles and some of the nationalism, patriotism and internationalism items, no measures were found that sufficiently expressed the sets of evaluative beliefs under investigation. Thus each concept was examined and a series of statements reflecting its perceived value or lack of value were generated. Items were pretested and some were reworded so that a greater range of response could be generated. All measures were presented in a seven point Likert format ranging from strongly agree (1) to strongly disagree (7). Items were worded both in support and in opposition to each belief, thus helping to lessen potential response sets. Items were randomly ordered into a questionnaire that consisted of 182 belief questions and 24 demographics.

Reliabilities were computed on each measure utilizing an internal consistency coefficient, Cronbach's Alpha (Cronbach, 1970). Table 1 presents the number of items, mean, standard deviation, reliability and a sample item for each scale.

Table 1   *Scale means, reliabilities and items**

Connect 1: Taking care of others
(6 items) Mean = 2.54   Stddev. = .72   Reliability = .68
Sample item
'People should take care of others.'

Connect 2: Taking everyone into account
(5 items) Mean = 2.45   Stddev. = .72   Reliability = .57
Sample item
'I believe in doing what's best for all concerned.'

Rights 1: Autonomy and individual rights
(5 items) Mean = 3.99   Stddev. = .99   Reliability = .62
Sample item
'Individual rights are more important than the common good.'

Rights 2: Valuing absolute rules and fairness
(6 items) Mean = 3.27   Stddev. = .92   Reliability = .59
Sample item
'We have rules about what's right that apply to everyone.'

War: Acceptance of war
(10 items) Mean = 4.91   Stddev. = 1.26   Reliability = .88
Sample item
'Sometimes war benefits us.'

*Maculininty: Acceptance of traditional male roles.***
(55 items) Mean = 4.23   Stddev. = .79   Reliability = .93
Sample item
'It is essential for a man to always have the respect and admiration of everyone who knows him.'

Family: Valuing the family
(6 items) Mean = 2.88   Stddev. = .92   Reliability = .78
Sample item
'It's important for me and my family to spend a lot of time together.'

Power: Valuing power
(5 items) Mean = 3.48   Stddev. = 1.00   Reliability = .72
Sample item
'It's important that people look up to me.'

Materialism: Valuing material things
(5 items) Mean = 4.09   Stddev. = 1.31   Reliability = .76
Sample item
'Money buys a lot of happiness.'

Nationalism: Belief that the US is the best

(4 items) Mean = 3.77   Stddev. = 1.14   Reliability = .62
Sample item
'The United States is closer to being an ideal country than any other nation.'

Internationalism: Belief in international cooperation
(6 items) Mean = 2.38   Stddev. = .811   Reliability = .63
Sample item
'The countries of the world should work together.'

Patriotism: Love of the United States
(5 items) Mean = 2.31   Stddev. = 1.10   Reliability = .84
Sample item
'I am proud to live in the United States.'

Buildup: Acceptance of nuclear arms buildup
(5 items) Mean = 4.42   Stddev. = 1.45   Reliability = .78
Sample item
'The United States needs nuclear weapons.'

Arms use: Use of nuclear weapons
(4 items) Mean = 4.83   Stddev. = 1.49   Reliability = .81
Sample item
'The use of nuclear weapons can be justified in certain situations.'

---

* All means are based on a 7-point scale: 1 = strongly agree; 7 = strongly disagree.
** Brannon and Juni (1983) short form.

Male roles. The short form of the Brannon and Juni (1983) masculinity scale was used to measure traditionalism of beliefs about male roles in society (Masculinity, MASC) Due to error three items were omitted, resulting in a 55 item scale. The Brannon and Juni scale showed excellent reliability (alpha = .93) in this study. Previous research had demonstrated the validity of the concepts (Brannon and Juni, 1983). This scale consists of items that tap a range of beliefs about how men should behave. It is composed of seven subscales, including: (1) Avoiding Femininity; (2) Concealing Emotions; (3) The Breadwinner; (4) Admired and Respected; (5) Toughness; (6) The Male Machine; and (7) Violence and Adventure.

Acceptance of War. The acceptance of war scale (WAR) measured an evaluative 'good/bad' dimension of beliefs about war. For example, an item worded in the direction of acceptance of war was, 'There are some situations in which we have no choice but to go to war.', and a lack of acceptance item was, 'Wars solve nothing.' Similarly, beliefs about the use of nuclear weapons (ARMSUSE), and nuclear buildup (BUILD) reflected an evaluative dimension of beliefs about these concept. These scales had reliabilities of .88, .78 and .81, respectively (See Table 1).

Moral Reasoning variables. Concepts of rights and interconnectedness were operationalized following Gilligan (1982), as well as Kohlberg (1964). Based on factor analysis and reliability testing, these resulted in two rights measures, belief in autonomy and individual rights (RIGHTS1), and belief in abstract, absolute rules (RIGHTS2). The reliabilities for these two measures were relatively low, as seen in Table 1. Similarly, the interconnectedness scale was divided into belief in taking care of others (CONNECT1) and belief in taking everyone into account (CONNECT2), with fairly low reliabilities of .68 and .57, respectively.

Family. Valuing one's own family (FAMILY) was represented by items such as, 'No matter what, my family comes first.', and showed a reliability of .76.

Variables related to patriarchy. As seen in Table 1, valuing money and material things (MATERIAL) showed a reliability of .76, and personal need for power (POWER) had a reliability of .72.

Nationalism, Patriotism, and Internationalism. Finally, based on the work of Kosterman and Feshbach (1989), three sets of measures were devised to reflect the concepts above. These measures showed mixed reliabilities of .62, .84, and .63, respectively. The present authors are concerned, however that the concept of nationalism was not sufficiently differentiated from patriotism in the short measure that was used in the present study.

3.3 Procedure

Questionnaires were distributed by nine graduate student assistants and a professor of psychology. An attempt was made to sample diverse populations in diverse settings in order to move away from a white middle class sample typical of college student research. Thus the sample included people on the street, friends and neighbors, as well as people in workplace, and recreational settings. Prior to participation, each subject read an information letter explaining the nature of the research and human subject considerations of anonymity, confidentiality and ability to withdraw from the research at any time.

4. Results and Discussion

Results of the simple correlations between measures and the construction of the covariance model through a factor analysis will first be presented. Following this, the test of the model with EQS, the structural equations program (Bentler, 1985), will be described. The nature of the resulting converged model will be discussed in terms of both its whole constellation and the relationships of its component parts.

4.1 Correlations

Table 2 presents the correlation matrix of the 14 constructed scales. The highest correlations were between the three measures of war, indicating some potential for validity of the measures.

4.2 Covariance Structure Model

Factor Analysis. The first step in creating a covariance model was to start with the underlying factor structure of the fourteen variables. The BMDP4M

Table 2 *Intercorrelations between variables*

	War	Masc	Nat	Pat	Int	Family	Power	Mat	Rights1	Rights2	Connect1	Connect2	Build
Masc	.51												
Nat	.42	.46											
Pat	.36	.16	.58										
Int	-.45	-.33	-.09	.02									
Family	-.08	.09	.15	.06	-.18								
Power	.28	.37	.19	.05	-.21	-.06							
Material	.27	.36	.41	.19	-.24	-.04	.47						
Rights1	.14	.30	.20	.04	.005	-.14	.29	.41					
Rights2	.24	.37	.32	.13	.52	.26	.11	.24	-.005				
Connect1	-.28	-.27	-.09	-.003	.47	.33	-.20	-.22	-.37	.05			
Connect2	-.24	-.17	.02	.05	.47	.30	-.17	-.13	-.18	.18	.44		
Build	.73	.47	.46	.38	-.44	-.02	.15	.29	-.13	.25	-.32	-.29	
Arms use	.65	.40	.42	.32	-.41	-.12	.20	.34	.21	.32	-.34	-.16	.65

R = .15, $p < .05$ n = 162

Figure 1   *Starting covariance structure model*

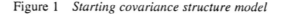

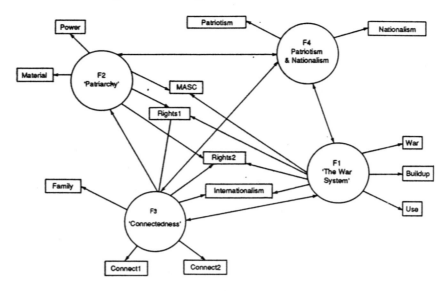

(Brown, 1977) factor analysis program with oblique rotation was used. Factor analysis is used as a starting point in order to simplify the initial identification of latent variables. A latent variable is a construct that is not directly measured, but accounts for variance in a set of manifest, or measured, variables. That is, a number of measured variables may touch on, but not completely measure a concept of importance, which then appears statistically as a latent variable in covariance modeling.

Four starting latent variables were identified in the factor analysis. Variables loading over .4 were included and variables loading over .3 were noted as smaller loadings. The first consisted of the three dependent variables (WAR, BUILD, AND ARMSUSE), plus negatively loaded internationalism and smaller loadings with negative RIGHTS1 and positive RIGHTS2 and MASC. This factor was labeled as 'The War System' factor, and accounted 26 per cent of the variance. The second factor consisted of power (POWER), materialism (MATERIAL), absolute rules (RIGHTS2), and masculinity (MASC). It was labeled conceptually as the 'Patriarchy' factor, and accounted for 8 per cent of the variance. Factor three consisted of internationalism (INT), negative autonomy (RIGHTS1), positive RIGHTS2, FAMILY, and the two interconnectedness scales, caring (CONNECT1), and taking everyone into account (CONNECT2). This was labeled as an 'Connectedness' factor (4 per cent of the variance). Finally the fourth factor consisted of nationalism (NAT) and patriotism (PAT) (1 per cent of the variance). As the factors were based on an oblique rotation, they were correlated with each other. These correlations were also used in the starting model described below to indicate initial direction and values for the links between the factors.

Starting Model. Based on the above factor analysis, a model was constructed (see Figure 1) and *EQS*, a structural equation computer program

Figure 2   *Converged covariance structure model $X^2_{66} = 63.34$, p = < .57*

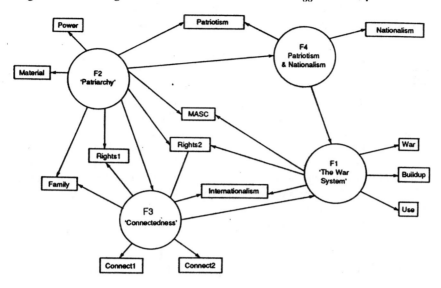

(Bentler, 1985) similar to LISREL V (Joreskog and Sorbom, 1983) was used to test whether the model fit the data (and vice versa). *EQS* allows for multiple, unidirectional and bidirectional relationships between and among latent variables and/or manifest variables. According to Bentler (1985), *EQS* allows the translation of 'substantive theory to the form of a model that can be statistically estimated and tested.' (Bentler, 1985, p. 7). *EQS* 'subsumes a variety of covariance structure models including multiple regression, path analyses, simultaneous equations, first and higher-order confirmatory factor analysis as well as regression and structural relations among latent variables.' (Bentler, 1985, p. 1).

As can be seen in Figure 1, the model is represented by the four factors in circles and the fourteen measured variables in rectangles, attached to the appropriate factors by arrows. In addition, the relationships between the factors are shown by double-sided arrows, for covariance and single-sided arrows for prediction. Thus factors 2 (F2), 3 (F3), and 4 (F4) predict to factor 1(F1) and covary with each other. The paths are positive in relating the variables unless a minus is indicated on the figure.

Results from EQS. By applying *EQS* (using a generalized least squares [GLS] solution for a normal distribution), both necessary and unnecessary paths are identified. Figure 2 presents the final converged model. All test statistics for the paths were significant.

The Chi Square statistic for 66 degrees of freedom was 63.324, with a significance level of .570. In covariance structure modeling, one wants to have the data fit the expected equations: Thus, a nonsignificant Chi Square is desired. All the statistics indicated a good fit between the model and the data. This fit shows that it was possible to describe this complex set of beliefs in terms of an interrelated model. It should be noted that this was not the only model that fit the data, but rather the best fit in accordance with the statistical feedback from the program. Thus the model should be viewed as a source of hypothesis generation rather than a test of hypotheses.

4.3 The Nature of the Converged Model

In describing and discussing the model, the entire constellation will first be described and discussed, followed by an analysis of some of the interrelationships of the component parts. The most important finding is that there appears to exist a comprehensive set of beliefs that are related to acceptance of war. The model can be best described in terms of its major constellation of four latent variables which form a circle with 'Patriarchy' predicting positively to 'Patriotism/Nationalism' and negatively to 'Connectedness'; whereas these latter two latent variables predicted positively and negatively to war, respectively.

Though it is difficult to describe the entire whole, several major implications can be drawn. First, the positive relationship of 'Patriotism/Nationalism' to the 'War System' indicates that, as Dyer (1985) has said, we may love our countries too much for their own good. It may however, not be just that we love them, but how we love them – that loving in the context of a dominant paradigm of competition and control needs to be better understood as a potential source of war. In contrast, the negative relationship of 'Connectedness' to the 'War System' presents a hopeful finding that perhaps as global interdependence is better understood, war will become less acceptable. Similarly, the caring and taking everyone into account (CONNECT1 and CONNECT2) aspect of this latent variable may indicate that all people have the ability to make war less likely by how they relate to people in their everyday lives. This 'Connectedness' latent variable and its relationship to war seems to support the views of Gilligan (1982) and others that there is a different way of looking at things when people per se are of more value than ideology. However, the positive relationship of RIGHTS2, valuing of absolute rules, with the connectedness latent variable raises questions. The link between connectedness and absolute rules may indicate, hopefully, that a system of moral reasoning based on abstract rules is not mutually exclusive from one based on connection with others.

The latent variable that has been labeled 'Patriarchy' may indeed represent underlying values of personal power over others (POWER), and material success (MATERIAL). The unexpected positive relationship of 'Patriarchy' with family values (FAMILY), but not with other forms of connectedness may represent a limit to caring only for one's own. The negative relationship of the patriotism manifest variable to patriarchy may also represent an individualistic orientation that does not allow one's heart to go beyond one's kin. Such a value set would clearly inhibit interconnectedness. The finding that patriarchal belief system as a latent variable was not a direct predictor of the war system, but rather operated indirectly through patriotism/nationalism and a lack of connectedness may indicate that its impact is more subtle, or give some information on how patriarchy may work to make war more acceptable.

The war system and patriarchy have two direct links in this model. The first is through the variable that measures the valuing of traditional male roles (MASC). The fact that this variable was associated with both latent variables is important. Its association with patriarchy is partly definitional. However its appearance in conjunction with with the war system indicates that the ideology of 'acting like a real man' may have far reaching social consequences. On a more hopeful note, as male roles change, perhaps our propensities toward war will also change (Hilsberg, 1989). In addition, more system-oriented measures of patriarchy, such as beliefs in hierarchies, have also been studied by Criss (1990) and have been found to relate to beliefs about war and peace.

The structure of the 'War System' latent variable may indicate the areas most intimately related to acceptance of war – valuing traditional male roles, discussed above, a lack of valuing of international cooperation, and an acceptance of absolute rules for for behavior (RIGHTS2). As mentioned above, the latter manifest variable was also represented positively on both patriarchy and connectedness latent variables. This finding appears to be paradoxical in that connectedness was negatively related to both patriarchy and the war system. However, belief in doing 'the right thing' may be common to the concept of connectedness as well as the other latent variables with which it is associated. There simply may be a difference as to what that 'right thing' is. For example, it could be possible that the higher one scores on acceptance of war, the more one believes 'the right thing' to be protecting national security through weaponry; the more one accepts patriarchy, the more one believes 'the right thing' to be a man having control of his individual world; and the more one accepts interconnectedness, the more one believes 'the right thing' is to find nonviolent solutions to problems. Indeed, Larsen (1986) defines problems related to acceptance of war partly in terms of a moral absolutism that prevents appropriate communication and compromise. Similarly, Watzlawick et al. (1974) have indicated that belief that there is one right way of doing things frequently contributes to impasses in communication and problem solving. The relationship of belief in absolute rules to three latent variables may point to a pivotal role for this concept in conflict and violence.

4.4 Summary

The fourteen measured variables successfully converged into a covariance structure model. All of the measured variables were related to at least one of four latent variables which were named the war system, patriarchy, connectedness, and patriotism/nationalism. Thus the respondents belief systems formed patterns interpretable in terms of the major concepts of the study. Two major findings focused around the direct contribution of human and global connectedness to the lack of acceptance of war, and the direct relationship of nationalism and acceptance of war. A third major finding was the indirect role of patriarchal beliefs in war acceptance through its negative relationship to the connectedness latent variable, and its positive relationship to nationalism. Two measured patriarchal beliefs were also directly related to war beliefs in the war system – specifically beliefs in absolute rules and traditional roles for men. Finally, the potentially paradoxical role of belief in absolute moral values was shown in its positive relationship to three latent variables.

5. Conclusion

Clearly, more exploration is needed to fully understand the relationships between these and other beliefs, values and attitudes and how war systems are maintained. The model presented here provides means for speculation on just where one might need to intervene in order to change a war system to a peace system. In addition, the measures need refinement and validity checks, and future samples should be representative. The concepts of peace and the nonviolent resolution of international conflict also need direct exploration.

However, the fact that this model fits the data is important. On a conceptual level, these data do suggest that beliefs of war being acceptable are embedded in a complex system of values. These values include a lack of connection with others and a nationalistic fervor driven by an individualistic, patriarchal system. In addition, as a statistical technique, covariance structure models seem to be applicable to the defining of the 'rules of the game' by which systems operate.

On a hopeful note, identification of such a system provides many points for change to be introduced. Most of the beliefs identified as contributing to the war system are such that individuals, in their everyday, lives can work for change, within themselves as well as with others. Professionals also have a role, for example, in teaching values clarification and tolerance for diversity, and personal empowerment, once they have examined their own values. Continued research on systems of beliefs, values, and attitudes that potentially mediate or impact war and peace is also recommended. When the covert rules of the game that support war are made overt, to reiterate Watzlawick, et al. (1974), the game can no longer be played in the same way.

Notes

1 The term 'beliefs' will be used to encompass concepts of evaluative beliefs, including attitudes and values, based on Rokeach (1968). Rokeach maintained that values are a particular kind of evaluative belief – an enduring belief that a mode of conduct or end state is desireable, and attitudes are an organization of beliefs around a specific object or situation.

2 Figures 1 and 2 do not include the error associated with each variable for reasons of clarity. Each variable that has an arrow pointing to it, has an amount of error (E)

in measurement. In the case of the factors, a 'disturbance' (D) represents the error that is not accounted for by its related manifest variables.

References

Bentler, Peter M. 1985. *Theory and implementation of EQS: A structural equation program*. Los Angeles: BMDP Statistical Software, Inc.

Brannon, Robert, & Juni, Samuel, 1983. 'A scale measuring attitudes about masculinity', *Psychological Documents*, 14(1) 6.

Brock-Utne, Birgit, 1985. *Educating for Peace : A Feminist Perspective*. New York: Pergamon.

Brown, M.B., ed., 1977. *Biomedical computer programs P-series*. Berkeley, CA: University of California Press.

Caplan, Nathan & Nelson, Stephen, 1973, March. 'On Being Useful', *American Psychologist*, vol. 28, no. 3, pp. 199–211.

Capra, Fritjof, 1982. *The Turning Point. Science, Society and the Rising Culture*. New York: Bantam.

Criss, Julie E., 1990. 'Patriarchal Structures in Acceptance of War and Peace: Values of Dominance. Competitive Hierarchy. Instrumentalism, and Masculinity'. Unpublished doctoral dissertation, California School of Professional Psychology, Los Angeles.

Cronbach, Lee J., 1970. *Essentials of psychology testing*. New York: Harper & Row.

David, Deborah & Brannon, Robert, 1976. *The forty-nine percent majority*. New York: Addison-Wesley.

Dyer, Gwynne, 1985. *War*, New York: Crown.

Eisler, Riane, 1988. 'The Chalice and the Blade', San Francisco: Harper and Row.

Feshbach, Seymour, Kandel, Elizabeth, & Haist, Frank, 1985. 'Factors influencing attitudes towards nuclear disarmament policies: The role of information and the value place on children', in Stuart Oskamp, ed., *Applied social psychology annual*, pp. 107–125. Beverly Hills: Sage Publications.

Gilligan, Carol, 1982. *In a different voice*. Cambridge: Harvard University Press.

Hilsberg, Bruce L., 1989. *Endorsement of traditional male roles and acceptance of war and peace*. Unpublished doctoral dissertation, California School of Professional Psychology, Los Angeles.

Holt, Robert R., 1984. 'Can Psychology Meet Einstein's Challenge?' *Political Psychology*, vol. 5, no. 2, pp. 199–225.

Holt, Robert R., 1987. 'Converting the War System to a Peace System: Some Contributions from Psychology and Other Social Sciences'. Paper presented at the Exploratory Project on the Conditions for Peace, Cohasset, MA.

Johnson, Paula, 1987. 'Values relating to acceptance of war: Impact of moral reasoning and gender', Paper presented at the annual meeting of the International Society of Political Psychology, San Francisco.

Joreskog, Karl G. & Sorbom, Dag, 1983. *LISREL V users guide*. Chicago, IL: International Educational Service.

Kohlberg, Lawrence, 1964. 'Development of moral character and moral ideology', in Martin Hoffman and Lois Hoffman, eds, *Review of child development research*, vol. 1, pp. 383–431. New York: Russell Sage Foundation.

Kosterman, Rick & Feshbach, Seymour 1989. 'Towards a measure of patriotic and nationalistic attitudes', *Political Psychology*, 10(2), 257–274.

Larsen, Knud, 1986. 'Social Psychological Factors in Military Technology and Strategy', *Journal of Peace Research*, vol. 23, no. 4, pp. 391–398.

Macy, Joanna R., 1983. *Despair and Personal Empowerment in the Nuclear Age*. Philadelphia: New Society Publishers.

McGuire, William 1973. 'The yin and ;the yang of progress in social psychology: Seven koan', *Journal of Personality and Social Psychology*, 26(3), 446–465.

Milbrath, Lester W., 1988, July. 'Making Connections: The Common Roots Giving Rise to the Environmental, Feminist and Peace Movements'. A paper presented at the annual meeting of the International Society for Political Psychology.

Reardon, Betty A., 1985. *Sexism and the War System*. New York: Teacher's College Press.

Roberts, Barbara, 1983. 'The death of machothink: Feminist research and the transformation of peace studies', *Women's Studies International Forum*, 7(4), 195–200.

Rokeach, Milton, 1968. *Beliefs, attitudes, and values: A theory of organizations and change*. San Francisco, CA: Jossey-Bass.

Schaef, Anne W., 1981. *Womens Reality: An Emerging Female System in the White Male Society*. Minneapolis, MN: Winston Press.

Schaef, Anne W., 1987. *When society becomes an addict*. San Francisco, CA: Harper & Row.

Spretnak, Charlene, 1983. 'Naming the Cultural Forces that Push Us towards War', *Journal of Humanistic Psychology*, vol. 23, no. 3, pp. 104–1 14 .

Watzlawick, Paul, Weakland, John, & Fisch, Richard, 1974. *Change: Principles of Problem Formation and Problem Resolution*, New York: Norton.

Weick, Karl E., 1984, January. 'Small Wins: Redefining the Scale of Social Problems', *American Psychologist*, vol. 39, no. 1, pp. 40–49.

17

Gender Psychology
and Issues of War and Peace

Benina Berger Gould

1. Introduction

The purpose of this study was to investigate five areas considered to – theoretically – represent the most common conceptualizations and important differences between females and males with respect to attitudes toward war: (1) perceptions as to the likelihood of war; (2) perception of loss; (3) expression of feelings; (4) acquisition of political knowledge; and (5) expression of solutions to the threat of war. Theoretical differences derived from the literature suggested the hypotheses that were tested.

The study was conducted within two weeks of the downing of the Korean Airliner 007 in 1983. This crisis was the stimulus common to the high school students who were asked the questions on this survey. A crisis provides a common stimulus to all young people, which they share through the media and reactions from family and friends.

The *first hypothesis* was: More boys will respond with 'yes' or 'no' to the question 'Do I think there will be a war?', whereas more girls will respond with 'maybe' when asked the same question. This was explored because research by Greenstein (1961,1965), who studied children grades 4–8, and Tolley (1973), who studied grades 3–8, showed that more girls than boys tend to give no opinion, no information, or guess answers about war and peace.

The *second hypothesis* was: 'More girls than boys will express global/macro loss or local/micro loss; more boys than girls will express personal/self loss'. This was based on the work of Chodorow (1978), who also theorized that females would express more local loss than males because of their concern with relationships.

Four effectual variables were investigated in *Hypothesis III*: the expression of fear, humanitarian concerns, anger, and blame. For example, Bauer (1976)

* Acknowledgements to Jeffrey B. Gould, M.D. MPH, and The Fielding Institute, Santa Barbara, CA, where original dissertation research was conducted.

and Croake (1969) suggest that girls are always more worried and fearful than boys.

Hypothesis IV, on the relationship of sex to political knowledge, explores four variables: reference to KAL 007, deterrence, world tension, and the technical limitations of fallout shelters. Geddie and Hildreth (1944), Greenstein (1961, 1965), Lane (1959), Hess and Tourney (1967) and Zwigenhaft (1985) studied the relationship of sex to political knowledge; they all found significant gender differences, with males being more knowledgeable than females.

Hypothesis V relates to males' and females' spontaneous expression of military or peaceful solutions to war; it was derived from the literature on hopefulness and belief in the future (e.g. Beardslee & Mack, 1982).

2. Methods

2.1 Respondents

The sample was derived from a data base collected in the two weeks following the Korean Airline 007 incident in September 1983. This study considers the responses of a subset of 231 respondents, 131 males and 100 females (Table 1).

In order to control for possible confounders (age, socio-economic status, educational ability) the respondents were restricted to California 10–12th grades from classrooms of mixed socio-economic status and mixed educational ability.

Teachers were asked to state, on a demographic sheet, the economic status, educational ability, and extent of nuclear war discussion, for each classroom. The analysis of these descriptions permitted segregating the ability of the class into groups of predominantly high ability, classes of predominantly low ability, and all others. For the purpose of this study, only those classes that were neither uniformly of high ability nor uniformly of low ability were considered.

2.2 Survey

Following the Berlin wall crisis in 1961, Schwebel had conducted a survey of high school students in New York State which asked three questions: (1) Do I think there is going to be a war?, (2) Do I care? Why?; and (3) What do

Table 1   *Sex and grade of respondents*

	10th	11th	12th	Total
No. of students	60	68	103	231
Females	26	27	47	100
Males	34	41	56	131

I think about fallout shelters? (Schwebel, 1965). The question about fallout shelters was retained in the present study even though these were no longer in use in 1983, to determine technical knowledge of males and females. In the two weeks following the shooting down of Korean Airlines 007 (1 September 1983) Schwebel's survey was repeated. The survey was administered by the classroom teacher using a standard protocol:

> A great deal is known about how world leaders and adults feel about nuclear war. This survey will help us to learn what students feel about nuclear war. There will be three questions. We will take 6 minutes to answer each question. I will tell you when 5 minutes have gone by. If you need more paper, raise your hand. Each student was given two sheets of paper and the teacher stated, 'Here is Question 1; please write it down. The question is then repeated and the students are instructed to begin.

On each questionnaire, the students wrote their sex and age.

2.3 Content Analysis of the Survey Questions

The questionnaires were blinded with respect to the sex and classroom of the respondent and randomly ordered by computer. Each questionnaire was scored by the author using the content dictionary developed by Gould, Eden and Berger-Gould (1986). The authors had reported that when each of them scored for the dictionary, agreement among their scores ranged between 80 and 95 per cent.

3. Results

In political psychology, stereotypes about men and women abound. With respect to the question 'Do I think there will be a war?', Greenstein (1965) and Tolley (1973) suggested that more boys than girls will respond with 'yes' or 'no', and more girls will respond with 'maybe'. Our survey found no evidence to support this hypothesis. The responses of boys and girls were statistically similar, and an equal number of males (24.4 per cent) and females (24 per cent) answered 'maybe' (Table 2).

The second hypothesis – 'More girls than boys will express global/macro

Table 2   *Comparison of responses to question 1:*
'Do you think there will be a nuclear war?'

	'Yes'	'No'	'Maybe'
Males	48% (63)*	27.5% (36)	24.4% (32)
Females	56% (56)	20% (20)	24% (24)

* $N = (\ )$
$X^2 = 2.0$
df = 2
$p = .37$

Table 3   *Percent who express loss in any of the three questions*

	Male	Female
Global	61.1% (80)	67% (67)
Loss	$X^{2*} = .86$ $p = .353$	
Local	38.9% (51)	58% (58)
Loss	$X^{2*} = 8.27$ $p = .004$	
Personal/self	62.6% (82)	67% (67)
Loss	$X^{2*} = .48$ $p = .489$	

Male $N = 131$
Female $N = 100$
* All chi squares df = 1

loss or local/micro loss; more boys than girls will express personal/self loss' – used content analysis to determine male and female expressions of loss in responses to all three questions. As predicted, more females expressed local loss; however, there was no evidence to support gender-specific differences in the expression of global, or self/personal loss (Table 3).

As predicted (Hypothesis III), more females than males expressed fear and humanitarian concerns (see Table 4).

Hypothesis IV concerned the acquisition of political and technical knowledge: 'Compared to girls, boys will have more knowledge of a) the political implications of KAL/007, deterrence, and world tension, and b) the technical limitations of fallout shelter.' There were no differences in males and females regarding such political knowledge, but a significant difference was found in male/female citations of the limitations of fallout shelters. (Table 5).

Hypothesis V explores male/female differences in relation to solutions to avoid nuclear war. It was hypothesized that 'Compared to girls, boys will offer more solutions to nuclear war.' We found no gender differences in the percentage of males and females who cited either a peaceful or military solution to war (Table 6).

4. Discussion

In developing Hypothesis I, the possible effects of age differences between Tolley's and Greenstein's work of young children and this survey of adolescents should have been considered.

Another factor not considered in formulating the first hypothesis was the type of question being asked: is it concrete or abstract? According to Gilligan (1982), women speak of caring and relationships, and need to relate to the here and now rather than to abstract or hypothetical questions. Because adolescent females in this study did not show greater ambivalence in answering the question 'Do you think there will be a war?' than did adolescent males, perhaps the question is being interpreted as a concrete question. This could be because it was asked at the time of a political crisis, the KAL incident, which seemed to threaten everyone; it was a prime subject in the media, and thus a very concrete event.

In relation to Hypothesis II, no gender difference was found in the expression of global loss. As expected, more females cited local loss supporting the work of Gilligan and Chodorow (Table 3).

For self-loss, no gender gap was demonstrated. This finding was not unexpected, given Chodorow's theoretical position that boys need to differentiate from mother at the Oedipal stage because of sexual tensions and society's values on masculinity. This is seen as creating a context where males are more concerned with self and the boundaries of self, and are less relationship-oriented. Perhaps the threat of self-loss due to nuclear war is so powerful that it overrides potential gender differences.

In response to Hypothesis III, the first finding, that females are more fearful then males, is in keeping with the literature on children's fears. Likewise, the

Table 4   *Male concerns and females who express fear, humanitarian, anger, and blame to any of the three questions*

	Male	Female
Fear	22.1% (29)	39% (39)
	$X^{2*} = 7.76$ $p = .005$	
Humanitarian	31.3% (51)	49% (49)
Concerns	$X^{2*} = 7.47$ $p = .006$	
Anger	42% (55)	46% (46)
	$X^{2*} = .37$ $p = .542$	
Blame	45.8% (120)	60% (60)
	$X^{2*} = 4.58$ $p = .03$	

Male $N = 131$
Female $N = 100$
* All chi squares df = 1

Table 5   *Political knowledge in answer to any of the three questions or the limitation of fallout shelters*

	Male	Female
Reference to Flight 007	9.9% (13)	16% (16)
	$X^{2*} = 1.91$ $p = .167$	
Reference to deterrence	20.6% (27)	14% (14)
	$X^{2*} = 1.70$ $p = .93$	
Reference to world tension	61.8 (61)	52% (52)
	$X^{2*} = 2.24$ $p = .134$	
Reference to limitations of fallout shelters	60.3% (79)	44% (44)
	$X^{2*} = 6.06$ $p = .011$	

Male $N = 131$
Female $N = 100$
* All chi squares df $= 1$
FE = one-sided Fisher's Exact Test

Table 6   *Military and peaceful solutions to any of the three questions*

	Male	Female
Military solutions	3.1% (4)	3.0% (3)
	$X^{2*} = 0.00$ $p = .981$	
Peaceful solutions	25.2% (33)	29% (29)
	$X^{2*} = .42$ $p = .517$	

Male $N = 131$
Female $N = 100$
* All chi squares df $= 1$

Table 7   *Summary of major findings of 13 content areas, by percent of respondents*

Variable	Overall n=231	Male n=131	Female n=100
Global	64	61.1	67
Local	47	38.9	58*
Personal/self	63	62.6	67
Fear	29.4	22.1	39*
Humanitarian concerns	38.9	31.3	49*
Anger	43.7	42	46
Blame	31.9	45.8	60*
007	12.6	9.9	16
Deterrence	17.7	20.6	14
World tension	57.6	61.8	52
Limitations of fallout studies	53.2	60.3	44*
Peaceful solutions	26.8	25.2	29
Military solutions	3	3.1	3

* significant gender difference $p < .05$

finding that more females express humanitarian concerns than males (Table 4) also supports previous research.

However, the third variable – anger – was not found to be excessive in males. The lack of a gender gap in male and female expression of anger in this survey may be related to the fact that this research measures only verbal responses, rather than observed aggressive behavior.

In Hypothesis IV, males did not express significantly more knowledge of KAL/007, deterrence, or of world tension; but they did evidence more knowledge about the limitations of fallout shelters. Male and female adolescents were both more expressive about world tension. In our survey, respondents were not asked specifically what they knew, and the expressions cited and coded were spontaneous answers to the questions.

The third variable of this hypothesis concerns the relationship of gender to expressed knowledge of the Korean Airliner Incident. Perhaps the issue of nuclear war is so prevailing and emotional that not only do males and females express similar knowledge about nuclear war, but they also express very little political knowledge about the issue (12.6 per cent any KAL/007, 17.7 per cent any deterrence: Table 7.

In relation to knowledge about fallout shelters more traditional stereotypes were upheld about females' lack of interest in technology relating to war, and males' being more knowledgeable about war technology. There was a significant difference in 16 male/female citations of the limitations of fallout shelters in Question 3, 'Do I believe in fallout shelters' (60 per cent males, 44 per cent females, p = .011) (Table 5) which suggests that the more direct a question regarding political knowledge, the better chance it will be answered. In relation to Hypothesis V about solutions, either peaceful or military, only 32 per cent of the students proposed a solution to war. This suggests that the questions asked were not sufficient to elicit solutions or that psychological and social issues interfer with students' formulation of solutions (Table 7).

The research of Bachman (1983) and Zwigenhaft (1985), which found boys to be more comfortable expressing solutions of how to end the threat of nuclear war, was not supported in our data, and the questions did not specifically ask for solutions. It is possible, as suggested in the previous hypothesis, that unless you ask adolescents directly, you will not get answers about political knowledge or solutions to war.

It is also possible that few solutions are offered because male and female adolescents feel powerless and that they have no future. In relation to Hypothesis V on solutions, either peaceful or military, there is limited research in the literature.

This feeling of hopelessness also may affect the teachers and parents of these adolescents so that they do not discuss the issue with them or impart knowledge in this area.

Hopelessness may create for adolescents a sense that they not only must live for today, but that they are not capable of effecting any change in the world. Although this study does not attempt to look at adolescence and efficacy, it is suggested that since there was only a small percentage of respondents who formulated solutions, most youth represent a group who are having difficulty envisaging any answer to the dilemma of the threat of nuclear war.

References

Bachman, J. G., 1983. 'American High School Seniors View the Military: 1976–1982', *Armed Forces and Society*, vol. 10, no. 1, pp. 86–104.

Bauer, D. H., 1976. 'An Exploratory Study of Developmental Changes in Children's Fears', *Journal of Child Psychology and Psychiatry*, vol. 17, pp. 69–74.

Beardslee, W. R., & J. E. Mack, 1983. 'Adolescence and the Threat of Nuclear War: The Evolution of a Perspective', *Yale Journal of Biology and Medicine*, vol. 56, p. 86.

Chodorow, N., 1978. *The Reproduction of Mothering*. Berkeley, CA.: University of California Press.

Croake, J. W., 1969. 'Fears of Children', *Human Development*, vol. 12, pp. 239–247.

Geddie, L., & G. Hildreth, 1944. 'Children's Ideas about the War', *Journal of Experimental Education*, vol. 12, pp. 92–97.

Gilligan, C., 1982. *In a Different Voice*. Cambridge, MA: Harvard University Press.

Gould, J., E. Eden, & B. Berger-Gould, 1986. *Youth's Perceptions on the Threat of Nuclear War following an International Crisis*. Presentation at University of California Conference on 'The Psychological Effect of the Nuclear Threat Conference on Children and Nuclear War', 1984.

Greenstein, F., 1961. 'Sex-related Political Differences in Childhood', *Journal of Politics*, vol. 23, pp. 353–371.

Greenstein, F., 1965. *Children and Politics*. New Haven, CT: Yale University Press.

Harris, L., 1990. Article in *New York Times*. 7 December, p. A27.

Hess, R., & J. Tourney, 1967. *The Development of Political Attitudes in Children*. Chicago,IL: Aldine.

Lane, R., 1959. 'Fathers and Sons: Foundations of Political Belief', *Journal of the American Sociological Society*, vol. 24 no. 4, pp. 502–511.

Schwebel, M., 1965. 'Nuclear Cold War: Student Opinion and Professional Responsibility', pp. 210–223 in M. Schwebel ed., *Behavioral Science and Human Survival*. Palo Alto, CA: Behavioral Sciences Press.

Tolley, H., 1973. *Children and War: Political Socialization to International Conflict*. New York: Teacher's College.

Zwigenhaft, R.L., 1985. 'Race, Sex and Nuclear War', *Genetic, Social, and General Psychology Monographs*. vol. 111 no. 3, pp. 283–301.